P9-CMB-188

Collective Bargaining in Sweden

Collective Bargaining in Sweden

A STUDY OF THE LABOUR MARKET AND ITS INSTITUTIONS

BY

T. L. JOHNSTON

Lecturer in Political Economy
University of Edinburgh

HARVARD UNIVERSITY PRESS
CAMBRIDGE, MASSACHUSETTS
1962

FIRST PUBLISHED IN 1962

PRINTED IN GREAT BRITAIN

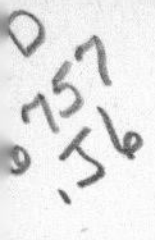

EX ANTE

SWEDISH experience with the problems of the modern welfare state has long excited the curiosity of foreigners in search of The Middle Way. Why this should be so is a vast and difficult question, to which no final answer will be attempted here. The Swedish national temperament, her homogeneous population, and the tradition of progress through careful discussion and compromise have provided a favourable environment for moulding the institutions of her economic and social life in a purposeful manner. Moreover, the Swedes have plenty of experience of organizing. The propensity to organize for all sorts of purposes is nothing short of incredible. It may be that it is the Americans who have publicized the Organization Man, but almost certainly his forefathers were Swedish emigrants, part of the vast army to take ship west, and settle in the Middle West, in the late nineteenth century.

Fortunately, he left enough of his relatives at home to enable us to find the twentieth-century Swedish labour market a fruitful laboratory for the study of collective bargaining. It is a tightly organized labour market, and it has experienced its share of industrial strife. But there has always been an underlying strain of sober realism at work, tempering excesses and pushing the collective bargaining system in the direction of a strong private system of government. The Swedes are not Teutonic in their thoroughness, but rather tenacious and pragmatic. The post-war discussion of wages policy has, for example, persistently and perseveringly tried to come to terms with the new problems of wage bargaining in a full employment economy. Through the whole system runs a strong sense of self-interest, dispassionate but materialistic; and this quality has meant that the system of industrial relations has shown a great awareness of the needs of production. In this country and labour market the economic aspects are never far from the forefront of men's minds.

No attempt is made in this book to argue that the Swedish system is pre-eminent, or ripe for export *in toto* to other countries. Indeed, one feature of Swedish industrial relations has been the willingness the Swedes have shown to absorb ideas from abroad and adapt them to their own needs and environment. As a small country Sweden has not, in this as in many other matters, been able to afford the luxury of isolation. It need not follow from this that Sweden is simply an importer of ideas. The main hope underlying this work is that there can be multilateral trade in the ideas governing labour relations. If this study of the Swedish system leads others to reassess their own perspectives and re-examine their particular and peculiar traditions and tribal customs, it will have served a useful purpose.

During the past decade I have accumulated scholastic debts in Sweden for which the conventional acknowledgements are a poor and feeble settlement. My indebtedness to the great Swedish authorities is obvious to all who know their work. Casparsson, Hallendorff, Lindbom, Schmidt, Geijer, Sölvén, Tingsten, Westerståhl, and others will undoubtedly find many of their ideas parading through the pages which follow.

The staffs of the libraries of the Swedish Employers' Confederation, the Labour Movement Archives, and the Social Institute of the University of Stockholm have been generous in allowing me access to written sources. Trade unionists, employers, and government officials have shown that they do not reserve their capacity for endurance and spirit of tolerance exclusively for the bargaining table by being willing to discuss with me, in person and in writing, many of the problems raised in the course of this study.

I am greatly indebted to Ulf Berggren, Bertil Bolin, Bo Carlson, Thorbjörn Carlsson, Erik Forstadius, Karl-Olof Faxén, Rudolf Meidner, Gösta Rehn, Fritiof Söderbäck, and the late Dr M. T. Rankin for their kindness in reading parts or all of the manuscript at various stages and giving me their valuable comments. Their willing help must not be taken to imply guilt by association on their part; I alone am responsible for the content.

The editors of *Economica*, *The Labor Law Journal*, and *The Scottish Journal of Political Economy* have kindly allowed me to use material which has appeared in some form in their journals. I should also like to thank the Carnegie Trust for the Universities of Scotland and the University of Edinburgh for generous financial support which made it possible for me to begin my work in Sweden by studying at the University of Stockholm.

November 1961

CONTENTS

EX ANTE *page* 7
INTRODUCTION 11

PART I. THE LABOUR MARKET ORGANIZATIONS

I. The Confederation of Trade Unions 23
II. Employers' Organizations 68
III. Unions of Salaried Employees 92

PART II. THE FRAMEWORK OF LAW

Introduction 115
IV. The Legal Status of Associations 118
V. The Rights of Association and Collective Bargaining 124
VI. The Law of Collective Bargaining 138
I. *Introduction* 138
II. *The Mediation Act* 139
III. *The Collective Contracts Act* 144
IV. *The Labour Court Act* 154
V. *Concluding Observations* 163

PART III. COLLABORATION AND BASIC AGREEMENTS

VII. The Genesis of the Basic Agreement 169
VIII. Economic Sanctions and Neutral Third Parties 176
IX. The Protection of Essential Public Services 182
X. The Success of the Basic Agreement 191

PART IV. JOB SECURITY AND INDUSTRIAL DEMOCRACY

XI. Job Security 205
XII. Works Councils 216

PART V. COLLECTIVE BARGAINING IN ACTION

XIII. Employment Agreements 235
XIV. The Bargaining Process 260
XV. Wage Rounds, 1939–60 276
XVI. Wage Changes and Wages Structure, 1939–60 292
XVII. Wages Policy 319
EX POST 338
APPENDICES 343
INDEX 353

INTRODUCTION

THE decade of the 1890s marked the beginning of an era of economic expansion in Sweden, a quickening in the tempo of activity, an upsurge and not a climacteric. It was the age of great Swedish innovators and inventions, which enabled Sweden to develop and profit from new technologies that were not dependent on coal as a source of energy. Her forest industry began the transformation from a sawn-timber industry, in which there had been an enormous upswing since 1850, to a timber-converting paper and pulp industry. The metal trades based on the mining and processing of ore, which in Sweden have a history going back at least to the thirteenth century, provided a sound technical framework and a highly skilled and inventive labour force for exploiting industrial inventions. Her third great natural resource, water power, could be utilized more effectively through the development of hydro-electric techniques.

Industrialism did not arrive suddenly, and changes in institutions, economic policy, and the supply and use of labour earlier in the nineteenth century marked the movement from a static to a dynamic economy. Gild restrictions were abolished in 1846, a Companies Act was passed in 1848, the Riksdag (Parliament) decided in 1854 to develop a state-owned railway system, and in 1864 an Economic Freedom Ordinance was passed which in theory provided a *laissez-faire* doctrine for economic activity, including the labour market. The supply of labour, increasing with the decline in death-rates, produced a rural population problem, which was reinforced by the enclosure movement. Before industrialism began to offer employment for the rural proletariat it was emigration, particularly to North America, that provided an outlet from 1860 onwards, and a peak figure for emigration of 50,000 was reached in the year 1887.

When industrialism did come the population continued to be widely scattered geographically, because of the absence of domestic coal deposits dictating location and the presence of a flexible electric power system permitting dispersion. The wide scatter of ore resources in Central Sweden and the large area of the north-east coast covered by the timber-working industry have also favoured a low population density. A feature still of Swedish industry is the absence of heavy industrial belts and Great Wens. The prevalence of small local labour markets has in turn raised problems of labour mobility which have become increasingly important in the current discussion of economic policy aimed at providing a flexible economic structure.

The shift from an agrarian to an industrial economy is reflected in the sectors from which the population drew its livelihood. Of the total population of 4·8 m. in 1890, 50% were dependent on agriculture, and only 16% on industry, but by 1910, when the population was 5·5 m., the absolute size of the agricultural population had begun to fall, and its proportion of the population had declined to 42%, while industry had more than doubled in size and increased its share from 16% to 27%.

The main demographic features of the twentieth century are reflected in the table below. The birth-rate, which was 27 per 1,000 in 1900, fell to 14 in the 1930s and, after a rise in the period 1942–8 (with a peak of 20·6 in 1944), it has again fallen below 15 per 1,000. Indeed in 1960 it was 13·65, the lowest ever recorded in Sweden. The death-rate has declined steadily from 17 per 1,000 in 1900 to little more than 10 in 1960.[1]

POPULATION IN '000s

Age-group	*1950*	*1960*	*1965*	*1970*	*1975*
MEN					
0–14	844	853·9	819·9	850·1	898·6
15–19	211	301·6	313·1	273·5	267·6
20–64	2117	2185·2	2276·0	2357·8	2377·6
65+	335	412·3	461·3	517·7	585·9
Total	3507	3753·0	3870·3	3999·1	4129·7
WOMEN					
0–14	806	808·3	775·9	805·7	853·0
15–19	205	288·1	298·1	259·1	253·2
20–64	2138	2183·9	2256·3	2320·6	2328·7
65+	386	485·1	544·2	609·8	680·8
Total	3535	3765·4	3874·5	3995·2	4115·7
Grand Total	7042	7518·4	7744·8	7994·3	8245·4

Source: *Statistisk tidskrift*, no. 6, 1960, pp. 357–60.

[1] There have been three population projections in recent years, (*a*) in *S.O.U.*, 1957 : 10, bilaga 3, p. 33, to the year 1970, on an assumed net immigration of 10,000 per year; (*b*) that used above, which assumed a similar net immigration rate, and uses the evidence of past time series for the fertility and mortality rates assumed; (*c*) Odd Gulbrandsen, *Industriproblem 1960*, p. 147–60 (Stockholm 1960); (*c*) gives higher figures than (*a*) and (*b*) because of its assumptions about fertility and mortality and the regional basis of calculation used.

Note.—The abbreviation *S.O.U.* used in the footnote above refers to *Statens Offentliga Utredningar*, which are reports of official committees of inquiry. The abbreviation *S.O.U.* is used throughout to refer to such reports, and particular reports are cited by year and number, e.g. 1957 : 10.

LABOUR FORCE BY SECTOR SINCE 1930

	'000s						*Percentages*					
	1930	*1940*	*1950*	*1955*	*1960*	*1965*	*1930*	*1940*	*1950*	*1955*	*1960*	*1965*
Agriculture, Forestry, and Fisheries	876	832	632	551	482	428	31·8	28·0	20·3	17·5	14·8	12·6
Building	157	192	244	272	292	312	5·7	6·5	8	8·6	8·9	9·2
Manufacturing Industry, Mining, and Handicrafts	782	878	1023	1053	1133	1198	28·4	29·6	32·9	33·4	34·7	35·3
Communications	179	202	251	254	258	262	6·5	6·8	8·1	8·1	7·9	7·7
Commerce	330	409	497	545	604	669	11·9	13·8	16·0	17·3	18·5	19·7
Public Services	190	262	344	384	419	454	6·9	8·8	11·1	12·2	12·8	13·4
Domestic Work	221	158	90	70	55	45	8·1	5·3	2·9	2·2	1·7	1·4
Unspecified	21	34	23	23	23	23	0·7	1·2	0·7	0·7	0·7	0·7
	2756	2967	3104	3152	3266	3391	100·0	100·0	100·0	100·0	100·0	100·0
Change		+211	+137	+48	+114	+125						

Source: *Balanserad expansion*, *S.O.U.*, 1957: 10, bilaga 4, Tables 16 and 23. The data for the period after 1950 are unreliable, and the labour force figures for manufacturing industry for 1955, 1960, and 1965 are residual. Figures for 1965 are estimated.

From the point of view of the labour market the significant population features are the rapid increase in the age-group 65 and over, and the rise in the 15–19 age-group from 400,000 in 1950 to a temporary peak of 600,000 by 1965. The implications of these shifts for work intensity, labour force participation, and vocational training are obvious.

The division of the labour force by sectors since 1930 also throws light on the main quantitative problems of labour relations.

The first interesting feature of this table is the small increase in the labour force in the period 1950–5, which imposed strains from the supply side of labour in relation to the demand. The shift away from agriculture towards industry, building, and the public services also draws attention to the strategic position of these last three sectors in the employment and organization of the labour force.

The classification of the working population by sex and occupational status shows two main trends in recent years. The first is a tremendous growth in the share of salaried employees in the labour force. Between 1930 and 1950 their number doubled from 425,000 to 843,000 and their share of the working population rose from 15% to 27%. Between 1930 and 1950 the increase in industry was 145%.[1] The second main feature is that the participation of women in manual work has declined, but female salaried employees showed the most rapid rate of growth in the 1940s.

Projections up to 1965 show a continued decline in the number of employers, a stable number (about 1,650,000) of manual workers, and the increase in the labour force falling almost entirely to salaried employees, with a growth in this group of 10% to 15% during each five-year period from 1950 to 1965,[2] giving in that year a total of 1,150,000 salaried employees. This enormous shift in the composition of the labour force has profound implications for the growth of trade unionism among salaried employees (discussed in Chapter III) and for the membership ceiling among manual workers' unions.

Other significant indicators for labour relations are the main industrial employers and average size of labour force per establishment. Employment in industry is dominated by the metal and engineering trades, which account for a third of the establishments and 44% of the manual labour force. The table opposite refers to establishments employing at least five persons. Both in industry and in other sectors, e.g. wholesale and retail trading, there are large numbers of firms with fewer than five employees.

[1] Erik Höök, *Tjänstemännen och den industriella omvandlingen*, p. 15 (Stockholm, 1953).

[2] See *S.O.U.*, 1957 : 10, bilaga 4, for details.

INDUSTRY, 1958

Industry	*No. of Establish-ments*	*Percent-age*	*No. of workers '000s*	*Percent-age*	*Average no. of workers per Establish-ment*
Mining	104	0·6	14·7	2·2	142
Metals and Engineering	5530	33·3	296·3	43·8	54
Quarrying	1132	6·8	32·2	4·7	28
Manufacture of Wood	2807	16·9	58·3	8·6	21
Pulp and Paper	331	2·0	50·9	7·5	154
Printing and Allied Industries	822	5·0	27·7	4·1	34
Food Manufacture	1950	11·8	44·7	6·6	23
Beverages and Tobacco	303	1·8	8·6	1·3	28
Textile and Clothing	1361	8·2	77·9	11·5	57
Leather, Hair, and Rubber Goods	621	3·8	25·4	3·8	41
Chemicals	547	3·3	24·5	3·6	45
Electricity, Gas, and Waterworks	1079	6·5	15·3	2·3	14
Total	16587	100	676·5	100	41

Source: *Statistisk årsbok*, 1960.

The average number of employees per establishment in industry is only 41, but this gives a misleading picture of the pattern of establishments by labour force size. In 1958 47% of the establishments in industry employed fewer than 10 workers, but they covered only 7% of workers in industry; 173 establishments (0·01% of the total number) each with over 500 workers accounted for 29% (197,000) of the 677,000 manual workers in industry. This pattern is inevitably reflected in the membership of the Employers' Confederation, which has a small number of large and a long tail of small firms.

These dimensions and changes in the structure of the labour force provide the framework for this study of the labour market. Questions at once arise about the organizations that have participated in this evolution, and their policies towards economic change. The shift in the labour force from manual to salaried employment highlights the interesting questions associated with trade unionism among salaried employees. The growth of the public sector clearly raises special collective bargaining problems. Other issues that arise involve a consideration of labour legislation, and the attitude of the law to the framework of industrial relations.

This book is divided into five parts. We begin in Part I with the labour market organizations. Pre-eminent on the employees' side is the Confederation of Swedish Trade Unions—popularly known as LO[1]—which was founded in 1898. One in five of the population is now a member of LO. The other main group representing employees, The Central Organization of Salaried Employees—TCO[2]—is a much more youthful organization, dating in its present form from 1944, but the trend to salaried employment gives the white-collar worker an increasingly significant and strategic place in the system of labour market institutions. On the side of the employers the most important group, historically and quantitatively, as the centre of countervailing power is the Swedish Employers' Confederation—SAF.[3] The public sector is, however, increasingly a strategic, indeed the largest individual, employer of labour.

In Part II the legislative framework is analysed. The main points that will be made there are, first, the relative absence of labour legislation, and, second, the tremendous controversy surrounding the subject of labour legislation in the first four decades of the twentieth century. Legislation, for example on the Labour Court, is undoubtedly significant: but private government has since the 1930s come to play a much more central part than public enactments in the Swedish system. This development is discussed fully in Part III, where we look at the forms this private government has taken, and the types of industrial action it has endeavoured to control through private machinery. Part III leads naturally to the topics of Part IV, the employer's prerogatives in 'hiring and firing', and the large questions of industrial democracy.

The essential rationale of the system of organizations and of the predominantly private arrangements for the government of the labour market is, of course, the whole range of problems centring on collective bargaining. This is studied in Part V, where we proceed from an analysis of the structure of the employment agreements found in Sweden, via the bargaining process that has been developed to arrive at and administer contracts, to a discussion of wages bargaining rounds since 1939, the impact of bargaining on the wages structure since then and, finally, an assessment of the major issues of wages policy which have since 1945 provided the central theme for labour relations.

The Swedish labour market has not by any means been distinguished by peaceful relations during the past sixty years of regulation by organization. Statistics for stoppages show how troubled and disrupted the industrial scene has sometimes been. By the same token

[1] Landorganisationen i Sverige. [2] Tjänstemännens Centralorganisation.
[3] Svenska Arbetsgivareföreningen.

the trend since 1935 has been a remarkable one, suggesting that some change took place in the 1930s in the climate of industrial relations. A brief commentary on the bare bones provided by the statistics helps to set the scene and give some perspective on labour relations.

STOPPAGES OF WORK

Period	*Number*	*Of which Strikes*	*Total days lost '000s*	*Period*	*Number*	*Of which Strikes*	*Total days lost '000s*
1903–7	1148	912	4411	1939–44	637	606	706
1908	302	229	1842	1945	163	163	11321
1909	138	102	11800	1946–50	319	316	365
1910–16	831	770	2383	1951	28	27	531
1917–19	1623	1540	4841	1952	32	31	79
1920	486	455	8943	1953	20	17	582
1921–2	739	656	5338	1954	45	44	24
1923	206	192	6907	1955	18	18	159
1924–7	895	804	5876	1956	12	12	4
1928	201	173	4835	1957	20	19	53
1929–33	956	873	10844	1958	10	9	15
1934–7	328	314	2847	1959	15	14	24
1938	85	83	1284				

Source: *Statistisk årsbok*.

In 1902, four years after it was founded, LO was involved in a public demonstration in the form of a political strike in support of the franchise question, the occurrence of which provided one of the incentives to employers to organize in SAF. In 1903 and 1905 the trade unions had experience of lock-outs in the metal trades, but in 1905 the collective agreement was formally recognized in that industry as a method of regulating the employment relationship. At the same time, the right of workers to combine in trade unions was formally conceded, while in the same year SAF established the proposition that the employer was master in his own house by including in its rules an article (the famous Article 23) to that effect. Although collective agreements grew rapidly in number and scope after 1905, a period of bitter relations followed, during which SAF developed the technique of the lock-out on a large scale, culminating in the Great Strike of 1909. This led to comprehensive, but unsuccessful, proposals in the Riksdag for the legal control of industrial relations, and also to considerable heart-searching on the part of the trade unions, enfeebled by their defeat in the strike.

Industrial relations were comparatively peaceful during the first years of the 1914–18 war, in which Sweden was of course a neutral, but the post-war period was marked by much unemployment, wage cuts, and bitter relations. The eight-hour working day and adult suffrage were approved by the Riksdag in 1919, and the first brave talk of industrial democracy led to inquiries and abortive proposals for works councils. Ultimately, the hostile labour relations of the 1920s inspired attempts to improve labour relations and make a new beginning, often by the suggestion of legal enactment, and in 1928 two Acts were passed, the Collective Contracts Act and the Labour Court Act, which endeavoured to regulate the central area of labour relations and industrial disputes. These enactments, which were bitterly opposed by the trade unions, constituted the first major legal intervention in industrial relations since the government provided mediation facilities in 1906 (revised in 1920).

In 1928 Sweden also had her due share of Mondism. A labour peace conference was held, but this positive development was abandoned when the Great Depression hit Sweden. Industrial unrest found a focus in the Ådal tragedy of 1931, when five people were killed by troops called out to ensure public safety during a labour demonstration. The bad industrial relations of the depression, highlighted by the ten-month stoppage in the building trades in 1933–4, led in 1934 to the appointment of an official committee (the Nothin commission) to investigate the problems of industrial peace. Its report was followed in 1936 by a momentous decision on the part of LO and SAF to endeavour themselves to promote better labour relations. In part this was the outcome of unsuccessful attempts to pass into law provisions designed to protect neutral third parties in industrial disputes. The year 1936 also marked a milestone in the evolution of the trade union movement from a predominantly defensive collective bargaining agency to a mature and socially conscious power group, aware of its responsibilities in the new welfare state which was being heralded by the rise to effective governmental power of the social democratic party.

In 1936, too, the movement of white-collar workers towards organized unionism began to assume significant proportions, spurred on by the passage of an Act to ensure the right to combine and to bargain collectively. The first Holidays with Pay Act was passed in 1938, and in the same year LO and SAF signed the Basic Agreement setting out a code of industrial relations practices for the purpose of improving relations between them. Since then the number of open conflicts has steadily declined. In 1941 the congress of LO made a thorough revision of the trade union movement's constitution, on the basis of the report of an LO Committee of Fifteen, in order to mould the structure and government of the movement to modern needs. In 1944 TCO became a central organization for salaried employees in both the private and public sectors.

The post-war period opened with a five months stoppage in the metal trades, but apart from a conflict in the foodstuffs industry in 1953 the period since 1945 has been one of industrial peace. In 1946 SAF and LO concluded an agreement by which works councils were to be set up. Other important developments have been the emergence of a strong organization for university graduates—The Swedish Confederation of Professional Associations—SACO[1]—and of a strongly centralized bargaining agency for the central government, the Ministry of Civil Service Affairs, set up in 1950. The dominant feature of labour relations since 1945 has, however, undoubtedly been wages bargaining in a full employment economy.

[1] *Sveriges Akademikers Centralorganisation*—The Swedish Confederation of Professional Associations.

PART I

The Labour Market Organizations

CHAPTER I

The Confederation of Trade Unions

IT would be tempting to deal with the trade union movement simply by analysing the current organization and government of the unions. This would have the commendable virtue of brevity, but it would suffer from the serious defects of over-simplifying and distorting the position. The fundamental point about the work of LO is that during its sixty years of experience it has shown one clear characteristic—that of following a Fabian-like policy of gradualism in its work. The evolutionary prospect portrayed in this chapter is an essential prerequisite for understanding the trade union view of contemporary problems of collective bargaining.

I. EARLY HISTORY

The Confederation of Swedish Trade Unions—LO—was formed in 1898. During the preceding twenty-five years the trade union movement progressed from a small number of local handicraft unions, via inter-union local committees, to organization in national craft unions. The first unions were formed in the 1870s among handicraft and skilled workers to deal with the problems that arose through the abolition of the gilds (1846) and the passing of the Economic Freedom Ordinance (1864), and to protect real wages in time of rising living costs. In the 1880s the trade union movement grew in response to the pressures of the population influx to the towns and through a developing political awareness among the working classes. The quickening pace of industrial growth in the 1890s and the rapid changes in the structure of production provided a new impetus.

The first attempt to provide organized contact between all local unions in one place was the setting-up in 1883 of the central committee for unions in different trades in Stockholm. It directed its activities to political as well as industrial issues, and almost at once became involved with the rising social democratic political movement. Whether the unions should become socialist was a question quickly resolved. More difficult was the organizational link between the political and union branches of the socialist movement, a problem which was not formally settled until 1909.

In the 1880s and 1890s increasing trade union activity made the unions a force in economic and political life, and trade unionists formed the overwhelming majority of party members when the social democratic party was constituted in 1889. Their participation helped to make the party more reformist than its early rigid Marxism intended. In turn, the party gave a big stimulus to the formation of unions after the dissolution of the Stockholm central committee in 1889, by emphasizing class solidarity, and providing organization and financial support. The party fulfilled many of the functions of a co-ordinating central body for the unions, and at the same time it had to draw the unions into political activity in order to gain numerical and financial strength for the franchise struggle. The franchise question was a powerful uniting influence. But while the party was primarily interested in organizing the whole of the working class, experience soon showed that craft and union problems required a separate and narrower basis of organization than that provided by the party. Despite the close ideological links, a move towards a separate and specifically trade union system of organization had already begun by the time the party was formed. The first national craft unions were organized in 1886 in printing and among postal workers. Throughout the 1890s the number of local and national unions rose rapidly, and national unions became the accepted method of organization. By 1899 there were thirty-two national unions. The year 1897 is a boundary line in the transition from a trade union movement which had been predominantly handicraft and skilled in character to one which, in response to the growing momentum of industrialism, also embraced industrial and unskilled workers. By 1900 there were about 70,000 trade unionists, comprising 15% to 20% of the total number of wage earners.

The rapid growth of national unions made the relationship between their form of organization and the general guiding role of the party in encouraging unionism a matter of some urgency. It was increasingly realized that the party form of organization was not suited to the needs of national trade unions, and in 1897 the fifth Scandinavian labour congress recognized there was a need for central national trade union confederations to co-ordinate the work of the national unions. At the same time, the link with the workers' political party was not to be lost. Thus in the same year the Swedish social democratic party conference authorized the unions to make the best possible arrangements for collaboration on union matters, while ensuring continued co-operation with the party. In August 1898, after discussion of preliminary proposals and various revisions, the Confederation of Swedish Trade Unions was founded and a constitution was adopted which set out the purpose and duties of this new central organization—LO.

LO was to consist of national unions covering specific trades, and a tripartite hierarchy of organization was adopted through (*a*) a congress, the supreme authority, (*b*) a representative assembly, and (*c*) an executive board (secretariat) of five persons, of whom the LO congress was to elect three, and the party two members. The function of LO was to act mainly as a central clearing house for trade union information and as an insurance office for the unions. The outbreak of every strike or lock-out was to be reported to the secretariat, but support from LO was to be limited *meantime*[1] to 'defensive conflicts', where the employer took the initiative in aggressive action by cutting wages, threatening the right to organize, or locking out workers who did organize. Where strikes were begun for defensive reasons some responsibility in considering them was given to local union committees, a sop to those who advocated more local independence than the powers being given to LO seemed to envisage.

These proposals about the purpose and duties of LO were approved after very little deliberation, for the main problem for discussion and decision was not so much the trade union aspects of a central LO, but rather the great issue of affiliation to the social democratic party, which had nurtured the unions over the past decade. There was general agreement that the unions and party should somehow be related. The formation of LO was not to prejudice co-operation with the party. But were the unions to be obliged to affiliate to the party? The congress decided that they should, within three years of joining LO.

LO made a slow beginning, partly because of the party affiliation issue, but by the end of 1900 it had twenty-one member unions and 44,000 members, and was becoming firmly established as the central focus of trade unionism in Sweden. From this point, however, our analysis must become more specific. The difficulties of internal organization that LO has had to overcome, and the problems that arose through the growth of a powerful employers' confederation —SAF—from 1902 were so many and varied that it is impossible to see twentieth-century Swedish trade unionism in a general setting. After 1900 the emphasis shifts to a consideration of particular problems. What have been the subsequent relations with the social democratic party? How has the original LO constitution stood up to the experience of negotiations and disputes with employers? Have the national unions retained their original position as the real centre of power? What principles of organization did LO adopt as the structure

[1] At the time it was anticipated that support would soon be given in all disputes, including those where the workers took the initiative. But a formal change in the LO rules to authorize support for 'attacking' disputes had to wait till 1941.

of the economy changed from handicraft production to large-scale industry? These are crucial questions, and they will be examined in the course of this chapter.

II. RELATIONS WITH THE PARTY

Despite the affirmation in the 1898 LO constitution about compulsory affiliation, the next LO congress of 1900 removed the compulsory affiliation clause and substituted, on the proposal of Hjalmar Branting, the leading social democratic politician, a declaration in the preamble to the LO constitution which stated that one of the aims of LO should be *to work for* the affiliation of every trade union to the local party organization and through it to the national party. This was considered a very satisfactory way of declaring the unity that existed between both branches of the working class in seeking political and industrial recognition. The formal party representation in the LO secretariat also ceased in 1900. But there was no clean break in the organizational links. At the same time the party revised its constitution, making the labour commune, a district body connecting various local groups with the central party, the primary unit of party organization. The commune could include local unions, and, moreover, the communes were themselves to be recognized as trade unions, and thus be represented at LO congresses. This development was criticized from the trade union side and, after the secretariat tried unsuccessfully at the next LO congress in 1903 to discontinue recognition of the communes as unions, the 1906 LO congress threw them out. This broke one formal link with the party.

But the clause in the preamble to the LO rules requiring it to work for affiliation to the social democratic party continued to attract criticism. In 1906 the LO secretariat made use of the curious argument that the position should not be changed, since it was the party congress that was entitled to make decisions about its form of organization. This amounted to 'an open confession that the leaders of the trade union movement felt bound by decisions arrived at by a non-trade union association'.[1] Under strong pressure from the two largest member unions the 1909 LO congress did decide, against the advice of the secretariat, to repeal the Branting declaration of 1900, and the LO constitution was purged of any suggestion of a link with other organizations. Since then there has been no provision in the LO rules about co-operation between it and the social democratic party. But that did not mean, and does not mean, that there was to

[1] Ragnar Casparsson, *LO under Fem Årtionden*, I, 150, 2nd edition (Stockholm, 1951).

be no co-operation. The 1909 LO congress accepted a resolution formulated by the chairman (Herman Lindqvist) which emphasized the solidarity existing between party and unions:

'This decision does not involve any change whatsoever in the ideological unity and solidarity of the labour movement, which from the beginning has bound together the Swedish trade union movement and social democracy. Congress considers that the social democratic party is the natural and obvious vehicle for the political aspirations of the Swedish working class.'

This declaration is as apposite today as it was then. The co-operation declared by this resolution is still cherished by the unions and the party. There is no official recognition of co-operation in union rules. The party rules allow union branches to affiliate collectively to the party through the local commune.[1] But, by a decision of the party congress of 1908, individual union members can in writing contract out of any obligation.

Subsequent discussion at LO congresses has proceeded along various lines. The vast majority, approving the collaboration between unions and party, have stressed that this is based on natural and more secure foundations than any formal provisions would ensure, and there has been no great support for proposals to reintroduce the explicit connexion into LO rules. Another line of approach, urging that the ties with the party should be severed and a politically neutral trade union movement established, has received short shrift. More problematical has been the voice, first raised at the 1922 LO congress —but not since the immediate post-1945 resurgence of communism, against which LO campaigned vigorously and successfully—that there were other (communist) working class parties too and these also deserved union support. Collective affiliation to the social democratic party could not, it was argued, be justified when there was more than one working class party. One form in which this issue has been posed is that of which political parties should be given financial support. The 1936 congress discussion is typical; LO reaffirmed its ties with social democracy, refused to recognize any other party as deserving of support and, with a small dissenting minority, voted funds for the social democratic election campaign. LO unions also provide financial support for the party.

Employers have on occasion attacked the LO link with social democracy, and frequent Riksdag motions have asked for legislation to prohibit collective affiliation to political parties. Nothing has come of such proposals. The stock reply has been that collective affiliation

[1] See *Grundstadgar for arbetarekommuner tillhörande Sveriges Socialdemokratiska Arbetarepart* (1960 edition), clause 1, section 2.

is not compulsory, that it is a matter for union branches, that there is provision for contracting out, and that no explanation for contracting out need be given.

The percentage of members of the social democratic party who are collectively affiliated through union branches has always been and remains high. In 1912 80% of the party membership of 65,000 were collectively affiliated, in 1929 the percentage was 71%, in 1933 67%; since 1945 about 60% of the party membership, which has crept steadily up to about 800,000 by 1960, have been collectively affiliated via union branches. The right to contract out is estimated to be exercised by less than 1% of members affected by collective affiliation. Dues for subscription to the local party commune are not collected separately through a political levy at union branch level, but are paid by the union branch from its funds on behalf of members not contracted out.

Apart from the strong political and financial ties through collective affiliation, co-operation is secured at top level through an informal council consisting of the party and LO leaders. This meets regularly to discuss questions of mutual interest. LO and the unions are also represented, and LO has a very powerful financial stake in the Labour Press (*A-pressen*). Until 1961, one-third of the dues paid to LO were earmarked for the Press Fund, and in 1960 LO subscribed about 6·6 m. crowns in this way.[1]

These ties between the party and the trade union movement have proved significant in determining union attitudes on two main issues: (*a*) government intervention in the negotiating machinery of the labour market, and (*b*) the choice between seeking material gains, e.g. retirement pensions, through collective bargaining or via legislation. On the first issue, as Part II will bring out, the trade union movement has pursued a fairly steady line of opposition to government intervention, even when, as has consistently been the case since 1932, the social democratic party was the sole or major party in power. The main argument against government intervention has been

[1] The Press Fund was set up in 1946 for the purpose of giving financial support to newspapers representing trade union interests. The original contribution was 20 öre per month for full-paying members, raised in 1956 to 50 öre per month. Lump sum grants are also made. It is obligatory on all members affiliated to unions in LO to pay this contribution, not by a clause in the rules but by congress decision. In the 1956 congress the LO secretariat said it considered it was obvious that no special congress decision was necessary for it to intensify educational and propaganda activity aimed at promoting the affinity between the social democratic party, LO, and the Labour Press.

In fact, the Press Fund has never been able to build up any reserves, because the demands made on it by the various newspapers LO subsidizes have exceeded its income from dues. In the period 1951–60 LO alloted 11 m. crowns more to the Press than the Fund brought in. LO has now decided to discontinue an explicit Press Fund, since it has not been able to operate in the way originally intended.

that the organizations themselves are better able to govern labour relations than the central government. At the same time, the party from its side has not been slow to let the unions know that the government in power reserves the right to intervene even in the labour market, although it would in principle prefer self-regulation by employers and unions. On material questions like hours of work, holidays with pay, and pensions, LO has chosen to seek a standard level of benefit via legislation. The predominance of social democratic governments since 1932 has in fact meant that LO has been able to widen its bargaining horizons whenever it felt that it was wise tactics to seek particular benefits through law rather than at the bargaining table. It reaps the best of both worlds.

Employers have practised essentially the same approach to the first issue: government intervention in the labour market. On matters of material content they have, however, preferred to seek a solution through collective agreements rather than in law. The unfortunate thing from their point of view is of course that in recent years they have not had much choice if LO felt a legislative solution was more in the workers' interests than a bargained agreement. The political squabble over pensions in 1958 provided an excellent illustration. SAF produced an outline pensions scheme in 1954 which it wanted to make the subject of collective bargaining. But it could not prevent LO from making the matter a political issue, when the alliance of party and unions was brought to bear in the political arena.

III. MEMBERSHIP OF LO

The absence of serious ideological or religious differences within the Swedish working class has enabled LO to avoid the challenge of any strong rival for the union loyalties of the manual workers. The syndicalists formed a Workers' Central Organization in 1910, after the major conflict of 1909, but it has never won very great adherence, its peak membership being 37,400 in 1924. Now it has about 17,000 members, mainly in building and forestry, and much of its significance as a body that was revolutionary in doctrine and decentralized in organization has disappeared with the acceptance of collective agreements by syndicalist sections. SAF has always stoutly opposed dealing with syndicalist groups, and, after an attempt to bring the syndicalists into LO had failed in 1929, LO has also set its face against negotiating along with syndicalist organizations. Only incidental references are accordingly made to syndicalist bodies here.[1] The consistently strong and successful opposition by LO to communist

[1] For an analysis of Swedish syndicalism, see Valter Åman, *Svensk syndikalism* (LO, Stockholm, 1938).

and Nazi influences has also made their impact a minor one in Swedish labour relations.

Membership of LO has shown a steady increase throughout its existence, apart from the period 1909–11, when the aftermath of the Great Strike took its toll of disillusioned union members. Beginning in 1912, membership recovered until by 1917 the previous peak of 186,000 members in 1907 had been passed. In only two other years, 1921 and 1933, has LO membership declined, and it has proved remarkably resistant to the usual explanation of union membership fluctuations correlated with the business cycle. The explanation is not simply some sort of vague 'working class solidarity'. LO tried hard during the inter-war years to promote the interests of badly paid groups, e.g. in farming and forestry, as a matter of deliberate and practical working class solidarity.

LO MEMBERSHIP IN SELECTED YEARS

Year	*Affiliated Unions*	*Branches*	*Men*	*Percentage*	*Women*	*Percentage*	*Total*
1900	21	787	42500	97·6	1000	2·4	43500
1910	27	1576	79500	93·3	5700	6·7	85200
1920	31	2799	247200	88·3	32800	11·7	280000
1930	37	5064	495700	89·6	57800	10·4	553500
1940	46	7862	813200	83·8	157900	16·2	971100
1950	44	8886	1038000	81·2	240400	18·8	1278400
1960	44	7930	1150900	78·0	334800	22·0	1485700

The most remarkable feature of LO membership in recent years has been the big increase in female membership. Since 1931 it has risen from 62,000 to 335,000 (an increase of 440%), while male membership has increased from 527,000 in 1931 to 1,150,900 (by 118%).

In the light of the statistics given in the Introduction on the manual workers' labour force, male membership of LO must be considered to be nearly at saturation point, and dependent for increases primarily on the growth of the male manual labour force. This is expected to be slow. While the drive to promote female membership and the LO policy in recent years of giving priority in wage rounds to women and badly paid groups (often the same groups) appear to have a sound basis in 'maximizing the membership function', the decline in the number of women employed in manual work does not provide encouraging growth prospects for LO over the long term. Demarcation problems with salaried workers' unions, particularly in commerce and the public sector, also lend point to the membership saturation problem of LO.

LO income is derived almost entirely from dues paid through the affiliated unions for their members. (Levies are permissible, but are not much used nowadays.) Dues have been increased at every congress since 1941, as the following table shows.[1]

	Monthly dues in öre	*Of which to Press Fund*	*Conflict support per week from LO (crowns)*
1923	40	—	—
1940	40	—	—
1941	50	—	6
1946	70	20	9
1951	90	20	12
1956	150	50[2]	16
1961	200[3]	—	25

In 1960 membership dues of 20·4 m. crowns comprised about 90% of LO's regular income. The main specified items of expenditure were for the Press (over 6 m. crowns, about 25% of total expenditure), depreciation (4 m. crowns), and salaries (over 1 m. crowns). In 1960 only 5,000 crowns were paid out in conflict support to the unions. The change in the significance of this item in recent years has been tremendous. Karlbom estimates that in the years 1899–1953 LO paid out 27 m. crowns in support, 21·6% of the total expenditure of 125 m. crowns in the period.[4] Since 1946 conflict support has become a minor item of expenditure, and the Press, administration, and educational costs of various kinds are now the main items of LO finance.

On capital account LO has now net reserves of some 37 m. crowns, compared with 511 m. crowns held by the forty-four member unions as assets. Financial power clearly rests with the unions.

IV. THE CONSTITUTIONAL POWERS OF LO

When LO was formed the emphasis in the financial support provisions was on giving aid in cases where the unions were attacked. This was inevitable when the unions have not yet gathered financial strength, and when the constitutional powers of LO were limited by a cautious desire to preserve a good deal of union autonomy. However, the growth in the financial and numerical strength of the

[1] Note: One Swedish crown (100 öre) is approximately equivalent to 1/4d. sterling, or 19 U.S. cents.

[2] Since 1955.

[3] The LO representative assembly was empowered by the 1961 LO congress to raise dues in 1964 or later, if it thinks fit.

[4] Torvald Karlbom, *Den svenska fackföreningsrörelsen*, pp. 95–96 (Stockholm, 1955).

movement, and the disadvantages of not having strong central powers which began to emerge through trials of strength with the employers' confederation, soon made the constitutional position of LO both a fascinating and fundamental subject for debate. Problems of internal discipline and co-ordination were solved empirically as they arose, but since 1941 the constitution of LO has been thoroughly revised to give the central organization very wide formal powers over its member groups.

Some tendency to centralization was of course inherent in the nature of the organization LO provided for the trade union movement. Any efficient development of the lock-out insurance service it provided would clearly bring LO into the centre of disputes, willingly or otherwise, as soon as these developed on any scale. Likewise, the very rapid centralization of power on the employers' side which allowed their leaders to arrive at agreements binding on the members was bound to react on the constitution of LO as soon as it had to negotiate with SAF on major issues. In 1907 and 1908, for instance, LO took part in negotiations along with the unions on disputes that had led the employers to adopt the technique of threatening lock-outs on a wide front. SAF was aware of LO's dilemma. In its report for 1908 it remarked that 'It has been shown that the organizations of the workers have not become strong enough to be able to take up a conflict with the existing employers' organizations, at least when economic conditions are not overwhelmingly favourable to the workers.' SAF argued that LO realized this, but had great difficulty in persuading its affiliates to toe the line.[1]

During the Great Strike of 1909 LO in fact exercised powers of leadership which it did not formally possess and the pessimism which defeat engendered within the labour movement found expression in much soul-searching at the 1909 LO congress. Previous congresses had taken no decisions which made LO a more powerful body in relation to the unions, but the experience of 1909 made the whole question of constitutional powers ripe for discussion. Many proposals for constitutional change were put forward, some arguing for centralization, others for the *status quo*, and some for a more decentralized arrangement. The secretariat itself proposed a new constitutional framework which would have involved far-reaching centralization through its becoming responsible for *all* disputes. At the same time, it was cautious enough to state that a decision about reforming LO could not, in its view, be made at once, and indeed only some preliminary steps seem to have been contemplated. In the debate

[1] Carl Hallendorff, *Svenska arbetsgifvareföreningen 1902–1927*, p. 102 (Stockholm, 1927).

the secretariat was reluctant to see more centralization, and the *status quo* remained unchanged.[1] A committee appointed to study the constitutional powers of LO endorsed this before the 1912 congress.

In fact, the period of self-criticism produced no important constitutional changes. In part this was the product of the decline in membership and the general ennui pervading the movement immediately after the defeat of 1909. There had been a crisis and the period of reaction took its toll. Equally important was the formation of the syndicalist central organization in 1910. To ask for increasing powers at the centre, when membership was falling and a bright new organization advocating decentralization was in the air, would have been a bad tactical blunder on the part of LO. In 1912 Lindqvist (the LO chairman) envisaged that by 1917, the year of the next congress, LO might be able to contemplate becoming an attacking organization. This proved an excessively optimistic forecast for a cautious Swedish trade union leader.

The centralization dilemma continued to recur, because the unions were always at a disadvantage when SAF presented a united lock-out front on any issue. As the successive LO congresses thrashed out the pros and cons of LO centralization there occurred a gradual shift in emphasis, away from the negative emphasis on defence against attacks by employers to a positive approach, which stressed the greater material benefits to be derived from central control in the union movement. At the 1922 congress it was agreed to give priority to badly paid groups of workers in deciding whether to approve conflicts. In succeeding congresses centralization for the purpose of promoting what was later to be called 'a wages policy of

[1] One change made in the 1909 congress was that the representative assembly was given the right to begin sympathetic strikes when employers attacked with a lock-out. Thus the initiative had to come from employers. (This became para. 7, clause 6 in the 1912 by-laws.) Some change was also made in the 1909 congress on the regulation of wages negotiations, the formulation being accepted that when one or more unions that had members employed in the same craft or industry or with the same employer planned wage claims, either independently or jointly, there would be co-operation among them to ensure agreement among all on the demands to be put forward. (This became para. 7, clause 7, from 1912.) It was also provided that negotiations could take place in common; decisions on proposals and on the beginning and terminating of conflicts would then be made 'in common' by the unions concerned in the wage claim. But this was not observed in practice, as the 1917 congress discussion and the 1933–4 building conflict show. In any case this new formulation on wage negotiation procedures did not give any greater powers of control to LO. Indeed, in the 1917 congress the LO secretariat said (in reply to motion 33, on consultation between unions on wage issues) that it was unnecessary to prohibit unions from arriving at separate agreements; and it might even be injurious, e.g. when it was advantageous for one or more unions to arrive at agreements even when this was not possible for all. The 1933 building dispute also showed that voting procedures for wage negotiations held 'in common' were often at variance.

solidarity' was discussed, but the secretariat was doubtful of the wisdom or practicability of infringing the autonomy of the unions. In 1931, after an inquiry, the secretariat still favoured the *status quo* on the issues of general co-operation within LO, inter-union collaboration on wage claims, and the LO obligation to lend support only in defensive industrial disputes. But then the pace quickened.

By the time congress met again in 1936 there had been a decided shift away from the *status quo* approach that had been preached since 1909. Three different elements contributed to this change, the building industry dispute of 1933–4, the government committee (the Nothin commission) on problems of industrial peace,[1] and the change in the attitude of the trade union movement to society and its understanding of social responsibility. This last was in part the result of the first two influences and of the rise to political power of the social democratic party; but it was also the fruit of a more mature attitude to problems of industrial relations, soon to be reflected in the Basic Agreement of 1938 between LO and SAF.

The conflict in the building industry was the most important labour dispute in Sweden in the 1930s. It not only hampered the government in its policy of stimulating public works during the depression. The way in which the dispute had to be settled raised some fundamental issues about the constitutional organization of the unions. After a strike over the terms of a new collective contract had been in force for ten months, union funds were drained, SAF was threatening a large-scale lock-out, and government intervention through compulsory arbitration was feared, the representative assembly of LO approved a secretariat recommendation that the conflict should be settled on the terms suggested by a mediation commission.[2] When the members of the unions affected voted on the proposals the outcome was that, although a favourable majority vote was obtained if all the votes of the unions concerned were taken together, two of the unions had, when taken separately, voted for rejection. One of the two, the Metal Workers, announced that the executive would overrule the adverse vote, since there was provision for this in its rules. But the other, the Bricklayers', did not think it could go against the wishes of its members. The LO representative assembly then 'enjoined' the unions affected by the conflict to accept the proposals, and the new agreement was signed. This procedure directed attention to the need for uniformity in the rules of LO unions. In fact, LO had been pondering this issue since 1930, and the representative assembly

[1] *Betänkande om folkförsörjning och arbetsfred* (Stockholm, 1935); *S.O.U.*, 1935 : 65 and 66.

[2] A similar problem had arisen in the paper and pulp industry in 1928. See Casparsson, op. cit., II, 95 et seq.

approved model rules in 1933. But the change came too late to influence the building dispute.

The dispute also had repercussions in the Riksdag, where in 1934 a whole host of motions on labour relations raised questions about the structure, organization, and activity of the labour market associations. The three-man Nothin commission was appointed in December 1934 to make a preliminary study of social intervention in economic life. In the sections of its report dealing with industrial peace the Nothin commission took up questions of voting in the trade unions, centralization of the right of decision, and the competence of organizations. It recommended that, before attempts were made to legislate, there should be an investigation into the possibilities of the labour market organizations themselves reaching agreement, so that outside intervention in the interests of securing industrial peace became unnecessary. In the commission's view a strong system of organizations was the best guarantee of social peace, and it made some positive suggestions for achieving greater control, particularly on the workers' side.

The Nothin commission had a powerful effect. One consequence of its report was the establishment of the Labour Market Committee by LO and SAF in 1936, the deliberations of which led to the Basic Agreement in 1938.[1] It also gave an impetus to reform and centralization of the constitution of the trade unions, and provided LO with a welcome lever with which to convince any of its individualist unions of the need for greater power at the centre. Earlier debates had shown that LO itself did not always oppose centralization, but feared it would lose the support of some unions if it did try to dictate action.

The 1936 LO congress agreed to a thorough inquiry into the tasks and objects of LO. One of the main features of the discussion was the emphasis placed on the increased responsibility of the trade union movement in society, the strengthened political position of the working class, and the need for a positive union attitude to social and economic problems, based on social control of the economy. The congress motion in which these ideas were propounded is a landmark in the development of a new phase of labour relations in Sweden,[2] although the constitutional powers of LO were discussed mainly with reference to collective bargaining and wages policy.

LO appointed a Committee of Fifteen in 1937 to conduct the inquiry, and in 1941 it published a comprehensive analysis of trade

[1] See below, Part III.

[2] This motion (no. 224) was the fruit of committee work in which all the LO industrial unions took part, though the motion was submitted in the name of the executive of the Metal Workers' Union. See Albin Lind, *Solidarisk Lönepolitik*, p. 8 (Stockholm, 1938).

unionism and its problems.[1] Though it ranged over a wide field, discussing relations with the state and problems of workers' influence, its constitutional proposals attracted the greatest discussion at the 1941 LO congress when the report was submitted to it. The main bone of contention was the proposed procedure for handling disputes and wage negotiations. Two developments since the 1936 congress helped to move the congress in favour of greater centralization. First, the signing of the Basic Agreement between LO and SAF in 1938 made it essential for LO to have more than paper guarantees for dealing on its side with union government. Secondly, the climate of opinion in 1941 in support of planning, self-discipline, and co-ordination was greatly favoured by the acceptance and experience of the war-time index wage agreements concluded between LO and SAF.

In addition to these factors there were, however, deeper forces which had been at work in the earlier discussions of the LO constitution and which now came to the surface in one major reform movement. Six strands can be distinguished: (1) a wages policy of solidarity had been increasingly advocated since 1922; (2) effective guarantees were needed in the rules to avoid government intervention; (3) LO was maturing into a statesmanlike responsible interest group; (4) there was pressure on the unions through the great centralization on the employers' side; (5) some of the existing rules were obscure; (6) from its beginnings in 1898 LO had intended quite shortly to begin giving financial support in attacking as well as defensive conflicts.

The rules adopted in 1941 (with later amendments) can be analysed under three heads: (*a*) the objects of LO, (*b*) the executive machinery through which it operates, and (*c*) the powers placed in the hands of the executive secretariat.[2]

(*a*) *The objects of LO*

Greater emphasis is now placed on the political aspects of trade unionism than had been the case since the *formal* link with the social democratic party was severed in 1909. Now LO is stated to be an association of the trade union organizations in Sweden, with the task of exercising the central leadership in the efforts of the movement to safeguard the interests of the wage-earners on the labour market and

[1] *Fackföreningsrörelsen och näringslivet* (Stockholm, 1941). This was the first of three comprehensive and lucid studies by the Swedish trade union movement of its place in contemporary society and economic life. The second is *Fackföreningsrörelsen och den fulla sysselsättningen* (Stockholm, 1951)—an abbreviated version was published in English with the title of *Trade Unions and Full Employment* (Stockholm, 1953). The third, *Samordnad näringspolitik* (Economic Expansion and Structural Change), was debated at the LO congress of 1961.

[2] For an invaluable commentary on the 1941 rules, and later amendments, see Arnold Sölvén, *Landsorganisationens Nya Stadgar* (Stockholm, four editions, 1942, 1947, 1952, and 1957).

in the economy, and in this and other respects of working for the development of society on the basis of political, social, and economic democracy. The emphasis on political democracy was new in principle, although in practice co-operation with the social democratic party has always been close. For the purpose of promoting these general objects certain more specific duties are laid at the door of LO, such as seeing that the trade union activity of the affiliated unions is carried on along uniform lines and with due regard to co-operation (the implication here refers primarily to the wages policy of solidarity, though this is not explicitly prescribed in the rules), while taking account of common interests, the rights of the individual, and the just demands of society. Other functions are to safeguard the interests of the wage-earners in legislative and social policy matters, and to collect and process statistical information in order to obtain a comprehensive picture of trade union activity and general labour market conditions. This last point is, of course, not new, but has gained in significance with the development of economic thinking and planning in aggregative terms. LO has also to promote the education of the members in political, trade union, and cultural matters, maintain international contacts, and provide financial support in conflicts on the conditions prescribed in detail.

(*b*) *The executive machinery*

The activity of LO is still carried on through the tripartite structure which was devised in 1898, a congress, representative assembly, and executive committee (or secretariat). Congress, the supreme decision-making body, is small and compact, and at present meets every five years. It consists of 300 delegates appointed by the unions (in the manner they determine) in proportion to their membership, with a minimum of one delegate per member union, plus the members of the representative assembly (about 125 at present) and the secretariat (13). Each delegate is entitled to one vote, and the representative assembly and secretariat members are entitled to speak and make proposals on any matter, and to vote on questions which do not relate to their conduct of the affairs of LO since the previous congress, or in matters where a decision of the representative assembly has been appealed to congress for final adjudication. Motions to congress can be raised in advance by every affiliated national union and by the local branches, and the secretariat is obliged to formulate and circulate its views on the motions submitted before congress meets. The distinctive features of LO congresses are the factual and objective approach, and the absence of hot air. Few political pronouncements are made. Apart from the phlegmatic national temperament, the explanations are to be sought in the following factors: (*a*) congress meets for one week every five years, which means there is little time for political demonstrations and high flights of fancy; (*b*) congress is small; and (*c*) a tremendous amount of preliminary preparation precedes the actual deliberations on the floor of the house.

Membership of the representative assembly, which is the supreme authority between congresses, consists of the secretariat and representatives of the affiliated unions, and is determined in proportion to membership.[1] The members are appointed by their unions immediately after the LO congress to serve for the period until congress next meets, and this provides continuity in membership for at least five years. The assembly normally meets twice a year, in the spring for a statutory annual general meeting, and in the autumn to consider collective bargaining problems.

The secretariat provides the necessary executive continuity. Since 1951 the secretariat has consisted of thirteen members of affiliated unions. Three of the members—chairman, vice-chairman, and secretary—are full-time paid officials elected by congress. They hold office until further notice, and are to all intents and purposes permanent officials. They are *ex-officio* members of the secretariat. The remaining ten members are part-time,[2] elected by congress for the period until it next meets. Besides the requirement introduced in 1941 that the secretariat members must (as a rule of convenience) reside in or around Stockholm, the ten elected members are, according to a rules amendment introduced in 1951, to be elected from national unions that carry on their activities in different sectors of industry and trade and of the labour market. In practice, the part-time members are always union chairmen. The secretariat normally meets once a week.

Formally, the secretariat is collectively responsible for policy, and arrives at decisions when at least seven members are in agreement.[3] But the position of the chairman is crucial and powerful. He is instructed to direct the activities of LO in consultation with the secretariat members. 'He leads the discussions at meetings of the secretariat, presents all the matters on the agenda, and is responsible for executing the decisions of congress, the representative assembly, and the secretariat.'[4]

[1] The formula is as follows: up to 10,000 members, 1 representative; more than 10,000 and up to 20,000, 2 representatives; over 20,000 members, 2 representatives, plus 1 for every additional 20,000 members, or part thereof.

[2] They are paid an honorarium, at present 1,800 crowns a year.

[3] When decisions are being taken to withdraw financial support from a union that rejects a secretariat proposal on wage negotiations a two-thirds majority is, however, required.

[4] LO has had nine chairmen: (1) Fredrik Sterky, a civil servant and office manager, 1898–1900; (2) Herman Lindqvist, a cabinet-maker, 1900–20; (3) Arvid Thorberg, a joiner, 1920–30; (4) Edvard Johanson, shoemaker, 1930–6; (5) Albert Forslund, a railway worker, 1936; (6) August Lindberg, a sawmill worker, 1936–46; (7) Gunnar Andersson, a metalworker, 1946; (8) Axel Strand, a cabinet-maker, 1947–56; (9) Arne Geijer, a metalworker, since 1956.

The central work of LO has become increasingly concerned with the provisions of expert information and advice, and LO employs in addition a number of experts, e.g. in law, economics, works councils, female workers' questions, work study.

(*c*) *The powers of the secretariat*

Apart from the routine tasks of administering the assets of LO, promoting international contacts, and shaping LO policy on legislative proposals, the main powers and duties of the secretariat relate to the centralization effected in 1941. There are four topics which contain the essence of the centralization, and on these the secretariat has formidable formal powers:

(*i*) internal disputes;
(*ii*) the plan of organization (implemented in 1951);
(*iii*) wages policy and negotiations;
(*iv*) procedures in disputes, and grounds for giving financial support.

These will be analysed in turn. All four involve major issues of policy.

(*i*) *Internal disputes*. Since the 1941 rules revision the secretariat has been empowered to examine *and settle* (previously 'try to settle') disputes that arise between affiliated unions, and to work for staunch and loyal co-operation among the unions. This on the other side involves general obligations on the part of the unions. When a member has obtained work in a sphere of activity (as laid down in the organization plan) of another union, the *organization* must collaborate in having his membership transferred to the new union. This new obligation on unions and their members[1] was reaffirmed and extended in 1951 to cover cases where, by a decision of the secretariat, the member is to transfer to another union.

Prior to 1941 disputes between unions could, on the request of either party, be referred to a special arbitration board appointed for the purpose. Now the secretariat acts as the board of arbitration, with no appeal against its decisions. Such disputes *are* to be referred to the secretariat for examination and settlement. The main reason for the change in 1941 was that most inter-union disputes refer to demarcation issues and organization boundaries, and it is considered more appropriate to have one body adjudicating on these rather than *ad hoc* arbitration boards.

[1] The position of individual union members is not explicitly regulated in the LO rules, since it is an association of unions. The rights and obligations of individual members are set out in the standard rules for the member *unions* discussed below.

(*ii*) *The organization plan*. In 1951 the secretariat became empowered to examine *and settle* questions concerning the interpretation and application of the plan of organization of LO. Express provision had previously been made only for cases where such questions were the subject of disputes between unions. In 1951 the secretariat argued that organizational problems could arise without there being a specific dispute, and that this was such an important matter that the rules ought explicitly to give it this power. LO need not therefore wait for organizational problems to be brought to it, but can pursue an active policy.

(*iii*) *Wages policy and negotiations*. The reformed rules of 1941 remained the same as before in stating that the secretariat had, when circumstances so required, to give support to the affiliated unions in negotiations on wages and working conditions. But, as the pre-1941 constitutional debate shows, there were considerable doubts about the formal powers of LO to participate in wage negotiations, and in practice the rule had been that the secretariat took part only when requested to do so by the unions.[1] Now formal powers have been given to the secretariat not only to participate, but to present proposals for an agreement to the organizations concerned in negotiations. A sanction was also introduced in 1941, providing that if a proposal made by the secretariat is rejected by the union concerned, and it is receiving financial support, the representative assembly (from 1952 the secretariat, which illustrates further centralization) may decide to withdraw it.[2] However, any such decision to withdraw support is qualified to the extent that it cannot be taken unless the conflict causes or can be *feared* to cause considerable inconvenience for other affiliated unions, for the trade union movement as a whole, or for vital social interests.[3] There is a right of appeal against such withdrawal of support to the representative assembly and to congress. This is a much cleverer sanction than that of *expulsion* would be. Here LO can appeal to 'the interests of society' if a union becomes recalcitrant, and a union is likely to have little bargaining strength, both inside and outside LO, if it resists the secretariat's policy.

An addition was made in 1941 to the old provisions dating from 1909 on wage negotiations, which recommended collaboration between unions negotiating for the same industry or trade. The building industry dispute had shown graphically that there was no clear formulation of the rules in the event of unions arriving at different decisions. To remedy this, it is now provided that such co-operation

[1] Sölvén, op. cit., p. 47, 4th edition (Stockholm, 1957).

[2] See footnote 3, p. 38.

[3] This particular clause has been reframed in this way since 1951, for reasons explained below.

is to take place *under the leadership of the secretariat.*[1] Another new provision is that this also applies when the employers' side takes the initiative in negotiations.

The secretariat has the duty of providing information on important wage negotiations and disputes to the organizations that are, or could be expected to be, affected by them, and on wage questions which may be important in principle or have wide practical significance the secretariat must call together for discussion representatives of the union affected.

The member unions are in turn obliged to keep the secretariat informed about important wage issues and disputes and (since 1951) are obliged to report the number of members affected. These obligations now apply irrespective of whether a conflict has in fact begun. The 1941 and subsequent wage policy provisions thus provide clarification and centralization on the most vexed questions of earlier wage policy discussions and wage negotiations. The provisions do not directly authorize LO to conclude agreements on behalf of member unions. It can put forward recommendations, and withdraw support. What can happen, and in recent years has become common practice,[2] is that LO can be empowered by the representative assembly to arrive at recommendations with SAF and (and here is the rub as far as union autonomy is concerned) bind itself to have these recommendations accepted. These formal powers give it considerable authority in ensuring success, though it is far from being the case that the pricing of labour services occurs only at LO level.[3]

(*iv*) *Procedures in disputes, and grounds for giving financial support: Permission to strike.* Increased central influence over the conduct of disputes formed an important part of the 1941 rules revision, not only because it was decided at long last to make formal[4] provision for support in strikes, 'attacking conflicts', but also because LO accepted the principle that it should adopt a responsible attitude to the pressures that strikes exercise on society. The 1941 formulation was not absolutely clear on this point. It stated that an organization affiliated to LO must not resort to a strike, including a sympathetic strike, covering more than 3% of its members without first obtaining permission from the secretariat. Strikes on a smaller scale than those

[1] The Nothin commission had suggested that when a wages dispute affected several unions in common LO should make the final decision. See *S.O.U.*, 1935 : 65, p. 109.

[2] The developing practice of centralized bargaining was given the formal seal of union approval by being incorporated, *without debate*, in the LO rules at the 1961 congress. See p. 265 for details.

[3] See Part V for an analysis of collective bargaining in operation.

[4] In fact LO had in recent years to an increasing extent given support in disputes that were in reality, though not formally, attacking conflicts.

covered by this '3% rule' might not be resorted to if they could be *expected* to lead to a lock-out of more than 3% of the members of the union *or* of members of other affiliated unions. This formulation did not clearly distinguish two separate questions. It did take account of a question of fact—whether 3% of the membership was affected—but it also raised a wide question of probability, based on anticipated developments in smaller disputes. The position was clarified in 1951.

In principle the secretariat did not like the '3% rule', and considered it would have been most logical to make LO permission mandatory in all cases, even although the rule clearly puts a severe limit on the freedom of action of affiliated unions. But in prescribing it LO hoped to avoid the practical difficulties of being troubled by disputes affecting less than 3% of a union's membership, and in addition it was generally only the larger conflicts that affected the whole trade union movement to such an extent that they justified control over them being placed in the hands of the secretariat. The broad intention was also to take account of expected developments, and the consequences of any strike, but it was extremely difficult to know *in advance* whether conflicts might lead to a lock-out of more than 3% of the union's members, or of members of other unions. Because of the difficulties of anticipating the multiplier effects of small conflicts, and because the 1941 formulation had only taken account of the possibility that other members might be locked out, and not, e.g. temporarily laid off, the 1951 congress agreed to add the following phrase to the clause: 'or if the strike can be foreseen to lead to the laying-off of members who, taken along with those directly affected by the strike, constitute more than 3% of the union's members, or can also be foreseen to lead to the laying-off of a significant number of members of other affiliated organizations'.

This is still vague, and still implies that the union could from the beginning reckon on a possible lay-off from work as an inevitable consequence of the strike, and there is thus scope for considerable differences of interpretation.

Refusal of strike permission. The provisions on strike permission are also vague in another respect. Provided the 3% rule was observed, and the difficulties of interpretation discussed above had satisfied LO, it was prescribed that permission to strike could *not* be refused *unless* the strike or lock-out to which it gave rise could be *feared* to cause considerable inconvenience outside the sphere of activity of the union concerned. This clause was amended in 1951. Instead of reading '*feared* to cause considerable inconvenience outside the sphere of activity of the union concerned', the phrase now reads 'feared to cause considerable inconvenience for other affiliated unions, for the trade union movement as a whole, or for vital social interests'. The scope has thus been broadened. The intention of 1941 *was* to take into account the social consequences of strikes: the 1936 LO congress discussion of social responsibility clearly implied this, the report of the LO Committee of Fifteen suggested it, and the Basic Agreement of 1938 between LO and SAF (particularly Chapter V) requires it. Moreover, LO had already bound itself in 1941, in the declaration of its objects, to take account of the interests of society. But the 1941 formulation was a compromise solution designed to appease the adherents of union autonomy (e.g. the compositors). The 1951 amendment explicitly allows LO to take account of the general interests of society in assessing the wide consequences of any direct action. This can be an extremely wide field. In wages policy, for example, LO can legitimately place the claims of one union against the wider interests of the movement or of society, if it feels they are paramount. Some protection against the discretion this gives to the secretariat is provided by the right of appeal against a refusal of strike permission.

Lock-outs. The secretariat also has considerable discretion in deciding what action to take in the event of lock-outs. When an employer or employers' organization begins a lock-out against members of LO unions it is the duty of the secretariat to decide upon appropriate action, after *consulting* the executive of the union concerned. If a large-scale lock-out is *threatened*, the secretariat is empowered, if it thinks necessary, to call a meeting of the representative assembly in order to discuss and decide on any measures the situation seems to require.

Blockading and boycotts. The declaration of blockades and boycotts is also carefully controlled. Only the executive of a union can declare a blockade or boycott that has binding effect, and the LO secretariat must give its prior agreement to a blockade or boycott in connexion with a strike for which LO approval is necessary or with a lock-out for which LO is giving financial support. A union cannot resort to a blockade which affects workers affiliated to other unions without the consent of these other unions or, if they cannot agree, the secretariat of LO. Since 1941 the LO secretariat, representative assembly, and congress have become entitled to begin sympathetic action in the form of a stoppage of work, blockade, or boycott covering any or all unions (provided they are not debarred by the terms of their employment from resorting to direct action).[1]

Conflict support. On the basis of these careful prescriptions governing direct action the secretariat of LO gives financial support as of

[1] Sympathetic action is permitted in law under the Collective Contracts Act of 1928. See Chapter VI.

right, in *all* conflicts, provided the rules have been observed. There is a right of appeal if support is refused.

V. THE NATIONAL UNIONS IN LO

Below the LO level, power in the trade union movement is centred in the national unions, of which the branches are dependent subsidiaries. Before the 1941 constitutional reform the national unions were generally considered to be the hub of the movement,[1] but the controls exercised by LO since 1941, both in its own rules and in the standard rules laid down for the member unions, make it very difficult to argue that the locus of government is now situated at the level of the national union. The unions are still the centre of financial strength, but not of constitutional power. The size and financial strength of the unions will be analysed before discussing their relations with LO and their branches.

In 1960 LO had a membership of 1,485,700, organized in forty-four unions with 7,930 branches.[2] The size distribution of unions is shown in the following table:

No. of members '000s	*No. of LO unions*
1–5	6
over 5–10	6
over 10–20	13
over 20–30	6
over 30–40	4
over 40–50	1
over 50–100	5
over 100	3

Easily the largest union is the Metal Workers' Union, with a membership of 286,000 (19% of the LO total), followed by the Building Workers' Union with 144,000, and the Municipal Workers' Union, with 119,000 members employed by local authorities on a wide range of jobs. The Union of Commercial Employees has 99,000 members and one of the largest untapped sources of potential membership. Ten LO unions have a majority of female members,

[1] Sigfrid Hansson, a prominent historian of Swedish trade unionism, was still able to write in 1935 that it was the national unions that were the hub of the movement, and that LO was in reality only the formal head. In writing of centralization, he considered it only in relation to what he termed the far-reaching powers of the executive boards of the national unions, *not* LO. See his memorandum on trade unionism in *S.O.U.*, 1935 : 66, p. 477 et seq. He expressed similar views in his *Från Mackmyra till Saltsjöbaden*, p. 23 (Stockholm, 1939).

[2] See Appendix 1 for a list of LO member unions.

over 80% in both the Hotel and Restaurant Workers' Union and the Garment Workers' Union. The drift from the land, the decline of textiles, and the growth of service industries have had a marked effect in recent years on union membership in these sectors, and the growth of the public sector has led to a rapid increase in membership among municipal employees, e.g. hospital staff (lower grades). The good export markets in engineering, paper and pulp, and wood products, have stimulated membership in these industries in the post-war period, and the Building Workers' Union has also expanded considerably.

The main sources of union finance are regular weekly or monthly dues, entrance and re-entrance fees, and *ad hoc* levies. The financial strength of the unions varies considerably according to the sector of the economy in which they operate and the benefits they provide. Entrance dues are in general fairly low; only seven unions charge as much as 10 crowns, and ten unions have at present no entrance charge. Re-entrance dues vary very much more between unions, and are on the whole higher than straight entrance dues, varying with the nature of the offence if a member has been expelled. In most cases the ordinary re-entrance charge, which is fixed by the union executive, does not exceed 20 crowns.

The ordinary dues also vary considerably, by union and by type of member. The table below shows the great increase in union dues that has taken place in recent years. It should be noted that these figures do *not* include dues to union branches, amounting to 50–100 crowns per member per year.

ANNUAL DUES OF FULL-PAYING MEMBERS OF LO UNIONS

	No. of unions	
	year	
Amount in crowns	*1950*	*1960*
less than 30	1	—
31–40	7	—
41–50	10	—
51–60	8	—
61–70	5	—
71–80	6	2
81–90	1	2
91–100	1	7
100–150	3	23
151–200	1	7
201–250	1	1
over 250	—	2

Source: LO annual reports, 1950, 1960.

As the table suggests, this is not unionism on the cheap. The three unions with dues over 200 crowns annually in 1960 were the Typographers', Lithographers', and Chimney Sweeps', the first two having extensive social welfare schemes.

Assets of the unions in 1960 totalled 511 m. crowns[1] (the LO net assets amounted to 37·5 m. crowns), and income from dues, 130 m. crowns, was 84% of the total income. The main items of expenditure were administration and dues to LO, and a surplus of income over expenditure of 38 m. crowns was carried forward to 1961.

Total assets, income, and assets per member vary enormously between unions, depending on the potential need for funds for conflicts and risks of unemployment. The Waterpower Personnel Union had the lowest *per capita* assets (11 crowns), and the Typographers the largest (1,980). The Metal Workers' Union had total assets of 148 m. crowns (27% of the total), a holding of 518 crowns per member.

The average holding of all unions was 344 crowns, but thirty-two unions had a per capita holding below the average. As with LO funds, so has the prevalence of industrial peace increasingly made union funds available for administration, propaganda, and education, rather than for support in disputes. In 1920 about half the unions had no assets, a marked contrast to the affluent position of 1960. Levies are now rather unusual.

Financial support is given by the unions to members in approved strikes and in lock-outs, and in cases of victimization by employers. Legal aid can be given in industrial disputes. Normally there is a qualifying membership period of three months before support is given, and a waiting period of six days. The amount of support is settled by each union, and at present ranges between 7 and 15 crowns a day, depending on family circumstances. Support is paid out through the branches.

Many unions also carry funds for unemployment insurance, which in Sweden is run through voluntary government-subsidized funds. These funds are not available for financing industrial disputes, unless unemployment existed when direct action broke out.

The rules of LO and the standard union rules provide that funds are to be held primarily in government bonds and other fixed-interest securities, but interest in holding some equities was expressed to the LO congress of 1956 by a committee of inquiry which had completed a study of the placing of union funds. Investment of LO and union funds in the shares of private firms has been expressly authorized since the 1961 LO congress. A central administration of union funds

[1] Excluding unemployment insurance funds, which are administered and accounted for separately.

and possibly a common fund for financing conflicts have also been considered. The latter would be a logical development of the increased centralization in wage bargaining, but it would involve a further shift away from the present distribution of financial strength within the trade union movement and is unlikely in the near future.

VI. THE GOVERNMENT OF THE UNIONS

Prior to 1941 the rules of LO stated that industrial and craft unions had a right to membership in LO, provided they recognized its objects and were willing to abide by its rules. The only other condition of entry was that the union collected a certain minimum level of dues from its branches for each member. However, LO did not in practice necessarily restrict itself to these criteria, for it also took into consideration such matters as the place the aspiring member union would occupy in the organization plan.

Under the new deal of 1941 there is no expressly recognized right of entry. National unions, and local unions that cannot gain membership of a national union, *may* be granted membership, on condition that they include in their rules four compulsory provisions, and otherwise abide by the rules of LO. The compulsory rules reflect the trend to centralization and the tightening up of organization in an attempt to achieve a certain amount of uniformity. They are briefly the following:

(*i*) the right of entry, the open shop;
(*ii*) the right to transfer membership;
(*iii*) the obligation to transfer membership; and
(*iv*) the power of veto of the executive of the union in bargaining questions.

Each of these is examined in turn.

(*i*) *The open shop*

Every worker *employed* in the sphere of activity of an LO union is entitled to join the union, with the exceptions where the union may legitimately refuse membership or expel a member.[1] The closed shop, which obliges an employer to employ only organized workers, has never been too serious a problem in Sweden, except for a short period after the First World War, when there was a high level of unemployment and some unions feared they might have to accommodate large numbers of unemployed if they allowed unrestricted entry. In 1926 the LO congress declared that a closed and monopolistic union policy conflicted with the principles of the trade union movement

[1] These are discussed below, p. 53.

and was not reconcilable with democratic and socialist philosophies.[1] The Committee of Fifteen, reporting in 1941, considered the open shop was so fundamental a right that an organization that did not recognize this basic tenet could not obtain or retain membership in LO. The 1941 formulation expresses the view, however, that it is going far enough to allow open entry to a union when the worker has obtained employment in the sphere of activity covered by the union.

Once employment has been obtained there is no objection to the exercise of pressure on individual workers and exhortations to join the union. But the 'union shop', which requires a worker to join the union within a certain period after obtaining a job, cannot be enforced, though LO is not unsympathetic to it, when the employer is a partner in SAF. 'Article 23' (now Article 32) of the rules of SAF explicitly reserves to the employer the right to employ organized or unorganized workers at his discretion. Outside the SAF sector the union shop does sometimes exist, e.g. in the co-operative movement,[2] and preference is given to organized workers by some non-SAF agreements.

The secretariat of LO has repeatedly stated that it is a matter for the parties to agreements to write a union shop clause into agreements, but that it is powerless to take the initiative with SAF on this question in view of the latter's insistence on protecting the negative right of association and refusing any hint of exclusive bargaining rights to union labour. The most recent LO pronouncement on the subject is somewhat equivocal,[3] by avoiding any declaration of principle for or against organization clauses and at the same time recognizing that the modern employer takes a positive attitude to trade unionism. LO is satisfied that experience shows that unions have been able to increase the percentage of organization among workers without the weapon of the closed or union shop. The 1956 statement can be interpreted as meaning that LO would not oppose

[1] See LO *kongress-protokoll*, 1926, motion no. 36, and secretariat *utlåtande* no. 4.

[2] The formulation here varies. In the co-operative agreements for food production it is provided that 'all personnel covered by the agreements are to be members of the union. It rests with the workers to control this.' The employer is not under any obligation to ensure that only union labour is employed, except when an approach is made to him on individual cases by the workers' side. In its agreements with the Metal Workers' Union and the Moulders' Union the co-operative movement expresses the view that workers should belong to their union.

[3] See LO *kongress-protokoll*, 1956, secretariat *utlåtande* no. 20, p. 397. Apart from SAF's opposition in principle, LO recognizes that 'the modern employer is aware of the usefulness to him of trade union organization in the workplace and therefore does not consider he is debarred from promoting it to the extent and in the way he finds possible. If in any sector conditions are such that it is considered appropriate and possible to have an agreement containing an organization clause the union concerned should investigate the possibilities itself.'

a union shop policy, though in practice this is probably unnecessary in the collectivized Swedish labour market. The Act of 1936 on the right of association does not provide protection for workers against pressure from the unions to organize.[1] It is SAF, and not the law, which appears as the defender of individual liberty, resisting any attempts by the unions to exercise job control through the union shop. At the same time, SAF does not oppose organization as such. The closed shop would of course be inconsistent with the LO rules safeguarding the rights of individual union members within the movement.

(ii) The right to transfer membership

A second condition for unions being members of LO is the *right* for the individual member of one affiliated organization who has found employment in the sphere of activity of another to transfer his membership to it without special payment. This clause is directed against unions that refuse to give up members, and is also intended to promote the LO organization plan. To further this latter aim, an addition was made in 1951 providing that members were entitled to transfer from one organization to another as a result of decisions made by the LO secretariat. But rights also imply obligations.

(iii) The obligation to transfer membership

In the pre-1941 rules individual members were obliged to transfer membership, but in 1941 the obligation was only placed on the affiliated organizations to facilitate such transfers. In 1951 it was made clear that the right of the individual member to transfer must also be supplemented by an *obligation* on his part to go. This is the third compulsory membership rule in LO.

Thus the secretariat, unions, and individual members are now formally involved in carrying out the organization plan of LO. It is recognized by LO that there can be no legal compulsion on a member to transfer, but the clause enables expulsion to be used as a sanction if a member refuses to go when he has found employment in another sphere or if the organization plan decrees that he should be organized elsewhere. The co-operation of the unions is ensured by making these requirements conditions of membership.

It is not LO's intention here to use the mailed fist in the interests of executing an abstract plan of organization based on industrial unionism, but rather to have these formal powers in hand as a last resort, while using the art of persuasion as the primary means.[2]

[1] The legal provisions governing the right to combine and bargain are discussed in Chapter V.

[2] This is discussed more fully below, pp. 61–66, with reference to the LO plan of organization.

(iv) The right of veto

The fourth requirement in national union rules is that the board (or executive council) of the union has the right to make the final decision in questions concerning the termination of collective contracts, the acceptance or rejection of proposals for agreements, or for resorting to direct action. Voting among the members on such issues is only advisory. This clarifies the type of issue which the 1933–4 building industry conflict raised. The Nothin commission questioned whether it was appropriate for proposals which had been agreed by negotiation delegations to be made the subject of voting by the members at all. It was desirable that both sides should be represented by delegates who had the power (the employers' side usually had) to arrive at definite decisions. The right of veto was in fact written into the standard LO union rules in 1933, and by 1941 only four LO unions did not have an express or implied right of veto in their rules. But the 1941 revision makes the clause on the right of veto a condition of membership of LO.

The standard rules provide that proposals for collective agreements are to be submitted to members affected for their examination, but this is not a *compulsory* provision. Likewise, the union is entitled to decide for itself the *manner* in which it obtains the views of its members, by vote or by delegate conferences, its voting requirements regarding the type of majority and whether a majority is based on those affected or those voting. More than half the unions reckon the majority on those *affected* by the proposals.

The right of veto inspires a clash of views about whether it is democratic to be guided by a majority vote of union members or by the views of the democratically elected union officials, and has been a perennial topic at congress.[1] The LO secretariat view has been that the board of a union would obviously only exercise its veto in exceptional circumstances, and would clearly take note of the opinion the members expressed in their vote. In 1946 the chairman stressed that the movement had representative democracy, and this (in contrast to the bad example of the syndicalists with their direct democracy) was a sign of maturity of the Swedish trade union movement.

Apart from these four obligatory clauses the unions must observe certain other rules, e.g. that the whole membership shall affiliate to

[1] By 1956 there were, however, clear signs that the opposition to the right of veto was becoming stilled. It is significant that all the protesting motions at LO congresses since 1941 have come from union branches, though spokesmen for some of the national unions have accepted it with reluctance. In the 1946 congress seventeen motions asked for the abolition or modification of the right of veto. In 1951 ten motions objected to it, while in 1956 only one motion asked for its abolition. It was not even mentioned at the 1961 congress.

LO, that the prescribed dues shall be paid. Otherwise, the union rules drawn up in standard form in 1941 are recommendations, and need not be followed. This distinction between mandatory rules and others (the majority) which are simply recommendations appears sometimes to be confusing to the unions. Not all the unions, for example, appear to appreciate how much discretion they have in determining voting procedures on wages issues. Another example is that the standard rules used to recommend provisions for honorary membership which the majority of unions follow. In 1956 LO refused to give a lead and remove this recommendation, despite the complaint by some that it was costly and out of date. LO stressed that this was a recommendation, which the unions were free to change as they thought fit. But in 1961 the clause in question was deleted from the standard rules.

The increased centralization in 1941 was reflected in the provision that LO may expel unions that flagrantly disregard the rules or decisions arrived at by its authorities in accordance with the rule and do not, despite reminders, take corrective action without delay. There was no express recognition of this right before 1941, though LO, like other organizations, enjoyed it. There is a right of appeal against expulsion through the representative assembly to the next LO congress. Affiliated unions can also disaffiliate on six months' notice. Unions that do not fulfil their financial obligations automatically lose their membership.

While the national unions have since 1941 lost a good deal of their previous independence, and can no longer be regarded as the constitutional centre of LO, their formal positions *vis-à-vis* their own branches was strengthened in 1951. The 1941 rules provided for workers to organize in local unions which were to form national unions. In 1951 it was stressed, however, that the national union was the main unit of organization, and the rules now provide that LO works for those employed in private, government, and local authority service being combined in national organizations which operate at the local level through branches in accordance with a plan determined by congress. Despite the very strict disciplinary code on certain fundamental matters, there is some flexibility in order to meet the particular requirements of individual unions. The Committee of Fifteen recognized that 'the unions must have the right to make provision for the special circumstances of the trade'. Within the framework of compulsory provisions, and standard rules which are only recommendations, there is considerable variety in the structure, organization, and financial position of the LO unions.

The national union is an association of all the workers employed in an industry or trade who should, 'in accordance with the LO plan of organization', belong to that union. Some unions do not include this last phrase, but specify the types of workers they do organize. Some unions go further than the LO standard rules by including in their objectives co-determination, industrial democracy, the socialization of production (about one-third of the unions include this declaration), hours of work, and overtime.

The organization of the national unions follows the LO tripartite structure of congress, representative or union assembly, and executive board, with in addition branch organization. Congress usually meets once every three to five years. Union congresses, like the LO congress, are compact, serious and dispassionate gatherings, carefully prepared, and held to a tight agenda covering major matters of policy on industrial questions. Each congress delegate has *one* vote. Union rules usually specify that the representative or union council members are to represent different districts, types of activity and size of branch in order to secure a really representative body. This council supervises the general activity of the executive board, which is not entitled to arrive at decisions in matters of principle or economic importance without prior consultation with the council. The executive usually consists of seven to ten members, the chairman, the secretary, and the treasurer being full-time officials. Decisions are made on the basis of more than half the total board membership being agreed. Apart from conducting the meetings of the board, the chairman is not endowed with any dictatorial powers. The strength of his position depends less on formal rules than on his own personality and guiding influence. In fact, he (and not the general secretary) is usually very powerful. Most unions have full-time officials who deal with negotiations, organization, education, works councils, and other matters.

VII. RELATIONS BETWEEN THE MEMBER AND THE UNION

In addition to the compulsory provisions which determine rights and obligations with regard to entry, transfer of membership, and collective bargaining, the rules provide other rights and obligations for the members. The individual member is entitled to submit motions to congress, for the branch can approve or disapprove, but cannot block them. He is eligible for election as a delegate to congress and is entitled to vote at the elections and be present at the counting of votes. He is entitled to obtain support in conflicts, to ask for legal aid, and to give up his membership.[1] He is also entitled to call for reference to arbitration as a final instance of disputes between him and the union on the following five issues:

[1] 'A member who has transferred to activity lying outside the sphere of activity of the union or of another union affiliated to LO, or who has become an employer or a foreman can, on payment of all the outstanding dues, have his membership terminated.'

(*i*) If he is expelled. Only in cases of failure to pay the prescribed dues is a *branch* authorized to expel a member, and expulsion is in any event automatic for this offence. Otherwise the *executive board* of the union *may* expel a member who has obtained membership by making false statements, who misappropriates the funds of the union in any way, who engages in strike and blockade breaking, or (a new provision since 1941, which was intended to give a union discretion to expel members of anti-democratic organizations) who has infringed the rules or instructions, or 'pursues or supports activity that is irreconcilable with the purpose of the organization, or otherwise behaves in a disloyal manner'.[1] In this last case the executive of the union may at its discretion, and as an alternative to expulsion, deprive the member indefinitely or for a specific period of his right to represent the union in an official capacity. The object in introducing this alternative was to cover cases where there is a closed shop agreement, and where expulsion would therefore be equivalent to a sentence of dismissal from employment.

(*ii*) A new ground for expulsion, to which no objections were raised, was introduced in 1951 to meet cases where immediate action is called for against a group of members, rather than individuals, who *clearly* and *deliberately* break the rules. The intention here is to enable the union to act more quickly than can be expected under the normal procedure governing expulsions, and refers in particular to unofficial strikes or a wilful refusal to obey a union decision to return to work. LO argued that in such cases action is necessary *at once*. This 1951 arrangement allows the union to act in cases where members wilfully flout the rules, or provisions arrived at by congress on the basis of the rules, and who, despite warnings from the union executive, fail to conform. The usual notification procedure (by letter) for expulsion can also be by-passed here. If more than one member is being expelled for the same reason they can be notified via the branch or a public announcement. This procedure is a powerful disciplinary deterrent to unofficial stoppages, and on several occasions since 1951 it has been brought successfully into action as a sanction against

[1] The LO congress of 1936 had declared, against the advice of the secretariat, that members of national socialist organizations could not be members of unions affiliated to LO. The secretariat was not sympathetic to the Nazis, but argued that the Nazis had so few adherents in Sweden that it would be unwise to raise the issue in this way. In December 1939, partly as a result of the Russian attack on Finland, the LO representative assembly issued a statement advising the unions not to allow themselves to be represented by communists. As a result, 'the communists in the trade unions were largely rooted out of official posts. Some unions went further and expelled members belonging to the communist party.' (LO *kongress-protokoll*, 1941, p. 262.) The 1941 formulation on expulsion and refusal of membership is more general, and gives unions wide discretionary powers in dealing with all forms of anti-democratic organizations. Some unions continued specifically to ban Nazis and communists from office.

members who objected to wage agreements negotiated by the union.[1]

(*iii*) In the event of other disputed matters between the union, branch, executive board, or members. There is also specific provision that a member who considers he has suffered unjustly through a decision of his branch or its board can appeal to the union executive.

(*iv*) If application to resign from membership is refused. There is little point in this clause. It does not really prevent (as might seem at first sight to be the object of the clause) a member from leaving the union if he chooses to do so, since he is automatically expelled if he fails to pay his dues for eight weeks. He then runs the risk of enjoying considerable unpopularity among dues-paying members, since his defection is generally made public.

(*v*) If membership is refused. Strictly speaking, this rule does not refer to the relationship between the member and the union, but the relationship of the union to a person seeking to become a member. Application to join a union is made through a branch, but final acceptance rests with the executive board of the union. In addition to the right of entry clause and any union age requirement, membership may be refused on those grounds which might lead to expulsion.

The arbitration procedure to which members can ultimately appeal in disputes falling under these five headings follows the provisions of the general arbitration Act. This provides for five arbitrators, two appointed by each side and the fifth jointly by them or, failing agreement, by the LO secretariat. Not all unions have adopted the standard rules on this point. Some specify that the union council or board is the highest court of appeal and decision in these disputes.[2]

Is there a case for arguing that an outside appeals body should be made mandatory, to overcome any secret victimization of members? There are points to be made on both sides. The provisions for treating expulsion try to keep the processing of such disputes *within* the movement itself. Though cases have occasionally reached the law courts, the legislature has been very loath to interfere in the internal affairs of idealistic associations,[3] and leaves them considerable scope

[1] The Collective Contracts Act of 1928 also places a heavy onus on organizations, and necessitates machinery in the union rules for curbing wayward members. See Chapter VI, Section III. The 1936 Act on the 'Right of Association' also requires organizations to restrain their members from violating the Act.

[2] E.g. the largest LO union, the Metal Workers' Union, which had arbitration arrangements for internal disputes prior to the 1941 reform, retains its own arbitration procedure, with the union executive having the right of final decision after the arbitration board has considered a problem referred to it.

[3] For cases where the law courts have on occasion dealt with expulsion from trade unions, see Folke Schmidt, *Kollektiv arbetsrätt*, 3rd edition, pp. 94–99 (Stockholm, 1958). Two main questions asked by the Courts have been: (*a*) the formal one of whether expulsion was in accordance with the rules; and (*b*) the material one, of whether membership is essential (e.g. if there is a closed shop agreement) to carrying on one's livelihood. In 1948 the Supreme Court ruled that

in regulating such matters between the organization and its members. In fact, LO goes a good deal further in these provisions in ensuring fair play than most other idealistic associations. SAF, for example, itself adjudicates on *applications* for partnership which are refused: but, under (*v*) discussed above, the trade union movement allows a right of appeal against a *refusal* of membership. This is a considerable privilege, for it means that an outsider can test the ground if any victimization by an LO union is alleged. This possibility is, of course, in keeping with LO's declaration in favour of an open trade union movement.

Union members have duties as well as these rights. They must work for the harmony and development of the union, obey its rules and decisions, and be loyal to the executive and other representatives of the union. They are obliged to supply on request statistical and other information about wages and working conditions. When members move between branches they are obliged to report their departure to the treasurer of the branch they are leaving, and report to the new branch on arrival. Their obligation to transfer from one union to another has already been discussed.

VIII. OTHER LEVELS OF UNION GOVERNMENT

(*a*) *The branches*

The branch of a national union is the local, geographically based, unit through which the national union carries on its activity at the local level. Sometimes there is more than one branch in a locality, depending on the industry or trade, but in general the branch comprises all the union members employed in that particular place. In relation to the national unions the branches are dependent organizations. A branch can neither leave nor be expelled from the union. Only individual members can. The only way in which the relationship between the union and the branch can be terminated is by the dissolution of the branch, which requires the approval of the union executive board. If a branch fails to carry out its duties to the union or refuses to obey the rules or decisions made on the basis of the rules the executive board may dissolve the branch and expel recalcitrant members.

The specific duties of the branch in furthering the work of the union include agitation and organization work, the promotion of appropriate forms of union organization at the factory level, the

entry to a union could not be refused if membership was essential for purposes of earning a livelihood. It should be noted that the Labour Court is not competent to deal with such internal disputes *within* a union or employers' group, since its jurisdiction covers the relations *between* employers and workers, particularly those arising out of collective contracts.

discussion of membership applications, the collection of wage statistics and other data the union requires, supporting the members in negotiations and agreements regarding wages and terms of employment, promoting educational activity, the collection of union dues, and disbursement of financial support during disputes. In addition to collecting the dues for the national union, the branch is entitled to impose dues on its branch members for the purpose of carrying on its own activity.

Branch business is conducted by a board of (usually five) members, consisting of a chairman, secretary and treasurer, plus ordinary members. In most cases these officials are active workers, running the branch outside working hours. The board members are elected at annual meetings, and hold office for a two-year term, with a right to stand for re-election. All elections take place by secret ballot, unless the branch members agree unanimously that voting is to be open. In other branch matters voting is open and by simple majority of those voting, unless the meeting agrees on a secret ballot. However, when issues voted on relate to wages, negotiations, and stoppages of work, a *two-thirds* majority in a *secret* ballot is necessary for terminating or arriving at an agreement or any other changes in conditions of work, and for decisions about work stoppages. Even then the union executive has the final say.[1]

Branch meetings are usually held once a month. Some rules provide for a representative assembly to take the place of the meeting of members as the supreme decision-making body, but this is not usual, since the branch is normally small enough to allow of branch meetings being open to all the members. The branch normally decides for itself whether it wants a representative form of members' meeting, although the rules of the Metal Workers' Union provide that representative assemblies are to be set up in branches where the membership exceeds 5,000. This is obviously necessary in such large branches, where direct member participation would be unwieldy. This indirect system is based on each workshop club or group having one representative in the assembly for every 50 members (in branches with more than 13,000 members 1 for every 100 members).

Since 1960 there has been a distinct trend towards rationalizing union organization by amalgamating branches, though not all unions are tackling the problem so drastically as the Commercial Employees' Union, which has reduced the number of branches from 260 to 40.

(*b*) *Factory clubs*

Where the branch is based on the locality and not the factory or plant, and covers two or more firms, factory organization is provided

[1] The specific procedure provided in national union standard rules for collective bargaining is analysed in Chapter XIV, on the bargaining process.

through branch subsidiaries, factory or workshop clubs. In fact, the club rather than the branch is the effective local *bargaining* agency. Its tasks are to spread information and carry on agitation on behalf of the union and the branch, to work for the promotion of good trade union relations, to prepare demands and seek to resolve conflicts, to act as local leader in the event of disputes, and to provide the information the branch or union needs. The board of the club deals with all questions submitted by groups or individual workers, and prepares wage claims. It represents the workers in negotiations with management and endeavours to settle disputes with management and between members. It is obliged to carry out instructions received from the union or branch, and in general exists to provide the factory nucleus of union organization when the branch does not coincide with the plant. This firm organizational structure at the factory level is tremendously important. It ensures that no separate shop stewards movement can by-pass the club, since the line of communication to management explicitly runs through the board of the club, who are union officials, elected by the rank and file. When local membership is too small to justify a branch, or where small craft groups exist, sections can be set up to look after the local interests of members. Again these are subsidiaries of the branch.[1] When there is *more than one* branch in a locality provision can be made, e.g. local government, for local co-operation between the branches. The Commercial Employees' Union has experimented since 1959 with local sections for young members under twenty-one. These have their own officials, but are subsidiary to the local union organization, which provides a contact man, a branch official. The intention is to attract youth, and provide education in union administration.

No provision is made in the standard rules for intermediary organizations between the branch and national union levels, but some unions have district organizations when the structure of the industry and the union make it necessary to have a wide geographical system of organization. The railways, telegraph and telephone service, forestry, and agriculture are typical examples of widely scattered activities which necessitate district organization. Other unions which cover heterogeneous forms of activity provide intermediate organization for industrial or craft groups, e.g. the Factory Workers' Union has industrial sections, and the Typographers' Union has national trade sections dealing with the problems of particular craft groups. In all cases the supremacy of the national union is clearly stated.

[1] A section of a branch is not simply a convenient internal administrative arrangement. It can have independent standing for the purpose of labour legislation. See, for example, Labour Court Judgement 1960/12, for a ruling on this point.

(c) Local central organizations

Co-operation between unions covering workers in different industries and trades is provided at the local level through local central organizations for the branches of all the unions in that place. They form a vital link in the chain of communications within the trade union movement. In part the local centrals are the equivalent of the local co-ordinating bodies that existed before, and immediately after, LO was formed. But there is a significant difference. The old bodies were mainly political in emphasis, indeed this was the main reason for LO removing the communes from LO membership in 1906. The modern local centrals are decidedly *not* political, and their present position is the outcome of careful regulation by LO to ensure that they do not become too political in their activity, or develop into rivals of LO and the national unions.

In 1906 the idea of such local bodies was not acceptable to LO, and the chairman at that time (Lindqvist) only favoured local co-operation *within* a union on certain specified conditions. But in 1912 Lindqvist, presumably feeling more certain of the strength of LO, asked congress to endorse (which it did) a proposal expressing the desirability of having local co-operation between the branches of different unions belonging to LO for two main purposes: (*a*) agitation and information activity, and (*b*) strengthening and making more effective unity in industrial disputes. It was stressed that such co-operation must not be undertaken in such a way as to interfere with the activity and rights of national unions. They must not become rivals to the unions or take over branch functions. In discussing reorganization and the industrial unionism principle, this LO congress also rejected the idea of allowing local central bodies to affiliate directly to LO, in case this weakened the framework based on national unions. A check on the local centrals was provided by the practice LO developed of examining their proposed rules to ensure there was a certain degree of uniformity and that they were not encroaching on the work of the unions. Model rules for any local centrals established were drawn up by the representative assembly in 1928, and these gave the LO secretariat considerable supervisory powers over them. Some local centrals were clearly prone to overstep their authority by allowing syndicalist influences to intrude and by declaring blockades and boycotts, for in 1931 the LO congress empowered the secretariat to dissolve local centrals that refused to obey its instructions and, in conjunction with the executive of a union concerned, to *instruct* union branches to disaffiliate from a local central that was carrying on disloyal activity. This provision is not in the rules but exists as a guiding principle. When the LO rules were revised in 1941 not much change was therefore necessary in the arrangements dealing with local centrals, since a basis of compulsory and uniform provisions had already been established, and LO had long made it clear that it would stand no nonsense from ambitious local centrals.

The activity of local centrals is financed out of the modest annual dues—estimated in 1960 to be 1·20 crowns per affiliated member—paid by the affiliated branches. The secretariat of LO has since 1917 been authorized to give them financial support, but that this has not been adequate is reflected in the frequent motions to LO congresses asking for funds. LO follows a system of granting funds to local centrals after each application has been assessed on its merits, and the annual LO vote to them has increased since the LO propaganda council was formed in 1945. It acts as the local centrals' overlord.

As local propaganda bodies the local central organizations undoubtedly serve an extremely useful function within the trade union movement in bringing together members of different national unions on a voluntary basis. Since they deal with general trade union questions like agitation, education, and propaganda, and are not allowed to become rivals to LO or the unions, they are not confronted with resolving the special problems of particular unions and trades. They have no powers in collective bargaining or industrial disputes.

A common form for their activity is for LO to arrange information meetings, LO paying the costs and supplying the speakers. Numerically, the local centrals have shown a steady growth, but in the past decade the number has remained at about 330 local centrals, covering over 80% of the members of LO and about 70% of union branches. Further expansion is likely to be restricted for geographical reasons, and the strengthening of links between local centrals at district level is regarded as the immediate organizational task.

(*d*) *Inter-union co-operation at national level*

The Swedish unions have not been immune from the vexed question of union mergers. The difficulties which unions in related trades and sectors of the economy encounter in trying to amalgamate led to a loose form of inter-union collaboration called a 'cartel' being evolved in the 1920s. 'Cartel agreements' to co-operate on matters of common interest in related occupations were set up in 1923 in the printing trades by the three unions in the industry: by the Paper, Forestry, Timber Floating, and Sawmill Workers' Unions in 1925; and a procedure for co-operation was agreed by the Metal Workers' Union and the Foundry Workers' Union in the same year. A building industry cartel was formed in 1926, and in 1929 the Food Workers' Union and the Commercial Employees' Union set up a consultative committee, later joined by the Hotel and Restaurant workers. The ten unions with members (now about 150,000) in the employment of the central government formed a cartel in 1937.

The unions in these various cartels co-operate on wages issues and disputes that arise during the period of validity of collective agreements. The government employees' cartel has an administrative structure to provide as far as possible for exchange of information and common policies. But in all the primary emphasis is on consultation, *not* decision-making, and some of the cartels are rather informal. Such cartel agreements, which are a loose form of confederation, form a useful addition to machinery for inter-union consultation. They are not given enough power to become rivals to LO, but they can exercise moral pressure which is intended to make for uniformity of attitudes in labour problems in the sector of the economy they cover. LO at first looked on these loose forms of agreement as transitional arrangements in the progress towards industrial unionism, but later regarded them as a more permanent form of consultation. In any case the cartel arrangement often applies to industrial unions which simply find it convenient to exchange views and keep each other informed of developments in their complementary sectors of the economy. In recent years there has again been an all-round revival of interest in passing beyond the stage of cartel consultation to complete mergers. Just as there is enthusiasm within individual unions for rationalizing by reducing the number of branches, so interest in merging unions in related branches of activity is growing, e.g. in forestry, paper and pulp; in clothing; in food, tobacco and drink; and in public employment. The number of LO unions is likely to be reduced considerably in the near future as a result of this trend.

The structure of the trade union movement can be summarized in the following diagram:

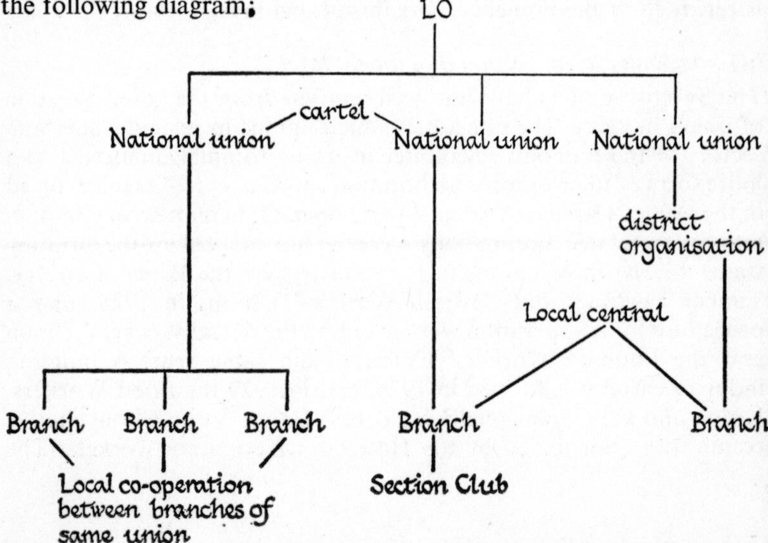

IX. THE LO PLAN OF ORGANIZATION AND INDUSTRIAL UNIONISM

The rules of LO now give it great powers over the structure of the movement through the provisions dealing with the plan of organization. Nevertheless, LO continues to take the view it has adopted throughout its history, that it can urge and coax the unions, but not compel them, to follow the plan of organization. The formation of the unions in the 1890s was not systematic, and mainly by craft. Only two unions, in sawmills and textiles, organized on an industrial basis, while the Transport Workers' Union and the Unskilled and Factory Workers' Union formed in the 1890s were rather heterogeneous in composition, the latter approaching to a general union. A methodical approach to the organization of LO groups, and demarcations between them, had to wait until the twentieth century. LO argued in 1903, for instance, that the primary problem was one of organizing workers into unions, rather than decreeing amalgamations and demarcations among them, but even at this early date in the life of LO it was hinted that an explicit organization plan would soon have to be devised. The 1903 congress accepted the view that there were administrative and practical advantages in concentrating as far as possible in large unions. But the time was not yet ripe for the introduction of compulsory provisions. LO hoped that developments in industry and experience would show the national unions the need to concentrate their organizations in order to be effective.

The growth of industry and of union membership, and the emphasis placed by the Swedish Employers' Confederation and the metal trades employers on the industrial form of organization, soon provided pressures for a specific plan of union organization. The metal trades employers' federation, for example, insisted on national agreements for engineering, and on *payment by degree of skill* rather than by trade or craft. It had to negotiate with eight unions, and only in 1908 succeeded in getting them all to sign a new national agreement for the industry. The advantages of having closely related trade groups in the same national union for bargaining purposes and for the conduct of strikes, and the difficulties that small craft unions could cause for other groups covered by the same employer when they brought about stoppages, helped to crystallize LO opinion very rapidly in favour of the industrial unionism principle. Apart from these obvious pressures, the Swedish trade union movement was helped in its gropings towards a coherent form of organization by two particular factors. The national craft unions were still comparatively young when LO began seriously to consider the form of organization, and craft boundaries had not become too sanctified. Moreover, LO aimed to organize national unions, which narrowed the problem to a discussion of the best organization plan for these national unions.

In 1906 the LO congress formally recognized the industrial unionism principle as an alternative to the craft principle. One of the strongest opponents of this recognition at the time was the Iron and Metal Workers' Union, which organized by the material worked upon. But it very quickly changed its mind, as a result of its experience in the engineering industry negotiations in 1908. After complaining in 1908 that the rules of LO allowed a union to organize by craft or industry, and maintaining that it was necessary to fix on one or the other, it came out very forcibly at the 1909 LO congress in favour of the industrial unionism principle. Preoccupied as it was with the major constitutional questions posed as a result of the Great Strike, the LO secretariat evolved a tactic of gradualism, by recognizing both principles, but also adding that there was much to be said for a division of union organization along industrial lines.[1] An organization plan committee appointed to study the question had its hands tied in advance through congress accepting a proposal by Lindqvist that it should decide on a successive adoption of the principle of industrial unionism.

The reorganization plan produced in 1912 provided for twenty-two industrial unions. At the time there were, for example, thirteen unions in housebuilding, and ten in the iron and metal-working industry. The committee proposed one union for each industry, while recognizing that the boundaries could not always be clearly defined because of the diversity of industry and trade. The secretariat struck a note of caution in its comments at the 1912 congress on the proposed plan. Experience of previous proposed union marriages had convinced it that too rigid an approach and a *requirement* of obedience to the proposals would meet with strong opposition. It recommended that congress should not make the scheme compulsory, but that the plan should serve as a guide which the unions were free to follow in forming industrial unions, 'in so far as the organizations concerned find it convenient'. There was to be no compulsion.

'It should be noted here that no coercion is being placed on hitherto independent unions, since the independence of no union can be considered unjustified as long as the majority of its members consider that affiliation to or amalgamation with a particular

[1] To congress Lindqvist, the LO chairman, put the matter more strongly: 'Technically it would be impossible to do away completely with the craft unions, but the development of industrial unions was a necessity which should be brought about as soon as possible.' LO *kongress-protokoll*, 1909, p. 85.

industrial union would be detrimental to the members or their interests.'

The secretariat of LO and the executive boards of the national unions were given the somewhat delicate task of working for the adoption of the principle of industrial unionism. In essence, this is still the task LO sets itself in organization matters, and developments since 1912 have consisted of attempts to put this principle into practice. The two organization plans drawn up since then, in 1926 and 1951, have tried on the one hand to follow the guiding principle that all workers in one industry should be affiliated to the same union, and on the other to ensure that the plan is sufficiently flexible to reflect the changing structure of the economy.

There has been little hardening in the attitude of LO to the problems of demarcation. In the 1917 congress it was recognized that questions of transferring workers from one union to another were very delicate, since from the beginning each union had decided for itself its composition and jurisdiction, and the secretariat did not see that it could go any further than to appeal to the unions to ensure that the 1912 plan was carried through by admitting workers to unions in accordance with the plan. In the 1922 congress the Metal Workers asked the secretariat to ensure that the change-over to the pure industrial principle was carried out by the end of 1925, though no sanction for non-compliance was discussed. One significant point made at the 1922 congress was that the industrial unionism principle would be an important weapon in organizing production along socialist lines. This theoretical argument is a most unusual one at LO congress discussions on organization, and perhaps owed its origin to the ideas about socializing production then in the air. The Swedish approach has been much more cautious and pragmatic, conditioned by considerations of the structure of industry and the need to mark out the inter-union demarcations in such a way that not more than one union bargains in any workplace.

A new plan to meet the changed structure of the economy was produced in 1926. It envisaged thirty-three national unions, organized by industry, with the exception of the public sector, where the 'ownership' principle was to apply.[1] Where the economic activity of several groups of workers belonging to different unions was interdependent, it was suggested that forms should be devised for

[1] The 1926 plan did recognize that special circumstances might justify a departure from the general principles. Some recognition of the craft principle was provided for in the proposed changes and arrangements for the building industry (significantly, as a result of changes on the employers' side, through the central building employers' federation joining SAF). One building industry workers' union was no longer considered so urgent.

ensuring close co-operation among them. The 'cartel' form was becoming popular at that time.

The importance for wage bargaining of having all the workers in a *workplace* in the same union has been repeatedly stressed since it was formulated in the 1926 plan.[1]

Problems of wages policy in relation to a plan of organization were prominent at the 1941 congress and, not surprisingly, in view of the congress discussion of centralization, the secretariat took a stronger line in hinting that more pressure might have to be put on unions which did not co-operate in operating the 1926 plan. In 1946, when a review of the plan was begun, the secretariat said the industrial unionism plan would not be abandoned, and the unions would 'as far as possible be consulted'. Nevertheless, the revised plan put forward in 1951, which provided for thirty-eight unions, stressed flexibility and inter-union consultation, and allowed for craft unions being retained, despite the basic industrial unionism principle; 'a plan that tried to be permanent would be an unfortunate thing, in the light of developments that took place in industrial life'.

In dealing with internal demarcation disputes LO has long made it clear that the requirements that workers doing a certain job should belong to a particular union, as provided in the organization plan, takes precedence over any claim by a union that its members have a 'right' to do a certain job. But in solving them LO has never seriously departed from the method of persuasion. True, there was some sabre-rattling in 1936, and in 1941 LO was given extended powers in dealing with demarcation disputes. Previously it was 'to try to settle' such disputes. Now it is empowered to decide which union is the legitimate one by reference to the nature of the jobs in question. But it is also provided that LO should seek the co-operation of the unions in such disputes, and this approach is clearly intended to be the basic one in the 1951 plan, despite the fact that it increased LO's formal powers to put the plan into effect. This approach has shown it can be very successful. Discussion between unions, which in 1948 led to a successful merger in the building industry, and in 1949

[1] The principle is set out on p. 104 of LO *kongress-protokoll*, 1926. In 1941 it was stressed as being the most important principle (LO *kongress-protokoll*, 1941, p. 292): 'The basic idea of the plan of organization is that there should be central control from the trade union side over the wages and working conditions of workers who are employed in the same branch of the economy. Where a uniform organization does not exist a certain amount of co-operation between different unions within the same sphere can of course help to eliminate some of the causes of friction but, in spite of the provisions to this effect in the LO rules, such co-operation has in many cases not occurred. A division of the workers in the same industry among several organizations must be detrimental to wages negotiation activity and give rise in many cases to unnecessary disputes among the unions.'

to a voluntary amalgamation between the Sawmill and Woodworkers' Unions, is recommended as the most appropriate method, and superior to formal rules. Though this can be a very lengthy process, it is yielding fruit in the gradual approach to a solution of some of LO's perennial problems of organization. One of these until recently was the Bricklayers' Union. Even after the formation of a unified Building Workers' Union in 1948 the bricklayers stayed outside, and the members consistently voted down attempts by their executive to persuade them to join the Building Workers' Union. In 1960 the bricklayers at last agreed to merge. Another problem union has been the Amalgamated Unions, a mixed bag of mainly unskilled industrial workers. Formed in 1897, it was never included in an LO plan of organization, yet flourished none the less. But in 1958, five years after the members rejected by a 10–1 vote an executive proposal that they should merge with other unions, the congress of this union unanimously accepted its executive's recommendation that it should transfer its members to other unions and cease to operate. It did so in 1961. Still outstanding is the problem of the Foundry Workers' Union, which was not included in the 1912 plan, but has consistently had good relations with the Metal Workers' Union, which is intended to absorb it. The Food Workers' Union, formed in 1922, covers a heterogeneous range of workers who deal with the processing of anything edible, and boundary problems exist here mainly with the Factory Workers' Union, which has been a catch-all since 1891 for workers who could not find a home in any other union in industry.

That amalgamations of unions and transfers of members are best brought about when those affected come to realize their value was the view LO propounded in 1956. Industrial unionism can be used as a basic pragmatic framework, but the plan cannot be logical or static when there is rapid technological change. Amalgamations must be worked for over a period, and frequently the members, as recent experience shows, take more time than their executives to adjust to the idea of change. The picture from the LO side is therefore one of tolerance and compromise, and LO has never sought to give a ruling on whether the vote of union members on merger proposals is binding or only advisory. Amalgamation thus proceeds by persuasion, and in recent years the unions have shown a great readiness to respond.

The change in organization towards industrial unionism has been in response to three main pressures: first, the changes in the structure of the economy; second, employers have organized by industry and have tried to bring about industry-wide agreements; a third pressure has been the support for the employer's view given in the judgements of the Labour Court.[1] These, rather than formal LO powers, have been the main pressures. But LO has worked with and not against them, and has adapted to the first two pressures. In fact, the 1951 organization plan committee of LO stressed that it did not wish to draw up organization boundaries which created difficulties in the labour market. If an employer wished to apply sensible arrangements in a workplace or tried to devise practicable arrangements the unions would not oppose him. 'Our forms of organization must not be pushed to the point of absurdity.'[2] This sensible attitude is of immense importance for flexibility in production methods and organization, through the avoidance of rigid forms of unionism and demarcation disputes. The Swedish trade union movement has recognized that it must be flexible in response to industrial change, and not vice versa, an outlook eloquently endorsed by the 1961 report on Economic Expansion and Structural Change.

The industrial union is not 'roses all the way', however. It has formidable problems of internal organization in reconciling traditional craft attitudes. Although the basic wages principle is that the wage rate is set according to the job done in an industry, and not by craft principles, wage differential problems occur, e.g. for electricians employed in different industries, and bus drivers employed in different sectors. The 'cross-rates' problem has to be lived with by the industrial unions, through allowing member craft groups to pursue sectional interests to a limited extent under the coverage of the industrial union, and by providing skill differentials in industrial and national agreements.

X. CONCLUSION

It would be imprudent to pass final judgement on LO and its member unions before we have considered the important problems that arise in the conduct of its bargaining with employers and the wages policy it has tried to pursue. We shall see in Part V, for example, that the formal constitutional rules analysed in this chapter do not provide a magic formula for wage bargaining. Nevertheless, certain conclusions can already be drawn about the trade union movement organized under LO.

[1] Labour Court Judgement 1929/29 pronounced that workers were considered to be obliged to carry out 'all work for the employer which is naturally connected with his activity and can be considered to come within the general trade qualifications of the worker concerned'. See Judgement 1950/57 for a recent formulation which does not differ in essentials from the 1929 ruling. This accorded with the employers' view of the priority to be given to the demand side in the allocation of labour. The whole range of questions relating to the issue of job security is taken up in Chapter XI.

[2] LO *kongress-protokoll*, 1951, p. 298.

Good and clear lines of communication have been established within the trade union movement, running from LO down to the primary unit of organization in the workplace. The powers of the different levels of union government have been clearly defined, and LO has not shirked the task of taking upon itself the formal leadership of the unions. It has moved slowly, cautiously, and pragmatically in doing so, but it has never been complacent or indifferent. It is easy to argue that in an international context the Swedish unions are small beer, and that their problems of scale are insignificant; but though the numbers involved may be small the unions have had to overcome considerable geographical problems of communication within the movement because of the wide dispersion of industry.

Much of the motivation behind LO policy has derived from a strong sense of working class solidarity, and concern for the whole working class rather than for individual sections of it. Paradoxically enough, this has been most clearly manifested, not when the workers were the underdog, but when the social democratic party became the leading political and governmental party. But the cohesion of LO is not purely ideological. A strong strain of materialism has pervaded its attempts to organize the unions in a manner favourable to production. There have also been considerable pressures at work from outside the unions. The opposition of SAF has always been a factor compelling LO to adjust the organization and constitution to suit the needs of the economy. Legislation and the threat of legislation have also been influential. The absence of unofficial strikes cannot be explained solely in terms of LO discipline and efficiency; the Collective Contracts and Labour Court Acts also make demands of the labour market organizations. We shall see the interaction of unions, employers, and the law at work in later chapters. The next step is to see how employers' organizations have developed in response to the challenge of unionism.

CHAPTER II

Employers' Organizations

EMPLOYERS' organizations in Sweden have been formed as a defence mechanism against trade unionism, but their activities in both the private and public sectors have had a powerful influence on the organization and policies of trade unions as well as their employer members. By far the largest employer grouping, and historically the pre-eminent organization, is the Swedish Employers' Confederation —SAF, and it will provide the main focus for the analysis of this chapter.

We saw in Chapter I that the trade union movement progressed very slowly over a period of fifty years to a compact and centralized system of organization. By contrast, SAF offers a picture of a highly centralized and co-ordinated body which grasped very quickly what its objects were, and what the most appropriate methods of structure and government were for the purposes it espoused.

The basis of employer organizations has been essentially practical. At first sight the foundation appears to be competition in all product and factor markets, with the exception of the market for labour services. In fact, it is not so much the possible positive benefits of having uniform labour costs and standard changes in labour costs which have motivated SAF, but rather the negative purpose of presenting a united front to prevent the unions 'whipsawing' individual employers. In addition, of course, as Part V will bring out, SAF is not opposed to wage differentials based on efficiency, and has found it neither expedient nor possible to control in detail the labour costs of its partners.

The formation of SAF in 1902 was preceded by several attempts on the part of employers to organize, but there are only isolated examples of employer organizations before the year 1890. There were difficulties in traditional industries, especially the iron ore mining and processing industry of central Sweden, where individualism was very strong and the villages were almost patriarchal societies. Organization was easier in new industries. Fairly rapid progress was made in the metal trades. From 1882 Stockholm engineering employers held meetings on matters of common interest, and tried to establish a common front in industrial disputes. A local mechanical engineering association was set up in Gothenburg in 1896, as a result of a wage claim by the local branch of the Foundry Workers' Union. Later in the same year a *national* metal trades employers' association was formed to promote the common interests and progress of the trade. It was organized in four regional sections, but did not acquire a strong and clear policy until 1902.

In the 1890s employer organization in other trades followed much the same lines as the trade unions, from local to national associations, in some cases via district arrangements. The problems, exemplified in the south of Sweden by organizational attempts there, were primarily those of finding a suitable form of organization for both small and large firms and for firms in different trades, and of providing both a strong central discipline to ensure sympathetic action in disputes and a mutual insurance scheme which made the costs of sympathetic action worth while through the united front an organization could present. A negative attitude on the part of many employers to the right of workers to organize, which resented not so much the local as the national unions and their close links with the social democratic party, produced many bitter disputes in the 1890s. The lesson the employers learned then was that they might be successful in stamping out organization in the short run, but a negative attitude must in the long run be replaced by organizing themselves into a positive opposition to the unions.

The political demonstration by the workers in 1902 in support of the franchise,[1] which was meant to be a political rather than an industrial gesture, precipitated action both in the metal trades and among other employers. The metal trades employers strengthened their organization at a national and regional level, and the association now limited itself expressly to questions relating to labour relations. Other questions could be discussed, but not made the subject of decisions.[2] The lock-out, which was the subject of carefully prescribed rules for decision-making, was to be the primary means of protecting the interests of members, but some mutual insurance was provided through financial guarantees based on the number of workers employed.

[1] Liberals as well as social democrats agitated for reform of the franchise. See Herbert Tingsten, *Den svenska socialdemokratiens idéutveckling*, I, 78 (Stockholm, 1941).

[2] This provision is still contained in the rules of the association (see revised rules of April 22 1953, § 32). After 1902 it did not in fact deal with many questions affecting the general economic interest of the members; but apparently this was felt to be a disadvantage, for in 1908 the chairman, J. S. Edström, proposed that the activities of the association should be extended. This led to a committee suggesting that the association should be divided into two sections, one for labour questions and one dealing with other questions of common interest to the members. This never came to fruition. The non-labour questions came to be treated by the Federation of Swedish Industries (Sveriges Industriförbund), which was formed in 1910, partly on the initiative of Edström.

In other sectors besides engineering the 1902 political strike galvanized the employers into organizing. Von Sydow, who was to become managing director of SAF in 1907, considered the strike was a pointer to employers, in that it convinced them that they must unite in counter-measures in the interests of 'sheer self-preservation'. To emphasize the 1902 strike as the primary factor leading to the formation of SAF is, of course, to exaggerate, for there had already been experience and talk of various forms of national and regional organization. The political events of 1902 were the occasion rather than the cause of the emergence of a national employers' association, though employers could rightly claim that the close, if somewhat obscure, relations between the unions and the social democratic party made it essential for them to organize in order to prevent the use of industrial stoppages for political purposes from becoming a habit. Certainly the employers took rapid measures to set up a confederation immediately afterwards.

The Employers' Confederation was constituted at a meeting of 'about forty' employers in Stockholm in September 1902. The constitution approved then, which had been drawn up earlier at various meetings of employers, still provides the essential framework within which SAF operates, despite many subsequent revisions. The two distinguishing features are: (*a*) control over the commencement of lock-outs, and (*b*) the payment of compensation during stoppages through a mutual insurance scheme. These characteristic features of SAF's powers and methods of operating derived from the experience of employers in South Sweden. They argued that it was not enough simply to set up a negotiating and investigating body. It must also be armed and ready to fight against the policy and tactics of the unions, *not* the unions as such. The leaders must have considerable powers of decision.[1]

If the constitution of SAF is analysed from the vantage-point of the rules as revised in 1961, it can be seen how little SAF has changed its basic purpose and forms of organization over a period of sixty years. The essential purpose is to promote the interests common to all employers. In particular, SAF aims to assist employers in industrial relations, and industrial relations alone, by welding them and their organizations into one joint body, furthering good labour-management relations, assisting affiliated employers in negotiations with organized labour, and providing compensation to affiliated

[1] 'Everything indicates that the men who planned and created the new organization had learned from the experience and mistakes of themselves and their colleagues in the preceding years, but also that they saw the future conditions of work to be so seriously overcast that they felt bound to sacrifice personal ideas, individual freedom of movement and also financial means.' Hallendorff, op. cit., p. 41.

employers for losses caused by labour disputes. Over the years the main changes that have occurred have involved widening and deepening the content of good labour-management relations, rather than amending the rules.

I. AFFILIATED EMPLOYERS

Membership of SAF covers employers' associations (the *Members*) in various industries. Partnership is granted to individual employers or companies (the *Partners*) who affiliate to SAF through their employer associations, the Members. Only until the year 1904 was the emphasis placed on the direct relations between the Partner and SAF. Since then the activities of the Confederation have been channelled through the Member associations, to allow SAF to concentrate on overall policy rather than the problems of Partners of particular Members. It is the Members who are entitled to a voice and to a vote in SAF. The Partners are, quite succinctly, obliged to pay dues and entitled to receive compensation for losses arising from industrial disputes.

In the original SAF rules there was some scope for local as well as trade associations becoming Members, but only one local association did join SAF (in 1906), and the Confederation now consists of associations organized along specific occupational and industrial lines, plus a General Group covering heterogeneous types of economic activity. The rules of Member associations have from the start required the approval of SAF.

II. ORGANIZATION OF CENTRAL AUTHORITIES

The original SAF tripartite structure of (*a*) a General Meeting as the highest authority, (*b*) the General Council, and (*c*) an executive Board, still exists, but the centre of power now lies primarily in the Board, and secondly in the General Council.

(*a*) The General Meeting, which meets annually, is not general in the sense of being open to all Partners. It is the Member associations that are entitled to speak and vote through their representatives, not the Partners, whose views are expected to reach the top via their Member associations. Each Member is entitled to one representative plus a further representative for every 3,000 wage and salary earners it covers. In 1960 the General Meeting had 300 representatives. Apart from the election of a Chairman, which takes place on the basis of one vote for every representative present, the voting procedure of the General Meeting is weighted according to financial liability, which in turn is based on the number of employees. The General Meeting has the usual duties of an annual meeting, but it has limited powers under the constitution, and one of its main contributions is to elect up to one-third of the members of the Board. Special Extraordinary General Meetings may be called for a specific purpose by the Council, Board, Members, or auditors.

(*b*) The General Council consists of one representative for every Member association, plus a further representative for every complete 20,000 employees covered by a Member. Again, the voting procedure is weighted, and is based on one vote for every Member plus an additional vote for every 5,000 employees. Apart from fixing the annual dues, and arranging other financial matters, the main power of the Council is as a body of reference for major lock-out decisions and their financial implications, and for other important matters which the Board refers to it, i.e. 'considers to be of such importance as to call for the decision of the Council'. It had seventy-two members in 1961.

Until 1928 the Council appointed the executive Board and managing director of SAF, and the original intention was that the Board should be subordinate to it, and receive instructions from it. This never happened, however, and in 1907 power became centred in the Board, both formally and in practice, and the managing director and two members of the Board were entrusted with the task of running the day-to-day business of SAF.[1] This centralization so soon after the founding of SAF was carried through because of the growth in the number of Members and Partners, and for the purpose of promoting administrative efficiency.

In 1928 the appointment of the Board was transferred from the Council to the General Meeting, in order to foster greater contact between SAF and the Member and Partners. Now, however, the General Meeting is empowered to appoint only one-third of the Board: the majority of the Board are chosen by the larger Members (each with more than 15,000 employees) *appointing* one member each. At present the Board has twenty-eight members, eighteen elected by the largest of the Members, nine elected by the General Meeting, and the managing director, who is an *ex-officio* member. It is not necessary to be a Partner or to represent a Partner, in order to be eligible for membership of the Board, but this rule very seldom operates in practice. Board members are almost always managing directors of SAF Partner firms. The Board elects its own chairman.

[1] The first managing director under this new arrangement was Hjalmar von Sydow, who soon became something of an ogre in the eyes of the trade union movement as the man who was prepared to lay about him with the lock-out club with great ruthlessness. For a somewhat more favourable picture of him by a fellow-employer, see *J. Sigfrid Edström*, a biography edited by K. A. Bratt, pp. 60–61 (Stockholm, 1953, Senare Delen).

SAF has had five managing directors: G. Falkenström (1903–7); H. von Sydow (1907–31); G. Söderlund (1931–41); F. Söderbäck (1941–7); and B. Kugelberg, since 1947.

(*c*) The Board, each of whose members has one vote, has formidable powers in its task of organizing, supervising Members, and making decisions about direct action. Further concentration is provided through the provision that the Board may, from among its members, appoint an executive committee of two to four members, plus the managing director, for dealing with both major and minor matters. The chairman of the Board is usually also the chairman of this working committee. The position of the managing director, who is appointed by and responsible to the Board, is quite fundamental. As well as leading the activities of the Confederation in accordance with the instructions he receives, he is empowered, without special authorization from the Board, to represent SAF in legal *and other* matters, and is entitled to call Board meetings. The working committee meets regularly, about once a fortnight, the Board once a month. The Council is unlikely to meet more than once in the year unless a grave emergency such as a lock-out threat arises.

There is thus considerable centralization in the organization of SAF. The Partners pay dues and receive compensation. They are entitled to receive the agenda of the General Meeting in advance, but cannot call a meeting. They have no power to call lock-outs, but can appeal to the Council against Board decisions on lock-outs and on Board assessment of damages.

The Members are entitled to a voice and a vote: but their voices and votes are weighted. In theory, the Partners in Member associations with less than 15,000 employees have an opportunity to participate in the election of one-third of the Board members at General Meetings, though the composition of the General Meeting is already weighted by size of association through a form of proportional representation. The majority of the Board will, however, always be appointed by the Members (at present 18) having more than 15,000 employees. Each Member is represented in the Council, though once again there is a form of proportional representation and a block voting procedure. This means that small Member associations may have no direct representation on the Board, depending on the persons elected by the General Meeting. In practice, one of the eight Board Members elected by the General Meeting represents the small firms. There is also a provision in the rules that if a 'relatively important matter' concerning one of the Members is dealt with by the Board a representative of the Member may attend and take part in the Board's deliberations on the subject.

These organizational arrangements are devised primarily in the interests of operating efficiency, not democratic representative government. The tremendous growth in its executive and professional departments in recent years testifies to the services SAF provides for the Partners. The increase in the number of small Partners in recent years also suggests that the Partners are looking for protection through solidarity in bargaining, rather than for some form of democratic government. At the same time, SAF has to carry its Partners with it in policy questions, through regular consultation.

III. FINANCIAL ARRANGEMENTS

These fall into two parts: (*a*) annual dues, and (*b*) mutual insurance obligations.

(*a*) Annual dues are paid by the Partners to meet the ordinary administrative expenses of SAF.[1] Entrance dues were abolished in 1948. The annual dues are fixed by the Council as a percentage of the wage and salary bill of the Partner in the previous year. Different percentages may be set for manual workers and other employees. Prior to 1961 the annual dues were based on the number of wage and salary earners employed by the Partners. Any surplus of income from annual dues over operating expenses is placed in an Insurance Fund, which forms the first line of reserve for giving financial aid in conflicts. In 1960, for example, SAF had an income of 37 m. crowns, of which 29·7 m. crowns was in dues, and a surplus of income over expenditure of 19·9 m. crowns was carried to the Insurance Fund, which totalled 165 m. crowns.

(*b*) Mutual insurance arrangements. A liability sum of 2% of the previous year's wage and salary bill (or up to 10,000 crowns, if the liability sum does not reach that figure) is fixed annually for each Partner, and the aggregate of these sums forms a Guaranty Fund which can be called upon *in emergency* to provide compensation for losses incurred through strikes and lock-outs. This basic financial arrangement, which dates from 1902, still distinguishes SAF. The General Council decides when the liability sums are to be called up, and not more than 10% of the total sums outstanding at any one time can be called up, in equal percentage from all Partners and at six-monthly intervals. The Partners' liabilities can be used by the Board of SAF as security for loans. The Guaranty Fund has not been called upon since 1925, and it is doubtful how far the Fund is of any real significance nowadays. In the early days of SAF, von Sydow considered that strike insurance *was* the truly distinguishing characteristic of SAF, and a great source of strength for its policy on lock-outs. In 1961 the Fund amounted to 300 m. crowns, and SAF thus had access to quick liquidity of 30 m. crowns (10%) in the event of a dispute. This is a small amount, both in relation to the size of

[1] Dues paid to SAF and its members are deductible for tax purposes, since SAF is formally a mutual insurance agency.

the first line of reserve, the Insurance Fund, and the likely cost of extensive conflicts.

In return for his liabilities the Partner in SAF is entitled to the benefits flowing from the provisions dealing with strikes and lock-outs. The main principle SAF follows is that it will try to compensate for losses, and the Board has great discretion. Minimum provisions are, however, set out in the rules, providing compensation of 0·025% of the wage and salary bill to the Partner for each day of a strike or lock-out lasting more than one week. Benefit is not completely automatic and 'as of right', for, in cases of general stoppages and in other cases where it is thought necessary, compensation may be reduced or cancelled by a decision of the Council. On the other hand, the Board may in special circumstances increase compensation, and this has been the usual practice since the war, or award it on a different basis. It may also authorize payment for strikes and (since 1961) for *lock-outs* concerning categories of employees other than manual workers.

IV. CONDUCT OF INDUSTRIAL DISPUTES

The conduct of direct action is strictly controlled by SAF in order to preserve its jurisdiction over Members and Partners. In the event of a strike being anticipated the Partner has no power to act on his own initiative, and there are sanctions against his acting rashly. He must report the matter to his Member association, which is required to take measures calculated to prevent a strike. If a strike has broken out, the Partner must inform the Member, which is enjoined to help him settle it. The Board of SAF must also be informed by the Member of any threat or outbreak of a strike.

Lock-outs, in which the initiative lies with the employer, are more significant. No Partner can call a lock-out on his own initiative. Nor can a Member. In all cases the Board of SAF must be consulted, and it has the power to approve a lock-out called for by a Partner or Member. There is a right of appeal to the Council if permission is refused. In two cases the Board cannot give approval on its own responsibility, but must refer to the Council for a decision: these are, first, if a Member asks for a lock-out which affects another Member and this second Member is unwilling to give lock-out support to the first Member; second, if the Board finds it necessary to call a lock-out affecting Members which have not approved of it. The Council makes the final decision, by a two-thirds vote, and specifies the Partners and groups to which the lock-out applies.

There has been a steady movement towards a concentration of power in this vital rule, with all the implications it has had for SAF's policy of locking-out on a wide front. Originally, the Board of SAF had power to decide on a lock-out in a limited conflict which might call for sympathetic lock-outs in the same branch of industry; and in serious conflicts covering more than one branch of industry the General Council had to approve the lock-out *unanimously*. Otherwise, the decision passed to the General Meeting, which needed a three-quarters majority.[1] This caused delay, and in 1907 a four-fifths majority instead of unanimity was introduced at the Council stage as a sufficient warrant of approval for a large-scale lock-out. This gave greater flexibility. However, there still remained the possibility of some lock-outs being referred to the General Meeting when more than one-fifth of the Council opposed the action proposed, and in 1928 reference to the General Meeting was deleted altogether in order to ensure rapid and effective action by SAF when the need arose. The General Council now makes the final decision, and only a two-thirds majority of those voting is required.

V. DISCIPLINARY CONTROL

Lock-outs ordered or approved by the General Council or approved by the Board are binding on all Member associations and Partners.[2] The original sanction here was that SAF could repudiate the obligation to pay compensation for lock-outs and strikes if the Partner or Member violated the procedure governing them. A further provision from 1902 governing strikes is that compensation can be refused if the Partner has taken unjustified measures that impair the position of the workers and this causes or prolongs a strike, or if the Partner refuses to take the action required of him by SAF in order to prevent or terminate the strike. The individual employer is thus prevented from being aggressive and aggravating workers. But on the other hand he is also prohibited, during the period of the strike or lock-out, from engaging or supporting workmen affected by the strike.

An additional sanction, introduced in 1904, is that Members and Partners who violate the lock-out provisions can be assessed damages by SAF. For Member associations no maximum is fixed, but for Partners the maximum penalty is their liability sum, or 10,000 crowns if their liability sum is less than this amount. The General Council

[1] This followed closely the provisions made by the Metal Trades Employers in 1902.

[2] In 1904 provision was made that Partners in SAF need not follow the lock-out decisions if the workers in their employment had not joined trade unions or given financial support to strikers in other work-places. This was a bait to tempt reluctant employers to join SAF. In 1920, by which time trade unionism was more widespread, this was again amended so that lock-outs apply to all workers of the Partner affected by them, unless the Board or General Council determine otherwise. It had been found difficult under the 1904 amendment to distinguish organized from unorganized workers, and there was also a fear that syndicalists might infiltrate if unorganized workers were kept on during conflicts.

can assess damages on Members, while the Board is empowered to do so in relation to Partners. SAF reserves the right to sue if damages are not duly paid. Partners can also be expelled immediately for these violations of the constitution.

Damages can also be assessed against employers who disobey orders from the top on matters other than strikes and lock-outs. This applies particularly to the provisions governing collective contracts and management prerogatives.

Provision is made for Members and Partners to resign from SAF or be given notice to leave, on six months' notice. Controversies between SAF on the one side and Members or Partners on the other are settled by three arbitrators appointed under the Arbitration Act. Unlike LO, SAF makes no provision for allowing membership *applications* which are refused to be taken to arbitration, for the Board has the final word on applications to join through a Member association.

VI. THE TACTIC OF THE LOCK-OUT

After it began to streamline its organization in 1905 SAF made great use of the lock-out on a wide front, and not simply in related sectors, as a method both of defending its Partners and of attacking the workers' side. Defensively, 'the counterpart of the organized strike is the lock-out. If this were not possible a strong trade union movement could kill one strong firm after another.'[1] It is tactically advantageous for a union to try to conserve its strength by fighting on a narrow front. SAF countered this by developing the technique of 'rolling up the front' into a major battle. Offensively, SAF used the lock-out in the early days to try to adjust the wage level to the state of industry, obtain uniform agreements, and develop a settled procedure for negotiations, whereas LO had to overcome the parochial and democratic ideals of the national unions. In 1908 and 1909 SAF, by contrast to LO, was able to roll a series of small disputes into the gigantic clash of the Great Strike of 1909, which left LO very feeble, and SAF triumphant. In later years aggressive use of lock-outs has given way to moderation, which it has also become easier to practice on both sides since the trade union movement developed countervailing power at the LO level. But the threatened large-scale lock-out by SAF in 1955, when union-level bargaining in the paper and pulp industry proved tough, suggests that the lock-out is not an antiquated weapon. Nor is it, however, an indiscriminate and coarse bludgeon, historically or tactically. The SAF rules provide the possible alternative of paying compensation in excess of the statutory amounts in case of emergency and for other valid reasons. This method could be used if

[1] *Industria* (the SAF monthly journal), 1928, p. 600.

a lock-out was considered too expensive or likely to meet with public disapproval, for it simply involves subsidizing an employer if he is attacked. It can help to keep the front narrow if SAF considers this is appropriate. Obviously, such a subsidy could not continue indefinitely, but the provision shows that the lock-out has not always been an inevitable sanction.

VII. COLLECTIVE CONTRACTS

Even more drastic centralization than that prescribed in 1902 and 1904 was introduced into the SAF rules in 1905, on collective agreements and on management prerogatives.

Since 1905 a Partner or Member wishing to enter into a collective contract with a national or local trade union must submit the draft agreement to the Board of SAF, and no contract may be entered upon without the approval of the Board. The significance of this clause for later policy in relation to wages can scarcely be overemphasized, for by it SAF came thus early in its career to have considerable formal control, though in practice it operates very informally, over the bargaining *behaviour* of its affiliates.[1] It should be noted, however, that it is a negative control over agreements the Members and Partners propose.

A new provision introduced in 1948 gives the Board of SAF powers, after having heard the Member concerned, to issue binding instructions about the application of the contract, about working conditions not regulated by the agreement (a wide field), and the procedure to be followed by the Partner in managerial questions to which the Board attaches major importance. This provision does not empower SAF to enter into collective agreements *on behalf of* the Partners and Members. Thus in central bargaining with LO, SAF must carry its affiliates with it *before* it can arrive at *recommendations* with LO.

VIII. THE MANAGEMENT PREROGATIVE

In 1905, too, SAF formulated the provision to be included in all collective agreements entered into by its Partners, that 'the employer is entitled to direct and distribute the work of his enterprise, to

[1] SAF estimated that in 1905, 107 Partners (44%) in SAF were covered by forty-six collective agreements, although this is considered to be a conservative figure. (See *SAF styrelse-och revisions berättelser 1905*, p. 3.) SAF introduced this provision, not so much because of the prevalence of collective agreements, but because its discussions with The Central Employers' Federation (CAF) suggested the need for uniformity. This formal control does *not* involve complete control over *content*. There is in practice frequently a discrepancy, often deliberate, between the wages rates (often minima) set out in an agreement and the wage actually paid. This is discussed in Part V.

engage and dismiss workers at his own discretion, and to employ organized or unorganized workers as he sees fit'. This clause ('Article 23', now clause 32) has subsequently been a real bone of contention in the private sector of the Swedish labour market. At the time it led to many conflicts in 1906,[1] and to a threat of a general lock-out by SAF. The December Compromise of 1906 between LO and SAF settled the issue of inserting this clause in collective agreements in the SAF sector, at least in the meantime. It was subsequently a major problem when the unions put forward demands for 'workers' security' and is discussed in detail in Chapter XI.

IX. SALARIED EMPLOYEES

No detailed provision is made in the rules of SAF for paying compensation to Partners in the event, admittedly more unlikely, of salaried employees involving the employers in disputes. SAF can pay abnormal compensation in emergencies, however, and the Board can authorize payment of compensation for strikes and (since 1961) lock-outs affecting 'categories of employees other than manual workers'.

These discreet references to salaried employees are in keeping with the slow crystallization of SAF's attitude to the growth of organization among salaried employees in the 1930s. Until then its attitude had been that it supervised the collective approach to the terms of employment of *manual* workers in firms that affiliated to it. After the passage of the 1936 Act on the right of association and negotiation SAF made a policy decision in 1937 by which it reserved the right to exercise its discretion about allowing Partners to affiliate to it for salaried as well as manual workers,[2] if an organization of salaried employees wanted to negotiate. At the same time SAF set up a department to help employers in negotiations with organizations of salaried employees.

The rapid growth of white collar unions soon made it necessary for SAF to adopt a more positive attitude, and in the rules revision of 1948 the scope of a partnership was widened to include all salaried employees working for a Partner. Whereas in 1937 the Partner could, with SAF approval, affiliate for his salaried employees (and many did so), the 1948 version provides that the Partner cannot join SAF merely in order to cover his relations with his manual workers. He

[1] This was also the crucial issue in the strike that took place in 1902 at the Separator Co. in Stockholm, following the political strike. The employer's side objected particularly to pressure being put on unorganized workers by those organized in trade unions.

[2] The managing director of SAF at that time, Gustaf Söderlund, took a somewhat negative attitude when he was a member of the commission whose deliberations led to the Act of 1936 by which the right of association was guaranteed in law (and from which organization among salaried employees derived immediate stimulus). See *S.O.U.*, 1935 : 59, pp. 149–55 (and also Chapter V).

must also allow his partnership to cover his salaried employees. The problems of bargaining with the growing numbers of salaried employees have become increasingly important in SAF's work.

The 1961 revision of SAF rules took some further steps towards removing the distinction between manual and salaried employees. There is no longer a separate *per capita* liability sum for the two groups, and the rules are now less explicit about differential annual dues for the two categories. Payment to employers in both strikes *and lock-outs* of salaried employees is now explicitly stated. The one remaining major difference is that the Partner's obligations do not yet include that of obeying a lock-out call that involves salaried employees. Whether the final step towards putting both groups on an equal footing is eventually taken will depend on the success of the Basic Agreements which SAF now has for salaried employees in industry. These are discussed in Chapter X.

X. TRADE GROUPS

SAF has continually striven to consolidate its organization on the principle it enunciated in 1904 of having employers belonging to the same trade in the same Member association. After the Great Strike of 1909 it made vigorous attempts to organize systematically by industry through amalgamations and by transfers from the General Group, and it tried in 1920 in a revision of the rules to form related trades into trade groups in order to make for closer collaboration between them. The Board did not think at that time that this concentration could be achieved by force. It merely recommended it.[1] At the same time the somewhat unwieldly General Group, which had been a refuge for all the firms that could not be fitted into one of the Member associations and had hitherto been directly controlled by the Board, was given a position of its own as a separate association with its own officials. Another new feature from 1920 was that conferences on policy were held once a month between the officials of the associations and SAF.

In 1928 a stricter control was introduced by which the Board of SAF became entitled to *decide* that associations with closely related fields of activity or other common interests should establish joint trade groups for purposes of consultation and collaboration. These groups do not have the right to make decisions about the activity of Member associations. They are similar in idea to the LO cartels, and, as with the cartels, the idea dates from the 1920s. But in SAF the organization of such groups is a matter for determination from the centre, by the Board, and is not left to the convenience of the individual groups, as in LO.

[1] SAF, *styrelse-och revisions berättelser* 1920, pp. 6–7.

XI. THE MEMBER ASSOCIATIONS

Although they are not responsible for the financial obligations of their member Partners to SAF, the Member associations are held on a very tight rein by SAF. Their rules must be approved by SAF, may not conflict with those of SAF, and cannot be altered without its approval. They must as far as possible be uniform, and include the obligation on the Members to be Partners in SAF and follow the provisions of its rules. Thus application for membership of the associations must be approved by SAF. Within this framework the trade associations are free to promote the interests of their members as they see fit in matters of industrial relations. In all important respects, e.g. in wage negotiations and conflict procedures, their rules are essentially reflections of the SAF constitution. The associations base their activity on the dues they levy, which are usually somewhat less than dues to SAF, and they can give economic support to their members in addition to that provided by SAF. In fact, however, the Members have no large funds of importance and, by contrast with LO, the funds of SAF are concentrated at the Confederation level, not the Member association (union) level.

The forty-four Members of SAF, with 920,000 employees, cover mainly manufacturing industry, handicrafts, and transport.[1] The Metal Trades Employers' Association, which joined SAF in 1917, is by far the largest Member, with 257,000 employees, 28% of the total covered by SAF. Next in size by employee coverage is the General Group with 87,000 employees, followed by the Building Employers' Federation (72,000), and the Iron and Steel Works' Association (62,000). The smallest Member is the peat industry, with only 100 employees. The Road Transport Association has the largest number of Partners (3,500) and covers 22,000 employees.

The following table shows the Members by size groups by number of employees covered:

Employees '000s	*No. of Member Associations*
less than 1	2
over 1–5	16
over 5–10	7
over 10–15	1
over 15–20	6
over 20–30	7
over 30–40	1
over 40–50	—
over 50–100	3
over 100	1

[1] See Appendix 2 for details.

The four largest Members account for 52% (480,000) of the employees, but a majority (twenty-five) of the Members have less than 10,000 employees, and twenty-six Members have less than 15,000 employees, the qualifying figure for becoming entitled to appoint a member of the Board. SAF has thus a considerable tail of small Members. A division of Partners by size of firm based on the number of employees also shows the predominance of small firms. This is, of course, a characteristic of Swedish industry.

SIZE DISTRIBUTION OF SAF PARTNERS AND EMPLOYEES, 1961

Partners' size by Number of Employees	*Partners*	*Manual Workers*	*Salaried Employees*
		Percentages	
–5	39·4	2·0	0·8
6–10	15·7	2·4	1·5
11–25	18·9	6·1	4·3
26–50	10·8	7·3	6·0
51–100	7·0	9·0	8·4
101–200	4·1	10·6	10·0
201–500	2·5	13·6	14·4
501–1000	0·8	10·2	10·1
1001+	0·8	38·8	44·5
	100	100	100

Source: SAF, 1961.

57% of the total number of Partners operate on a scale which necessitates their employing ten workers or less, but they employ only a small proportion of the total number of employees SAF covers. The 125 firms (0·8% of the Partners) each with over 1,000 employees constitute the most important group. SAF is a confederation of small rather than large Member associations and of small and medium-sized firms; but the few large firms and Member associations are the most important employers of labour. This is reflected in the procedure for selecting the Council and Board, where representation is predominantly by size of Member and Partner, as measured by number of employees, rather than by the number of Partners a Member has. The other extremely significant aspect of the table above is that the employment of salaried workers is of concern primarily to the large firms (those firms with over 1,000 employees accounting for 44·5% of the total number of salaried employees covered by SAF). In some of the large firms the number of white-collar workers in fact exceeds the number of manual workers. For large SAF firms, therefore, the salaried employees present a larger collective bargaining problem than manual workers, and the devising of a salary policy has become a matter of great urgency.

The percentage of Partners with less than ten employees has tended to increase in recent years, partly because of the accession to SAF of new members operating in small-scale industries (e.g. Bakeries), but this trend is not the result of a general shift towards small-scale firms in the economy. The explanation is to be found in two factors: (*a*) the specialist services in economic, technical, administrative, and educational matters which SAF can now offer when its funds are not primarily needed for the conduct of industrial disputes, and (*b*) the protection against the upward pressure on wages which workers (more than unions) exercise in full employment. The large-scale employer can resist this latter pressure more easily—though he may also be a more willing accomplice, since he can more probably absorb 'wage drift' increases—but the small firm needs the protection which SAF can provide through its overall strategy.

Since 1958 the work of SAF has been organized in four departments directly responsible to the managing director: Negotiations, Expert and Information, Training, and Finance and Administration. SAF prides itself on having a central cadre of experts to advise on wages, salaries, legal matters, job techniques, works councils. General research is concentrated at the SAF level, and SAF claims to be able to provide a professional and cheap service for small firms in these various fields. A statistical bureau has operated since 1912, and Partners are obliged to let the Board have any data it may require. In recent years there has been considerable emphasis on the development of human relations, with research into problems of training and information. A special Council for Personnel Administration was set up in 1952 with SAF grants to study and promote research in the scientific aspects of manpower problems, such as industrial psychology and physiology. This is one of the most significant pointers to the development of the constructive co-operation in the labour market which has become evident in recent years. It is, of course, not a purely altruistic move, but has a sound basis in the efficient use of scarce labour services in a full employment economy. SAF also has a special institute for training supervisors and a residential management training centre.

In summarizing the historical development and position of SAF the main feature that emerges is the speed with which it realized that it must have power and sanctions over its Partners and their collective contracts and strong financial resources, if it was to be an effective instrument of labour relations. The purpose is essentially practical. From the beginning there has been an insistence that the only way to have an effective policy was to have strong centralized powers, not simply for the conduct of external relations but in order to ensure cohesion within the Confederation. The obvious reason for this is that the Partners may very well be business rivals, and prone to step out of line unless they have solidarity thrust upon them. It is hardly true to say there has been a *trend* to centralization within SAF, in the same sense that new principles have been introduced with experience. The forms for action and of centralization have changed, but the essential features of central control have been evident since 1905, and changes made in the light of practical experience, for instance in the power to decide on lock-outs, have been introduced to ensure rapid and decisive action. The alterations made in the rules in 1948 reflect this, for they are largely technical in character rather than novel in principle.

That SAF was able to develop a strongly centralized organization from the beginning is due also in part to the fact that it preceded the vast majority of its member groups, unlike LO. SAF began from scratch and had to show practical results. The offensive spirit it showed in the period 1905–9 was evidence that it meant business. Its insistence on national organization, on industry-wide agreements, and orderly negotiation procedures has also had a powerful influence on the trade union movement. Much of the pressure within LO for industrial unionism reflects the attempts by employers to establish industry-wide collective contracts.

XII. RELATIONS WITH OTHER EMPLOYERS' ORGANIZATIONS

SAF has always been willing to expand and develop collaboration with other groups of employers. In this aspect of its work it spent the first fifteen years wooing the metal trades and engineering employers, whose association only joined SAF in 1917. The Central Employers' Federation (CAF), formed in 1903 and covering building and handicrafts, was dissolved in 1919, and its groups then joined SAF. In the early years there was frequent collaboration between SAF and these two outside groups, and indeed many of SAF's tactics on particular questions were derived from the metal trades and building employers practices. It was the building employers who in discussion convinced SAF of the need for a policy on collective contracts, reflected in the clause SAF introduced into its rules in 1905. The metal trades provided a lead in the use of the lock-out threat, and in insisting on the development of negotiation procedures. But SAF's mutual insurance principal was a stumbling-block to consolidation, particularly for the Central Employers' Federation, while the metal trades employers did not approve of SAF covering handicraft employers. By 1919, when these two major groups had been included in SAF, a comprehensive organization had been created for industry and, to a lesser extent, for handicrafts. Both on strategic and financial grounds the inclusion of the metal trades association was a major step forward for SAF.

SAF formed a consultative committee in 1910 with three employer organizations outside industry and handicrafts—those in commerce, shipping, and agriculture—in order to promote the common interests of the employers' federations represented in the committee. In practice this consultative committee does little more than maintain the representation of private employers in certain public bodies, e.g. the Labour Court. Some of the organizations in the private sector outside SAF (in banking and newspapers, for instance) also collaborate on certain matters, e.g. statistics on salaries. A major obstacle to the newspaper proprietors joining SAF is that there is a complete ban on economic sanctions in the newspaper industry under the terms of central long-term peace treaties.

It is mainly in the public sector that employers' organizations exist which are not Members or associates of SAF, as the table below shows. The figures are approximate, and rounded.

EMPLOYERS' ORGANIZATIONS

Private	*Employees*
Employers' Confederation—SAF	920000
Agriculture and Forestry	146000
Commerce	110000
Shipping	25000
Newspapers	29000
Banking and Insurance	27000
Co-operative Movement	50000
Public	
Ministry of Civil Service Affairs	350000
Collective Bargaining Board	80000
Government-owned Companies	4000
Federation of Municipalities	100000
Federation of Rural Councils	50000
Federation of County Councils	50000

Private and public enterprises account for 80·5% of the national wage and salary bill (as against 84% in 1939), the central government for 7·4% (5·5% in 1939), and local authorities for 11·3% (7·9% in 1939).

The significance of this table does not lie solely in the quantitative data about numbers of employers and employees. SAF certainly has the lion's share of manual workers, and is broadly accepted as the wage leader for the employers in the economy. But there are also important differences in the principles on which the various employer groups conduct their activity. Apart from the obvious difference that the public sector does not have the same profit-maximizing objective as the Partners of SAF, an important distinction between private and public sectors can be drawn on the basis of the bargaining weapons (e.g. the lock-out) which are available for use. As between SAF and the co-operative movement there are significant differences stemming from the sympathetic relations which in principle exist between LO and the Co-operative Union. Quantitative data alone do not give the full flavour of the differences in ends and means that exist between different employer groups. Qualitative differences are also important. It is worth looking at some of the differences that exist.

The public sector: (a) central government

The growth in public employment, the legal position of certain civil servants, and the emergence of a strong employers' organization to counter the growth of strong unions among civil servants have posed particular problems for this sector. Different groups of civil servants have a different status in bargaining. One distinction, not always clearly or uniformly applied, is that between employment in accordance with the terms of a collective contract and according to an official 'salary scale'. Another related, but not wholly identical criterion, is that of the 'official responsibility' of certain civil servants, which may mean that they can neither be dismissed (thus depriving the government of the lock-out weapon) nor be permitted to withdraw their labour (in this way being debarred from striking). Legislation to cover responsible officials among civil servants was passed in 1937 which denied them the full bargaining rights set out for everyone else in the Act of 1936 on the rights of association and negotiation. Their bargaining rights were limited to a right to be consulted but not to negotiate in the full sense.[1] The employer alone decided, and the salaries and conditions of employment are still in law laid down in statutory regulations by the Riksdag.

In practice, however, the employer's side has changed the bargaining procedures in fact, though not yet in law, in the direction of the procedures followed in the private sector. For civil servants proper the Riksdag, while formally and historically remaining the final

[1] The details of this legislation are given in Chapter V.

instance in making employer decisions, has since 1945 increasingly become a rubber stamp. A Ministry of Civil Service Affairs, under a cabinet minister, was formed in 1950 to carry on the work of negotiation on behalf of the employing central government, and it has gradually evolved the practice of concluding collective agreements in fact, though not in law, with the organizations representing civil servants, which it then presents to the Riksdag for approval. It has been clear since 1952 that the Riksdag has little power to change these agreements. It must either accept them as a whole or reject them as a whole. The locus of the central employer bargaining power which has been developed resides in the Ministry and its officials, not the Riksdag. The Ministry has also been instrumental in centralizing bargaining with all the staff associations in order to prevent whip-sawing. The civil service is now one large bargaining unit.

This change has increasingly been recognized as inevitable, so much so that it is now proposed to set up a bargaining agency empowered in law to conclude collective contracts with civil servants.[1] These developments in the public sector are often regarded mainly as legal and constitutional problems, but in fact the main aspect is economic, involving the bargaining pressures which can be exercised by both sides to affect the pricing process, e.g. striking, locking-out, giving notice of dismissal, resigning, infringing security of tenure. Some of these sanctions are admittedly obscure in law.

For about 80,000 employees of the central government and its agencies who are employed under the terms of *collective contracts*, there is no formal difference from the private sector in bargaining rights and obligations. The Riksdag is not directly involved at any stage as the employer, and only indirectly through the general voting of funds for the payment of wages and salaries. Bargaining for *these* civil servants is now conducted through a special Government Collective Bargaining Board, which was set up in 1947 to co-ordinate the employer side of the bargaining structure. The main groups covered by the Board are: (i) communications, e.g. the railways, postal and telegraph services, power plants, road construction; (ii) defence establishments; (iii) miscellaneous agencies, e.g. the Mint, tobacco and alcohol production; (iv) a few government-owned companies. Collective contracts covering these various groups have developed over the years in different ways. The main impetus to the setting-up of this co-ordinating body came from the expansion in the defence sector during the war, which made some uniform employer policy necessary.

[1] For the most recent report on this issue, see *Statstjänstemäns förhandlingsrätt*, *S.O.U.*, 1960 : 10.

In all, 80,000 employees are covered by about eighty-five contracts with which the Board is concerned. It is instructed[1] to take account of general trends in wages, and promote uniformity of conditions of employment for similar work. The Board consists of a chairman plus four members, and has a secretariat which assembles collective bargaining data and helps with negotiations. The powers of the Board vary for the different agencies whose work it co-ordinates. In the case of communications and miscellaneous activities the Board assists them as a central negotiating agency, but they sign and are the formal parties to contracts, though they must have the prior approval of the Board. This provision is similar to SAF powers over the contents of its Partners' contracts. In the case of defence establishments the Board chairman leads a separate but subsidiary seven-man bargaining delegation which is entitled to arrive at agreements which are formally binding on the appropriate department. In the case of government-owned companies, which have just over 4,000 employees, the role of the Board is more that of a consultant.

The main weight of ensuring that a uniform policy is followed by the various agencies and boards which conclude collective contracts as agents of the government falls on the chairman, who is given an extremely powerful position. He is entitled to lead all important bargaining work from the employers' side, and, in fact, the Board cannot make any important decisions without him. The Board is urged to co-operate with corresponding organizations in the municipal and private sectors. With the latter, e.g. SAF, it is difficult to envisage formal collaboration on such matters as lock-outs, since the Board could never bind itself by any policy decisions SAF makes. There can be no more than informal co-operation and exchange of views in this direction, and this is the level at which arrangements for co-operation between central and local authorities have been in force since 1950.

(*b*) *Local government*

The same general trend has occurred for local authorities, where employer bargaining power has increasingly become centred in the central employer organizations. The three organizations (which do not confine themselves to labour market issues) are the Federation of Municipalities, with about 100,000 employees, and the Federation of Rural Councils and the Federation of County Councils, each with approximately 50,000 employees.

Until 1944 the position of local authorities was similar to that of central government in the emphasis on decentralized bargaining, and

[1] For the most recent instructions governing the work of the Board, see *Svensk författningssamling*, 1959, no. 528, of September 4, 1959.

each local authority's wage and salary board was the effective bargaining agent. But the movement towards centralized bargaining by the three local government federations was more rapid, formally and in fact, than in central government.

In 1918 and 1939 the Federation of Municipalities, which dates from 1908, had tried to arrive at some degree of uniformity in the conditions of employment of salaried staff, but nothing more than a general framework within which local negotiations took place was agreed until 1945. In that year the Federation reached a central agreement with the unions by which standard conditions of service were to be applied in unchanged form by the municipalities. For manual workers on collective contracts a similar centralization occurred in 1948, replacing the local system of negotiations used since about 1910, and in 1954 a co-ordinated negotiation procedure was agreed with the LO and TCO unions. Similar reorganization and centralization of bargaining took place in the two other federations in 1944 and 1945.

The main pressure in favour of centralized bargaining in local government has also come from the employers' side, in order to prevent whipsawing, particularly of the smaller authorities. Formal legislative approval of the centralization has been given since 1954, when an Act was passed which clarified the constitutional position of a local authority by allowing an employers' federation to bargain on its behalf. Local authorities are now specifically empowered to delegate their powers of arriving at terms of employment to the Federations, with binding effect for the local authority. Legally, the individual authorities are still the parties to collective contracts through their wages and salary boards. But in the case of the Municipalities' Federation, which bargains for about 200 local authorities, there has since 1951 been a clause in its rules which requires the members, on pain of expulsion, to follow recommendations which are formulated by the central bargaining delegation of the federation. This delegation has about twenty members, appointed for three-year periods by the congress of the Federation. Though reference to the Federation of disputes that arise is not yet formally part of the uniform negotiation procedure, the Federation helps members in bargaining issues and disputes that arise at local level in order to achieve co-ordination of policy and interpretation.

Further co-ordination on the local authority employers' side is provided through the three Federations consulting one another on common problems, though the Municipalities' Federation has a more heterogeneous and wider range of bargaining problems and counterparts than the others. With central government, which is the wage and salary leader for public employment, the local authorities have had a consultative committee since 1950 to co-ordinate policy on matters of common interest. But a uniform policy is not always possible, for technical and economic reasons.[1]

The main difference between the public employers' groups and SAF is that the former do not accumulate large insurance funds and use a lock-out weapon, primarily because many aspects of public activity are considered to involve essential public services. Nevertheless, bargaining pressure can be exercised in various forms, e.g. through withholding salary increases (as the central government threatened to do in 1952 for certain groups) and by refusing to pay salary bonuses to employees involved in disputes (a tactic used in 1955 by the Municipalities' Federation). On the side of the employees there are similar difficulties about withdrawing labour through striking if the employees in question are responsible officials, but again pressure can be and has been exercised by giving notice of resignation and by blockading new or vacant posts.

The co-operative movement

Enterprises in the co-operative movement organize for bargaining purposes in a special Bargaining Organization, which assists the members in industrial relations and in bargaining, concludes contracts where several enterprises are involved, and provides assistance in the event of open conflict. The main emphasis in this employers' organization is, however, placed on promoting good relations between the co-operative movement in general and its member firms in particular on the one hand, and the employees of the movement on the other. A central agreement of 1946 between the Co-operative Union and LO sets out the sympathetic relations existing between the co-operative movement and the working class, makes explicit the wages principles which should be observed by the co-operative movement, and provides a negotiation procedure for the consideration of disputes that arise.[2]

The wages principles imply that the Co-operative Union is essentially a wage follower, not a wage leader, and the generally sympathetic relations between LO and the movement make the sanctions of direct action less important in practice, since they are seldom used. None the less, in principle they can be.

CONCLUSION

Important bargaining implications can be drawn from the discussion of employers' organizations in this chapter. While there is no unified

[1] For a criticism of the difficulties in co-ordinating the public sector employers' front see *Svenska Stadsförbundet, styrelsens och revisorernas berättelser*, 1957–60, pp. 40–41.

[2] This is discussed in Chapter X.

employer front covering the whole economy, the centralization long practised by SAF and the trend to increased centralization in central and local government now provide a few key points in the main areas of the labour market. A clear nucleus of employer bargaining strength can be identified in SAF, which is the leader, and additional nuclei in the public sector. The fact that there are few such centres of power means that wage and salary differential problems, and consequential wage and salary changes, can readily be pin-pointed through the increasingly tight control which the employer groups exercise over their members.

In principle, therefore, the development of employers' organizations in the Swedish labour market has reached the stage where a handful of key figures could provide the employer members of the 'round-table conference' which in many countries is often regarded as the prerequisite of a national wages policy. This may very well be the next stage in the development of the bargaining system. The important points to take from this chapter, however, are that the organizational structure for centralized bargaining has been thoroughly developed first, and in the public sector it is the employers who have pushed through an increasingly centralized system of bargaining. This is less true of SAF in its relations with LO, for LO has contributed largely to co-ordinated bargaining with SAF through its wages policy of solidarity.

CHAPTER III

Unions of Salaried Employees

THE most distinctive feature of the structure of the Swedish labour market in the last twenty-five years has been the rapid growth in the number of salaried employees.[1] The organizations claiming to represent their interests in relation to employers accordingly provide a fascinating study in a new form of trade unionism. Three main organizations will be discussed in this chapter:

TCO: The Central Organization of Salaried Employees, with 394,000 members;

SACO: The Swedish Confederation of Professional Associations which has 57,000 members;

SR: The National Federation of Civil Servants, 16,000 members.

The tremendous growth since 1930 in the absolute and relative share of salaried employees in the labour force, and the assumptions of population and labour force projections that this trend will continue, have been noted in the introduction. The rate of increase since 1930 has been fastest in industry and in the public service, as the following table shows.

SALARIED EMPLOYEES BY SECTOR
'000s

	1930	*1940*	*1950*
Agriculture and forestry	15·2	22·6	24·6
Industry and handicrafts	79·3	112·0	198·0
Communications	43·6	55·9	83·3
Commerce	140·0	211·4	270·7
Public services and professions	112·8	188·0	255·1
Domestic service	1·2	5·2	4·0
Other	—	8·0	10·5
Totals	392·1	603·1	846·2
As percentage of total gainfully employed	13·5	20·1	27·1

Source: based on Fritz Croner, 'Salaried Employees in Modern Society', in *International Labour Review*, 1954, LXIX, 98–99.

[1] Some idea of the wide sweep of the term 'salaried employee' can be obtained from the list of TCO member unions given in Appendix 3.

Within industry the total number of employees increased in the period 1948–58 by 78,000, of whom salaried employees accounted for 54,000, and manual workers for only 24,000. In all industries the salaried employees increased their absolute and relative share of the total employees during the same period. The metal and engineering trades employ 51% (96,000) of salaried employees in industry. If we look at the female labour force we find that in recent years all the increase has fallen to salaried employees, but the vast majority (e.g. over 90% of the female members of the Union of Clerical and Technical Employees in Industry—SIF) are employed in office and commercial rather than technical work. We have already noted that, in industry covered by SAF, the large firms are the most significant employers of salaried workers.

These trends have been of enormous significance for the collective bargaining and wages and salary structure of the post-war period, and we shall be looking at them more closely in Chapter XVI. But what has caused the growth in the number of salaried employees? Fritz Croner, the leading Swedish authority on the subject, classifies the causes under four heads—industrialization, rationalization, commercialization, and socialization.[1]

A partial explanation obviously lies in the change in the structure of the economy from a predominantly agrarian to an industrial and manufacturing economy, which was particularly rapid in Sweden. The growth in service industries and in the public sector have also contributed to a big rise in the numbers of administrative personnel. In industry the conscious trend to 'rationalization', particularly since the 1920s, has necessitated larger numbers of planning, costing, administrative, accounting, and technical staff.[2] Many of the new specialized office tasks are simple, routine jobs. But the growth in white-collar work is due not only to these structural changes from the demand side. The term itself has changed its meaning, and has lost much of its nineteenth-century flavour, when the white-collar worker was the boss's man, occupying a position of personal trust and dependence. Rationalization and mechanization, and specialization of function, have removed the personal link, and the term salaried employee has come to cover not only the all-round boss's man but the employee engaged in routine work for which no particular

[1] See Fritz Croner, *Tjänstemannakåren i det moderna samhället* (Uppsala, 1951), and his two articles (in English), one in *International Labour Review*, LXIX, February 1954, 97 et seq., 'Salaried Employees in Modern Society': and the other 'The Swedish White Collar Worker', in *Tjänstemannarörelsen*, 1953, no. 6. For a sociological study of white-collar workers in Sweden see E. Dahlström, *Tjänstemännen, näringslivet och samhället* (Stockholm, 1953).

[2] Höök, in his study of salaried employment in industry, considers that from two-thirds to four-fifths of the change is to be explained by factors associated with the process of industrial transformation. See Höök, op. cit.

scholastic qualifications are necessary. Every salaried employee no longer carries a managerial baton in his knapsack. Prospects of promotion are less, although even the slightest chance of promotion may serve to make the salaried employee feel he is in some way 'different' from the 'ordinary' worker. This Croner thinks is, in fact, a fundamental distinction between white-collar and manual workers. The opportunity for promotion still exists for salaried employees, and this is a sort of highest common factor among them, whereas the manual worker has to become a salaried employee in order to progress within the firm. On the supply side, the growth in educational facilities has also weakened the superior position of the salaried employees, at the same time as the progress of democratic education has increased his numbers. Yet there are qualifications to the simple idea that demand and supply have combined to reduce the status of salaried employees. The demand for many specialist skills is continually rising, and there is a shortage of qualified people. None the less it is true to say that there has been a lowering in the general status of the white-collar worker. This levelling down process has been one of the greatest incentives to organization. By the 1930s the salaried employees realized they would have to organize if they were to be able to share in the fruits of increased production. The Act of 1936 which guaranteed the rights of negotiation and association in law provided a tremendous stimulus to organization among them; indeed the Act was intended primarily for salaried employees.

The definition of a salaried employee has proved a controversial topic. There is no clear definition in labour law in Sweden. The Collective Contracts Act of 1928 makes no special provision for them, and the Act of 1936 resolved the problem of definition by coining a new word for employees (*arbetstagare*), which is a more comprehensive term than the previous 'worker' (*arbetare*). The only special distinction in law is that made for the group of responsible public servants who have to fulfil certain obligations of service.

A practical upper boundary has been reasonably easily agreed, but at the other extreme the demarcation between salaried and manual worker has frequently provoked acrimonious controversy between LO and TCO groups.[1] The paradoxical distinction has sometimes been employed that members of LO unions are workers, and those in TCO unions are salaried employees. Other criteria, such as the size of income, or period of payment, are precarious. Distinctions drawn on the basis of manual versus non-manual work also cause

[1] See Fritz Croner and Sven Jonasson, *Tjänstemän och arbetare* (Stockholm, 1959).

difficulty, particularly when skilled compositors (in LO unions) are compared with typists (in TCO unions).[1]

When one asks why salaried employees in Sweden have formed separate organizations instead of joining LO, only a partial explanation is offered by attempts to classify groups by the tasks they undertake. Other factors can be listed. The conditions of employment of salaried employees have been determined more on an individual basis than in the case of manual workers, and there has been less pressure for collectivized forms of employment and standard rates. Salaries have taken account of individual training and responsibility, and differentiation is the rule, not the exception. The position of salaried employees in the event of industrial disputes has also been a factor marking off salaried employees, in particular foremen and public servants. For these reasons employers, both in the private and public sectors, were long reluctant to concede bargaining rights to salaried employees, and it was with the support of legislation that the white-collar workers were able to begin organizing in strength from 1936. Again, salaried employees have not in general shared the view of LO unions that organization for industrial purposes is inevitably accompanied by combination for political purposes, and all the white-collar unions stress that, as organizations, they are politically neutral.

Some of the distinctive characteristics of salaried employment have been changed as a *result* of organization. Salaries *are* becoming more collectivized, fringe benefits no longer offer an attractive differential, the position of salaried employees in disputes has been regulated, and in any case they are now themselves prepared to use the strike weapon where this is legal. But these changes do not invalidate the point that there were sufficient differences twenty-five years ago to make salaried employees organize separately from LO, and enough still remain to keep them apart from LO.[2]

I. ORGANIZATIONS OF SALARIED EMPLOYEES

Partly because the concept of salaried employee covers a vast multitude of personnel functions, the organizations that have been developed have not been homogeneous or become integrated under

[1] Croner takes a functional approach, distinguishing the *duties* of salaried employees under four heads: supervisory, planning, administrative, and commercial functions. Per G. Stensland, *Tjänstemännens ekonomiska och sociala problem* (Stockholm, 1937), takes a similar approach.

TCO's job nomenclature follows Croner's functional approach closely, and distinguishes five types of work: general administrative, technical, social, commercial, and accounting and technical office work.

[2] By way of illustration, an apparently minor but in fact a very important problem which exercises salaried employees much more than manual workers is the regulation of inventions made by employees.

one central body corresponding to LO. There are early examples of white-collar trade unions. A Marine Engineers' Union was formed in 1848, and the National Union of Bank Employees dates from 1887. A Journalists' Union was formed in 1901: foremen began to organize in 1905. The right of association and negotiation were among the main preoccupations of early work, but in the 1920s conditions of employment such as pensions, sick pay, and holidays with pay became important issues, and some co-operation took place between unions. In 1921 the Union of Bank Employees tried to promote inter-union collaboration, which in later years took up specific problems like pensions and unemployment for joint consideration.

Out of this co-operation grew the Salaried Employees Central Organization (DACO), founded in 1931 mainly on the initiative of railway clerks and bank employees, and consisting of eight organizations and 20,000 members in the *private* sector. DACO was to be a central co-ordinating organization and look after the common interests of salaried employees. It was not given any great powers as a central body, though within a few years it was complaining that member organizations ought to consult and inform it about matters that might affect other members, and at least raising the issue of general direction from the centre.

In 1937 the salaried employees in the public sector formed a Central Organization of Salaried Employees (TCO), covering eight organizations and 40,000 members. There had been attempts in the 1920s to form a central organization for both the public and private sectors, and when TCO was formed a collaboration committee between it and DACO was set up. Both organizations benefited from the legislation of 1936, 1937, and 1940 on the right of association and negotiation,[1] and in 1944 they were able to agree on a merger in a new central organization, which continued the name of the public sector organization, TCO—the Central Organization of Salaried Employees. The main object in amalgamating was to create a unified and strong trade union movement among salaried employees. 'In modern Swedish society it appears to be inevitable that if a group wishes to maintain and advance its interests it must do so through organized co-operation. It has been a great disadvantage to salaried employees in the past that their organizations were split. The differences of view that have existed between salaried employees in private and public service have been a direct hindrance to their obtaining the proper appreciation that they would probably have enjoyed otherwise.'[2]

[1] See Chapter V for details.
[2] *DACO–TCO kommitténs betänkande*, p. 15 (Stockholm, 1944).

The subsequent history of the new TCO has brought 'proper appreciation' on a scale far exceeding the most hopeful expectations of 1944. In fifteen years TCO has more than doubled its membership.[1]

TCO MEMBERSHIP, 1944–60

Year	No. of affiliated organizations	Members '000s Male	Female	Total
1944	38			180000
1946	40			222000
1948	47			254000
1950	43			272000
1952	45			308000
1954	42	200	123	323000
1956	41	212	133	345000
1958	37	230	135	365000
1960	36	241	153	394000

The thirty-six unions in TCO cover a wide range of salaried employment, for TCO has not grown according to any particular plan of organization or organizational principle. About 60% of the membership in sixteen unions organize vertically, corresponding to the industrial unionism principle in LO, in that salaried employees in the firm, irrespective of duties, position, and training are included. Foremen, teachers, nurses, and warrant officers cover more homogeneous craft groups, and organize horizontally.

Fifteen of the TCO unions, covering 55% of the members, operate mainly in the private sector of the economy, while twenty-one of the unions, with 45% of the members, are in the public sector. The rate of growth of membership has been roughly the same in the two sectors in the past decade.

Women are more strongly represented in the public sector unions, accounting for 53% of the total of 178,000 TCO members in public employment. In some of the public sector unions, e.g. nursing, primary school teachers, and in general administration, women are in an overwhelming majority. In the private sector unions about a quarter of the total membership of 202,000 are women, and they are most strongly represented in pharmacy, insurance, catering, commerce, and banking.

TCO has a majority of very small unions. Twenty-five of the member unions have fewer than 10,000 members, twenty of these

[1] See Appendix 3 for a list of TCO member unions.

less than 5,000.[1] By far the largest union, the only one with more than 50,000 members, is SIF, a rapidly expanding and skilfully directed union with 107,000 members (30,000 of them women) almost entirely employed in private industry and covering a wide vertical range of functions. Next in size is the Foremen and Supervisors' Union, a craft group with 43,000 members in both private and public employment. In the private sector the Foremen's Union has achieved almost 100% organization. The two major problems facing this separate foremen's union, arising out of the 'in between' position of foremen in an enterprise, are their neutrality in industrial disputes, and the extent to which their terms of employment, especially wages, are to be collectivized.

TCO is described in its rules as an association of national organizations of salaried employees, with the task of exercising the central leadership of the movement and safeguarding the common economic and social interests of the salaried employees. In order to fulfil this objective, TCO has to promote organization, draw up a plan of organization, safeguard and promote bargaining rights, protect the interests of members in relation to the government, represent the organizations in matters of common interest, protect the legal position of members, collaborate in investigations into the conditions of work and employment of salaried employees, and promote education and training.

One fundamental feature of the TCO objectives which was stressed in 1944, but not written into the rules, is the political neutrality of the central body *and* its affiliated organizations. By this is meant that while TCO should favour democratic ideas, it must not support a political party in any form, nor become involved in expressing support for a party at election or other times. Lobbying of the various political parties is of course legitimate. Individual officials of TCO are not debarred from participating in political life, and they have been urged to do so. This distinction between organizations and their officials has not always been a happy one, and in 1958 it produced a serious crisis within the TCO organizations, when it proved difficult to follow the principle of judging a political issue like the national pension scheme 'on its merits'.[2]

The organization of TCO is based on the three levels of a Congress, General Council, and a Board. Congress, the supreme authority, now

[1] That this proliferation of small organizations makes for expensive trade unionism is recognized by TCO. See *TCO kongress-protokoll*, 1955, p. 65. The annual cost of running unions with less than 4,000 members was 51 crowns per member, twice as much as the cost per member for unions with over 20,000 members.

[2] See the TCO Board reminder on political neutrality of January 7, 1958, and the TCO–SIF peace treaty of February 1958, for an even stronger reminder, reproduced in *TCO styrelsens och revisorernas berättelser*, 1958, pp. 42–43.

meets every third year, and consists of 200 delegates from the member unions, which are entitled to submit motions to Congress, plus the executive Board. Each Congress delegate has one vote. The General Council, elected annually, consists of 100 representatives appointed by the affiliated unions and usually meets twice a year, in the spring for an annual meeting, and in the autumn for discussion of collective bargaining issues.

The executive Board has a full-time chairman and nine part-time members drawn from among the full-time officers of the affiliated unions, and appointed for the period from one Congress to the next. The Board employs the director,[1] secretary, and other full-time officials. The director's position is a key one in the hierarchy, in that he is primarily responsible for the day-to-day running of TCO. Though not a member of the Board, he is obliged to be present at its meetings.

One of the most significant powers of the Board is that of assisting organizations that *want help* in bargaining in the way it thinks appropriate. Help in negotiations may, however, only be given if the organization binds itself not to accept proposals for resolving a dispute that are rejected by TCO. Since 1949 the rules have been amended to provide that the initiative for TCO participation in negotiations need *not* come from the side of the member organization. The Board now has the power to participate, 'when circumstances require', in the negotiations of the organizations on matters of principle or of general importance, where the results of the negotiations affect several affiliated organizations directly or indirectly. A corresponding obligation is placed on the unions to invite TCO to take part. Since 1948, too, the organizations have been obliged to notify the TCO Board before giving notice of direct action affecting other unions, and since 1955 of all direct action, as a prerequisite of TCO support, so that the Board can decide whether it is able to support it. This is intended to avoid the dilemma of TCO being confronted with a *fait accompli*. This centralizing tendency so short a time after TCO was set up has stemmed primarily from the post-war collective bargaining environment, in which TCO has sometimes played an important part in taking the initiative, e.g. for wage restraint, or co-ordinated negotiations.

But TCO has not moved inexorably towards centralization, and, in fact, its central control is very limited. Over its two major member groups its powers are almost negligible. Since the battle of 1958 with SIF, when a very serious disruption was narrowly averted, it has been made perfectly clear that the union goes its own way in bargaining.

[1] At the 1961 TCO Congress the posts of director and chairman were assigned to *one* person, but the rules are still formulated on the assumption that the two posts are separate. This can cause confusion, e.g. in the provisions that the director is engaged by the Board and is required to be present at its meetings.

The independence of the Civil Service Section within TCO has also been strengthened since 1949. When TCO was formed in 1944 a separate section was established for civil servants to look after their particular social, economic, and legal interests; and membership of the section is compulsory for civil service unions in TCO. Since 1946 the section rules have been incorporated in the TCO rules, and the section is led by a Board of eleven members chosen from among the representatives of civil service unions in the TCO General Council. Prior to 1949 the chairman of TCO had the right to take a matter that was being raised in the section before the whole Board of TCO, if he felt that it raised important matters of principle for the whole body. But in 1949 the rules were amended in order to indicate more clearly that the civil service section is independent in matters that refer exclusively[1] to the economic, social, and legal interests of civil servants. The section now decides such matters for itself, though the chairman and director of TCO are still entitled to be present and to speak at its meetings. This unique position reflects the special problems of employment in the civil service and the post-war trend to centralized bargaining in the civil service through the Ministry of Civil Service Affairs. The Section can arrive at *binding* agreements on behalf of its member unions.

The TCO unions covering employees in local government retain more of their independence than the individual civil service unions do in their section. A TCO Municipal Salaried Employees' Committee was set up in 1951 to look after questions of common interest in this sphere of negotiations. In addition to general administrative staff it covers specialized categories of nurses, policemen, midwives, handicraft teachers. The arrangement here is that in matters that are of *common interest to several organizations* the individual unions are not entitled to arrive independently at final decisions for presenting bargaining proposals, nor to accept or reject such proposals from employers. They can proceed independently on matters affecting only their own particular union and its members, but must keep the committee informed.

In 1950, following the consultation which was formally begun on the employers' side in the public sector, the civil service section began the practice of inviting representatives of local authority unions to its Board meetings, to ensure an exchange of views on matters of common interest.

[1] That this may be difficult to interpret is suggested by the requirement (TCO by-laws, § 21, clause 2) that in questions affecting organizations outside the section it stands in the same relationship to TCO as the non-civil service organizations. The position of the director *vis-à-vis* the section also stresses that he is in essence a transmitter to the section for its views of matters that arise: he 'assists the section in its activity and carries out its decisions' (§ 27).

Co-operation is also arranged for other special groups. A committee for salaried employees in private service was formed in 1953, but its position is not very strong, particularly when the Union of Clerical and Technical Employees is able to pursue an independent policy.[1] As far as SAF is concerned its bargaining counterparts are the above union and the Foremen's Union, not TCO. Other inter-union consultative arrangements for discussing professional or craft matters exist for engineers, teachers, and foremen. So far a special council for women's interests has been rejected, on the grounds that it is dangerous to label particular problems as 'female only'. These various arrangements for collaboration among member groups in TCO are designed to overcome the weaknesses inherent in such a heterogeneous organization.

Financially, TCO itself is not strong. Dues to the central organization have been, and still are, light. Affiliated unions now pay to TCO 9 crowns annually per member,[2] and 50 crowns annually per organization. TCO income from dues in 1960 was 3 m. crowns. One quarter of the *per capita* subscription is allocated to a central Support Fund which TCO set up in 1949. It had assets of 5½ m. crowns in 1960. TCO has made strenuous efforts in recent years to build up this fund, and it has increased fourfold since 1953.[3]

Financial strength is centred in the unions, and some of the individual unions are much better off than TCO. In 1960 the Union of Clerical and Technical Employees in Industry had capital assets of over 50 m. crowns, 470 crowns per member, while the Foremen's Union had over 19 m. crowns, 449 crowns per member.[4] The unions in the private sector had assets of 94 m. crowns, 435 crowns per head; in the public sector union assets amounted to 48 m. crowns, 270 crowns per head. The *per capita* holdings at union level compare very favourably with those of LO unions.

Dues to individual unions vary considerably, ranging from 50 to 200 crowns annually, and are generally higher in the private than the public sector. But the public sector unions have recently begun to

[1] See *TCO kongress-protokoll*, 1958, p. 31, for a report by the TCO director which poses the dilemma of union autonomy in this sector versus collaboration with the central organization.

[2] In 1944 the annual dues were 50 öre per member, raised successively to 1 crown (1947), 3 crowns (1950), 6 crowns (1953), 8 crowns (1959), 9 crowns (1962).

[3] The original TCO Guaranty Fund for the private sector was discontinued in 1955. The basis was similar to the SAF liability sum principle, in that each organization pledged a certain amount per member (10, latterly 5 crowns) if required for the conduct of disputes. Since 1958 the Civil Service Section has developed a Guaranty Fund, based at first on liability sum of 50 crowns per member in the Civil Service member organizations, now increased to 100 crowns.

[4] The largest *per capita* holdings were in the Union of Navigation Officers (1,075 crowns), the Marine Engineer Officers' Union (647), and the Bank Employees' Union (635).

build up their financial strength in case of disputes. The average annual dues in 1960 for members in the private sector were 167 crowns, and for civil servants and municipal employees 115 crowns. Much of the overall increase in financial strength dates from 1955, when the TCO unions were urged to strengthen their financial position.[1]

To date there has been no great need for fighting funds within TCO's sphere of activity. Threats of direct action in the form of strike notices are frequent enough, but only occasionally has a stoppage actually occurred. In 1921 the marine engineers struck for four months, and in 1946 a major dispute threatened in the banking industry over the principle of collective contracts and salary scales. A mediation commission resolved the dispute in time. TCO and the Union of Clerical and Technical Employees supported the bank employees, and this dispute was in fact a landmark in bringing home to TCO the need for financial reserves.

Emergency legislation has on occasion been threatened against public servants in TCO, e.g. policemen (1947) and nurses (1951). Merchant marine officers have had two disputes, in 1948 and 1955, which the government threatened to resolve by legislation. In 1955, which was a year in which TCO groups tried to restore differentials, there were strike notices and lock-out discussions concerning salaried employees in the electrical and engineering industry, and some minor disputes occurred elsewhere in which both blockading and black-listing were used. TCO issued declarations of sympathy. In 1957 another major dispute in banking was resolved peaceably, again at the eleventh hour. Recent increases in dues, and the Guaranty Fund for the Civil Service Section, indicate that the TCO unions intend to be able to afford disputes in future if necessary.

Membership of TCO is not open to organizations as of right, despite TCO's comprehensive sweep. Provided an organization of salaried employees is a national one, and is not operating in a sector already covered by a TCO union, it *may* be granted membership by the TCO Board. Refusals of membership can be appealed against to the General Council and Congress. Member organizations must also fulfil certain obligations when they become members and in order to retain membership. They must recognize the principle of the open shop for persons employed in their sphere of activity, allow members of other organizations to transfer to them when they have obtained employment in the new sphere, abide by the organization plan and accept the ruling of the Board on demarcation disputes, provided

[1] In 1954 the average dues for TCO unions in the private and public sectors were 97 and 74 crowns respectively, and average capital holdings per member 265 and 82 crowns respectively.

they have been referred by one of the organizations involved. Rules governing the transfer of members are also recommended. The collective bargaining obligations have already been discussed. No stress is laid in the TCO rules on the sanctions for enforcing these duties of the member organizations, but the threat of expulsion is clearly intended as the deterrent to waywardness.

Apart from these requirements TCO does not prescribe any normal union rules, and there is considerable variation in their content. In general, the union is controlled by congress, meeting at intervals of several years, and the day-to-day running of the union is entrusted to an executive, sometimes assisted by an advisory council. As with LO unions, the branch is the local unit of organization, although there may sometimes be district or county organizations instead of, or as organs for co-operation between, branches. The branches promote recruitment, collect dues, statistics, and other information, carry out and obey decisions of the executive, conduct local negotiations and ensure that agreements are observed, and generally act as the local focus of union activity. Usually the branch is constructed on a geographical basis, but plant-based clubs occur in large firms in industry for both the Union of Clerical and Technical Employees and the Foremen's Union, and the bargaining rights of these local agencies have in recent years been clarified through central agreements with SAF.

Special local TCO committees (rather along the lines of the LO local central organizations) have been set up in seventy-two places to act as propaganda and contact bodies for all TCO union members in the locality, and as clearing houses for information. TCO does not take any initiative in forming them, but their rules must have its approval. They must not engage in party politics, or represent local branches in purely trade union matters. Some financial support is given by TCO, but the main finance comes from the union locals.

A plan of organization has been one of TCO's recurring ambitions since 1944. Two plan committees (appointed in 1949 and 1952) have made proposals which were accepted in 1956 as the principles for organization.[1] The aim should be to have only one organization confronting an employer (the industrial unionism principle); but this can be modified if the organizations do not represent the same categories of salaried employees, if the terms of employment are not determined uniformly, or if the group is a fairly independent one in regard to its terms of employment.

Separate civil service unions can continue to exist, despite having one employer, the government, but the criterion should be that each

[1] See *TCO kongress-protokoll*, 1955, pp. 134–6, 'Principprogram för TCOs organisationsplan'.

union deals with a special group with particular conditions of employment which justify a separate organization. Distinctive craft groups, particularly nurses, can continue to cover members of the group employed in different sectors. Two basic requirements should be fulfilled by an organization: (*a*) it should have enough members to be effective, and (*b*) it should be willing to collaborate in negotiations with related unions.

In fact, however, the Board recommends a gradual approach to organization problems and a tactic of persuasion. Its formal powers to settle demarcation disputes are limited to cases *referred* to it, and it is unwilling to use any compulsion. The organization plan is regarded as a general rational framework. One of the thorny organization problems is that of foremen, particularly in the public sector. This was resolved in 1956 by a compromise of setting up an advisory foremen's council for supervisors in the employment of central and local government.

TCO has considerable demarcation problems with LO unions. Because there is no watertight definition of a salaried employee, demarcations at once arise. The desire to 'maximize the membership function' has not only trade union but also political and ideological aspects,[1] since TCO members offer both an industrial and political prize to suitors eager to exploit this grey area. Competition has been particularly acute in central and local government, commerce, and insurance.

Before 1949 LO and TCO had a committee for the purpose of regulating particular boundary problems, but in 1949 co-operation was broadened through the establishment of a consultative committee consisting of four representatives each from LO and TCO, which it was intended should deal with wider issues than simply demarcation disputes. In recent years LO has been making overtures to discuss common issues of wages policy in the committee, but so far it is mainly with demarcation disputes that the committee has been concerned. It has had some success in agriculture and the entertainments industry. A compromise in the demarcation dispute in commerce was reached in 1959 through the mediation of the LO–TCO committee. The local authority sector has also arrived at workable demarcation agreements, to which LO and TCO did not object.

In view of the clouded boundaries between manual and white-collar work, demarcation disputes will continue to arise and require a solution on an empirical basis. It is doubtful whether TCO has

[1] See LO *kongress-protokoll*, 1956, p. 296: Sten Sjöberg: 'We compete with a TCO organization which is about as strong numerically as that part of our union (Telecommunications) which organizes telephonists. The boundary line is fairly clear: those who are not afraid of the labour movement and social democracy belong to us, those who feel the opposite belong to the other organization. The front is stable.' (The Conservative, Liberal, and Social Democratic Parties all have salaried employee councils which direct propaganda at white-collar workers.)

enough control over its organizations to prevent them stirring up demarcation disputes, while LO from its side says it cannot dictate to the unions on matters of external jurisdiction. In view of the shifting structure of the labour force away from manual work and the rapid growth of salaried employees' unions, LO has of course no great urge to make the boundaries completely explicit.

Within TCO there are considerable strains and stresses arising out of the attempt to provide a central organization covering both the private and public sectors. Two of these are particularly pressing: (*a*) the position *vis-à-vis* TCO of the Union of Clerical and Technical Employees in Industry, and (*b*) the relatively independent position of the Civil Service Section.

The Union of Clerical and Technical Employees in Industry (SIF) pursues a bargaining policy of having general conditions of employment regulated in national collective agreements. But salary policy is decentralized at the local level. Despite recent experience of general and centrally negotiated salary increases at the SAF–SIF level, there is still considerable scope for local bargaining to take account of individual circumstances and competence. Politics and pensions produced a clash of views between TCO and SIF in 1957–8, and this was heightened by the union concluding an agreement with SAF on negotiation procedure and security of employment of salaried employees in industry, without the prior consultation with TCO which the TCO rules required on such an issue.[1] The union was able to dictate terms to TCO for staying inside the organization,[2] since it can stand on its feet without TCO, but TCO could hardly expect to survive in the private sector if half its members in the private sector were to be withdrawn by SIF.

The Civil Service Section is also very independent of TCO, both formally and in practice. Much of the centralization of the past decade in the Civil Service Section has resulted from the central bargaining which the Ministry of Civil Service Affairs has sponsored, and the section rationalized its negotiation arrangements through

[1] TCO had immediately previously recommended certain principles to be followed on the issue of security of employment, and it pointed out publicly that SIF had not followed these. The Basis Agreement which caused this controversy is discussed in Chapter X.

[2] See *TCO styrelsens och revisorernas berättelser*, 1958, pp. 42–43 for the text of the agreement between TCO and SIF, one of its member unions. TCO recognized that the rules of TCO were based on the idea that the unions were largely independent: political neutrality was again stressed: the distinctive nature of TCO as against LO was emphasized: the General Council of TCO was enlarged in a way which favoured SIF representation: and TCO agreed that the Civil Service Section should in its decisions speak in its own name and not that of TCO.

The implications of this compromise, which was a victory for the Union of Clerical and Technical Employees, were recognized by the director of TCO at the 1958 congress. See *TCO kongress-protokoll*, 1958, p. 34.

setting up its own advisory bargaining council in 1957. TCO has not much more than an advisory role to play. The collectivization which is inevitable in government employment does not always coincide with TCO's general ideas about differentiated salaries.

To unite such groups in one central movement is extremely difficult when there is no 'working class solidarity' with a political emphasis to provide a common bond. Solidarity based on the defence of salaried employees' privileges against attack by LO is rather a negative rallying cry, and a positive programme is not easy to devise when there is such a large flora of organizations, and wide differences among members in occupation, training, responsibility, and salary scale. It would be disastrous for TCO to preach a wages policy of solidarity when it covers groups with annual salaries ranging from 7,000 crowns upwards. An attempt was made in 1955 to interest the TCO congress in a Programme of Action, but the Board gave it a cool reception, and the director of TCO argued that it was more appropriate to build up financial resources and promote an active personal interest among members than to produce a programme. The Board of TCO is rather suspicious of ideologies. TCO's dilemma is that it is politically neutral as an organization. Attempts in various quarters to promote the ideology of a middle-class political party have not been convincing. The goals round which TCO must build solidarity are practical issues like salary policy and social benefits. But such denominators are far from common among its groups, and in principle TCO preaches a salary policy of reward according to *individual* qualifications and competence. It is extremely doubtful whether in its present structure TCO can hope to achieve a unified white-collar trade union movement. This becomes even more evident when the salaried organizations standing outside TCO are analysed.

TCO is not the only central organization for salaried employees, though it is certainly the largest. In the light of its rules there seems at first sight no reason why it should not cover all white-collar workers, since it aspires to do this. It is comprehensive enough in aim and it does cover employees in both public and private sectors. But it has been found to be *too* comprehensive. The concept of salaried employee covers a wide variety of personnel and training, and not all salaried employees have consented to enter into the vertical structure which TCO aims to become, preferring in some cases to organize in small but significant groups.

The largest group of salaried employees outside TCO is organized in SACO,[1] which was formed in 1947 as an association of organizations for professional workers who have passed examinations at a

[1] *Sveriges Akademikers Centralorganisation*—The Swedish Confederation of Professional Associations.

university or similar institution, or have specialized training based on the matriculation examination. SACO is essentially a craft movement, using the specific organizational principle of academic training. It now has thirty-four member organizations and 57,000 individual members, as against 15,000 in 1947. About half the members are employed by central government, a quarter by local authorities, and the remainder are in the private sector or self-employed.

Organization began first among young graduates, mainly because of the bad economic conditions during probationary years of service and the heavy burden of repaying study loans. The lawyers took the lead in 1947 in extending their organization to cover all lawyers, not simply apprentices.

SACO is non-political, and the most important principle governing its activity is that it organizes on a horizontal or 'craft' basis. The criterion of eligibility is a university degree or a profession, and each craft, e.g. doctors, lawyers, dentists, organizes as one association, irrespective of the place and sector of employment. There are many reasons for using this principle of organization. In part it was because professional groups were being squeezed by wage developments that they adopted this principle of organization, since SACO believes that the craft principle gives bargaining strength. Small professional groups might in its view be sacrificed in large vertical unions in the interests of the majority. A narrow front is considered a good bargaining strategy, though this has become less important in the public sector with the growth of central bargaining. Another reason is that the horizontal groups, e.g. doctors and dentists, often move between sectors, which makes industrial unionism less appropriate. Finally, and this is the main reason, SACO member organizations are not only trade unions but also *professional* organizations, interested in undergraduate and post-graduate education and training for professions, and in standards of professional conduct, as well as the conditions of supply of their particular skills.

As a central organization of university trained professional workers, SACO safeguards their economic and professional interests, and carries on its activity through an annual congress, executive board, and special advisory committee for particular groups.

The member associations are mainly small, twenty-one of the thirty-four having fewer than 1,000 members each, and of these six have fewer than 100 members. The largest groups are the Association of Secondary School Teachers (12,000 members), the Association of Graduate Engineers (8,000), the Swedish Medical Association (7,000), the Lawyers' Association (5,600), and the Dental Federation (4,500). These five account for 65% of the membership. Some intriguing associations travel under the banner of SACO, from university teaching staff, recently merged into one union, to the federation of clergymen (2,300 members), librarians, social and natural scientists, physiotherapists, architects, curators of museums, pharmacologists, and veterinary surgeons. Dues vary enormously between the associations, ranging from 50 crowns per annum for professors to 290 crowns for pharmacologists.

SACO itself is not strong financially. Its main source of income is from annual dues of 20 crowns per affiliated member, and it has an emergency fund for use in disputes of only 165,000 crowns, intended not so much for financial support to members on strike as for appropriate office expenditure during disputes. As an alternative to a central fighting fund, SACO has now begun the practice (to strengthen its bargaining hand) of asking the unions to guarantee for each member employed by central and local government a sum of 100 crowns, which (like the SAF and TCO Guaranty Funds) can be called up in emergency. The amount available on this basis in 1960 was 2½ m. crowns. SACO has repeatedly urged its member unions to build up their own fighting funds, which now amount to 7·5 m. crowns, and which it is hoped to make transferrable between unions if necessary.

The member organizations are free to promote the interests of their members, but must ensure that they do not harm SACO or other affiliated organizations. They are required to include in their rules provisions binding their members to be loyal towards their organization, to follow its advice, and to respect agreements it concludes. The member organizations must also keep SACO informed on important matters, and of any direct action they may be planning. The most important bargaining provision is that the organizations must respect agreements entered into by SACO as their representative. As a corollary, the organizations have since 1960 been required to participate in any direct action on which the Board may decide. It is becoming increasingly common for SACO to bargain on behalf of its organizations in the public sector. Centralization on the employers' side has to some extent made this inevitable, but in addition SACO has fought hard during its short lifetime, and with considerable success, to ensure that its members' craft interests are not submerged by the other salaried employees' organizations, at any rate in the public sector. In the private sector, on the other hand, SACO has made little impact on the salary bargaining leadership exercised by the Union of Clerical and Technical Employees.

The third central organization for salaried employees is the National Federation of Civil Servants—SR[1]—which caters exclusively for senior civil servants and officers of the armed forces,

[1] *Statstjänstemännens riksförbund.*

Higher civil servants first organized in 1904, and the present SR was formed in 1946 through a reorganization of the Civil Servants' Board dating from 1917. SR is the central organization for forty-two federations of civil servants in the middle and higher salary ranges, with 16,000 members. Only two of its member organizations have more than 1,000 members, the Association of Civil Servants in Postal, Railway and Telegraph Services (5,800), and the Officers' Association (4,800 members), and together these accounted for two-thirds of the total SR membership. Five associations have less than 10 members, and fifteen have between 11 and 50 members.

SR claims as its main virtues compactness and homogeneity. Its criteria for organizing are straightforward. The employer is the central government, and salary grades provide the ranges of civil servants with whom it is concerned at national and departmental level. The main reason, both in 1917 and 1946, for forming central organizations was the deteriorating salary position of senior civil servants, and SR is concerned to safeguard the interests of this small and compact group. It has gained the confidence of the government as a body competent to speak on their behalf, and is represented at central negotiations along with TCO, SACO, and the LO civil servants' cartel.

The organization is the usual tripartite structure. Each organization has a contact man to foster contacts between the Board and the organizations, and together the contact men form the Members' Council, an *advisory* body which meets to discuss major questions concerning salaries, pensions, etc. The Board is not obliged to consult it, but it provides a good channel of communication for transmitting information on important questions.

The member organizations can bargain independently about matters affecting only their own organization, but SR must be informed if the matter affects others, and it can decide to take part in the negotiations. There is provision for bargaining delegations to be appointed by the Board for central bargaining, which is conducted by SR, and for extra meetings to discuss major questions, e.g. new salary scales. SR has thus to a large extent overcome the problems of small isolated groups through providing good communications, and also by giving the Board wide powers in the increasingly common central negotiations.

II. COLLABORATION BETWEEN SALARIED EMPLOYEES' ORGANIZATIONS

Just as there are stresses within TCO, so between TCO, SACO, and SR there have at times been strained relations because of the conflicting criteria on which they base their organization. TCO aims to cover everybody in a vertical scheme, SACO singles out academic qualifications, and can thus appeal to groups already in TCO or SR, while SR confines itself to the senior civil servants.

When SACO was being formed TCO deplored the breach it was making in a united salaried employees' front[1] and unsuccessfully suggested giving some SACO groups a separate position within TCO. TCO also tried to persuade SR to join it for an experimental period, but failed. There was some co-operation on specific issues. Between SR and SACO relations were at first harmonious. But in 1951 and 1952 the various groups clashed on salary grading and cost-of-living bonuses in the civil service. SACO isolated itself from the organizations by giving notice of direct action for some groups, and declaring blockades. The government retaliated by including in its salary proposals to the Riksdag a clause to the effect that a salary bonus would not be paid 'to employees belonging to organizations that give or have given notice, or resort or have resorted to direct action in connexion with salary negotiations'.

TCO and SR for their part accepted the proposed salary revisions, and accused SACO of having infringed an agreement they had made among themselves when negotiations began that no direct action would be taken during the course of negotiation.[2] From the dispute SACO gained in organizational strength and membership, particularly among secondary school teachers. But relations with TCO in particular were subsequently very strained.

What conclusions can be drawn about unionism among salaried employees in the light of the analysis of this chapter? Membership is certainly buoyant, and the scope for growth greater than in any other group in the Swedish labour market. But the crying need is clearly for a more unified system of organization among salaried employees. This is unlikely to come to pass in the near future, for there is a fundamental clash between the principles of industrial and craft unionism. It was because graduates were being squeezed by manual workers and lower-grade salaried employees that SACO organized them in the first place. Having done so with considerable success it is unlikely to abandon the craft principle in favour of the vertical organization favoured by TCO and, in private industry, by the Union of Clerical and Technical Employees.

An appropriate, but at this stage a formal, solution would involve the reorganization of salaried employees vertically by sector of the

[1] See *TCO styrelsens och revisorernas berättelser*, 1947, p. 45.

[2] See *Resultat utan konflikt*, an SR brochure; *Vad gäller striden*, a SACO publication: and *Statstjänstemännens förhandlingar 1951–2—papperen på bordet*, a joint publication by SR and TCO, for the acrimonious history of the dispute.

economy. This would mean in the private sector, for instance, that the Union of Clerical and Technical Employees would become the explicit focus for *all* privately employed salaried employees, organizing vertically, and including SACO members working in the private sector.[1] This union could then act as salary leader for the private sector, setting the pace, e.g. for the banking and insurance unions. In the public sector the TCO Civil Servants' Section could then form a central organization for civil servants, and expect to be able to act as wage leader for local authority employees. SR could be absorbed by it, or continue to exist as a compact, specialized federation for senior civil servants, but including senior civil servants now organized in TCO.

This reorganization would overcome the existing weaknesses of TCO—at least compared with LO—as an excessively heterogeneous grouping of unions, with little or no power over the present Union of Clerical and Technical Employees and the Civil Service Section. TCO would in effect disband. One disadvantage *vis-à-vis* LO, however, would be that the demarcations between salaried and manual work might become even more obscure, and the subject of greater poaching, than is the case at present.

Such a solution is unlikely in practice, because the term salaried employee covers such an enormous range of skills, training, and salaries, and such a wide variety of objectives, that there would be every likelihood of splinter groups forming and breaking away. In the meantime, collective bargaining for salaried employees in both the private and public sectors is liable to suffer from occasional explosions in the salary structure, set off by one of the existing top organizations pushing the claims of a particular craft or industrial group. SACO, with its emphasis on percentage salary differentials and on career earnings (and therefore an interest in the rate of progression of the tax structure), has little in common with some of the large TCO groups.

At the moment the attempts of the rival organizations to emulate one another through their bargaining strategies give the salary structure a strong propensity to move upwards. This indeed is precisely why the Ministry of Civil Service Affairs has insisted on centralizing bargaining with all the civil service unions. It would be difficult for all the salaried employees' unions to agree voluntarily on

[1] There is no clash between this union's policy for salary principles in industry and that of SACO, which also favours individualized remuneration in industry, rewarding and encouraging knowledge, responsibility, and performance. See a SACO guide to employment in private service: *Akademiker och högre tjänstemän i enskild tjänst*, SACO, 1958. Where a clash could occur is that the Union of Clerical and Technical Employees would not agree unequivocally that academic qualifications are necessary qualities for top-ranking salaried employees.

some sort of co-ordination at present. But the recent centralized bargaining trends in the economy may soon force them to think of some form of collaboration in all sectors, and even of reorganization. It is in this group of labour market associations that the most interesting developments can accordingly be looked for in the future.

PART II

The Framework of Law

Introduction

THE analysis of Swedish labour legislation in this part deals particularly with the system that has been built up to promote industrial peace. There is much protective legislation, governing for example hours of work, accident prevention, unemployment insurance, holidays with pay, and national pensions, some of which has been controversial when it affected the economic interests of the groups closely. The analysis here will, however, be confined to the legislative machinery developed specifically for the furtherance of industrial peace.

The activity of workers' and employers' organizations in Sweden has never been a matter to which the Riksdag could turn a blind eye. The growth of the organizations, the methods they have used to protect and advance their interests, and the problems of the 'rights' and 'obligations' to which this process gives rise, have all at various times been considered by the legislature. A positive flood of legislative proposals has tackled such problems as the right of employers and workers to combine and carry on negotiations, the settlement of disputes in a peaceful manner, the provision by the government of machinery to help the parties resolve disputes, the interpretation of contracts in force, and the drawing of boundary lines to protect vital social functions from the effects of industrial conflict. Sometimes suggested legislation has aimed simply at codifying the practices that have developed in the relationships between employers and unions, while at other times attempts have been made, and occasionally succeeded, to pass legislation which would provide a new framework for the conduct of labour relations.

Not much legislation has in fact been enacted. This seems at first sight a paradox, in view of the emphasis in Swedish society on 'the rule of law'. The main centre of regulation and government is the parties themselves. To date, legislation has been passed which deals, in chronological order, with three main areas: a mediation system (1906), collective contracts and a Labour Court (1928), and the rights of association and collective bargaining (1936). The main distinction that has governed attitudes to legislation has been that between justiciable (*rätts*—legal) disputes and non-justiciable (*intresse*—interest) disputes. Procedures for regulating legal disputes, which involve the rights and obligations that arise out of the contracts concluded between the parties, have been regulated since 1928 by the Collective Contracts Act and the Labour Court Act. Non-justiciable disputes, on the other hand, still remain unregulated in law, the government going only so far as to provide mediation machinery.

The legislation of 1928 was in the main codifying law, giving legal form to the content of the collective relationships built up since the turn of the century by the parties to agreements. But the framework of procedure and law that has grown up has only come into existence after much bitterness and disagreement, trials of strength, and political controversy. Its progress has now been hindered, now promoted by the political complexion and policy of the party (or parties) in power and in opposition, by the particular economic conditions prevailing at the time and by the relative strength of the organizations of employers and workers.[1] The views of all these groups have fluctuated with the growth of experience, and in accordance with the power and strategic position they have occupied in the political and economic scene. One distinguishing feature has, however, been the empiricism with which the legislative approach has been faced. Sixty years ago, in the prevailing liberal climate of opinion and during the period when unions and employers' organizations were striving to establish themselves, there was uncertainty about the action in law which was appropriate to the government of their activity. By the time opinion had crystallized the labour market organizations had themselves acquired wide powers of private government. Nevertheless, labour peace is not by any means entirely the product of self-discipline and sweet reasonableness. Quite frequently the labour market parties have been forced into activity for self-regulatory purposes just because the government was contemplating some form of intervention in their affairs.

In sum, there has been little legislation for three good reasons: (*a*) the labour market parties have themselves built up a system of regulation; (*b*) changes in political power made for a shifting evaluation of the virtues of government intervention; and (*c*) the trade union movement has continued, during the thirty years of social democratic government, to argue that there is little need *in practice* for legislation to codify what is accepted procedure between it and employers.

The analysis of the law can be divided into the treatment of two main groups of problems. The first is the position in law of the organizations in the labour market, both in respect of their internal government and their rights to have external relations with other groups through being empowered to bargain. These issues are taken up in Chapters IV and V respectively. The second range of problems concerns the settlement of disputes, justiciable and non-justiciable, that arise between parties which are recognized, *de facto* or *de jure*,

[1] The various points of view put forward in the debates and discussions on legislative proposals and their political aspects are analysed in great detail by Jörgen Westerståhl in his *Svensk Fackföreningsrörelse*, especially Part III, Förhållande till staten, pp. 235–425 (Stockholm, 1945).

as having bargaining rights. Chapter VI, the Law of Collective Bargaining, deals with the various aspects of this group of problems. A third potential area of labour law, which in Sweden has not been the subject of legislative enactment—though of innumerable legislative proposals—centres on the broad area of 'the public interest'. The protection of neutral third parties and, on a broader canvas, of society, against the strength and influence of the labour market organizations has been made the subject of private government since LO and SAF concluded the Basic Agreement in 1938, and it is taken up in Part III.

CHAPTER IV

The Legal Status of Associations

LABOUR market organizations in Sweden are not subject to any legislation requiring them to register or account publicly for their funds, or to submit to government supervision of elections and voting. The internal government of the organizations is a matter for their own regulation, and the arrangements for the control of their bargaining rights leave them with much discretion. There has been considerable discussion of their legal position, but no legislation has been passed. The only method of discovering the status in law of trade unions and employers' associations is therefore to survey the discussion and see, in a negative way, what has happened.

By defining the position in law of associations *other than* those for idealistic purposes[1] the legal position of the latter has been clarified but never defined in law. The positive definition on which the distinction is based is that governing associations for *economic* purposes. These are distinguished in law from associations for idealistic purposes, which comprise a mixed bag, ranging from temperance, free church, and other voluntary associations to labour market organizations. It is therefore necessary to look at the definition of economic associations and the law governing them in order to see, by implication, the position of idealistic associations like trade unions and employer associations.

Associations for economic purposes have been regulated in law since 1895. The most recent Act on economic associations, which came into force in 1953, defines the term in a narrower way than the previous Act of 1911, in order to distinguish economic associations from companies. The term 'economic association' is now reserved for co-operative associations in the narrow sense, that is, co-operative

[1] A committee of inquiry which reported in 1903 defined an association for idealistic purposes as one that 'fulfils religious, philanthropic, political, social, scientific, artistic or communal aims, or strives to look after professional matters, or otherwise has a purpose other than that of promoting the economic interests of the members through economic activity'. A difficulty recognized then, and in the later discussion in the 1930s, was that any attempt to single out and provide for legislation on trade unions would be difficult, and savour of class legislation, if the definition of idealistic associations was as comprehensive as this in fact is. The same difficulty occurred in providing legislation to cover the right of association and negotiation, and in dealing with neutral third parties in industrial disputes.

associations of at least three *persons* who are *active* in some way in the association, which 'promotes the economic interests of the members through economic activity in which the members themselves participate, as consumers or suppliers, by their own labour or through making use of the services of the association, or in other such manner'. These associations *may* register and come under the provisions of the Act. But again, as in the 1911 Act, there is some implied compulsion to register, in that until it has registered an economic association cannot possess rights or incur liabilities, nor plead, petition, or defend itself before a court of law or other authority. When they have registered the economic associations are required to keep books. They are subject to fairly detailed legislative requirements to prevent the association from being used purely for purposes of profit. If it were used for this purpose it would be brought under the Companies Act and be subject to a different and higher scale of taxation.

Paradoxically, therefore, an economic association has to register before it can enjoy in law, *de jure*, the rights which non-economic associations have explicitly enjoyed *de facto* since 1910.[1] The distinction drawn by the old Act of 1911 and the 1953 Act on economic associations is that associations for idealistic purposes do not pursue economic activity directly or actively on behalf of their members, whereas economic associations do. Nevertheless, the demands made at various times for legislation on idealistic associations have paid attention to what these non-economic associations do, and whether their actions are against the public interest. This aspect became particularly important in the discussion of the 1930s, but the proposals for legislation made prior to 1910 were concerned mainly with the *uncertainty* that existed about their position in law.

This uncertainty was removed by the *de facto* recognition of idealistic associations. In 1907, for example, LO argued that the experience of twenty-five years of trade unionism had not created any need, on the part of the unions or of society, for legal intervention in their activities through registration provisions and either compulsory or permissive definition of their legal status.[2] In most cases relations between wage-earners and wage-payers were regulated by mutual agreement, without the intervention of the courts. Registration of associations would be the thin end of the wedge and the first step towards the development of legislation aimed against the trade unions, and in particular at making them responsible for the acts of their

[1] Moreover, if they choose not to register they are regarded in law as unregistered economic associations, and then lack the legal capacity enjoyed *de jure* by registered economic associations and *de facto* by idealistic associations.
[2] See LO *berättelse* for period April 1906–April 1907, pp. 31–33.

members.[1] LO was convinced that the judicial relations being developed through the activity of the labour market organizations without the intervention of law were the best guarantee of mutual obligations being fulfilled. This view has persisted, on this and on other aspects of proposed labour legislation. This attitude also found support in the practice then being developed and sanctioned by the courts, which began to grant recognition of full legal rights to unregistered idealistic associations as soon as they had a settled form of organization, a board, and fairly comprehensive rules. These are still the rough criteria used.

When in 1910 legislation on collective contracts was being discussed the Minister of Justice in fact stated that the legal position of idealistic associations was already settled *in practice*, in that associations that had the settled form of employers' and workers' organizations were considered to be competent bodies in law.[2]

Possible resort to the law courts in order to settle disputes about the legal obligations of collective agreements was also settled by the practice employers and trade unions adopted. There has never been any great inclination on the part of unions and employers to sue each other in the public courts. Almost the only case of note arose out of the 1909 conflict, and this was settled in 1915 in the Supreme Court by a decision that in principle a collective agreement was binding on the parties, and that a union could sue and be sued for damages under the common law as a legal person, irrespective of incorporation.[3] In the particular case at issue, no damages were awarded,

[1] A common solution advocated at that time, e.g. in the 1903 proposals, was to make registration voluntary, but to impose the condition that only by doing so could they acquire full legal status. The early legislative proposals all made distinctions of this kind. If they chose not to register idealistic associations would have no legal status (the 1903 proposal), or they could be sued but have no right to sue (the unsuccessful 1910 and 1911 proposals). The 1903 proposals did not provide that such associations should be responsible for the acts of their members. The restrictions of the 1910 proposals would in practice have compelled the associations to register, in order to offset the liability to be sued by the right to sue. Later proposals do not attempt such distinctions. A 1938 proposal, for example, which conformed with existing practice, suggested that all associations would have full legal capacity, whether registered or not. In a report (*S.O.U.*, 1949: 17), *Betänkande med förslag till lag om registrerade föreningar m.m.*, which formed the basis for the 1953 Act on economic associations, it was again suggested that idealistic associations should be given the opportunity to register if they wished, the reason advanced being that this would have legal advantages, e.g. in property transactions. It was not anticipated that many idealistic associations would register, and no action was in fact taken on this proposal.

[2] See *Proposition 96*, 1910, p. 60.

The Mediation Act of 1906 gave this *de facto* recognition to unions and employees' organizations, as did the practice of concluding collective agreements, although it is true that when the Mediation Act was passed some doubts were expressed that this legislation would not be thoroughly effective until the legal position was clarified and legally binding collective contracts were in existence.

[3] For a discussion of this case, see Folke Schmidt and Henry Heineman, *Enforcement of Collective Bargaining Agreements in Swedish Law*, p. 3, *University of Chicago Law Review*, XIV, February 1947, and James J. Robbins, *The Government of Labour Relations in Sweden*, pp. 90–91 (Chapel Hill, 1942).

because sympathetic action (during the dispute of 1909) had not been explicitly debarred in the contract. But this was exceptional. The labour market organizations kept clear of the law courts for enforcing agreements and settling interpretation disputes, by themselves devising procedures, e.g. private arbitration. The collective agreements could in the main be enforced by sanctions or negotiations set in motion by the parties themselves. Ultimately, the practice they developed was largely incorporated in the Collective Contracts Act of 1928. A further reason for avoiding the law courts was the great delay in hearing cases. Six years elapsed before the case mentioned above was settled, mainly because of the lengthy judicial process in Sweden which (until 1948) was based almost entirely on written process. One of the main virtues of the Act of 1928 was the speed with which cases could be resolved.

Since it was the practice to by-pass the law courts, and because the associations had been recognized in practice as competent to act in law, the discussion of the legal status of idealistic associations lapsed. When it flared up again in the 1930s emphasis was no longer placed on the uncertainty attaching to their legal position, but on their activities. The problem now was to control and regulate them in order to prevent abuses, particularly those that were prejudicial to neutral third parties on the labour market, to the government and society, or actions that involved decisions which raised doubts about the nature of the rules of idealistic associations (e.g. the building industry dispute). All these were vital questions in the discussion of industrial peace in the 1930s.

The Nothin commission expressed the view that on the one hand the *de facto* recognition of idealistic associations made further regulation of their legal capacity in external matters unnecessary, while on the other the internal government of the associations ought in the first instance to be regulated by the associations themselves. In fact, the labour market organizations tackled problems both of internal government, in LO's revision of its rules, and external activities, in the Basic Agreement signed in 1938. This voluntary solution made it unnecessary for the Riksdag to attempt to resolve the dilemmas which haunted it in 1934–6: (*a*) of enacting legislation against labour market organizations only, and not against other idealistic associations,[1] and (*b*) of whether it was possible by law to control the direct activities of these parties against neutral

[1] In 1934 the second standing committee appeared to consider legislation need not cover the whole field, but in 1935 it found that a *general* investigation into idealistic associations would first be necessary (*Utlåtande* no. 37, 1935) before legislating about a particular type of idealistic association. The Nothin commission also thought (like the report of 1903) that any legislation would have to be much wider in scope than labour market organizations only.

third parties without first defining an idealistic association in law, or vice versa.[1]

Proposals for defining the legal status of idealistic associations along the lines of the *de facto* position were circulated in 1938, and the views of SAF and LO at the time represent from the other side the zeal with which they themselves were trying to rid their organizations of the internal weaknesses of government and the external abuses of power which had precipitated many of the demands for their regulation in law. SAF propounded the argument that society must rely on the willingness and ability of the organizations to guide developments in the direction that was best for society. If intervention took place via legislation the organizations could no longer accept their share of responsibility for the development of social affairs and of labour market organizations in the country.[2] The LO secretariat opposed regulating idealistic associations in law, but emphasized that it was not opposed *in principle* to legal regulation of matters coming within the field of activity of the trade union movement. In this case it could see no *need* for such legislation *in practice*.[3]

Optional registration for idealistic associations was suggested in 1949 in connexion with the revised law on economic associations, but SAF, TCO, and LO all opposed such legislation on the grounds that it would be simply confusing, and the head of the Department of Social Affairs suggested that the proposal should not be made law.[4]

SUMMARY

The main strands in this matter have been the negative attitude to the definition in law of idealistic associations, and the *de facto* recognition by the law courts. But it would not have been possible to leave the position of the labour market associations so formally obscure in law if they had not been able to show that legislation is not needed. To do this they have had to demonstrate that they can order their internal affairs and external relations in such a way that they do not commit abuses and alienate the goodwill, or at least tolerance, of society. At times, particularly during the 1930s, they came very near to doing this. It is only because they have devised adequate internal constitutional arrangements (as in the revision of

[1] In 1936, when the legislation on the right of association was being discussed, the second standing committee (*Utlåtande* no. 58, 1936, p. 77) felt it would be easier to settle problems of neutral third parties in labour disputes if the legal status of idealistic associations had first been clarified.

[2] *Industria*, 1938, p. 643 et seq. 'The absence of legislation on the basis for carrying on the activity of idealistic associations has not been disadvantageous to these organizations or caused any anomalies.'

[3] See LO's statement of October 17, 1938. *Fackföreningsrörelsen*, 1938, II, 412.

[4] See *Proposition 34*, 1951, p. 63 et seq., and especially p. 71.

the LO rules) that the law has not intervened; and the pressure of proposed legislation has been an important factor in the development of self-government to promote labour peace. The social conscience of the labour market organizations is not merely spontaneous, but in part also induced by the threat of legislation.

This is a flexible approach, for it means that the internal structure of government can be suited to the needs of the various groups like LO, SAF, and TCO, and it means also that the machinery for the conduct of industrial disputes can be geared specificially to the labour market and take account of its special problems. Indeed the matter has been carried further in Sweden for, under the Basic Agreement between LO and SAF concluded in 1938, which is analysed in Part III, the labour market organizations have become important private agents of the government in the labour market.

CHAPTER V

The Rights of Association and Collective Bargaining

WHEN the Economic Freedom Ordinance of 1864 heralded the move away from a status society there was no need to provide for regulation of the activities of trade unions, since they were almost unknown in Sweden. In any case, clause 16 of the Constitution implied that the right of association was guaranteed, subject to those who combined observing law and order. The 'fundamental strain of liberty' which the Swedes take pride in identifying in their constitutional history implied that there was no question of combination being a conspiracy. But there was no positive guarantee of the right of association if employers cared to oppose trade unions, and towards the end of the nineteenth century many bitter labour disputes were fought because they did. Many of the battles which employers waged over the right to form unions were successful, in that they were able to force workers to leave the unions they had joined.

But the successes were very much in the nature of a Pyrrhic victory,[1] and the foundation of SAF in 1902 was explicit recognition of the fact that trade unions had come to stay, and could not be repressed by employer measures to prevent workers combining. The most noteworthy attack of all on the right of association took place, however, as late as 1906, at Mackmyra. This was a conflict which marked the end of the autocratic attitude of the patriarchal employer and the beginning of the era in which workers' and employers' organizations recognized each other.[2]

Legislation to guarantee the right of association was called for on various occasions in the early years, but the labour movement modified its views when it succeeded in having the right recognized in practice. The employers' interest in recognizing the right without legislation was in turn based on their fear that if the right of association was guaranteed in law they might lose their absolute control over the terms on which they were prepared to recruit labour.

[1] Hallendorff, op. cit., p. 17.

[2] Sigfrid Hansson, *Från Mackmyra till Saltsjöbaden*, p. 6. It is noteworthy that SAF refused to give support to the employer when it was discovered that the conflict had arisen because of the refusal of the firm to allow workers to belong to a trade union. See Hallendorff, op. cit., p. 74.

The famous December Compromise of 1906 between LO and SAF was satisfactory on this point from SAF's point of view, primarily because it stipulated that the employer was the sole judge of the demand for labour, and the unions could not control the supply by insisting on closed shop arrangements; but the Compromise also recognized the right to organize, and provided a procedure which entitled the workers to demand an investigation through their union if they considered that the employer had exercised his prerogative over hiring and firing to make dismissals in circumstances which could be interpreted as an attack on the right of association. The new metal trades agreement of 1905 had also recognized the right to combine, while the Mediation Act of 1906 was based on the assumption that there were organizations in existence on the labour market which might need conciliation.

As far as manual workers were concerned, therefore, the right of association, and with it the right of negotiation, became generally recognized in and through the growth of collective agreements. There were of course abuses. But the principle had been conceded, and the question only became important again as a matter of principle when salaried employees began to organize. The distinctive feature of the discussions which led to the Act of 1936 regulating the rights of association and collective bargaining was the attempt to clarify and safeguard their position. The Labour Court set up in 1928 in conjunction with the Collective Contracts Act was only entitled to take up cases concerning the right of association where a collective contract existed. It very quickly recognized that the very process of entering into a collective contract implied a positive right to combine, which need not be expressly stated. But if no collective contract existed, and this was the case for the vast majority of salaried employees, the Labour Court could not act.[1] There was a gap.

Logically, it would have been more appropriate to regulate the right of association and negotiation in law before setting up a Labour Court to interpret a collective contracts Act. But the fact that logic did not prevail serves to emphasize the practical approach. Manual workers did not need this right in law. They already had it in practice. It was only when salaried employees began to organize (e.g. in DACO) in the 1930s that the guarantee of these rights in law became a goal and, when achieved in 1936, a boon for salaried employees. How far they enjoyed these rights before 1936 was obscure. Inquiry

[1] See Robbins, op. cit., p. 287 et seq., for an analysis of three main classes of breach of the contractual right of association: (*a*) inducements to persuade a worker not to join or to leave a union; (*b*) discrimination against a worker because of his membership of a union; (*c*) discrimination on the grounds that a worker has participated in the activities of the union or has appealed to it to act on his behalf.

showed[1] that the right to combine was 'on the whole recognized', while the right of negotiation varied for different sectors of the labour market and between different types of organization, and was not widespread among salaried employees. The fundamental problem to consider was the method of protecting employees who were not well enough organized to be able to safeguard their own interests and were in addition reluctant to resort to direct measures.

Two approaches were possible, either to regulate in law the form and content of the individual employment agreement or to provide in law for the right of association and negotiation which manual workers had possessed *de facto* since 1906. Ultimately, the second approach triumphed in 1936, but only after an abortive attempt to recommend that the individual contract of employment should be regulated by law. In the early years of the twentieth century, and in 1910 and 1911, proposals had been made to do precisely this for manual workers, but they were rejected, and the individual employment contract came to be regulated largely by the collective contract. Now, however, a special departmental committee of inquiry proposed that permissive legislation should be passed which regulated the *content* of individual employment agreements and provided *procedures* for entering into and terminating such agreements.[2] Confusion was caused by some of the recommendations on the content of contracts. There were to be certain compulsory provisions on material content, dealing with sickness pay, and holidays with pay, for which specific provisions were suggested for the three groups into which the committee divided employees. (LO objected to this 'class' division.) These could be permissive where collective agreements regulated the matters in question.

This would have meant some dualism for parts of the labour market, and such a legal regulation of some of the terms of employment was quite out of character with the stress placed in Sweden on the voluntary negotiation of the content of contracts, at least for manual workers. From the point of view of the interest organizations the explanation was that LO was not particularly interested in salaried employees and their problems,[3] while SAF was reluctant to make many concessions to them.

No legislation was passed on the basis of this report. The remedy in fact, as LO for example grasped, was not to legislate on the form

[1] *S.O.U.*, 1935 : 59, p. 101. *Betänkande med förslag till lag om förenings-och förhandlingsrätt.*

[2] *S.O.U.*, 1935 : 18. *Betänkande med förslag till lag om arbetsavtal.*

[3] The editor of LO's paper, Sigfrid Hansson, was an enthusiastic supporter of trade unionism among salaried employees. LO itself made some very pertinent comments on the report mentioned above, and it later endorsed the legislation giving legal protection to salaried employees.

and content of agreements, but to guarantee to employees who had so far been unable to bargain collectively the right to do so. Collective norms for employment would follow if the rights of association and negotiation were recognized. The committee took this point, and in a second report it proposed legislation to guarantee these rights.[1]

I. THE RIGHT OF ASSOCIATION

The Act[2] governing the rights of association and collective bargaining was only passed into law in 1936 after considerable misgivings and amendments, and it is a narrowly framed enactment. It applies to relations between employers and employees, with the exception of public servants who occupy 'positions of responsibility' and whose legal status is governed by the penal code. The right of association it deals with is not general, but refers to the labour market only, and with associations which look after the interests of employees or employers in matters affecting conditions of employment and other relations with the other side. The right of *association* covers the rights for employers and employees (1) to belong to associations; (2) to enjoy membership; (3) to work on behalf of the association; and (4) to work for the formation of an association.

Thus the Act only regulates the *positive* right of combination. No legal protection is provided for the negative right of association, the right to be unorganized, e.g. by banning compulsion to organize.[3] Three reasons were given for this restriction: (*a*) that no legislation on such a far-reaching issue could be confined to the labour market; (*b*) that compulsion to organize is an *internal* matter for workers and for employers, and the Act does not intend to prescribe conditions about the government of the internal affairs of trade unions or employers' associations, but to provide for each side to be able to exercise the right of combination with regard to the other; and (*c*) the right to combine is only in fact regulated to the extent necessary to guarantee the right of *negotiation*. The primary object was to help

[1] *S.O.U.*, 1935 : 59. SAF, through its representative in the committee (Gustaf Söderlund), opposed legislation. He did not deny that there had sometimes been abuses against the right to combine, but thought it wiser to endure some slight injustice than to have legislation.

[2] *Lag om förenings-och förhandlingsrätt* den 11 september, 1936 (no. 506).

[3] The negative right of association, providing protection against compulsion to organize, had a chequered career in the various legislative proposals put forward by official committees during the early 1930s. See *S.O.U.*, 1933 : 36 (The Bergendal report on third party neutrality in labour disputes): *S.O.U.*, 1934 : 16 (the report of the thirteen-men commission): *S.O.U.*, 1935 : 59: Proposition 31, 1935, and Proposition 240, 1936: and the statements by the second standing committee in 1935 and 1936, for shifting emphasis on the merits and demerits of protecting the negative right, and of providing a legal solution restricted to the labour market only.

organizations of salaried employees to obtain this right, and this is the essential practical point which explains the limitations of the Act.

The positive right of association is, rather vaguely, 'to be inviolate'. Violation is not directly defined, but is deemed to occur if certain purposive action is taken. When, either from the side of employers or employees, *measures* are taken against anyone on the other side for the *purpose* of persuading him not to join an association, to leave an association, not to make use of his membership of an association or not to work on behalf of the association or for the formation of an association, violation has occurred; and likewise if from one side measures that *injure* a party on the other side are taken because this second party is a member of an association, makes use of his membership, or is active on behalf of or for the formation of such an association. The sanction is damages, discussed below.

This protection is provided only for those *in employment*. For example, an employer who refuses to engage a worker because he is organized in a certain union is not guilty of violating the right of association.[1] Thus an employer is not prevented from systematically avoiding the employment of members of a certain union. The union has *no* independent right of association, since the right only arises through having individual members *in employment*. Two changes were made here in 1940. First, even beyond the contract area an organization can now claim damages if the right of association of its *members* in employment has been violated and its activity is therefore impaired. Secondly, violation of the right of association can occur through a measure being adopted for the purpose of fulfilling the provisions of a collective or other contract.

This second provision is intended to deal with 'organization clauses', various forms of the closed or union shop. The right of association does not *debar* organization clauses, but it takes precedence over them if there is a clash between them, and it cannot be made permissive or contracted away. If an employer dismisses a member of *one* organization because he has a closed or union shop agreement with *another* organization he is guilty of violating the right of association. An unorganized worker has no protection, however, against organization clauses. In such a case the employer would be obliged to dismiss unorganized workers, since the right of association only arises through joining, or attempting to join, an association.[2]

One exception to the Act is that provision may be made indivi-

[1] See Folke Schmidt, *Kollektiv arbetsrätt*, 3rd edition, p. 155 (Stockholm, 1958). That this is so is obvious, in the case of SAF partners, from the fact that the 'management prerogative clause' in the SAF rules still exists and gives the Partners freedom to discriminate between organized and unorganized workers in selecting their labour force.

[2] Labour Court rulings on organization clauses have been the subject of considerable disagreement among the members of the Court.

dual or collective agreements specifying that foremen[1] may not be members of unions that are designed to look after the interests of persons employed under them. This was merely a codification of the practice on which SAF had, for instance, insisted since 1907, and which had been conceded in earlier legislative drafts, e.g. in 1910. Foremen can of course, and do, organize in their *own* union.

Cases arising out of this statutory right of association are taken up for decision by the Labour Court, which thus had its competence extended to cover the statutory right and not only the contractual right, as was the case between 1929 and 1936. The Court has to deal with measures, and the purpose of the measures, in adjudicating on cases, mainly dismissals, concerning the right of association. The burden of proof lies mainly with the employer side; once the workers' side has shown that a dismissal was probably an attack on the right of association, the employer must show that there were other good reasons, independent of the right to combine, such as a shortage of work, or misbehaviour on the part of the worker.[2]

The sanction for breach of the right of association is civil damages, but there is no limitation (by contrast to the maximum damages of 200 crowns against an individual workman under the Collective Contracts Act) on the amount of damages that may be awarded by the Labour Court. Damages can be claimed for personal suffering, and for encroachment on the injured party's interest in following his occupation without let or hindrance. The amount of damages may be reduced by the Court in the light of the degree of culpability, or the assets of the guilty party, and complete exoneration from the obligation to pay compensation may also be granted.

II. THE RIGHT TO BARGAIN COLLECTIVELY

The right of association is more fundamental than the right of negotiation as a principle of individual liberty, but the Swedish legislation of 1936 is not idealistic on this point. It aims to regulate the right of association only to the extent necessary to ensure the right to bargain collectively. Chapter 2 of the 1936 Act, on the right of negotiation, channels negotiations on the *employees*' side through their organizations. The right of negotiation can be exercised by an individual employer or an association of employers, and by associations of employees. These various persons or associations are entitled

[1] A foreman is defined as a person who is employed as the employer's representative to lead, allocate and control work that is carried out by persons subordinate to him, and in which he himself does not participate except on rare occasions. By Labour Court rulings, it is now sufficient for the foreman to lead, allocate *or* control work, without having any general managerial function. See Labour Court Judgement 1939/87.

[2] See Labour Court Judgement 1937/57.

to call for negotiations on the regulation of conditions of employment and of other relations between employer and employee. This right involves the other side in an obligation[1] to enter into negotiations either in person or through representatives at a meeting and, when required, to present proposals for resolving the subject of negotiations. This *can* be a non-justiciable or a justiciable dispute (see the Mediation Act, Chapter VI). The party wishing to call negotiations informs the other side, and, if the other side so asks, representations must be made in writing, setting out the question(s) on which negotiations are desired. Meetings for negotiations are to be held as soon as possible, and the parties are enjoined to agree on a time and place for the meeting without delay.[2] If the other side wishes, minutes are to be kept and signed by both parties. There is of course no *obligation* to arrive at agreement, since this would imply, in the case of non-justiciable disputes, some measure of compulsory arbitration as an ultimate solution.

The only matter on which the parties may agree to depart from the rules of this Act is by agreeing to some other arrangement about negotiation procedure in a collective contract. Möller (the Minister of Social Affairs) here met the wishes of LO, which wanted the provisions on negotiation procedure to be permissive, since LO unions already had settled negotiation procedures. The Act thus sets out the *principle* of the right and obligation to negotiate, but the parties may agree on *procedure* in their collective contracts. For manual workers' organizations these new provisions meant little, as the above dispensation shows, and Chapter 2 of the Basic Agreement of 1938 was soon to provide a further voluntary codification of procedure. For salaried employees' organizations, however, these rules immediately confronted the employer with an obligation. SAF did not like it and could not agree with the provision which introduced compulsion to negotiate[3] and provided the tremendous

[1] The sanction is civil damages, as set out in the Mediation Act, NOT this Act. If one party refuses to negotiate with the other side that other side has no means *itself* of demanding that the legal obligation to negotiate is fulfilled. But it may ask for the assistance of an official mediator under the Mediation Act. If such a request is made by employers or trade unions covering at least half of the employees affected by the dispute the mediator is obliged to put his services at the disposal of the party. It follows from the Mediation Act that the mediator is entitled, when one of the parties requests, to ask the Labour Court to instruct the recalcitrant party to enter into negotiations or run the risk of paying a fine. This provision has been applied on only one occasion.

[2] No employer may refuse an employee reasonable time off for the purpose of his participating in negotiations on a question for which he has been appointed to represent his association.

[3] See the reservation by Gustaf Söderlund (the managing director of SAF) in *S.O.U.*, 1935 : 59, pp. 149–55. In this reservation Söderlund also expressed his *general* distrust of labour legislation, an attitude that was clearly significant in the development of the private negotiations between LO and SAF which led to the Basic Agreement of 1938. See below, Chapter VII.

stimulus to the growth of organizations among salaried employees which was discussed in Chapter III.

III. REGISTRATION PROCEDURE

Indeed the Act went even further, for under Chapter 3 of the Act, which is now almost obsolete, it provided certain facilities for the exercise of the right of negotiation where no settled negotiation procedure yet existed. At the time SAF expressed its dislike of this chapter, LO termed the registration arrangements a bureaucratization of the negotiation procedure, and the Minister (Möller) had in fact endeavoured to leave this chapter out of the Act. The rules it provides are interesting in showing what sort of provisions would be tolerated in helping infant salaried employees' organizations to obtain bargaining rights, and they also show by contrast the sort of thing which LO and SAF would never have accepted for their part of the labour market at that stage in their development.

The procedure provides for several stages. (1) Registration of trade unions (the Act does not here provide for employers' registering) with the Social Welfare Board, giving data about rules and officials. (2) This registration involves an obligation to submit all disputes that arise between the registered union and employers which cannot be settled by the parties to negotiation before an independent chairman before direct action may be taken. (3) The obligation to keep the peace automatically becomes mutual, and both sides are required to attend for negotiations on the call of the independent chairman. (4) The independent chairman, appointed by the Social Welfare Board, may attempt to resolve the dispute. If he fails he can recommend voluntary arbitration with the approval of both parties, failing which he must, on the request of one side, ask that a Board should be appointed who make *proposals* for settling the dispute. (5) If either side refuses to accept proposals these may, on the request of either party, be made public, in order to exercise moral pressure. The Swedish terminology refers to this Board as a board of arbitration, but it is more correctly regarded as a board of conciliation with moral powers of persuasion which is entitled to recommend, but not to impose, a solution, and to use publicity for the purpose of exercising pressure. (6) If this is unsuccessful, the peace obligation for the particular issue lapses; proposed sanctions must be indicated within one month, at seven days' notice. Meanwhile the independent chairman retains the initiative to invite the parties to reopen negotiations. The mediators appointed under the Mediation Act do not deal with disputes arising under the procedure of this chapter, for the whole approach is quite different from that with which the official government mediators are primarily concerned.

Very few associations have registered with the Social Board under Chapter 3 of the 1936 Act, and those that have are small salaried employees' unions. It was of course entirely in their interests that this special registration procedure was devised, and there is a clearly recognizable thread running through the procedure, based on the assumption that certain employers may have to be dragooned by the device of registration into negotiating with organizations that are not strong enough to use force. The largest union to use the procedure at one time was the Foremen's Union. Now the provisions of Chapter 3 apply only to six registered associations,[1] no association has registered since 1948, and this chapter of the Act could well be repealed. Nevertheless, in its time Chapter 3 ensured by its very existence that many salaried workers' unions did gain recognition. The law provided machinery for forcing employers to negotiate if they did not do so voluntarily. Chapter 3 marks a milestone in the evolution of white-collar unions to a position of equal standing with other groups on the labour market as organizations entitled to bargain about terms of employment on behalf of their members.[2]

IV. THE SPECIAL BARGAINING POSITION OF PUBLIC SERVANTS

The Act of 1936 regulates the right of association to the extent that is considered necessary in order to promote bargaining through negotiations in which the employers' and workers' organizations are regarded as equal parties, free and able to use their bargaining strength. But the Act excluded from these rights employees of the central and local government who occupied 'positions of responsibility'. The governing factor in this cleavage was the need for the government to be certain that essential public services would be performed without interruption. Secondly, established civil servants had security of tenure in order to ensure their independence of the government of the day, of political parties, and of the public. These circumstances were incorporated in the terms of employment of such public servants, who were guaranteed a certain salary, and security of tenure. This at once limited the freedom of the employer to use bargaining sanctions such as the lock-out to settle their terms of

[1] For an analysis of this chapter, see Tredje kapitlet, by Carl Chr Schmidt, in *De första decennierna—En bok on HTF*, pp. 69–87 (Stockholm, 1957).

[2] Paradoxically, the few cases before the Labour Court on the right of association of salaried employees did not favour the employees' side. The first case of this kind after the passage of the Act was the Kungälv case (Judgement 1937/57) which for a long time convinced salaried employees that the protection of the right to combine was 'largely a paper guarantee'. See Geijer, in Geijer and Schmidt, *Arbetsgivare och fackföreningsledare i domarsäte*, pp. 65, 79 (Lund, 1948). But this did not prevent salaried employees' organizations from flourishing.

employment. But on the other side the bargaining position of established civil servants was weakened by the provisions of the penal code and the Constitution, which made it a dereliction of duty and a criminal offence for them to withdraw their labour.

The government could not therefore envisage a bargaining model for such civil servants along the lines of that implicit in the Act of 1936. A special decree[1] of 1937 accordingly attempted to provide some limited arrangements for civil servants, and an Act[2] of 1940 regulated the position of responsible officials employed by local authorities.

Instead of a two-sided collective bargaining procedure and process, the decree of 1937 provided for *consultation* between government departments or agencies and organizations of civil servants to which the government *conceded* this right of consultation. All rights of decision were reserved unilaterally for the employing authority. At departmental level provision was made for a limited obligation to *inform* the unions of any proposals relating to changes in or new conditions of work, salaries, and their application. Matters affecting individual civil servants (e.g. promotion) could also be taken up for this limited type of negotiation. The staff associations could ask for negotiations and discussions; but it was not intended that the right of the authorities to decide should be infringed. The employers' side also reserved the right to discontinue negotiations. The unions were only entitled to be consulted and to air their views.

While it did not explicitly provide for the right of association this decree clearly implied it, and it stimulated organization among civil servants. An attempt was made to ensure that the unions being consulted were representative of the staff by the requirement in the decree that applications for this right to negotiate were to be submitted to the government, and include copies of the rules, and information about officials and membership. No attempt was made to grant exclusive bargaining rights, and the provision was not very effective, because the government usually recognized an association as soon as it had fulfilled the formal requirements. The government has not exercised any pressure to rationalize bargaining through reducing the large numbers of unions claiming to represent civil servants, arguing that in principle it is inappropriate for the employer, the government, to regulate the manner in which civil servants are organized. The clause dealing with recognition was dropped in 1954, and at the same time more flexible arrangements were introduced for informing the staff side of proposed changes.

In fact, the whole trend in this sector in recent years has been away

[1] *Kungörelse angående förhandlingsrätt för statens tjänstemän* den 4 juni 1937 (no. 292).

[2] *Lag om förhandlingsrätt för kommunala tjänstemän* den 17 maj 1940 (no. 331).

from the special treatment of responsible officials towards a collective bargaining system which is very similar to that of the private sector. The growth in public activity and in civil service unionism, and the trend to centralized bargaining for civil servants in the 1940s, have made the 1937 decree old-fashioned. Central bargaining was not envisaged by the decree, for it only gave a vague formulation that the government could negotiate through representatives with the staff associations, and did not explicitly provide for the type of central negotiations at the level of the Ministry of Civil Service Affairs which have developed in practice.

Various attempts have been made to clarify the legal and constitutional position in order to keep it abreast of practice.[1] The criteria used for the 1937 decree have not proved satisfactory. The definition of responsible official has proved a poor criterion, because the public sector has grown haphazardly and no systematic attempt has been made to apply the 'permanence of tenure' rules to new types of activity. In fact, they have been applied to many new types of public activity which could equally well have been undertaken by private companies. Permanence of tenure and responsibility have not always coincided. The related criterion of employment on salary plan, which was meant to cover employees whose services were indispensable to the community, has also been applied in a slipshod fashion. The bargaining weapons available to civil servants and the government have also been ill-defined. There may be no right to strike, but there is no limit on the use of the employment blockade, and unestablished civil servants can give collective notice to withdraw their labour: from the side of the government too pressure has on occasion (e.g. in the SACO dispute of 1952) been exercised by threatening to withhold salary increases.

The most recent proposals put forward by Ekblom[2] endeavour to provide a legal solution to match the practice of recent years, by abolishing the decree of 1937 and promoting a system of collective contracts. There will not be a complete movement to full equality of bargaining rights, however, through an extension of the rules of the private to the public sector. Certain subjects will be expressly exempted. The employer's prerogative on working rules, engaging, promoting and dismissing staff, and disciplinary questions, are to be retained as limitations on the subject-matter of bargaining. The central subject for bargaining is to be salaries.

In dealing with direct action, and the problems of permanence of tenure, Ekblom has suggested that 'responsibility of office' will

[1] The two main inquiries into this whole question have been *S.O.U.*, 1951 : 54, *Stats-och kommunaltjänstemäns förhandlingsrätt*, and *S.O.U.*, 1960 : 10, *Statstjänstemäns förhandlingsrätt*.

[2] In *S.O.U.*, 1960 : 10.

continue to be used as a criterion, but in principle the link between responsibility and industrial disputes should be severed.[1] The penal code will not be applied where the employer locks out or the staff *associations* withdraw labour. Permanence of tenure will be retained, but only for certain of the traditional categories of government administration where the government interest is predominant, and cannot be entrusted to private enterprise (e.g. defence and justice). This was the original intention; and in order to ensure the government fulfils its duty to the public these indispensable civil servants are to be debarred from striking. Unestablished civil servants will have the right to strike.

Finally, Ekblom suggests that the competence of the Labour Court, which cannot at present deal with civil service salary contracts (since in law they are still not contracts, but promulgated orders), should be extended to include civil servants, and the Mediation Act should be applicable to them.

While this problem of bargaining rights for civil servants is still regarded primarily as a constitutional question, there is no doubt that the real issue is an economic one. It is the growth of public activity and the development of unionism which have outmoded the provisions of the decree of 1937. There has been a swift movement away from the cleavage established in 1936 between responsible officials and others, and from a position which Robbins, for example, thought would be permanent. 'With due allowance for the indistinctness of this line in certain sectors, we may safely conclude that the collective contract system may not rise in its future growth above that theoretical ceiling. It cannot expand so as to include government employees who are, to speak broadly, official and not merely auxiliary to the official governing function.'[2] The fact that this is no longer a realistic statement is a measure of the changes that have occurred in this sector within fifteen years. The implications for wages policy are enormous. The government, via the Ministry of Civil Service Affairs, is in effect collaborating in the development of a collective bargaining system for public activity, and is making no pretence of having an objective salary policy, based on justice or fair comparison. The economic model of the bargaining process in the public sector is now based on bilateral organization, which means that freedom to negotiate must be permitted. The government has washed its hands of any

[1] Op. cit., p. 38.

[2] Robbins, op. cit., p. 126. In fact, of course, these developments towards collective contracts in the public sector endorse Robbins' development thesis, that there are four stages in the process of development towards a mature collective bargaining system, from (*a*) mutual acceptance of the principle of combination; through (*b*) growth in the associational structure; (*c*) a collective contracts system, to (*d*) the final stage of private governing organs for functional areas.

attempt to follow the 1937 policy, of simply announcing its intentions and discontinuing discussions at its discretion. It has now adopted a bargaining model, subject to the restrictions the Ekblom proposals impose. To put the point another way, the government is not looking to the public sector to give a lead in wages policy by elaborating bargaining principles but simply accepting a collective bargaining system based on organizational strength.

The Ekblom proposals apply only to central government, unlike those of the 1951 report, but they would clearly also provide a lead for local authorities in systematizing their relations with their 'responsible officials'. Following on the Act of 1936, their position was regulated by a Local Government Employees Collective Bargaining Act of 1940, which regulated the right of negotiation along much the same lines as in the 1937 decree for civil servants. Here also the right of negotiation covers general conditions of work, employment, and remuneration, and their application. But the employer's right to decide was in no way infringed.

One difference was that, whereas the civil servants' organizations were conceded the right of consultation in relation to a specific department, the procedure for local authorities is that the Social Board concedes the *general* right to negotiate to an organization of salaried employees, which must then apply to a particular local authority in order to be allowed to negotiate. The intention was that the individual local authority had the final power of decision, but in 1954 local authorities were specifically given in law the right to delegate their powers of decision in bargaining to associations of local authorities. This does not in principle alter the formal position of the 1940 Act governing the right the organizations of employees have to be consulted. It is simply a practical recognition of the trend towards centralized bargaining that has in fact taken place.

SUMMARY

The legislation of 1936, 1937, and 1940 on the rights of association and collective bargaining has been successful in providing these rights for salaried employees, and in giving a lead to 'responsible officials'. But no attempt has been made in Sweden to develop a comprehensive set of legal principles guaranteeing both the positive and negative rights to combine. There is no protection in law[1] against compulsion to organize—the major defence is provided by SAF. The right of association is purely functional and auxiliary to the right to bargain collectively, which is considered the main object in view. This

[1] The penal code does of course provide protection against violence, libel, etc., as means of pressure to organize.

necessitates some provision allowing people to organize, but the right to bargain is given a higher standing than the right of association pure and simple.

This approach emphasizes the willingness in the Swedish system to accept collectivization and to apportion to the collective contract a central place in the system of labour relations. There is little scope for individuals to stand outside the system. Another lesson to be drawn from the discussion of this chapter is that the law can help to encourage bargaining but, as the recent experience of the public sector shows, it cannot stand out against organizational pressures that stem from a growth of activity in that sector of the economy. It can lead and encourage, but not repress.

CHAPTER VI

The Law of Collective Bargaining

I. INTRODUCTION

THE legislation of 1936 and later years analysed in the last chapter was designed to extend collective bargaining to all salaried employees except 'responsible officials', but even in that sector there has been a surge towards a system of collective agreements governing the terms and conditions of employment.

The collective contract has been the main focus of labour legislation in Sweden, and the twentieth-century discussion has been primarily concerned with the collective form of contract as the one to be regulated. Three main problems can be distinguished as central to a system of collective contracts:

(1) How is the process of *negotiating* such contracts to be regulated: to what extent are the parties to be allowed to exercise pressure by the use of economic coercion? How far does the government promote peaceful solutions by providing mediation or arbitration machinery?

(2) When the contract has been *concluded*, what enforcement machinery is to be established for resolving disputes about interpretation? Is a Labour Court, arbitration in an alternative form, or mediation to be employed? Can sympathetic action be allowed when a contract is in force? What sanctions are appropriate for breaches of contract?

(3) What limitations does the public impose on the freedom of the parties to handle disputes arising under both (1) and (2) in such a way that neutral third parties may be harmed, and vital social interests impaired?

The first two groups of questions have in Sweden been tackled by legislation, but the third has been resolved by agreement, and will be taken up in the next part.

These first two groups of questions fall broadly under the headings of non-justiciable and justiciable disputes respectively. Non-justiciable disputes involve disagreements about matters which are not regulated by contract or statute, and no legal rules or norms are provided for their solution. Justiciable disputes, on the other hand, involve disagreement about the rights and obligations that arise from the provisions of a statute or contract, collective or individual. These cannot always be resolved by reference to legal norms, but in general, since there is an agreement, a contract or a statute in existence to be interpreted, they are more suited to a legal approach than non-justiciable disputes are.

Since both non-justiciable and justiciable disputes involve economic interests, it is confusing, and inappropriate, to translate the Swedish word *intresse* (used to refer to non-justiciable disputes) by 'interest' or 'economic'. A worker may be concerned about the wage terms of a proposed contract, and can make a non-justiciable (interest) dispute of it: but he will also be interested in the wage he earns as a result of applying and interpreting the contract once it has been concluded on his behalf by the union and he becomes entitled to benefits (and has obligations) under the contract. Both are economic and interest disputes in the widest sense, but the first is a non-justiciable, the second a justiciable dispute.

Swedish legislation on collective contracts has endeavoured to preserve a distinction between non-justiciable and justiciable disputes, but in some of the frequent and comprehensive proposals for legislation made, e.g. in 1910, 1911, 1916, and 1928, the distinction has not always been clearly and finely drawn. Nevertheless, practice has shown that the parties to collective contracts make a distinction, and the legislation which has been passed has endeavoured to respect it.

Problems of resolving non-justiciable disputes in Sweden quickly led to the Mediation Act of 1906, revised in 1920, and this is dealt with in Section II. The regulation of collective contracts once they are in force, and the justiciable disputes that arise out of them, has been a much more controversial subject, which was only finally resolved in 1928 with the passage of the Collective Contracts and Labour Court Acts. These will be analysed in Sections III and IV respectively of this chapter.

II. THE MEDIATION ACT

The current Mediation Act[1] was passed in 1920, and it continued the essential geographical basis established by the first Mediation Act of 1906, by which the country is divided into eight (before 1950, seven) districts, each with a government-appointed mediator. The geographical basis is flexible, in that the mediator can operate outside his district for a specific branch of activity, e.g. for a national agreement. Further flexibility is provided through the provisions that the government can appoint special individual mediators, who may or may not

[1] *Lag om medling i arbetstvister* den 28 maj 1920 (no. 245).

be drawn from the ranks of the district mediators, or *ad hoc* mediation commissions, usually to work along with the district mediator. Such commissions are usually composed mainly of people with experience as mediators. The intention is that special mediation commissions should be used sparingly, and it is not the intention, though it happens in practice, that the various forms of mediation should be successive instances, but rather alternatives.[1]

Initially the powers given to the mediators to use their good offices in labour disputes applied to *all* types of dispute that threatened labour peace, but in fact, and particularly since the passage of the Collective Contracts Act of 1928, they have been predominantly concerned with non-justiciable disputes about the proposed terms of new agreements.[2]

The district mediators have the duty of following closely the conditions of employment in their districts. They meet employers and unions when they ask him for help.[3] More important in theory than practice is the provision that the mediator is empowered to intervene when a serious labour dispute appears to be threatening. An amendment to the Act, passed in 1931 at the behest of salaried employees' organizations, obliges the mediator to call parties together on the request of an organization of employees covering more than 50% of the employees affected. This is unimportant in practice.

The mediator can ask the parties to refrain from direct action while negotiations are in progress, but he cannot prohibit work stoppages. The Warning Act, passed in 1935, provides an additional string to the mediator's bow by requiring parties to a dispute to give seven days' notice of a stoppage of work (a strike or a lock-out, not a blockade or a boycott) to the other side and to the mediator. This is frequently the way in which the mediator is brought into a dispute. Notification of intended direct action must contain a statement of the reasons for the proposed action. The Warning Act is a procedural

[1] On one occasion, in 1955, an additional instance, a government commission (the name chosen to distinguish it from ordinary mediation commissions, which are nevertheless appointed by the government) was appointed to act mainly as a co-ordinating commission for the negotiations which were outstanding when SAF threatened direct or sympathetic lock-outs affecting 500,000 workers. The situation was considered so serious that the government introduced this additional instance into the negotiation procedure on that occasion.

[2] Formally, the Mediation Act cannot apply to the regulation of the terms of employment of responsible public officials, discussed in the last chapter. But under the Ekblom proposals mentioned there the Mediation Act will extend to the system of collective contracts being proposed for these government officials.

[3] A general shift over the years in the mediator's task has been that he is now involved mainly in trying to *prevent* stoppages. In the early days he was more of a fireman, called in usually *after* a stoppage had begun. See *Sociala Meddelanden* 12, 1956, for a series of articles on the mediation system. See also Howard E. Durham, 'The Place of Mediation in the Swedish Collective Bargaining System', in *Labor Law Journal*, pp. 536–45 (Chicago, August 1955), for a very perceptive analysis in English of the system.

one, and it is not a breach of contract to fail to give notice, but there is a sanction, the liability to be fined a maximum of 300 crowns in the public courts.

In the Mediation Acts of 1906 and 1920 there were no provisions of sanctions for failure to attend for negotiation on the call of the mediator, though the 1920 Act formally 'required' attendance. But the legislation of 1936 provides that such cases may now be brought before the Labour Court. Only a few cases have occurred, and only one fine has been imposed by the Court. The Act of 1936 also provides that parties to negotiations have not only a legal obligation to negotiate, but also to present proposals. The mediator cannot in theory, therefore, be confronted with passive resistance.

The core of the Mediation Act is §6, which provides that the negotiations the mediator convenes and conducts are primarily for the purpose of enabling the parties to arrive at agreement in accordance with the offers or proposals they *themselves* make. But the mediator is entitled, if and to the extent that he considers it likely to promote a good solution of the dispute, to urge the parties to accept adjustments and concessions which are considered to meet the case.

The mediator has no other function than that of seeking to bring about agreement. He has no duty or powers to try to embody certain provisions or principles in agreements. His sole task is to work towards an agreement that both sides are likely to accept, irrespective of its intrinsic merits or economic implications. He is entitled to bring pressure to bear, but not to dictate. All that he is instructed to try to do along these lines is set out in a royal decree.[1] Where a settlement of a labour dispute is reached through the direct or indirect assistance of the mediator he ought to endeavour (*a*) to have such provisions introduced into the contract as are designed to prevent disrupting stoppages of work in future, and (*b*) to work for such contracts being given a clear and unambiguous formulation. Again, in practice the mediator confines himself to the unresolved issues, and does not attempt to mould the perfect collective contract.

Mediators are formally controlled through the Mediation Office of the Department of Social Affairs, which co-ordinates their activity and promotes co-operation between them. Mediators are appointed

[1] *Kungörelse* (no. 898) of December 31, 1920, especially § 6.

The distinction between mediation and arbitration is made perfectly clear in the Act, as the following procedure shows. If agreement cannot be reached during the negotiations the mediator may recommend the disputants to allow the dispute to be settled by (*a*) a board of arbitration or special arbitrator; or otherwise (*b*) to allow one or more persons, whose verdict the parties bind themselves to follow, to arbitrate between them. The mediator could help to brief the arbitrators. *But he may not himself act as an arbitrator in industrial disputes.*

Arrangement (*a*) above has never been much used, and has fallen into disuse. Arrangement (*b*) is used very occasionally.

by the government for a specific period or indefinite period, but in fact their tenure depends entirely on the success with which they gain the confidence of the parties to disputes.

The formal provisions of the Mediation Act are not inflexible or detailed, and the law is dependent for its operation on the way in which the mediators in practice make use of the wide powers of discretion they have.[1] The Act only provides a framework of mediation machinery, and the mediators and the parties apply it to suit their own needs and wishes. The innovation by the parties of the impartial chairman in negotiations, by which one of the official mediators may be asked to take the chair from the beginning of negotiations, in the hope that he will be the mediator if and when the negotiations pass beyond the exploratory to the conciliatory stage, is an example of an attempt to fit the machinery of the Act to the desires of the labour market parties.

The only principle which stands out as inviolable, and which is essential to the whole approach in Sweden to the settlement of industrial disputes, is that the mediator is not in any sense making awards or dispensing justice. He is not arbitrating, but conciliating.[2]

Non-justiciable disputes are thus settled by negotiation, mediation, voluntary arbitration, or open conflict. The labour market organizations have held pretty consistently to the view that non-justiciable disputes must be settled by the arrangements they themselves care to make, aided by the government mediation machinery just analysed. It is true that in the early days the unions advocated arbitration on all issues, but when the first Mediation Act was passed in 1906 the chairman of LO, Herman Lindqvist, said the unions no longer felt so much in need of arbitration. They favoured mediation, but opposed compulsory arbitration of non-justiciable disputes. SAF has taken a similar view, but it was critical in 1906 even of the discretionary powers given to mediators, and in 1911 opposed any suggestion of a permanent mediation commission. The employers would, it argued, be unable to oppose a mediation proposal that had the backing of a government body. The result in fact would be the same as in the Australian system—state-fixing of wages. And once the government had its foot in the door Sweden would be on the high-road to an arbitration system, which SAF opposed.[3]

In effect, this was a tribute to the mediation system which, though government-sponsored, is not a direct instrument of government

[1] Durham, op. cit., p. 543. 'The absence of control is based on the theory that the primary mediatory relationship is between the mediator and the parties rather than between the mediator and the government.'

[2] The place of the mediation system in the post-war bargaining process is discussed in detail in Chapter XIV.

[3] *Industria*, 1911, p. 125 et seq.

policy. Both sides learned to praise the mediation system, because it did not deprive them of their own judgement and responsibility for bargaining decisions and their consequences.

The unanimity of view on the part of LO and SAF on this issue is reflected in the statement on compulsory arbitration of non-justiciable disputes which the secretariat of LO made at the 1926 congress:

'A law on compulsory arbitration in non-justiciable disputes must mean that the State takes upon itself the obligation to guarantee through its agency that the workers will enjoy the highest standard of living that the economic situation will allow at any one time, and that the employers obtain guarantees that wages will not be set higher than the general economic conditions prevailing will permit. The State cannot, however, give such a guarantee, since economic science can not yet serve as a satisfactory guide in judging these questions. Practical statistics are in addition far too inadequate to form the basis for a general judgement of these matters. Nor can the State give the workers a guarantee that employers will be willing to carry on their activity at the wage determined by arbitration, any more than it can guarantee that employers will be able to obtain workers at the wage determined. Thus the State seems to lack the prerequisites for being able to estimate what wages should be fixed at any one time, and for guaranteeing that business firms continue their activity at the wages fixed or that workers work for those wages. The employers' and workers' organizations are also in agreement in vigorously opposing legislation for compulsory arbitration of non-justiciable disputes. As far as private enterprise is concerned, therefore, SAF and LO are in complete agreement that compulsory arbitration in non-justiciable disputes is neither desirable nor appropriate.'[1]

Soon afterwards LO, in submitting its views on methods of determining minimum wages to the delegation for international co-operation on social policy, expressed opposition to legislation for determining minimum wages via wages boards. Such legislation was not desirable in Sweden. In the 1930s LO toyed only briefly with approving minimum wage legislation for agriculture, and has otherwise adhered to the arguments set out above against government fixing of wages.

The conviction of the labour market organizations that non-justiciable disputes would continue as long as there was opposition of economic interests, and that intervention by the government in such disputes would undermine the freedom of contract of the labour

[1] LO *kongress-protokoll*, 1926, *Utlåtande* no. 31, p. 329. The Report of LO's Committee of Fifteen, *Fackföreningsrörelsen och Näringslivet* (1941), p. 159, considered this still expressed the general views of the trade union movement. The arguments used, it will be noted, are all *practical*.

market, was endorsed by the Nothin commission. It took the view that non-justiciable disputes over wages and the distribution of income, and in particular disputes about the content of new contracts, could not be avoided. But compulsory settlement by the government of non-justiciable disputes that arose seemed to the commission to be out of the question at that time, for it would require so many regulations that the consequences could not be foreseen. It held the same view about an arbitration institution, and considered the best path along which to advance was that of achieving better contact and co-operation between the parties to labour contracts.

There was a definite difference between justiciable and non-justiciable disputes. In non-justiciable disputes the outcome was usually determined by the supply of and demand for labour, cost of living, market prospects for the finished products, and the bargaining strength of the organizations. In the case of an export industry foreign competition was sometimes decisive. Thus it was not legal rules, but economic strength and power, that determined the outcome of a non-justiciable dispute, unlike a dispute about rights. Compulsory arbitration in a wage dispute must therefore be based on an evaluation of the significance of the wage-determining factors. As to principles for arbitration, 'In our country as in others it would be extremely difficult to determine such principles.'[1] In any case neither employers' nor workers' sides considered the time was ripe for arbitration procedures in wage disputes. The commission recommended longer period contracts and various forms of wage adjustment mechanisms to reduce the area of conflict.

The implication of rejecting any form of arbitration for non-justiciable disputes was that there might well be open conflicts, and therefore a need to control direct action. The government could not always be expected to remain neutral and 'look the other way' unless there were some procedures for dealing with the complex problem of disputes that prejudiced the public interest. These are discussed in Part III.

III. THE COLLECTIVE CONTRACTS ACT

In the late nineteenth century, when the collective contract was beginning to assume significance as a regulator of the terms of employment, it was recognized that justiciable disputes should not be resolved by force, but regulated by agreement or by seeking redress in the law courts. Private arbitration of industrial disputes could be arranged under the terms of the general Arbitration Act of

[1] *S.O.U.*, 1935 : 65, p. 114.

1887, and provision for this was frequently made in early collective agreements, because the trade unions in particular considered that justiciable disputes ought to be settled in this way. But resort to arbitration under the Act was not always happy. Experience showed that such a procedure was too formal and time-consuming, and that collective agreements were frequently too technical for arbitrators to understand. This led the parties to devise their own arrangements for having arbitration of justiciable disputes. In Riksdag discussion of the special problems of labour relations there was generally a cautious attitude, e.g. in the discussion in 1887 and 1895 of arbitration of justiciable disputes, with considerable emphasis on the freedom of contract and the newness of collective labour problems. The wisdom of devising special arbitration arrangements in law for labour disputes was questioned.

After SAF was formed, LO and the employers continued to develop their own arrangements. In 1908 they reached agreement on a formulation which would help to resolve the difficulty of deciding whether a dispute about the content of an agreement was a justiciable or a non-justiciable dispute. SAF had taken the view that it was frequently difficult to tell whether a dispute that developed about the content of an agreement was one of interpretation, or a non-justiciable dispute that had not been covered by the negotiations leading to the agreement. It therefore favoured having negotiations on all disputes; and it could be decided then whether to refer a dispute to arbitration or to regard it as one which might possibly lead to open conflict if it could not be settled by negotiation. A formulation was agreed between LO and SAF providing that

'if disputes arise about the interpretation and application of agreements in force or disputes between the parties for *other* reasons, these disputes must in no circumstances give rise to an immediate stoppage of work on either side, but negotiations on the matter are first to take place between the parties involved and thereafter, if no agreement has been reached, between the employers' organization and the national trade union involved.'

In 1920 legislation was passed, which LO considered was essentially based on this 1908 agreement, providing for (*a*) a Central Arbitration Board (similar in composition to the Labour Court which replaced it in 1928) and (*b*) special arbitrators.[1] Both instances dealt with disputes about rights which were referred voluntarily by *both* parties for a binding decision through arbitration. The

[1] *Lag om särskilda skiljedomare i arbetstvister* den 28 maj 1920 (no. 248). This act is still in force, but no special arbitrators have been appointed since 1949.

legislation provided a useful supplement to the private arrangements made by the parties through arbitration, negotiation, or direct action.[1]

The settlement of justiciable disputes was, however, taken a stage further in 1928, by statutory enactment which obliged the parties to have justiciable disputes arising out of collective contracts settled peaceably, in the last resort by a special Labour Court constituted for the purpose.[2] A great deal of invective surrounded the 1928 enactments. LO now argued that voluntary arbitration of justiciable disputes was superior, in that both parties agreed to refer. This gave moral strength.[3] In addition (using an SAF argument of 1908) it was often difficult to know whether a dispute was about interpretation or was a non-justiciable question. Legislation was unnecessary, unjust, and likely to be biased. LO feared a legalistic approach would lead to complete legislative control over contracts. When the Act had been passed LO counselled its member unions to see that the text of new contracts was clear and unambiguous in order to avoid the Act becoming a 'full employment Act for lawyers'. Before it was passed the labour movement staged protest demonstrations in which about 400,000 workers took part.

SAF approved of the introduction of legal provisions that interpretation disputes must be settled peacefully, and in the last resort by a court. There was a need for a permanent court in order to obtain the best competence and specialized knowledge, and it was necessary to give it enough powers so that its judgements were

[1] LO argued in 1927 that since 1913 less than 1% of the total number of stoppages, covering less than ½% of the workers affected by stoppages, had been due to interpretational disputes; though SAF countered this by arguing that these figures gave no indication of situations where a dispute existed. For figures supporting the LO claim that legislation was unnecessary see also motion no. 282, *Upper Chamber*, 1928 (by Thorberg, Möller, Wigforss, Sandler and others).

[2] *Lag om kollektivavtal* den 22 juni 1928 (no. 253), and *Lag om arbetsdomstol* (no. 254) of the same date.

[3] See LO *verksamhetsberättelse*, 1927, p. 93 et seq.

There had been a gradual shift in LO's attitude with the years. In 1910 (see LO *verksamhetsberättelse*, 1910, p. 15, and motion no. 272, Lower House, 1910, by Lindqvist, the LO chairman, and others) LO approved a Labour Court in principle for the settlement of rights disputes, but did not like the proposed Act on collective contracts which the Court would have had to administer. In 1916–17 Lindqvist and the representative assembly of LO were not opposed in principle to the settlement of justiciable disputes by arbitration in a Labour Court; but the LO congress of 1917 (see *kongress-protokoll*, 1917, pp. 138–43) over-ruled the secretariat and expressed strong opposition to legislation.

The social democrats also changed course. In 1926 the social democratic Minister of Social Affairs (Gustav Möller) had stated (Westerståhl, op. cit., p. 365) that the time was ripe for the settlement of rights disputes by compulsory arbitration, though not necessarily by law, and, as he stated in the debate in the Upper House on May 25, 1928, certainly with the co-operation of the parties. The social democrats were alienated by the political crisis of 1926 and the change of government which brought the liberals to power, and this explains much of the heat generated over the legislation of 1928.

respected. In addition, SAF thought that the coverage of the labour market by it and LO was not sufficiently comprehensive to enable the problem to be resolved by agreement.

The sources of the 1928 Acts are to be sought in the practice of the parties in resolving their disputes by machinery they devised themselves, and in previous legal debate and proposals, e.g. in 1910, 1911, 1916, and 1920. But in 1928 legal rules for collective agreements were prescribed for the first time, and the organizations were deliberately invited to play a major part in administering and interpreting the Acts.

The basic thread running through the enactments is that a dispute about the way in which a collective agreement is to be interpreted must not be settled through the pressure of economic sanctions. The parties may themselves agree on procedures for resolving such disputes peaceably but, in the last resort, they will be resolved by judicial process before a specially created tribunal, the Labour Court.

(*a*) *The provisions of the Collective Contracts Act*

The Act contains no specific provisions about the content of collective agreements. Nor are they defined directly, but only by means of a clause (§1) setting out the manner in which such agreements are to be drawn up. 'Agreements between employers or associations of employers and trade unions or other similar associations of workers about the conditions that are to be observed in employing workers, or otherwise dealing with the relations between employers and workers, shall be drawn up in writing.' As well as providing that collective contracts are to be in writing (which also covers acceptance by letter or acceptance of the proceedings of negotiations in approved minutes) so must notice of termination of an agreement be given in writing or by telegram. Provision is made for the eventuality of letters and telegrams going astray, but the procedure for terminating is in practice much less formal.

There is no legal definition of the criteria by which the competence of an association to conclude a collective agreement are to be assessed, the procedure being based on the practice that had been approved by 1910 for 'idealistic associations'. On the side of employers an individual employer can conclude a collective agreement, but an individual worker or group of unorganized workers cannot conclude a collective agreement with the other side. The individual worker is normally covered by a contract of service (*arbetsavtal*) into which he enters —frequently verbally—with an employer on taking up employment, but the individual employment agreement is generally related to and indeed based on a collective agreement. Economically, historically, and legally the main function of the collective agreement is to provide a framework of standards in the light of which the individual employment agreement is regulated.[1]

The collective agreement establishes norms about content, and a framework of rights and obligations which the parties bring upon themselves when they enter into agreement with one another. It provides at least minimum (though sometimes standard) conditions for the employer to observe, although he is not always debarred from being more generous than the terms of a collective contract provide.[2] Collective agreements can be national, district, local, or plant level in scope, though the national agreement is the most important form.

Under §3 of the Act the supremacy of the collective norms is indicated by the provision that individual employment agreements may not deviate beyond certain limits from it, for if 'agreement has been reached between employers and workers who are bound by the same collective contract on conditions that involve a departure from the collective contract, then such an agreement is not valid beyond the limits of the deviation allowed by the collective contract'. The collective norms take priority, even though they may be discretionary. Only the parties to the agreement, acting together, can change the collective agreement, not individuals. The collectivized nature of the employment contract is a rule which the Labour Court has applied strictly. At the same time, the rule is not necessarily exhaustive. It is possible to avoid the problem of deviation from the collective contract norms—and this is particularly true, and standard practice, for salaried employees in private employment—by excluding salary provisions from the contract. Here the policy is one of avoiding, not evading, the collective norms, because both sides have preferred

[1] There is no comprehensive legal regulation of the individual contract of service in Sweden. Attempts have been made at various times (e.g. in 1910, 1935) to introduce such legislation in order to fill the gap left through the effective disappearance of the pre-industrial contract of service between Master and Servant (which was formally repealed in 1926). The main sources governing the individual's terms of employment are: (*a*) collective contracts; (*b*) regulations, e.g. in the public sector; and (*c*) legislation covering such matters as hours, holidays, workers' protection, etc. Interest in the individual contract of service has revived since the Union of Clerical and Technical Employees in Industry began to publish in 1942 a series of booklets on various aspects of the subject for the guidance of salaried employees (who in general have been more affected by individual than collective terms of employment), and through the recent book by Folke Schmidt, *Tjänsteavtalet* (Stockholm, 1959).

[2] For a discussion of Labour Court interpretations of cases where wages in excess of standard rates have been paid, see Lennart Geijer and Folke Schmidt, *Arbetsgivare och fackföreningsledare i domarsäte*, pp. 215–25 (Lund, 1958). The implications of such overpayment, e.g. in the form of wages drifting, are however in practice more important economically than legally. The important practical point is that the Labour Court is not intended as, and has not been used as, an agency of price (wage) control in practice. In full employment the employer is in any case a willing partner with the worker, rather than the union, in such overpayments.

individual to collective salary norms for white-collar workers in industry.

There is no provision in Swedish law for extending the coverage of the terms of a collective contract to parties standing outside it who operate in the same sphere, but such parties can agree to apply its terms to their relationship. This frequently happens when unorganized employers apply the material terms of SAF Partners' contracts to their own activity. However, although there is no legal provision providing explicitly for extension, the clause in the Collective Contracts Act which allows sympathetic action to be used (discussed below) means that in certain circumstances the terms of collective contracts can be extended by the exercise of bargaining pressure on employers who have not concluded collective agreements.

A collective contract does not bind specific named persons, but contracts concluded for a trade group or an area are also binding on the *members* of the association, whether they join the association before or after the agreement is concluded. They are not bound by the agreement if they are already bound by another collective contract. Nor do members cease to be bound by a collective agreement merely through leaving an association. The Labour Courts deal with such cases as they arise and according to the circumstances.

The rights and obligations of associations and members are not identical under the Act, e.g. only an association can give notice of termination from the workers' side, and the parties to an agreement may agree that certain rules bind only them, and not their members;[1] at the other extreme, the individual worker's liability for breach of contract is limited.

The position of unorganized workers under the Act is not defined. In theory an employer bound by a collective agreement might be tempted to conclude an individual employment contract with unorganized workers that deviated from the collective agreement. This has not been a major issue in Sweden in fact, because of the high organization percentage (and hence its omission from the Act), but the Labour Court has primarily stressed the supremacy of the principle of collective norms by ruling[2] that collective agreements also apply to unorganized workers unless specific provision to the contrary is made in the collective agreement. The employer is generally under an obligation to the union, not to the unorganized workers, to apply the terms of the agreement to non-union labour in order to prevent price cutting. The principle the Labour Court advanced was that it was natural to assume that employers bound

[1] The problems of the extent to which clauses in contracts apply at both the organization and personal level, or at the former level only, are discussed in Folke Schmidt, *Tjänsteavtalet*, pp. 25 et seq.

[2] Judgement 1932/95.

by a collective contract must not apply worse conditions than those set out in the agreement to workers who stood outside the workers' organization but were employed on work referred to in the agreement. It was not necessary to make express provision in the agreement to this effect. It was quite sufficient that this should be the parties' intention. This general principle would apply unless the parties made some other provision in the contract. This general principle is in keeping with the whole collectivizing nature of collective agreements. If this were not the general rule employers might have an incentive to employ unorganized workers at rates of pay below the contract rates. In addition, the general rule coincides with the view that it is no concern of the employer to establish whether his employees are organized or not, but of the unions.

(b) The collective contract as a peace treaty

The provisions of the Act follow closely here the views expressed by the labour market organizations, as these had crystallized by 1928. There is not a complete ban on direct action, no general prohibition of sanctions during the period of validity of contracts. But the intention is to promote peace, and where the Act allows direct action it imposes far-reaching limitations on this freedom under four heads. During the period of validity employers or workers bound by the collective agreement must not resort to stoppages of work (lock-outs or strikes, blockades, boycotts, or other comparable *measures*) in the following four cases:

(1) On the grounds of a dispute about the validity, existence, or correct meaning of an agreement, or on the grounds of whether a particular action violates the agreement or the provisions of the Act. Thus the parties may not resort to direct action merely because they disagree about the provisions set out in the contract.

(2) In order to bring about alterations in the terms of the agreement.

(3) In order to enforce provisions aimed at coming into force after the contract has expired.

(4) In order to assist others in cases where they are not themselves entitled to resort to direct action. This prohibits the giving of help to someone who has himself repudiated his obligations under a collective agreement or the Act. Otherwise, *purely sympathetic action is allowed.*

These four grounds involve the Labour Court in a wide range of problems; for example, about whether direct action was taken; if so, in what form; by whom; with what intention and object? The remit of the Labour Court thus extends beyond justiciable disputes in an interpretative sense, because the peace obligation under (2) and (3) may cover unregulated non-justiciable disputes, while (4) allows sympathetic action by a party even when it is bound by a contract.

Direct action in connexion with unresolved non-justiciable disputes is not banned by the Act. In principle, economic sanctions can be used over a matter not regulated in a collective contract while the contract is in force covering other subjects. The procedure on disputes agreed by LO and SAF in 1908 recognized that the boundary line between justiciable and non-justiciable disputes might be difficult, and in theory the 1928 formulation could open up a wide area of possible conflicts. But the principle endorsed by the Labour Court has been that it interprets the liberties of the parties with regard to unresolved disputes in a very *narrow* way. It has ruled that direct action may not be taken on an unresolved dispute by one party, if the other side asserts in good faith that the dispute relates to a matter regulated in the contract, *until* the Labour Court has decided whether the dispute is an unresolved non-justiciable dispute.[1] This in practice clarifies the peace obligation. The Labour Court has followed the basic rule that its function is to promote industrial peace.

(*c*) *Sympathetic action*

The right to sympathetic action is not limited by this Act to certain kinds of primary conflict or to certain kinds of sympathetic measures. The only requirement under the Act is that the side being supported, i.e. involved in the primary dispute, is itself entitled to resort to economic sanctions. This means in practice that sympathetic action usually occurs when the primary conflict is a non-justiciable dispute, for in most cases a party is freed from the peace obligation of the Act only when it is not bound by a collective contract. The provisions on sympathetic action make far-reaching modifications to the peace obligation, because of the insistence (particularly on the part of SAF) that purely sympathetic action is a fundamental bargaining weapon. The sympathetic lock-out and secondary boycott are permissible.

[1] Labour Court Judgement 1930/79 stated: 'The legislator has pre-supposed that a dispute concerning rights arising out of a collective contract ought naturally to be resolved by judicial process, and in applying the prohibition it is not important which of the parties is ultimately found to be in the right in the actual dispute at issue.' Just as a party that considers direct action to be legal is inconvenienced by this rule, even if his interpretation is subsequently found to be correct, so a party that benefits from the rule in the short run may be penalized if his interpretation is subsequently held to be wrong. Thus, when one side protests in good faith that a dispute is one about rights, and not an unresolved non-justiciable dispute, it can be held liable to pay damages if its interpretation is held to be ill-founded. (Judgement 1936/9.) See Geijer and Schmidt, op. cit., p. 276 et seq.

SAF was very anxious to assert the right to sympathetic action soon after it began its activities, and in 1907 it persuaded LO to accept a clause in contracts allowing it. Subsequent debate[1] concerned the end to which such sympathetic action could be directed, whether to enforce new provisions in contracts, regulate 'matters of principle', have amendments made to existing contracts, or whether it should be restricted to an expression of pure sympathy. The 1928 Act settles for this last formulation.

The right to take sympathetic action is one that is still valued by both sides in the labour market as a means of widening the area of conflict. It is on such strategy that SAF can base its lock-out threats and try to force agreement by widening the front.[2] More fundamentally, it has been argued that if purely sympathetic action were to be banned disputes might not be resoluble without outside government intervention, which neither side wishes.

The intention of the sympathetic action clause in the Collective Contracts Act is to allow a party to help others without itself aiming to gain anything itself, but the Labour Court has sometimes had to take account of the nature and intent of the sympathetic action. In form such action may appear to be an expression of sympathy, but difficulties of interpretation can arise if the sympathetic action is really intended to serve another purpose, e.g. influencing the terms of employment for one's own area of contract.

The peace obligations set out under the four headings discussed are mandatory, and apply even if a collective contract contains provisions which conflict with them. The Act takes precedence over any attempts to agree to *wider* uses of economic sanctions. But it only sets a minimum list of peace obligations, and the parties to a contract may if they wish make the peace more secure by prescribing additional limitations on direct action and accepting more onerous obligations. This is done in some cases by prohibiting all forms of economic sanction during the validity of a collective agreement, as in local government, and sometimes longer, e.g. in the newspaper industry.

(*d*) *The enforcement of the peace*

The Act provides obligations for both associations and their members. Strong pressure is put on organizations to avoid the use of the illegal sanctions prescribed here by the imposition of two obligations, one indirect, the other direct. If an association *or* a member (a local union branch or individuals) is bound by a collective contract the

[1] E.g. on *Proposition 96*, 1910.

[2] Limitations on, and the effects of sympathetic action on neutral parties, are regulated by Chapter 4 of the LO–SAF Basic Agreement, discussed in Chapter VIII.

association may not arrange or otherwise contrive the use of economic sanctions which are prohibited, nor may it lend support and aid to illegal direct action to which a member has resorted. This obligation on organizations, even when they are not directly party to a contract, is in keeping with the strong centralization over the use of economic sanctions which SAF has always had over its Members and Partners and which LO strengthened in the rules revision of 1941. Secondly, an organization (national union or branch) which *is* a *direct* party to a contract is also obliged to endeavour to *prevent* its members from resorting to illegal direct action or, if this has already begun, is obliged to endeavour to have it discontinued.

This is an extremely powerful deterrent to unlawful stoppages and unofficial strikes, as the series of cases before the Labour Court in 1954–5 on dockers and in 1960 on the oil workers section of a branch of the Transport Workers' Union showed. From the point of view of collective bargaining it also reinforces the 'right of veto' a union has over the terms of a proposed contract. In this respect the law supports the collective price-fixing to which a union may agree. Constitutional rules of labour market organizations are reinforced by this obligation in the Act.

The peace is also enforced by provisions for damages. The sanction under the Act for breach of the provisions is civil damages, which may not be converted to penal sanctions such as imprisonment. The main rule is that employers, workers or associations that do not fulfil their obligations in accordance with their collective contracts or this Act are liable for any damage to which this may give rise. In judging the extent to which damage has occurred the Labour Court takes into consideration not only the purely economic or material damage, but other factors such as the importance of maintaining the contract. Economic damages are limited to the actual amount of damage caused (though this may sometimes be difficult to prove), but exemplary damages may also be awarded even if an action, such as a breach of agreement through the employment of more apprentices than the agreements allows, causes no direct economic loss.[1]

The Labour Court has considerable discretion in assessing damages and taking into consideration 'extenuating circumstances'. The amount of damages may be reduced if this is found to be reasonable in the light of the slight guilt of a party causing the damage, the position of the party injured in relation to the origin of the dispute, the size of the damage, or other circumstances. The Court may also grant complete absolution from the obligation to pay damages.

Only modified damages may be assessed on an individual workman.

[1] See Östen Undén, *Från arbetsdomstolens praxis*, p. 34 (Uppsala, 1932).

Following the alterations made (after LO protested) by the second standing committee, the Act provides that the damages assessed on an individual workman may in no case exceed 200 crowns.[1] There is no limit to the amount of damages that may be awarded against an organization, whether of employers or workers, or against an individual employer. In principle the Act does not provide for collective responsibility to pay damages, for if several persons (individual workers and employers, and their organizations) are responsible for the damage caused, the damages are allocated among them in accordance with the amount of the damage for which each has been proved responsible. Organizations are not liable to pay damages assessed against their individual members, but they may agree to do so.

It has frequently been disputed how far the 200 crowns rule is permissive. Can it, for example, be modified by a clause in a collective agreement prescribing *higher*, rather than lower damages for breach of contract? The Labour Court held on one occasion that the parties could agree, explicitly or by implication, that damages *exceeding* 200 crowns could be imposed on an individual employee for breach of contract, but the question must not necessarily be judged uniformly for all breaches of agreement. Confining itself to the particular case at issue, it held that the 200 crown rule was permissive for the particular type of breach of contract under judgement.[2] On the other side, agreements to modify claims for damages to less than 200 crowns, or renounce any claim to damages at all, are permissible.

The Labour Court has other sanctions it may use. It can issue a decree instructing that certain actions are to be taken or discontinued on the part of an association or individual. It may also terminate a contract through the default of one side, if the breach is of fundamental importance for the agreement as a whole, and if the other side so requests. This sanction is seldom used.

IV. THE LABOUR COURT ACT

The Labour Court was set up at the same time as the Collective Contracts Act in 1928 for the purpose of administering the Act and interpreting the provisions of collective contracts. The Labour Court is a judicial body, concerned primarily with declaring what the rights and obligations of parties to a collective contract are when disputes about it arise. Popularly, it has been called a court of arbitration, but that obscures its essential function. It is not at all concerned to adjust

[1] This is no longer a serious deterrent, because of the rise in real incomes and in the general level of prices.

[2] Judgement no. 1953/23.

differences of opinion, to compromise or conciliate, but to adjudicate on what collective contracts mean in the light of the Act when disputes about them arise. It does not have complete jurisdiction over justiciable disputes, since the parties are free to arrive at alternative *peaceful* methods of settling disputes about collective agreements. It can be by-passed by writing private arbitration clauses into collective agreements with the consent of both sides.[1] Again, collective contracts usually provide that if disputes arise about them there shall first be negotiations between the parties and their organizations. Only thereafter can the Labour Court accept jurisdiction. The negotiation procedure must be exhausted first. But no direct action can be taken over justiciable disputes, and the Labour Court is a final court of judgement. No appeals can be made against decisions.

The Labour Court is the only instance of its kind in the country. It is similar in composition to the Central Arbitration Board set up in 1920, which it replaced. In fact, it represents the instance *par excellence* of the Swedish flair for entrusting the government process to private interest groups. The majority of the members of the Court are lay members, representatives drawn from the labour market interest groups, a practice which was envisaged when the first Labour Court proposals were put forward, and defeated, in 1910. But the primary criterion for its composition is that it is a court of experts in law and in the special problems of the labour market. The Court consists of a chairman and seven (originally six) members. Three of the members, the chairman (who has since 1931 been the only full-time member), vice-chairman and one other member are independent members appointed by the government from among persons who cannot be considered to represent the interests either of employers or employees. The chairman and vice-chairman must be learned in law and have a knowledge of the duties of a judge, while the third independent member must have experience of and knowledge of labour conditions and related questions concerning labour agreements. These independent members are appointed for a specific period. The other five members are appointed for two years at a time, two on the recommendation of LO, two on the recommendation of the consultative council of SAF, and the fifth, 'the special member', by TCO. The special member was first appointed in 1947, and he participates in place of one of the LO members in cases involving salaried employees. All five members appointed by the interest groups are required to have experience of and knowledge of labour conditions. They are in no sense directly representative of

[1] For some time after the passage of the Act a considerable element in the trade union movement favoured the by-passing of the Court by writing such provisions into collective agreements.

their own side. The intention has been to bring together a representative group of persons competent to contribute expert knowledge on the complexities of collective contracts and to apply this knowledge in a judicial manner.

The Labour Court has its seat in Stockholm, and its main task is to pass judgement on—to take up and settle—disputes of the following kind relating to collective contracts:

(1) The validity, existence, or correct meaning of a contract.
(2) Whether certain procedures conflict with collective contracts or with the Collective Contracts Act.
(3) Questions relating to the consequences of such procedures, e.g. whether economic sanctions taken were illegal or violated contracts.

The competence of the Court includes cases relating to individual employment agreements that are covered by provisions in a collective contract, though it is not empowered to deal with disputes that arise over individual contracts of service which are not based on collective contracts. Such disputes are taken before the ordinary law courts.[1]

The Court can give rulings on test cases when asked. This provides some economy in the use of its time. A further labour-saving device is the general rule that cases are channelled through organizations. An individual member, or former member, of an association bound by a collective contract cannot plead before the Labour Court unless he has first shown that the organization has refused to take up his case. If anyone wishes to raise a case in the Court against a member or former member of an association that has concluded a contract the organization must also be summoned.

Non-justiciable disputes can *not* knowingly be referred to the Labour Court, even if the parties are agreed to do so. It has no jurisdiction over impending contracts, but deals with existing contracts and the problems that arise out of them.

Since the Labour Court was intended to be an expert body and one that reached decisions quickly, its procedure is worthy of study. Here, and particularly prior to 1948, the year when Swedish legal procedure was reformed, there was a remarkable contrast with the normal slow and tedious process of the law courts. This is not accidental. Two main principles underlie the working of the Court. Its proceedings should be informal and oral, and it should arrive at

[1] This dualism in interpretation of labour contracts has led to a recent revival of interest in the proposal that the Labour Court should be given competence to deal with interpretational disputes arising out of all contracts of service, collective or individual.

decisions swiftly. The Court meets on the summons of the chairman, a quorum being the chairman plus four members. The 'non-independent' members must be equally represented, and the 'special member' must be present if the case deals with salaried employees. The Court can meet outside Stockholm if it wishes, and the chairman and two members (one from each side) may visit factories in order to get the feel of a case. The chairman may also instruct a legally trained official of the Court to investigate details about the case he may wish to have, provided this does not involve the rejection of a case.

There are two stages in the treatment of a case, a preparatory stage, and the hearing. A party wishing to bring a case before the Labour Court must first submit a *written* application for a summons against the other side, setting out the circumstances, his demands, and any written evidence he has. When the summons has been issued and the defendant has replied the case is prepared in writing. The views and replies of each side can be passed back and forward for comment and elucidation. This preparatory stage almost invariably ends in the form of a meeting before the Labour Court.

When the preliminaries are over the parties are called to the main hearing before the Court, which forms the second stage. The Court procedure is a rapid and highly informal one, and every endeavour is made to dispose of a case after one hearing. The judgement of the Court is sent by post to the parties as soon as possible after a case has been heard, and usually within four to eight weeks. The judgements give an account of the dispute, the reasons for the judgement, and the decision. Minority and dissenting opinions of members of the Court are recorded.

Since the Collective Contracts Act contained only basic rules, and because there was an absence of legal rules in Swedish labour law, the Labour Court has had to evolve its own particular judicial approach to the problems falling under its jurisdiction. It has also developed certain rules to help it in its work. The basic principle it has sought to apply is to ask what the joint intention of the parties was when a disputed provision was drawn up. The situation prevailing before the contract and the protocol of negotiations have been called in to help the Court on this question. Secondary rules employed by the Court involve asking questions as to whether a particular disputed clause (which is in writing) is clear in itself, whether a party proposing a provision has fulfilled the obligation to clarify what he understands the proposed provision to mean, what the practice is if a similar provision is applied in other spheres. In addition, the Court frequently relies on general principles by analogy with other areas of law. Not surprisingly, the Court has sometimes found difficulty in reconciling and applying these rules, and in obtaining unanimity among its members.[1]

Some general principles have been enunciated or pronounced by the Labour Court. The sanctity and prior claims of the collective contract is an obvious ruling. It has taken the view that the collective contract is meant to promote labour peace, and has therefore generally interpreted the peace obligation widely, though the employee side members have on the whole adopted a more liberal attitude to what direct action (e.g. on sympathy) is permissible. It has endorsed, not always unanimously, as a general principle the employers' prerogative over hiring and firing, as set out in the SAF rules. It has ruled on the application of contracts to unorganized workers, and explained that a worker is obliged to carry out any work which is naturally connected with his employer's main activity *and* for which he has the appropriate trade qualifications. In examining the concept of the right to organize prior to the Act of 1936 it endorsed the general principle, though in later years some cases showed the lay members to have a vested interest in defending organization clauses, a difficulty only overcome by a ruling of the legal *ombudsman* (an official watchdog who safeguards the interests of private individuals against administrative injustice by officialdom). Some of its rulings, e.g. on holidays, the concept of an employee, have clarified the position for subsequent legislation.

Statistically, the work of the Court can be summarized in the following way (see table opposite).

The vast majority (88%) of cases taken before the Labour Court have been brought by the workers' side. In the short run the employer will determine issues of interpretation, and the only way in which the workers' side can ultimately secure a firm ruling is by taking the employer before the Labour Court. Employer submissions to the Court have dealt mainly with the scope of the obligation to perform work, and illegal economic sanctions.

[1] For a very useful study of the dissenting opinions in the Labour Court see Geijer and Schmidt, op. cit. Five main groups of reservations are analysed by Geijer from the point of view of the legal interpretation which the dissenter(s) seemed to put on the problem. In almost every instance a dissenting employer or employee member of the Court gave the benefit to his own side, employers to employers, employee members to workers. In the view of the authors this was *not* because they were explicitly biased. They consider that the interest group members have tried to be objective and judicial in their approach and to avoid a compromising attitude; but the explanation given (op. cit., p. 358) is that it is difficult to get rid of a party viewpoint acquired through long experience in the labour market, and difficult not to see one's own side through 'rose-coloured spectacles'. Employer and official members of the Court are found to be more legal in outlook, and disposed to look backwards for rules and precedents, while the workers' representatives, who have recorded the largest number of dissenting opinions, have been less bound by legalism, and shown a worthy concern for changing social ideas.

Year	No. of cases decided	Year	No. of cases decided
1929	65	1945	103
1930	115	1946	82
1931	140	1947	82
1932	204	1948	87
1933	186	1949	77
1934	189	1950	68
1935	154	1951	54
1936	123	1952	41
1937	152	1953	57
1938	134	1954	52
1939	141	1955	44
1940	122	1956	44
1941	157	1957	38
1942	103	1958	43
1943	116	1959	39
1944	106	1960	39

Source: Geijer and Schmidt, op. cit., p. 21, Table 3, and *Arbetsdomstolens domar*.

The increasing unanimity of the Court is reflected in the decline in the number of reservations; 40% of all judgements in the early years were the subject of reservations, but the figure has now fallen to 10–15%. The Court has issued about 3,100 judgements, an average of 100 a year, but the table shows that since the war there has been a decided downward trend in the number of cases. The Court is not considered by the present chairman to have been overwhelmed with work, at least in relation to the number of cases that was originally anticipated.[1] The question can of course be put from the other side, and one can ask why the Court has had many cases to deal with at all. The first chairman of the Court, Lindhagen, shed light on this point when he once said that he would like to have the opportunity to demonstrate how a collective contract should be expressed in order to avoid interpretational disputes. The answer of one of the lay members of the Court was that there would then be no collective contracts! The parties to a contract do not necessarily want the meaning of agreements to be crystal-clear, particularly if a doubtful clause can be applied in their favour.

What of course is not shown by statistics, except through the decline in the number of cases coming before it, is the manner in

[1] See *Arbestdomstolen 1929–1953*, a jubilee publication (Stockholm, 1954).

which the Labour Court indirectly influences the whole collective contract nexus. Its judgements provide rulings on the interpretation of collective agreements which in some respects, as discussed above, enunciate principles, but which in most cases provide a ruling carefully limited to the particular circumstances of the dispute at issue. Whatever the ruling, the decisions of the Court are noted by the parties, and new agreements are modified and moulded to take note of its judgements. In this way the wording, meaning, and significance of collective contracts are continually subject to scrutiny, and the indirect influence of the Court, in addition to its rulings in 3,000-odd cases, is enormous.

Many of the simpler issues the Court had to tackle in its early days are now settled directly; and the Court is also less likely to be concerned with complex problems that may involve matters of principle or precedent. Apart from cases by or against employers bound by contracts who do not belong to an employers' association, the most likely sphere of expansion in the Court's work in future is that formed by the rapid growth in collective contracts for salaried employees. The appointment of the special member in 1947 gave a hint of this, though in fact the number of cases before the Court involving salaried employees has not shown any upward trend.[1] But if the Ekblom proposals for extending the collective contract system to the area of the public service from which it has hitherto been banned so far become law, then the Labour Court will be faced with a new range of problems springing from the special circumstances surrounding employment in the public service. Another possible sphere of expansion in its work arises from suggestions that the Labour Court should be made competent to deal with disputes that arise out of individual as well as collective contracts of employment.

Already the Labour Court has acquired additional functions since it began operations in 1929. It has jurisdiction over the enforcement of the Act of 1936 on the rights of association and negotiation, irrespective of whether a collective contract exists, since the right of association is a statutory if functional one. It also has powers (little used) to deal with cases under the Mediation Act, where a mediator refers a case of a party which has not fulfilled its obligations to negotiate. The Court also deals with certain cases under the Holidays Act[2] and with legislation governing dismissals on grounds of military

[1] The Basic Agreements which SAF concluded in 1957 and 1959 for salaried employees in the private sector in fact by-pass the Labour Court. See below, Chapter X.

[2] A recent Judgement (1960/14) illustrates the activity of the Court in a number of ways. Asked jointly by an employers' association and union to give a ruling on the meaning of the ninety days sickness qualifying period under the Holidays Act, the majority of the Court (two of the law members plus the employer members) ruled that ninety days meant calendar days, not working days, basing

service, marriage, pregnancy, and the activities of workers' safety representatives.

Various points of general principle arise out of the work of the Labour Court. It is sometimes argued that its rulings have served to intensify collectivization in the labour market. This can clearly not be advanced as a criticism of the Labour Court, but of the system of collective contracts which was already firmly established. The role of the chairman of the Court has always been powerful and dominant, and it is well known that the first chairman, Arthur Lindhagen, viewed the Court as a judicial tribunal, seeking and applying legal principles. The practice that has grown up is for the chairman to draft proposed judgements or alternatives after the hearing and send them out to the members. But there is a safeguard against any excessive legalism from the chair by the very fact that the lay representatives form a majority of the Court. On occasion the lay majority has united to agree a decision with which the law members of the Court disagreed. But it too can be prevented from practising excessive self-interest. The law can be changed, and, as has happened, the legal *ombudsman* can question the legality of its decisions. Thus there are checks and balances which prevent excessive domination by the chairman or the lay members.

Another criticism is that the Labour Court, and in particular its law members, has sometimes attached excessive importance to precedents. 'Once the Labour Court has taken up a position it is difficult to bring about changes.'[1] In one important matter, the employer's prerogative, it has shown a tendency to stick to a strict contractual interpretation of the employer's right to hire and fire, although the whole climate of social opinion has led to a considerable modification in practice of the employer's right to dismiss without giving reasons. At the same time, some respect for precedents is necessary in the working of the Court.

The Labour Court is only a small part of the process of law-making, and in any event the trend has subsequently been to avoid legislation and concentrate on solutions to outstanding problems through private arrangements. It has not proved the thin end of the wedge and initiated a legal invasion of the labour market. In addition, these outstanding problems are matters which centre primarily on the terms of future, not existing, contracts. What the Labour Court has done is to play a fundamental part in ensuring respect for the

this judgement on the discussion at the time of the passage of the act of adjustments in sickness insurance. The minority (one law member plus the workers' members) preferred an interpretation which in their view was more in accordance with the general construction of the act, that ninety days meant ninety working days. The ruling is one of general interpretation.

[1] Geijer and Schmidt, op. cit., p. 347.

provisions of collective contracts once they have been concluded. The change in the attitude of the unions to the Court reflects the usefulness of its function, and is a tribute to the success of the legislation in practice.

At various times in the 1930s motions were put before the Riksdag asking for the repeal[1] of the two Acts of 1928, and the question recurred at LO congresses. The Transport Workers' Union, with a large number of complicated local contracts, has been the most enduring critic of the Court. The secretariat stated in 1931 that since their attempts to prevent the passage of the Acts had failed the unions could not spurn the opportunity for the workers to be represented in the Court and thus have an influence on its activity. There was no question of boycotting it.[2] In 1936 the secretariat stressed how important it was to ensure that clauses in contracts were clear and unambiguous, since the Court could only make its judgements on the basis of the content of the contract or in the light of the meaning the parties wishes to express through the provisions,[3] and the congress approved a declaration that justiciable disputes 'do not belong to the type of dispute for whose solution direct action is to be recommended'.[4] At the same time, and later in 1939, LO stressed the weak position of the worker *vis-à-vis* Court rulings on cases concerning the termination of employment. The solution here was not, however, to seek repeal, but to have introduced into contracts provisions which protected the worker and provided correctives against abuses by the employer. The Court interpreted contracts, and the content of contracts was based on strength, but just for that reason LO argued that the appropriate approach was for the unions to work for a stronger position finding expression in the clauses of contracts. The remedy to the weakness in the worker's position was not to be found in abolishing the law, but in ensuring that the contracts it had to interpret were favourable from the unions' point of view.

When the Labour Court celebrated its silver jubilee in 1953 tributes to its impartiality and important contributions to the promotion of industrial peace were paid by employers and workers. E. D. Kärrfeldt, the treasurer of the Building Workers' Union, was one of those who had demonstrated in 1928 against the proposed laws, but in 1953, as a member of the Court, he said that 'the Labour Court has been accepted and gained a surprising amount of goodwill if one

[1] The trade union movement would not have accepted repeal alone, but would have insisted on a return to the arrangements under the Act of 1920 on the Central Arbitration Board.

[2] LO *kongress-protokoll*, 1931, secretariat *utlåtande* no. 23, p. 355.

[3] LO *kongress-protokoll*, 1936, *utlåtande* no. 3, p. 244 et seq.

[4] Ibid., p. 559 et seq.

recalls the opposition then. It has worked perfectly from the start and no voice is now raised in favour of its abolition. Its judgements are respected, although the losing side naturally grumbles.'[1]

Other legislation which has been of some significance in industrial relations should be mentioned. The penal code has not been applied to labour relations to any great extent, apart from the public servants who are 'responsible officials'. Strike breakers were protected under the code in 1897. The most important enactment under this heading was the Åkarp Act of 1899, which provided penal sanctions against persons who *attempted* to coerce anyone to take part in a stoppage of work or who prevented anyone from returning to work or from accepting a job that was offered. An attempt in 1905 to provide penal sanctions for labour disputes which endangered vital social interests failed. In 1914 the maximum penalty under the Åkarp Act was reduced to imprisonment instead of penal servitude, and the Act was repealed in 1938. During its lifetime about 800 persons were sentenced under provisions of the penal code relating to labour relations, mainly the Åkarp Act, while about three-quarters of the cases were dealt with by a fine. Apart from the penal law sanctions, prosecutions have occasionally been made under the law of libel, which prescribes limits to methods permissible in applying economic sanctions.

An Eviction Act was passed in 1936 which limits the right of an employer to use eviction as a pressure in industrial disputes. This was a sanction frequently used in early labour disputes, but the Act has not been important in practice. Employers no longer evict and the tied house is not important in industry.

V. CONCLUDING OBSERVATIONS

Legislation has been used very cautiously in regulating industrial relations in Sweden. There has been no great propensity to legislate among any of the major interest groups, and the main emphasis in LO and SAF attitudes, for example, has been practical. Some governments have shown a greater interest in seeking legislative solutions than others, but disagreement among the political parties on both principles and practice produced a range of pressures, both for and against law. This meant that any legislative proposal was thoroughly aired at successive stages, and likely to be passed only after considerable delay. At the same time, the growth of a strong collective bargaining system through powerful labour market associations, which showed that a detailed system of legal regulation was unnecessary, has enabled legislation to be confined to two main matters.

[1] Reported in *Morgontidningen* (June 24, 1953).

The Mediation Act provided a framework for handling non-justiciable disputes. But it did not ban the use of economic sanctions, and left plenty of scope for the system to be moulded by the mediators and the parties to suit their needs. The legislation of 1928 on collective contracts is also general in character. The intention is that the Labour Court interprets contracts, but there is nothing to prevent the content of contracts from evolving, and the mediation system encourages it to do so, in response to the strength and needs of the organizations. The legislation of 1936 on the rights of association and collective bargaining was an effective endorsement of the central position of the collective contract.

Indeed, all the legislation has concentrated on furthering the pre-eminence of the collective bargaining system. In the main the law has codified the practice that had evolved, with the exception of the Act of 1936, which did pave the way for collective bargaining among salaried employees, though it did not of course develop any new principles. Another point to be drawn from the Swedish attitude to labour law, which is illustrated by the existing conflict between law and practice in the public sector, is that the law must set a realistic framework and must adjust to the pressures of economic change and bargaining strength.

It is evident from the absence of any arbitration provisions for resolving non-justiciable disputes that economic sanctions may well be used, and the Collective Contracts Act presupposes that economic sanctions are permissible unless specifically regulated. Legislation has not listed the types of direct action which may be employed in labour markets, apart from minor enactments like the Eviction Act, nor has it distinguished types of dispute or sectors of the economy for legal control. This means that there are large areas of labour relations where economic sanctions can be deployed.

The absence of legislation here does not mean that the legislature has been indifferent. On the contrary, repeated attempts have been made to legislate on economic sanctions and the control of economic sanctions was the burning issue of Swedish labour relations in the 1930s. In theory the Labour Court could have provided, and the labour movement feared it might, a convenient agency on which to hang new functions and duties for the purpose of controlling labour relations. But this did not happen. Why?

The answer is to be sought in the new developments in the government of labour relations which took place in the 1930s, as a result of which considerable private jurisdiction has become concentrated at the level of SAF and LO. Constructive co-operation in the Swedish labour market, which is the subject of the next part, is based essentially on the presupposition that private arrangements can provide a suitable alternative to legislative enactment for the control of sensitive areas of labour conflict. Under the Basic Agreement of 1938 SAF and LO have created a special tribunal, the Labour Market Board, which has arbitral and conciliatory functions on both justiciable and non-justiciable disputes. It deals as a conciliatory agency with problems of recruitment, lay-off and dismissal of labour, it acts as a board of arbitration in regulating economic sanctions, particularly those against neutral third parties, and it can take up for discussion any conflict situation that threatens essential social functions.

The idea of settling disputes privately, without resort to law, has thus developed at a sophisticated level in the Swedish labour market. This is the major achievement of Swedish labour relations in the decade of the 1930s.

PART III

Collaboration and Basic Agreements

CHAPTER VII

The Genesis of the Basic Agreement

IN discerning the change in attitude and atmosphere which developed in the Swedish labour market organizations in the 1930s there is a distinct danger of being wise after the event. Nevertheless, with that caveat in mind, certain strands can in retrospect be distinguished as leading towards the central discussions which produced their first fruits in the Basic Agreement of 1938 between LO and SAF.

Co-operation and top-level discussion between SAF and LO were not completely new. Before the major conflict of 1909 there had been central discussions on general matters of principle, reflected in the December Compromise and the agreement of 1908 about sympathetic action, subjects which were again taken up in the Basic Agreement. But after 1909 there was an interlude, lasting over twenty-five years and coloured by the post-1909 weakness of LO and then by the First World War and its aftermath of economic disruption.

A revival of collaboration was suggested in the initiative which the minority social democratic government took in 1926 in appointing a nine-man labour peace delegation, with three official members and three each from SAF and LO, to investigate appropriate measures for promoting industrial peace. The intention was that these discussions would produce a common basis for assessing the advisability of furthering industrial peace by labour legislation or in other ways. But this move was premature, for the Stripa conflict of 1926 over the use of unemployed workers during a labour dispute, on pain of withdrawal of unemployment relief, brought about the fall of the social democratic government, and the new liberal government pushed on with proposals for compulsory arbitration of justiciable disputes. Despite the unrest in the labour movement when the Acts of 1928 were passed, the conservative government which took office a few months later was able to bring the parties together for a top-level two-day conference, at which discussions took place on the possibilities of improving labour relations. (This labour peace conference is usually referred to as the Swedish attempt at Mondism.[1])

[1] So-called after the Mond-Turner conferences begun in Britain in 1927 on the initiative of Sir Alfred Mond (Lord Melchett).

The primary emphasis was placed on relations at the shop-floor level, not on changes in the formal relationships between the labour market organizations. Another labour peace delegation of SAF and LO plus official representatives was formed. Again, it proved abortive in the short run, for soon after the Ådal tragedy of 1931 LO (against the advice of the secretariat) withdrew its members from the small committee which had succeeded the delegation.[1] But the experiment had shown there was some evidence on both sides of a willingness to come together and discuss mutual problems that lay outside the immediate nexus of collective contracts.

The beginning in 1932 of the era of social democracy provided the next impetus. As a minority government in 1932, the social democrats had to hearken to repeated demands from other parties for legislation and this posed a dilemma for both the party and LO. As the government in power, the social democrats had to take a wide view of the public interest (e.g. in the building industry dispute), and could not logically deny the right of the legislature to intervene in the labour market when its attitude was so positive to social legislation in other spheres. The dilemma for LO was posed by Möller, the Minister of Social Affairs, in 1934, when LO was discussing Professor Bergendal's proposals for legislation to protect neutral third parties in industrial disputes. He pointed out that LO could not adopt a purely negative attitude, both because of the moral issue, and because the social democrats could not completely block legislation.[2] LO responded with a declaration that it was not in principle opposed to legislation in the labour market. In any event LO was co-operating in the work of the Labour Court, and was not able to argue that legislation was out of the question. LO had to be constructive, both because it had worked for its political ally having the opportunity to show that social democracy was a superior political system,[3] and because the social democratic government could not, as a minority government, stand out against law.

But neither the LO nor social democratic attitude to labour legislation was very enthusiastic. The 1926 social democratic initiative had invited co-operation, and in 1928 the leaders of the party deplored the Collective Contracts Act as stifling the emerging spirit of co-operation in the labour market. It is true that when he appointed the Nothin commission in 1934 the Prime Minister, Per Albin Hansson, did appear to envisage there would be labour legislation,

[1] The secretariat's views were moderate and constructive. See LO *kongress-protokoll*, 1931, secretariat *utlåtande* no. 23, p. 355 et seq.

[2] Westerståhl, op. cit., p. 386 et seq.

[3] This moral aspect, with the emphasis on social responsibility, had become fully articulate by the time motion 224 to the LO congress of 1936 precipitated the move towards the 1941 revision of the LO rules.

after full and impartial inquiry, and he stressed that it must be with the collaboration of the labour market organizations. But at the same time he drew attention to the fact that the question of labour peace was really part of a much larger question—disputes about economic interests in the widest sense—and this focused attention on the difficulties of legislating for labour disputes alone. In 1935, too, he suggested that many of the evils that had been taken up in the debate on legislation to control economic sanctions could be removed by the organizations themselves. Nor in 1935 was the government slow to withdraw its support from its own proposition[1] when it learned that the opposition would vote against it. In principle it was not a bad proposition from the labour point of view, for it had taken most of LO's objections into account and was acceptable to the unions. Throughout the years 1933–5 the impression in fact is very much one of the social democratic government responding to the avalanche of Riksdag motions by reluctantly proposing measures to remove many of the abuses in labour relations. It was not prepared to legislate for its own sake, and in general was much less enthusiastic about legislation than the other parties that had tasted political power about that time. Social democratic philosophy at the time seems to have envisaged a political society of strong interest groups and organizations.

That LO distrusted legislation, and preferred discussion with SAF as a lesser evil, is a familiar but not conclusive argument. More plausible as a source was the lack of any tradition of legal enactment for the government of the Swedish labour market, and a preference for private and flexible arrangements.

Some sort of 'power equilibrium' between LO and SAF is frequently cited as a reason for the emerging climate of opinion which favoured discussion rather than law in the 1930s. This is a vague concept, and difficult to identify by overt industrial relations behaviour. It is just as arguable that declarations such as the one made by LO in 1926, setting out its own and SAF's opposition to compulsory arbitration of industrial disputes, required some sort of responsible self-government on the part of the organizations. Some control over direct action was essential, just as some sort of internal cohesion was important. LO had already grasped this latter point in 1930 by initiating discussion of standard rules for the member unions. To put the point bluntly, if LO and SAF were to preach self-government in non-justiciable disputes they had sooner or later to show they could govern. The circumstances of the early 1930s brought this inescapably to the fore.

The Nothin commission, reporting at the end of 1935, had a

[1] *Proposition 1935 : 31.*

powerful effect in bringing the two sides together. While it did not completely reject the idea of legislation on certain aspects of industrial relations, it placed the primary onus on the voluntary approach. SAF and LO had to do something. The Nothin report is much more influential than developments in Norway earlier in the same year. The Swedish Prime Minister drew the attention of the Riksdag to the Norwegian Basic Agreement as an illustration of what might be achieved voluntarily.[1] But Norway is clearly not a fundamental source as far as the unions were concerned, for the trade union mouthpiece used it in a negative way, as an argument against legislation, not as a positive lead for top-level discussions in Sweden between LO and SAF.[2]

What significance as a pointer to the SAF–LO discussions had the change in the leaders on both sides at this phase of industrial relations? Von Sydow retired from SAF in 1931 and was succeeded by Gustaf Söderlund. Albert Forslund, who had known Söderlund previously when Söderlund was engaged on government work,[3] became chairman of LO in 1936.

It is tempting to see in the departure of von Sydow a landmark in the change of attitude on the part of SAF, for although he was not quite the exponent of iron laws of wages that the workers (and cartoons) made him out to be, and had, for example, taken part in the labour peace conference in 1928, he had been at the SAF helm since 1907, during periods when industrial relations were very bad indeed. His successor in command, Söderlund, and the new SAF chairman, Edström, had at least a chance, given a favourable economic climate, to adopt a conciliatory attitude to LO.

Söderlund made an important statement in a speech at the LO school (in itself a significant pointer) in 1935.[4] It would be most advantageous if the labour market parties concentrated on ordering their affairs themselves, not only in relation to collective contracts, but in other matters as well. This involved the two sides in the obligation to be responsible and exercise restraint, and to do everything possible to arrange their relations in such a way that society did not feel obliged to intervene. One prerequisite of the organizations fulfilling this task was that the relevant problems were taken up for careful analysis and study. It was high time both sides realized that in the long run neither could enjoy the protection and assistance

[1] For an analysis in English of this Norwegian agreement, see Walter Galenson, *Labor in Norway*, p. 192 et seq. (Cambridge, Mass., 1949).

[2] See *Fackföreningsrörelsen*, 1935, I, 150.

[3] See *J. Sigfrid Edström*, a biography, edited by K. A. Bratt, Senare delen, p. 137. In a discussion of labour market legislation at a meeting of a liberal club (frisinnade klubben) in February 1936, Forslund and Söderlund found their views were very similar and decided to discuss the matter further.

[4] *Motsättningen mellan kapital och arbete* p. 22 (Stockholm, 1935).

of the government for its interests and at the same time retain its freedom in other spheres. This, *ex post*, can almost be regarded as an invitation to the discussions which began the following year. The LO journal welcomed the idea of having Söderlund address trade unionists. It was something new, and would do everyone good. A free exchange of views would be beneficial.[1]

Formally, however, it was LO that took the initiative in the spring of 1936, which led to the discussions with SAF. The secretariat thought the report of the Nothin commission and its recommendations in favour of voluntary agreement provided an avenue that ought not to be left unexplored, and Forslund persuaded the representative assembly to approve the secretariat proposal that it should convene discussions with SAF. Söderlund had confirmed that SAF was not interested in legislation and was prepared to collaborate in reaching a voluntary agreement. The discussions began in May. In the autumn of 1936 LO persuaded its congress, despite some distrust of SAF and of legislation which was voiced, that it was high time that (to quote Forslund) 'we make at least one serious attempt to take up the problem of relations between the two sides and their methods in the many aspects of labour relations, so that the wishes and views of both sides can be crystallized'.[2]

While the discussions were in progress Söderlund again spoke at the LO school,[3] on the problem of whether the organizations could retain their independence of the State. Much government intervention had been asked for in the past, both by employers and workers. The workers had obtained legislation on protection at the place of work, on accident compensation, hours of work, and unemployment insurance, while employers had been given protection against competition. Reforms had been obtained the political way. But the labour market parties had now learned mutual respect, they were conscious of their strength, and therefore of the practical consequences of excessive demands. All this promoted economic insight and responsibility. If both sides were agreed in principle and in the long term not to surrender their rights of decision over wages and the forms in which the organizations pursued their activity, there would be no risk of their independence being taken from them. The danger would arise when one side saw that government intervention was in its interests.

In sum, many factors contributed to bring about the Basic Agreement through the SAF–LO discussions. The most important was that

[1] *Fackföreningsrörelsen*, 1935, II, 58 et seq.

[2] LO *kongress-protokoll*, 1936, pp. 305–6. See also motions 159–65 and secretariat *utlåtande* no. 5. Only seven reservations were made at the congress to the secretariat *utlåtande* favouring the continuation of the discussions.

[3] See *Två anföranden i LOs skola*, August 19, 1937.

the insistence by both sides on self-regulation of non-justiciable disputes could not long persist, and survive such events as the depression and the building industry dispute, unless the organizations made their system of private government effective. The other circumstances proved auspicious in their timing by providing incentives and channels for coming together. The minority position of the social democratic government served to push LO into an awareness of the choice between self-government and law, and to make SAF aware of the potential power of social democracy. The new men at the top on each side provided the channel of communication for beginning discussions, and there is no reason to doubt their genuine co-operative spirit as well as their strong self-interest in preserving private government. The Nothin commission acted as the catalyst, by focusing the issues and by making the choice plain for LO and SAF to see. This combination of favourable circumstances and people proved epoch-making through the agreements which have followed from the discussions begun in 1936.

The 1938 Basic Agreement is divided into five chapters. Chapter 1 deals with a Labour Market Council which SAF and LO agreed to set up as a central instance for dealing with matters arising from the Agreement. Chapter 2 prescribes a negotiation procedure, which is an essential part of any system of peaceful industrial relations. Chapters 3, 4, and 5 take up for regulation specific problems which the organizations or society had found to be pressing. Thus Chapter 3 deals with the questions of the termination of contracts of employment, dismissals, laying-off, and re-engaging of personnel, all matters relevant to SAF's traditional attitude expressed in Article 23 of its rules. Chapter 4 considers the limitations on economic sanctions and protection of neutral third parties, while Chapter 5 regulates the handling of disputes that threaten essential public services.

LO and SAF undertook to have the Basic Agreement accepted voluntarily by their member associations, and when adopted it has the binding force of a collective contract. We shall look in this chapter at the machinery provided by the Labour Market Council and deal subsequently with the topics of Chapters 2 to 5.[1]

THE LABOUR MARKET COUNCIL

The idea of having a central Council arose during the discussions within the SAF–LO committee. In particular, it was felt that the

[1] The use of economic sanctions and protection of neutral third parties is discussed in Chapter VIII: the protection of essential public services in Chapter IX: dismissals, layoffs, etc., in Chapter XI: and negotiation procedures in Chapter XIV.

Labour Court was not a suitable instance for dealing with the problematical disputes involving neutral third parties, and the Council was devised as a special forum. It is a negotiating and in some cases an arbitrating body, consisting of six members, three appointed by LO and three by SAF. As a negotiating body, the Council has both general and specific functions. It also acts as a reference board in disputes that arise which threaten essential public services (Chapter 5), and in connexion with specific problems of job security (Chapter 3).

In matters in which it acts as a negotiating and discussion body the Council reaches its decisions by simple majority. Since decisions may only be reached when all the members are present, and there is in *these* matters no provision for a casting vote, the implication is that decisions will be unanimous, or that at least one member of one side will vote with the other side.

As an arbitration instance the Council considers *and* settles disputes about the use of economic sanctions and protection of neutral third parties under Chapter 4 of the Agreement. Provision is made here for a jointly appointed impartial chairman to take part in discussing and settling such issues where the Council cannot reach agreement by itself, in order to avoid possible deadlock. This private arbitration instance is in effect a substitute for legislation on the difficult questions of economic sanctions which had provided much of the ammunition for legislative demands.

The original intention was that the Council should also act as a permanent forum for the discussion of major issues of common interest to LO and SAF, but in fact the *committee* which drew up the Basic Agreement has fulfilled this role. The Council can be involved in a consideration of problems where immediate and delicate issues are in dispute between employers and employees, and therefore it is not entirely a suitable forum for dealing in a reflective and informal manner with long-term problems as well. With typical empiricism, and almost by accident, SAF and LO have continued the Basic Agreement committee as the forum for discussion of wider problems, and have avoided the dualism that would have arisen through the Council being at once an arbitrating, negotiating, and debating body.

CHAPTER VIII

Economic Sanctions and Neutral Third Parties

STRIKES, lock-outs, blockades, boycotts, and purely sympathetic action are considered to be permissible in Swedish industrial relations unless there are specific restrictions upon the use of coercive pressure, such as those provided in a limited form by the Collective Contracts Act. In pursuing his interests a party is free to exercise a wide range of bargaining pressures in order to bring the other side to accept his demands in the negotiating of a new contract. The argument enunciated by the labour market organizations in support of this position has been that the best guarantee of peace is that contracts should have been entered into voluntarily. There are of course some safeguards, in the rules, e.g. of SAF and LO, in agreed bargaining procedures, and in the Mediation Act, which make it necessary for parties to exhaust the bargaining machinery before resorting to direct action.

But it is clear that problems may arise, and did in fact arise, where abuses follow from the unrestricted use of economic sanctions in non-justiciable disputes. Should there then be restrictions on the forms economic sanctions may take? Or rules as to the persons against whom they may be exercised? These two questions are dealt with in Chapter 4 of the Basic Agreement. An even wider question, whether economic sanctions ought to be controlled in particular sectors where essential public services are at stake, is treated in Chapter IX.

The control of and limitations on particular types of direct action, and protection for neutral third parties, played a prominent part in the various demands made during the 1930s for labour legislation. The outcome was that in Chapter 4 of the Basic Agreement LO and SAF were able, though not without the shadow of possible legislation hanging over them, to regulate these problems. They had been thoroughly aired, in familiar fashion, through demands in the Riksdag for legislation, inquiries, further inquiries, and legislative proposals that failed to pass through the Riksdag.[1]

The various stages encountered similar problems, of whether the scope of the legislation could be confined to labour disputes, what

[1] Five stages can be distinguished:

(*a*) The investigation by Professor Bergendal, 1929–33, which was primarily a methods of economic sanctions should be controlled, the definition of a neutral third party, particularly with reference to strike-breakers, and the sanctions to be used to enforce the law. The legislative discussion was of considerable help to LO and SAF in determining the form and content of Chapter 4, for it explicitly takes account of the problems of scope and definition encountered in the four previous stages.

The machinery for handling the provisions of this chapter centres on the Labour Market Council as the final instance, after the checks of negotiation procedures and organizational rules have been exhausted. It acts as a board of arbitration in taking up and settling disputes about the interpretation and application of the provisions of the chapter. The Council can under this chapter be reinforced by an impartial chairman, who has a casting vote if the organization representatives cannot reach agreement. The Council must obviously be able to make a definite decision where the interests of neutral third parties are involved. The neutral parties protected need *not* have signed the Agreement, since the very essence of economic sanctions may be to exercise pressure on parties standing outside, i.e. neutral to, the dispute which has led to direct action being taken.

I. FORMS OF DIRECT ACTION

Direct action is defined as strikes, lock-outs, blockades, boycotts, or similar action, and notices of termination of contracts, which are undertaken for purposes of exercising pressure or of retaliation. Such sanctions, open or veiled, *are completely banned* under Chapter 4 if the object is to persecute *anyone*, a party to a dispute or a neutral, on religious, political or similar grounds, or for the purpose of preventing him from pleading before a court of law or giving testimony, or assisting a public officer, or for purposes of retaliation for his action in this respect. *After* a dispute has been settled, retaliation is banned against anyone who has in any way been connected with a dispute. He *then* becomes protected from action by his own or any other side. LO insisted that retaliation *during* a dispute was permissible, an argument it had advocated since the days of the December Compromise, when it declared that trade unionists were opposed to working with strike-breakers.

fact-finding inquiry, but also contained a preliminary draft of legislation. See *S.O.U.*, 1933 : 36.

(*b*) A commission of thirteen persons again studied the question in the spring of 1934. See *S.O.U.*, 1934 : 16.

(*c*) The social democratic part presented a proposition, 1935 : 31, which was rejected, the government voting against its own proposition.

(*d*) The Nothin commission report. See *S.O.U.*, 1935 : 65.

(*e*) The Basic Agreement itself.

Complete protection is also given to family businesses. A family business is defined as 'anyone who, without any assistance other than that of his wife, his children, or his parents, is engaged in trade or undertakes work for his own account'. There is also a complete ban on economic sanctions if the purpose is to seek illegitimate favours by inducing anyone to pay or forgo wages—extortion blockades. These forms of pressure were in fact very infrequently encountered by the time Chapter 4 was devised.

II. PROTECTION OF THIRD PARTIES

The problem of defining and safeguarding third parties arises because it is not always possible to confine a dispute to the direct disputants. An attempt is made here to allow people standing outside a dispute to maintain a neutral standpoint in relation to both sides. But they must be and remain neutral.

A neutral third party is not defined directly in the Agreement,[1] but primarily by the negative approach of stating the circumstances in which an outside party is non-neutral.

Broadly, where economy sanctions against another party are forbidden third parties are also given at least as much protection. Even where economic sanctions like the strike, lock-out, blockade, and boycott are allowed against another party, they must not be directed against a neutral third party for the purpose of bringing pressure to bear on a party to the dispute in the following circumstances:

(*a*) in disputes about the negotiation of collective contracts;
(*b*) in disputes about the negotiation or application of individual contracts of employment;
(*c*) in competitive disputes over job opportunities;
(*d*) in order to induce a party to join or prevent him from leaving a labour market organization.

(*c*) and (*d*) involve disputes between workers, and the employer is then a neutral party. But if there is an organizational clause in a contract, the workers can use pressure against him in disputes under (*c*).

There are qualifications to (*a*) above, which considerably modify third party protection. We have already seen that the Collective Contracts Act of 1928 specifically permitted purely sympathetic

[1] The definition of a neutral third party in the earlier stages of the discussion had caused some difficulty. Bergendal took a very wide view, and defined a neutral third party as anyone who was not a party to a labour dispute and had observed neutrality in relation to it. In *Proposition 31*, p. 45, Möller defined neutral third parties as 'independent tradesmen who stand completely outside the primary conflict and observe neutrality in relation to the parties to it'.

action. The Basic Agreement likewise allows economic sanctions to be used against third parties for purely sympathetic purposes, i.e. provided the object is to support a party to a dispute by extending the scope of the original dispute concerning the drawing up of a collective contract. The sympathetic action must not have an independent purpose. But the Basic Agreement, unlike the Act of 1928, provides limitations on the forms of direct action. This is limited to strikes, lock-outs, labour blockades (of workers or a workplace), and a boycott of goods intended for or emanating from an enterprise carried on by a party to the *original* dispute. The secondary boycott is thus permitted in the form of exercising pressure on others by refusing to handle goods.

Having provided protection for neutral third parties, with the exceptions above, the Agreement then goes on to define non-neutral third parties, to whom this protection is not afforded. A non-neutral third party is:

(*a*) A member of an organization which is involved in a dispute, if he has neglected any obligations to his association which do not conflict with these provisions, and an advantage accrues to the other side. Not surprisingly, solidarity with one's organization is expected in the highly collectivized Swedish labour market.

(*b*) A blockade breaker—those who engage in work during a dispute, i.e. those who remain at or take a job affected by a dispute. All strike-breakers can be attacked, provided the dispute is legal and authorized by the rules of the union. Again, this was a rule on which LO insisted.[1]

(*c*) Any employer who engages workers locked out during a dispute.

(*d*) Anyone who during and in connexion with a dispute gives financial help to one of the parties, or assists him by changing the nature of his own activity.

[1] Bergendal had suggested protecting against retaliation those who remained at work (and the thirteen-men report specifically protected unorganized workers who remained at work), but not those who took work. LO argued along working-class solidarity lines that economic self-determination was a fiction in modern society, especially for the working class; and e.g. most collective contracts covered unorganized as well as organized workers—the Labour Court had said this was a tacit rule in contracts unless specific exception was made—and it was the organized workers who concluded them. Proposition 31 went the whole way to meeting LO's view by deleting protection as a neutral third party to *any* strike-breaker. It was on this issue that the Proposition foundered. The conservatives were not prepared to accept such a clause, the social democratic government was not prepared to agree that strike-breakers were neutral, and on this deadlock the social democrats also voted against their own proposition.

Retaliation against strike-breakers during a dispute is permitted, but not after the dispute has been settled.

(*e*) Anyone who has a controlling interest in a company that is a party to a dispute, or is a partner in an unlimited liability company that is a party to the dispute: and any company or partnership in which a party to the dispute owns a dominant share or is a partner.

III. PROTECTIVE WORK

In all these cases above protective work can be carried out without status as a non-neutral third party being lost. Protective work is exempt from economic sanctions and enjoys neutrality, irrespective of which side takes the initiative in a dispute. It is defined as:

(*a*) Work of such a kind that it must be carried out in order to bring production to a halt in a technically satisfactory manner.
(*b*) Work that is necessary to avert danger to human beings, or damage to buildings or other installations, ships, machinery, livestock, or damage to stocks of goods that are not used during the dispute for the purpose of maintaining the production of an enterprise or for disposal to a greater extent than is necessary in order to prevent deterioration or decay to which the goods may, because of their nature, be exposed.
(*c*) Work which a person is obliged by law to carry out, e.g. the seamen's Act, and work for neglect of which a penal code sanction could be invoked, e.g. public officials.

These definitions of protective work are general,[1] and SAF and LO assumed that a more precise definition would be agreed for their appropriate sectors by the national unions and employers concerned, and that, in order to avoid the problems, e.g. of strike breaking, a firm's ordinary labour force would undertake to carry out the protective work where an enterprise did not undertake production during a dispute. A similar formulation is used in the negotiation procedure agreed in 1954 for local authorities.

There are no special laws or provisions dealing with picketing.

Chapter 4 of the Basic Agreement provides considerable modifications to the practices which had been used at various times, and of the possibilities of their use in future. Direct action is not by any means banned. All the provisions are concerned to do is to set out a code of rules to keep the fighting clean. Nor does the codification

[1] But not so general as, e.g. the definition proposed by the report of the thirteen-men commission, viz., 'work that cannot be postponed without there arising danger to human beings, or damage to buildings or other property, domestic animals, ripe grain, machinery, stocks of goods, etcetera'. LO objected to the 'etcetera', and to the inclusion of 'ripe grain', which would have put agricultural employees in a very weak position *vis-à-vis* their employers.

of direct action through the SAF–LO agreement necessarily mean that the government has renounced all claim to take note of their success in practice.

The agreement form is more flexible than legislation would be, and it can be, and has been, adapted to suit particular needs of contracting parties in different sectors of activity. This is the main practical advantage over law. Another advantage is that the various legislative proposals had great difficulty in deciding on appropriate sanctions. Bergendal and the thirteen-men commission thought there would have to be penal sanctions: Proposition 31 favoured having a special court in which moderate civil penalties would be imposed. There would have been difficulties in agreeing on provisions for damages, which would often be difficult to prove, particularly for third parties remote from the immediate conflict. A third advantage, one of principle and perhaps most fundamental of all, is that the onus of operating economic sanctions in an industrial relations system has been placed on the institutions of the labour market, not the government and its law-enforcing agencies.

So far the Labour Market Council plus the impartial chairman has only been used on two occasions under the provisions of this chapter, in 1953 and 1954, one case concerning the interpretation of protective work and the second the legality of sympathetic action.[1] It is unlikely that the provisions will be used a great deal, not only because their very existence provides a code, but because any organization bound by the Agreement is obliged to seek to prevent its affiliates from resorting to the economic sanctions banned in this chapter, and to seek to have them discontinued if they have already been applied. The provisions have also served as a code outside the SAF–LO sector.

[1] Schmidt, *Kollektiv arbetsrätt*, p. 233, footnote 19, discusses these cases.

CHAPTER IX

The Protection of Essential Public Services

THE Basic Agreement goes further than regulating economic sanctions which may be shady and may injure third parties. It extends the idea of third parties to include the whole of society, and in Chapter 5 it sets out certain procedures for handling disputes that threaten essential public services.

This is an old problem, and one of the most complex issues, not only in Swedish labour relations. Many of the legislative proposals for controlling industrial relations have demanded protection of the public interest, and as early as 1882 a Riksdag motion had wanted gas and waterworks to be exempt from direct action. Amendments to the penal code that were suggested in 1905 focused primarily on the public sector activities as potential sources of disputes threatening essential services, and the public rather than the private sector has throughout been the main centre of attention in proposed solutions to the essential services difficulty.

Various criteria were put forward for defining such disputes—by the nature of the activity and type of production, by its purpose, and by the duration and scope of the dispute. When the Nothin commission examined the question it thought that a definition ought to take as a starting-point the purpose or object which the activity in question was designed to serve. If, for example, the activity did *not* aim primarily at providing for the economic interest of some employer it seemed that as a rule a work stoppage would then involve important social functions. This focused attention on 'service industries' where the profit motive was secondary, and in particular on the public sector.[1]

In cases where economic interest was the predominant motive, and some approximation to profit maximization is a reasonable guide to the motivation of the private sector, the Nothin commission considered that speedy action to prevent the outbreak of disputes where social interests were at stake could take various forms. Possible solutions were to prolong the period of validity of an existing

[1] The Nothin commission proposals for the public sector or, more broadly, service industries, are discussed below, pp. 187–8.

contract, authorize that a mediation proposal should be given the force of a contract, or prescribe arbitration. Emergency legislation to facilitate these approaches could be provided through a general powers Act which enabled intervention to take place within prescribed periods.

Such solutions were hardly calculated to appeal to LO and SAF. More in keeping with their outlook was another point the Nothin commission made, that these proposed solutions were not intended to prejudice the effectiveness of the normal bargaining and mediation machinery, nor to remove from the organizations their own responsibility for resolving disputes.[1]

Chapter 5 of the Basic Agreement does not use any of the Nothin solutions, since ultimately they are all inconsistent with the contractual freedom of the parties. It takes an extremely empirical approach to the problem of defining conflicts that endanger essential public services. In the view of SAF and LO no approximately satisfactory demarcation of spheres of activity could be made which was objective and generally accepted.[2]

The balancing of opposing interest which such disputes involved was in the SAF and LO view unsuitable for reference to a court of law.

Sölvén points out that no satisfactory delimitation is possible. However, 'as a distinguishing feature in principle of a function that is vital to society could be stated its importance for *providing the public with the necessities of life: the maintenance of public order and safety, and the maintenance of public health and other essential social services* (his emphasis). To such spheres of activity belong

[1] *S.O.U.*, 1935, 65, p. 125.

[2] 'The very fact that the public interest is always dependent on the *scope* of a prevailing labour conflict makes such a prefixed demarcation impossible. A particular activity is rarely in itself of such fundamental importance to the community as to warrant its protection against all conflicts. On the other hand, a conflict that is in itself by no means directed against any essential public functions may yet through its manifestations to some limited extent impede or even prevent activity that is essential for providing the general public with safety of life and health. (Thus not only the *nature* of the activity is important, but also the scope and effects of the conflict.) Consequently, since the need for avoiding or limiting a particular conflict is directly dependent on *the circumstances of each case*, no other solution appears to offer itself than that of allowing the balancing of conflicting interests to assert itself in each individual conflict, with due regard also to the interests of society as a whole. A review of the open conflicts that have occurred in Sweden in the past shows that one cannot reasonably charge the parties on the labour market with having in their internal labour disputes disregarded the truly essential interests of society. On the contrary, the organizations on each side have consciously endeavoured to prevent their disputes from hazarding these interests. Nevertheless, and in order to establish more favourable conditions for efforts of this nature, the Committee proposes a more settled form for the consideration of questions that arise about measures to be taken with a view to preventing labour conflicts from disturbing essential public services.' *Preamble to the Basic Agreement*, pp. 10–11.

gas, electricity, and waterworks, the police force, fire service, care of the sick, cleansing, and also other activity *in so far as* it involves the maintenance of the above.'[1]

Chapter 5 of the Basic Agreement, which takes up socially dangerous disputes, differs from the other four chapters. First, it applies irrespective of whether affiliated organizations have accepted the Basic Agreement. Secondly, it applies whether the conflict situation does or does not affect a party affiliated to LO or SAF. Such disputes are more liable to occur in fact outside the sphere of activity of SAF, in the public, not the private sector.

SAF and LO undertake to take up promptly for joint consideration any conflict situation where protection of any public interest is called for. The right to ask for consideration by LO and SAF of such disputes is not confined to them. It may be asked for by either of the two organizations, by a public authority, or by any other similar body representing the public interest in question. In the one dispute which has so far produced a positive SAF–LO recommended solution the initiative was in fact taken by such public bodies as the Medical Board and the State Railways.

The machinery for discussion operates through the Labour Market Council, which *considers* questions of preventing, limiting, or settling the dispute. No provision is made for the independent chairman taking part in deliberations under Chapter 5, and the Council consists of three representatives from the LO and SAF side respectively. Neither the preamble to the Agreement nor the chapter gives any guidance about how decisions are arrived at. No provision is made for a vote, nor for a ruling by the chairman, if a majority view cannot be reached. The underlying intention here is clear, that only by a joint expression of opinion can the Council fulfil its function. If a majority has been obtained in favour of preventing or settling a conflict what action is to be taken? Both SAF and LO undertake, each on its own side, 'to take immediate measures for bringing about a settlement between the parties concerned'.

What the Council does is first to consider whether and, if so, to what extent the dispute is endangering essential social functions; secondly, to try to find a solution on which the majority of its six members can agree; and, thirdly, then to try to persuade the parties to agree on a solution.[2] This is deliberately vague, because of the

[1] Sölvén, *Huvudavtalet*, 2nd edition, p. 209 (Stockholm, 1948).

[2] The SAF commentary on the Basic Agreement, *Redogörelse för huvudavtalet*, p. 13, states: 'In this connexion the Labour Market Council is to endeavour to find the most appropriate method of regulating working conditions. It rests with the central organizations to try, with the means of pressure at their disposal, to have such decisions executed in the form of an agreement between the parties involved.' As is suggested by the analysis in Part 1 of the government of LO and SAF, the pressures available can be formidable.

conviction that such disputes involve a 'balancing of opposing interests', and each case must be considered on its own merits. No provision is made for the Council publishing its views.

In such disputes it may in principle be likened to a private court of inquiry. It is not stated formally to be a board of arbitration, but rather a deliberating and recommending body. There is in fact a very strong presumption that the Council will arrive at a majority recommendation when the public interest is felt to be involved, and of LO and SAF being able to bring pressure of an unspecified nature to bear on the parties to a dispute on their respective sides. Behind the acceptance of the Basic Agreement lay strong pressures from Riksdag motions, the Nothin commission, and the government, so that both sides have an interest in arriving at agreement and making it work. Otherwise the law may step in.

Chapter 5 has only been put to the test once so far,[1] when in 1953 a dispute arose in privately owned electric power stations which threatened to develop into a conflict that endangered essential public services. The main issue was a wage dispute; the workers in these power stations argued they had lagged behind the government-owned power stations in wage improvements in recent years.

The number of personnel directly affected by the dispute was about 2,000, of whom 400 were technicians, and 1,600 were installation, linesmen, and distribution workers. It was estimated that from 25 to 30% of the total national electricity supply would be lost in the event of a strike. After unsuccessful mediation attempts and two mediation proposals had been rejected, before and after LO had given the Electrical Workers' Union permission to strike, the Medical Board and State Railways Board informed the mediation commission independently that they intended to ask for the dispute to be brought before the Labour Market Council. (The Telegraph Board also asked later.) The strike was therefore delayed. The mediation commission stated it would call the parties together again as soon as the Council had discussed the question. It discussed the matter for three days, heard the parties, and succeeded in arriving at a unanimous recommendation. The disputants therefore had before them when they resumed negotiations with their mediation commission a proposal

[1] The Council has had two other cases before it. The first, in 1944, was brought by the Government Food Commission when it feared that a slaughterhouse dispute in Stockholm would endanger food supplies in time of crisis. The Council rather let the matter rest, for it was not felt to be a dispute for which the Chapter 5 provisions need be invoked, and it was settled by agreement. SAF proposed to take another wartime dispute, in the rubber industry, before the Council, but LO put pressure on the workers' side to avoid the necessity of a reference. The second dispute to reach the Council was in 1953, just before the electricity dispute discussed above. A dispute in the foodstuffs industry was not considered by the Council to endanger essential social services. This case is discussed below, p. 187.

(not made public) behind which stood the deliberations, recommendation, and authority of LO and SAF. Not surprisingly, the dispute was at once settled peacefully.

In fact, there is a very strong presumption that in such disputes the Board will arrive at a recommendation, because both sides have the common interest of avoiding government intervention. This is the essential idea underlying the whole Basic Agreement. Given this circumstantial bias in favour of a settlement made on the basis of a recommendation from the Board, there is considerable justification for saying that in fact the Council will in such disputes be a board of arbitration.[1] Whether the power of the two sides is based on statutory rules or moral pressure, there would be a grave risk for the whole structure in either of the associations involved going against the recommendation the Council produces.

It is clear from the experience of Chapter 5, and its sparing use, that neither LO nor SAF would wish to have wage disputes referred to the Labour Market Council as a matter of habit.[2] There are two main reasons. First, it would mean that a final stage was introduced into the wage bargaining system *after* mediation had failed to bring about a settlement acceptable to both sides. Nothing would be more calculated to undermine the whole edifice of the mediation system, and bring the mediation arrangements into dispute, than the Labour Market Council standing in the background as a final semi-arbitration body. A second point, which arises from the post-war practice of recommending general wage policies and increases, is that SAF and LO would not relish having cases brought to the Council, since each side might then be forced to depart from the general policy it was trying to pursue in the year's wages round. Thus SAF and LO will clearly be reluctant to take wage disputes to the Council unless some outside authority explicitly brings the matter before them under

[1] *Aftontidningen* (LO's mouthpiece) expressed the view in a leader ('Privata kraftverken') on June 4, 1953, that the Council had in practice functioned as an arbitration board. LO, itself, however, is on record (in its statement in 1952 on a proposed Labour Market Council for the public sector—see LO *verksamhetsberättelse*, 1952, p. 190) as saying that the Labour Market Council is not an arbitration board, under Chapter 5. Formally, this is correct, for there is no means of knowing whether its recommendations are adopted in unchanged form by the parties. Nor need it be one or both of the parties to a dispute that refer a matter to the Council for its views. But LO added in its 1952 statement that there was a strong presumption that any recommendation by the Labour Market Council would be accepted by the parties. Further confusion was added in 1955 during the shipping dispute, when the trade union signatories of motions submitted to the Riksdag on the subject (*Upper Chamber*, 1955, motion 540, and *Lower Chamber*, 1955, motion 667) clearly accepted the idea that the Council *is* an arbitration body under Chapter 5.

[2] Sölvén, in *Fackföreningsrörelsen*, 1956, II, p. 418, questions whether in fact it was the intention at the time Chapter 5 was devised that economic disputes could be referred to the Council.

the terms of Chapter 5. In any event they will be able to use the other methods their rules provide for influencing the bargaining behaviour of their member groups.

The provisions of Chapter 5 posed other problems in 1953: (*a*) the wage differentials between private and public undertakings in the same type of economic activity, and (*b*) the way in which workers employed in activity which is found to be essential to society may be deprived of the strike weapon and therefore lose considerable bargaining power.

Another dispute in 1953 which did end in a conflict was that in the food processing industry. At first sight this seemed even more likely to be labelled a socially dangerous dispute, for the whole of the food processing industry with the exception of the co-operative movement's section closed down. For five weeks the Swedish public marched on co-operative bread. Although the Labour Market Council discussed aspects of protective work in connexion with this dispute, it was not considered to be one that endangered essential public services.

This dispute raised all the thorny problems about the criteria for defining a dispute that endangers essential services. SAF and LO were clearly reluctant to label it as such, and on this occasion, in contrast to the electricity dispute, they were not forced by a request from an outside authority to take the dispute up in the Council. This is perhaps the key factor in considering the different treatment accorded to the two disputes.

Formally, the Council is not prevented from taking up disputes outside the SAF–LO sector, and is indeed obliged to do so if asked. Significantly, such disputes are in fact much more likely to occur *outside* the common SAF–LO area of the labour market, in central and local government and in public undertakings. At the time the Basic Agreement was concluded, it was argued in conservative motions submitted to the Riksdag that organizations in the public sector would not admit that the SAF–LO Labour Market Council was competent to discuss such disputes, and the employers' side in particular would be reluctant to allow a body on which it had no representation to take up disputes outside the LO–SAF common area. In addition, groups standing outside LO and SAF would not be subject to the same moral pressure as employers and unions directly involved in SAF and LO to reach agreement on the basis of a Council recommendation. Legislation was therefore asked for to cover this gap in the treatment of disputes threatening essential services.

The particular problems of the public sector had already been examined by the Nothin commission, but no action was taken by the government on the basis of its recommendation that experts should investigate whether and to what extent industrial disputes could be prevented in cases where the activity was *not* designed primarily to promote the economic interests of some employer. The distinction between economic and non-economic activity did not coincide with that between the private and public sectors at the time the commission reported,[1] and the rapid growth of government activity in the past twenty years has blurred any such distinction even more.

One approach suggested for the public sector in recent years is that a separate Labour Market Council should be created to deal with its problems under this heading.[2] The trend towards a system of collective contracts for civil servants, and the proposal for a new government agency to carry on collective bargaining for civil servants along similar lines to the present Collective Bargaining Board, suggest that a separate Labour Market Council for the public sector is now a much more realistic prospect than it was even ten years ago. The main objection voiced in the past to a public sector Council has been that it might produce opinions designed to influence the parties to a dispute (and there would be little point to it if it did not do precisely this), one of whom in certain cases would be the Riksdag. This difficulty of bringing pressure to bear on the legislature will disappear if the Riksdag abandons its formal position in wage and salary determination for civil servants. A practical difficulty confronting a Labour Market Council in the public sector would be that the groups are not so homogeneous as SAF and LO. Nevertheless, in principle it is now possible to think seriously of a public sector body parallel to the SAF–LO Council.

Despite these existing and potential institutional arrangements, the difficulty of defining and handling emergency disputes remains. Three cases since the war show that the Riksdag will never be able to ignore disputes in either the public or private sectors if these are felt to endanger the public interest, and it must keep emergency legislation up its sleeve as the final sanction.

Since the war the government has intervened in two disputes in the public sector, the first the 1947 police pay dispute, when it was held that the maintenance of public order and safety justified the passing

[1] The Nothin commission was aware of this. Examples of non-economic activity which it mentioned were the police, fire service, cleansing, and hospitals; local authority establishments for lighting, power, water, and gas, for although these were in certain cases carried on as business undertakings, business profit was seldom the determining motive, but rather the supplying of a necessity to the public. Government enterprises with a monopolistic position, such as postal and telegraph services, were closely comparable. More doubtful were government enterprises that competed with private, such as railways and the waterfall board. See *S.O.U.*, 1935 : 65, pp. 116–17.

[2] See *Lower Chamber*, 1952, motion 297, by two conservative party leaders, and *S.O.U.*, 1951 : 54, p. 120, for a favourable view of such arrangements.

of a special enforcement-of-duty Act.[1] Compulsory arbitration was not considered an adequate solution, since it did not force a party to work on the terms of an arbitration award. The second case concerned nurses in 1951, when the government presented a Proposition proposing compulsory arbitration for a dispute about salaries,[2] supplemented by enforcement-of-duty if necessary.

In both cases agreement was reached through mediators before the legislation was required. Both these cases were typical of the type of public sector activity which the Nothin committee had discussed. The third case, in the private sector, was more controversial, when compulsory arbitration was proposed in 1955 of a dispute between the Shipping Federation (which is not a Member of SAF) and the Master Mariners. The Proposition[3] was withdrawn when the dispute was settled by mediation. The controversy arose because the government interpreted the public interest in a much wider sense, arguing that there would be grave damage to the *economy* of the country if the dispute was allowed to lead to a stoppage. This aroused considerable opposition in the Riksdag. *All* disputes exercised economic pressure and were liable to involve economic losses for the parties themselves and for society as a whole, depending on the scope and duration of a conflict. Society should be prepared to pay a certain price for the value of a free labour market.[4] This was of course simply an echo of the traditional hostility to government arbitration of non-justiciable disputes.

CONCLUSION

In the last resort private institutional arrangements for dealing with emergency disputes may prove inadequate, and emergency legislative powers are then necessary. That is not to say that the SAF–LO Labour Market Council has been a paper treaty. On the contrary, by its very existence it has shown the parties to labour disputes in the SAF–LO sector what pressures may be brought to bear on them if they do threaten to overstep the narrow dividing line between disputes that are not and are socially dangerous. It is arguable also that if there had already been in existence a Labour Market Council for the public sector then the two disputes discussed above could have been handled by it. It is important to have the institutional

[1] *Proposition* no. 326, of June 27, 1947. The proposed sanction of imprisonment for failure on the part of the police to carry out their duties was modified by the Riksdag (see *Riksdag skrivelse* no. 500, 1947) to comprise fines only.

[2] See *Proposition 212*, 1951, and *Proposition 213*, recalling *212*.

[3] *Proposition 197*, 1955.

[4] See especially *Upper Chamber*, 1955, motion no. 540, by Yngve Möller, Åman (TCO director) and Geijer (then chairman of the Metal Workers' Union).

pressures as a check on irresponsible action, and these the LO–SAF Agreement provides. But, as the Agreement recognizes, the definition of socially dangerous disputes remains intractable in principle; each case must be treated on its merits. What the Swedish experience of these problems suggests is that disputes are less likely to reach the critical stage when they are recognized as having become socially dangerous if the private organizations themselves make arrangements to provide control and prevent emergencies from arising.

CHAPTER X

The Success of the Basic Agreement

How successful has the Basic Agreement been? The answer can be set out in a number of dimensions.

There was some initial suspicion in the trade union movement, which was reflected in the subsequent LO congress motions, mainly dealing with the problems of workers' security discussed under Chapter 3 of the Agreement. There has been practically no criticism of the idea of the Agreement, but only of the specific clauses (particularly those on security) which particular groups have found operating to their disadvantage. This is a wholly healthy sign.

Some of the early trade union suspicion seems to have been engendered by the fear that the Agreement meant intervention in the internal affairs of the unions. What in fact it did directly was to provide a framework for the conduct of relations between the labour market organizations, and between them and society. Indirectly, it is true, it did involve more control over the internal government of the unions, since the parties accepted the obligation to exercise responsibility and keep order in their own houses, as the 1941 rules revision of LO illustrates.

In terms of worker coverage, the Basic Agreement was accepted by sixteen LO unions in 1961, and roughly 560,000 LO members were directly covered. This represented 80% of the workers covered by SAF. In addition, agreements modelled on the Basic Agreement have been adopted in other sectors (discussed below). For this reason alone figures of statistical coverage are not conclusive. But, more fundamentally, it is impossible to assess the success of the Basic Agreement purely in quantitative terms. If we look at the activity of the Labour Market Council, we find that most of its work has been concerned with dismissals under Chapter 3, while it has had only one dispute before it which was considered to endanger essential public services. But its success cannot be gauged on the basis of what it does. In the case of Chapter 5, for example, its existence is a deterrent to parties allowing disputes to go before it. No figures can show how far the Basic Agreement has promoted labour peace just because its procedures provide machinery for settling disputes.

The positive ideas of collaboration on which the Agreement was based have, however, undoubtedly yielded a great deal of fruit. It was not the original intention that the labour market committee which drew up the Basic Agreement should be a permanent body, but in fact it has endured, since it was found that informal summit discussions between LO and SAF leaders on matters of common interest could produce agreement on many questions, sometimes informally, but also in the form of new agreements. The committee has fulfilled the contact function that was envisaged for the Labour Market Council in the 1938 Agreement. Subsequent agreements arrived at through the committee cover matters of common interest and dispute:

1942: agreement on workers' protection at the workplace (revised 1951);
1944: agreement on vocational training;
1946: agreement on works councils;
1948: agreement on work study.

In the sphere of less formal agreement the committee has produced a report on women in gainful employment, which led to the establishment of a labour council for women's questions. It has also discussed thorny issues such as the comprehensive national health scheme (1955), hours of work, problems of wages policy, and structural problems of various sectors of the economy.

The co-operation leading to and stemming from the Basic Agreement can claim some of the credit for the peaceful relations between the parties that have on the whole prevailed since 1938. Some allowance must be made for the fact that a period of abnormal war years followed immediately on the conclusion of the Agreement, and both sides were willing to subordinate their own interests to those of the nation. The post-war era of full employment has also provided a favourable environment, in which disputes, apart from the big metal trades disputes of 1945, have been infrequent. But there seems no good reason why the Basic Agreement should succumb in the event of a depression and large-scale unemployment. The framework it provided for the conduct of labour relations has now become standard practice for a whole new generation of employers and trade unionists, accustomed to channelling their bargaining strength and grievances within the framework provided by the Basic Agreement and to practising the informal exchange of views and argument which the 1936–8 discussions pioneered.

Some criticism was made when the Agreement was signed that it represented the thin edge of the wedge, that there might be a ganging up of employers and workers against the consumer, a vertical combination of industry against everyone else. This was no doubt a natural reaction, when *both* sides were agreed on the desirability of avoiding social intervention in the labour market. But the fears have proved unfounded. The Prime Minister was very quick to point out that the Saltsjöbaden agreement gave good cause for satisfaction, since in a democratic society this method was more valuable than legislation. The spirit behind the agreement was a good guarantee of relations on the labour market. But at the same time he said that he would not hesitate to put forward the necessary measures if the labour market did become turbulent. The Basic Agreement would have to prove itself, and the State did not henceforth renounce all interest in and concern for labour problems.

One additional word of warning should perhaps be added on the other side, to compensate for the excessive enthusiasm of some foreign commentators about the Basic Agreement. Undoubtedly it was an achievement, but Edström, speaking in 1939, reminded us that 'behind the present fairly harmonious relations between the parties lay nearly forty years of development, full of unremitting organization work and many unsuccessful attempts to co-operate: nor did we wish to conceal that we still had a very long way to go to anything that could be called an ideal state on the labour market'. 'We (the labour market committee) took the view that people abroad had to a great extent exaggerated the so-called "middle way policy" we were considered to represent. We weren't nearly as clever as we were made out to be.'[1] The Basic Agreement did not spring up overnight. It was the culmination of many years of experience, sometimes good but frequently bad, of industrial relations and also the beginning of the technique of high-level personal contacts which is now so important in the centralized wage bargaining rounds.

OTHER BASIC AGREEMENTS

One of the most significant aspects of the Basic Agreement is the manner in which it has served to inspire similar developments in other sectors.

The Basic Agreement most similar to that of SAF–LO is the Basic Agreement for state-owned companies, a small group covering about 4,000 workers. Concluded in 1947, this Agreement contains chapters on negotiation procedure, works councils, notice of dismissal and layoff, local safety services, apprentice training, limitations on economic sanctions, emergency disputes, and a central Council. The central Council of four persons corresponds to the SAF–LO Labour Market Council, and has similar duties and competence.

[1] *J. Sigfrid Edström*, Senare Delen, pp. 150–1.

I. THE CO-OPERATIVE MOVEMENT

In the co-operative sector a Basic Agreement concluded in 1946 between LO and the Co-operative Union (KF) differs markedly in several respects from the SAF–LO Agreement. The LO–KF Agreement set out machinery for handling disputes which replaced the conciliation arrangements LO and the Co-operative Union had drawn up in 1926. These had provided that no work stoppage of any kind must take place before negotiations had been held at the local and union level, and if necessary in a central conciliation board. This had three representatives from each side, and its function was to try to take all possible steps to bring about a settlement.

The 1946 central agreement is much more detailed. It provides for a three-tier negotiation procedure as before, but makes separate arrangements for dealing with justiciable and non-justiciable disputes at the summit. For interpretational disputes a central Tribunal is set up, with two members from each side and a jointly appointed impartial chairman who takes part when the Tribunal is examining and settling legal disputes. Such disputes must be referred to the Tribunal by *both* sides before it can fulfil the function which in the last resort the Labour Court would otherwise perform.

For non-justiciable disputes a conciliation board of two persons, one from LO and one from the Co-operative Union, endeavours to conciliate the parties if no agreement is reached at the earlier negotiation stages. If conciliation fails, the two sides can resort to economic sanctions, but only after the *Tribunal* has had an opportunity to express its views on the dispute and the conciliation board has again met the parties to try to reach an agreed solution on the basis of the Tribunal's views. The Tribunal can also act as a board of arbitration in non-justiciable disputes if *both* sides agree.

There are similarities to and contrasts with the SAF–LO Basic Agreement in these arrangements. The negotiation procedure is reminiscent of Chapter 2 of the Basic Agreement, and the Tribunal is given functions in relation to dismissals[1] similar to the Labour Market Council under Chapter 3 of the Basic Agreement. But the co-operative sector agreement contains no explicit provisions codifying economic sanctions or about socially dangerous disputes. The main difference, however, is that the SAF–LO agreement does *not* have an explicit role in collective bargaining, whereas the essential purpose of the LO–Co-operative Union arrangements is to administer the wage policy agreement which the two sides agreed at the same time in 1946.

[1] Not under the agreement discussed here, but under the Works Council agreement for the co-operative movement.

The co-operative movement occupies a special position as 'the other side' in the collective bargaining of LO unions, for it is recognized that there is some affinity between the two movements, in working-class membership, in their interest in economic democracy, in the fact that the consumers' co-operative movement does not have profit maximization as its rationale, and in the primary interest of providing good quality goods for the consumer at the lowest possible prices. The problems of wages costs and prices that arose in this context when the co-operative movement became an important employer of labour were not satisfactorily resolved by the 1926 conciliation arrangements, and three basic principles were agreed in 1946 as a guide to the collective bargaining in this sector:

(1) that co-operative enterprises are not to be burdened by higher wage and other labour costs than private firms in the same sector;
(2) that the co-operative firms will not pay lower wages or apply worse conditions than those of other rationally conducted firms in the same branch, since it can be assumed that co-operative enterprises will be conducted at least as efficiently as other forms of enterprise;
(3) that, given their position as model employers, burdened by labour costs equal to those of private enterprise, the consumer co-operative enterprise ought, in consultation with the trade union movement, to strive to create security of employment and good working conditions for their employees.

The wording of these principles, which must be looked at together, implies that the co-operative firms will not pay any *better or worse* wages than comparable firms in private ownership. It means in practice, as the 1953 food industry conflict brought out, that the co-operative movement will not be a wage leader, but follow in the wake of the private sector. This simplifies any attempt to set a pattern for economy-wide bargaining on the part of SAF and LO, since there is no question under the agreement of the co-operatives taking a lead; but this implication has not always been clear to some of the branches of LO unions which conclude contracts with co-operative firms.[1] The phrase 'model employer' does not mean that the *highest* wages are paid, but is more likely to have significance for the other conditions of employment. In fact, until the recent spread of fringe benefits and social legislation, the co-operative movement was a model employer in the sense that it took a sympathetic and generous view of these private welfare benefits.

[1] See LO *kongress-protokoll*, 1956, pp. 470–3.

II. THE NEWSPAPER INDUSTRY

Labour disputes in the newspaper industry always attract public attention, and focus on the vexed question of national emergency disputes. Freedom of the press is one of the fundamental freedoms written into the Swedish Constitution; and the newspaper industry therefore occupies a very sensitive position in the conduct of its industrial relations. There are several reasons why the industry devised its own arrangements. The Newspaper Employers' Federation is not a member of SAF. The provisions in the newspaper industry also owe a lot to the work of Sten Dehlgren, an enlightened employers' representative, who had for many years been conscious of the direct manner in which the production of newspapers touches the public interest. The Nothin commission, with its support for voluntary peace treaties in industry, provided an additional stimulus.

The industry has since 1937 accepted the implication that any stoppages would endanger essential public services. By means of long-term peace treaties the newspaper industry is virtually guaranteed industrial peace, since compulsory arbitration is provided for *all* disputes that arise. This is a considerable extension of private industrial jurisprudence beyond the usual contractual and also legislative provisions, e.g. of the Collective Contracts Act, which allows sympathetic action, and the Mediation Act, which does not debar direct action. The first of a series of long-term peace agreements was signed in 1937, and agreements to keep the peace for periods up to eight years have been in force ever since.

Both the private newspaper employers and the social democratic newspaper proprietors (*A-pressen*) abide by the agreements, which cover typographers, teletype operators, lithographers, bookbinders, distribution workers employed in newspaper sub-offices, and drivers. So far the agreements have not been extended to cover journalists, office employees, and delivery staff (who are in the main part-time women workers). These omissions are more formal than truly important, for two reasons. Economically, none of the groups excluded is large enough to carry on a strike for any length of time, and, secondly, great pressure could be brought to bear on them if they tried to bring about any direct action in the newspaper industry. The delivery girls, for example, are members of the Union of Transport Workers. It is difficult to envisage a strike staged by these members of the Transport Workers' Union, which is affiliated to LO, when other LO unions which are contracting parties to the peace treaties are numerically superior.

The procedure set out in the peace treaties is designed to ensure rapid settlement of disputes that do arise. These may be about the interpretation of agreements, or non-justiciable disputes which arise in the annual collective bargaining negotiations.

For the settlement of disputes about rights, the machinery for considering *and* settling them proceeds via local negotiations to a board of arbitration if necessary. This board sits in Stockholm, and consists of five members appointed for one year at a time, each side appointing two members and these four choosing the fifth. The intention is that the disputes should be settled speedily, and certainly within fourteen days. Both sides are obliged to ensure that their members do not violate this procedure or the decisions of the board, on pain of expulsion, and each of the central organizations is liable to pay damages to the other if it does not keep its part of the treaty. Very few disputes are ever taken as far as the arbitration board, most being settled at an earlier stage, and in any case precedents normally provide a guide to the parties in the event of a disputed matter.

Disputes in connexion with new contract negotiations which occur from year to year are obviously more complex than rights disputes, where the legal interpretative function is paramount. For non-justiciable disputes the procedure set out is that an impartial chairman is first appointed to try to mediate between the parties. Disputed issues on which no agreement can be reached are to be referred by this impartial chairman to a separate board of arbitration. The obligations of the parties in relation to the decisions of this board are the same as for rights disputes, in that the decisions of the board are final and must be adhered to by the parties concerned and their members. The non-justiciable disputes tribunal is, however, more permanent in its composition, because its members, who consist of three independent persons, are appointed for the full period of the peace treaty, and not simply for one year at a time. The parties appoint the chairman and one member or, failing agreement, the Social Board appoints them. The third member is the chairman of the rights disputes board. The existence of two tribunals conforms to the accepted distinction between justiciable and non-justiciable disputes.

Some attempt is made in the peace treaties to give guidance to the arbitration board for non-justiciable disputes. It is provided that, 'in addition to what the parties themselves adduce and support with reasoned argument', the board shall have regard to the following matters: (*a*) the legitimate demands of the public that newspapers should be published; (*b*) the cost-of-living index; (*c*) the classification of cost-of-living areas; (*d*) the general wage situation; (*e*) working conditions and arrangements; and (*f*) a reasonable standard of living and terms of employment for the workers. There is ample scope here for the wisdom of a Solomon being tested, and it is perhaps fortunate that the one economic dispute which has been before this board so far was a cost-of-living problem in 1941. Again, this comparative inactivity on the part of the arbitration board is typical of the Swedish dislike for having non-justiciable disputes settled by arbitration.

The parties here have clearly felt it to be in their interests to reach agreement before recourse to arbitration becomes necessary.

These peace treaties in the newspaper industry are *not* altruistic. Both sides benefit materially from them. The employers are guaranteed continuous productive activity. Nor have the unions in the newspaper industry abandoned all their tactical weapons, for the peace treaties have certain bargaining advantages. Directly, they can be used as a bargaining tool, and the original agreement of 1937 was only concluded, for example, when the peace agreement had written into it provisions for three weeks holiday in the year (then a very favourable fringe benefit). In 1954 renewal was made contingent on pension improvements. Indirectly, too, the peace treaties guarantee that the unions in the printing industry will always have a high proportion of their members in employment who could give financial support to other members in sectors where labour could be withdrawn. Thus there are real benefits to be derived from long-term peace.

III. SALARIED EMPLOYEES

The growth in the number and organizational strength of salaried employees is reflected in two Basic Agreements which have been concluded for the SAF sector in recent years, the first in 1957 with the Union of Clerical and Technical Employees in Industry, and the second with the Foremen's and Supervisors Union in 1959.

The 1957 agreement between SAF and the Union of Clerical and Technical Employees provides, first, for the setting-up of a labour market committee for the purpose of extending collaboration through top-level discussion in an informal manner on matters of mutual interest. It consists of twenty members, ten appointed by each side. No specific rules of procedure or tasks are provided, in order to promote the maximum freedom in the exchange of views. In essence, this committee becomes parallel to the SAF–LO committee set up in 1936 from which the Basic and subsequent SAF–LO agreements have stemmed.

Secondly, a uniform negotiation procedure is established for all disputes, running if necessary from local negotiations to the national union and employers' association level, then to a Trade Council at the national union level, and, in non-justiciable disputes, to a Salaried Employees' Labour Market Council. In interpretation disputes about a collective or private contract, local negotiations are if necessary followed by negotiations between the Union of Clerical and Technical Employees and the SAF Member association. If no agreement on a solution can be reached by the end of these two stages, each of which must have been instituted within three weeks of negotiations being requested, *both* sides can agree to refer the matter to a Trade Council for a final decision. This consists of five members, two appointed by the employers' association concerned, two by the union, and the fifth, the chairman, jointly by the two sides. Alternatively, one side can ask that the matter be referred to a court of law. Trade Councils cannot, however, adjudicate on disputes about the right of association, which are the prerogative of the Labour Court.

The same procedures of local, national, and trade council instances can be used for non-justiciable disputes. *Both* sides can agree to refer such a dispute to a Trade Council for final decision, i.e. to voluntary arbitration. Alternatively, *either* side can take the matter to a higher instance, by requiring within three weeks that the question should be referred to the Labour Market Council for its *opinion.* If SAF is the employers' bargaining agent it can require the reference. The Council consists of six members. SAF and the union each appoint two, and each side also appoints a representative of the employer and employee respectively for each particular case. Each member has one vote, and the quorum required is all six members. Unless the parties agree otherwise, the opinion of the Council *is made public.*[1] This contrasts with the SAF–LO Labour Market Council, which in such cases would work behind the scenes and not publish any recommendation it made. It is clearly meant to be influential, if necessary through the pressure of public opinion. Again, this difference in approach emphasizes the awkward problems that can arise when salaried employees bargain with, and are also the representatives of, the employer. Neither side wants open conflict.

The disputes with which the Salaried Employees' Labour Market Council is likely to be concerned are primarily salary disputes. This

[1] The clause is rather formal: 'Requests for a statement of opinion from the Salaried Employees' Labour Market Council are to be made in writing to the Council. Details are to be given of the claims and of the circumstances on which the request is based. The Council will be responsible for giving the opposite party an opportunity to make a statement and, moreover, the Council is entitled to call for such other written or verbal statements as may facilitate its reaching a decision.

'A summons to attend the meeting is to be issued by the Council not later than two weeks after the submission of the case to it. The meeting is to be held as soon as possible after the issue of the summons. Should either party call for speedy handling of the case, it is the duty of the Council to do everything possible to meet this requirement.

'The opinion of the Council is to be submitted in writing to both parties simultaneously. Unless otherwise agreed by the parties the findings are to be made public.'

again contrasts with the SAF–LO Council, which would not want to handle such disputes if possible. The Salaried Employees' Council may also be asked to give opinions on cases of an employer giving notice of termination of employment to a salaried employee who has been employed for at least twelve months, after the local and union-level negotiations stages have been exhausted.[1]

After the Council has given an opinion on a matter referred to it, the parties have full freedom to act, e.g. to use economic sanctions. But each side binds itself to refrain from threatening or taking aggressive action during the three-week period in which non-justiciable disputes can be referred to the Council, unless they have agreed not to refer it. If it is referred, the ban on direct action applies until the Council has issued its opinion. If the two sides in a non-justiciable dispute agree to remit it to their Trade Council, no aggressive measures are to be instituted or continued, since they are binding themselves to accept its decision.

One of the main aspects of this Basic Agreement is the strengthening of the local negotiation procedure, which is essential to the union's policy of favouring local salary negotiations. Local negotiations take place between the employer and the salaried employees' organization within the company, and, if there is no organization, both parties are recommended to appoint representatives for establishing contact.[2]

The central agreement concluded in July 1959 between SAF and the Foremen's and Supervisors Union provides for essentially similar procedures and instances, through local and national negotiations, Trade Councils, and a Foremen's Labour Market Council. A foremen's labour market committee of twenty-four persons, twelve from each side, has also been set up to discuss questions of mutual interest. The main differences from the SAF agreement with the Union of Clerical and Technical Employees are that the foremen's agreement contains provisions dealing with the foreman's position as the representative of management, his obligations in the event of disputes, and the execution of protective work.

The flora of Basic Agreements reviewed above provide a rich variety of codes for the conduct of industrial disputes. Some resemble the 1938 SAF–LO Agreement closely in the procedures adopted;

[1] The general issue of security of employment for salaried employees is discussed in Chapter XI.

[2] If both sides agree, local representatives outside the company may be allowed to take part in negotiations. A further provision which considerably strengthens the union's influence is that the salaried employees have the right to be represented at negotiations between an employer and his *workers* which directly or indirectly affect the salaried employees or a particular salaried employee.

others have moved much further in the direction of providing machinery for dealing with wage disputes and the content of agreements. The SAF–LO Agreement stops short at regulating bargaining procedures and, with the exception of Chapter 5, does not intervene in the actual wage-fixing process. The groups reviewed above who have allowed wage and salary-fixing to become the possible subjects of settlement by arbitration either occupy a special position in the labour market, e.g. the co-operative movement, the newspaper industry, and salaried employees, or operate in wage bargaining primarily on an individual basis, e.g. salaried employees in industry. For this last group the possibility of arbitration in salary disputes represents a significant departure on the part of SAF. It is clearly the price that has had to be paid to ensure peace and order among employees occupying positions of trust, and whose decentralized salary fixing could otherwise, in the absence of negotiation procedures, permit small-scale disputes at the local level.

The main success of the Basic and subsequent Agreements has been in the encouragement given to peaceful compromise through well-ordered negotiating procedures and codes of conduct. The Basic Agreement set a new tone, of which it was itself at once the product and the pioneer. This is amply demonstrated by the change that has come over the most sensitive aspects of labour relations, workers' security, and employers' sovereignty, which are analysed in the next two chapters.

PART IV

Job Security and Industrial Democracy

CHAPTER XI

Job Security

TWO aspects of the problem of security of employment have enjoyed particular prominence in the Swedish labour market: (*a*) job security, or, if this is looked at from the employer's side, the management prerogative in employing labour; and (*b*) security in the wider sense, of contentment at work based on knowledge and participation, which is covered by the broad term 'industrial democracy'. Despite the moral overtones and appeals to constitutional liberty, both issues have a strong economic content. Industrial democracy in Sweden is strongly geared to productivity, while the narrower issue of job security, which will be discussed in this chapter, can largely be analysed in terms of demand and supply.

I. JOB SECURITY

The management prerogative, expressed so clearly in Article 23 (now 32) of the rules of SAF,[1] involves full freedom for the employer to control his demand for labour through:

(*a*) selecting his labour force by quality, not by the criterion of the union in which the workers organize. Since the early part of the century there has been little opposition by SAF to the right to organize as such, but strong resistance to all forms of organization clauses, like closed and union shop arrangements and preferential hiring;

(*b*) reallocating the labour force in accordance with the requirements of production;

(*c*) making marginal adjustments in the size of the labour force in the light of product markets and relative factor prices.

From the supply side the unions have been concerned to control (i) the amount of labour supplied, (ii) its quality, and (iii) access to work through union membership. Despite SAF's 'Article 23', unions have succeeded in having many of the supply aspects regulated in collective contracts, e.g. through clauses on apprenticeships. Nowadays, agreements usually contain provisions providing a period of

[1] For a general study of Article 23, see Valter Åman, *Paragraf 23* (Stockholm, 1939).

notice of termination of employment of manual workers of seven to fourteen days. It is provisions that allow the employer to terminate employment without notice on grounds, e.g. of misbehaviour, that have proved controversial.

The 1906 December Compromise between SAF and LO was in principle a victory for the demand side, in that SAF was able to resist all pressure to channel the supply of labour services through the unions, but at the same time the employers qualified their prerogative by agreeing that dismissals which might be interpreted as attacks on the right of association could be made the subject of review through agreed machinery. The demand side triumphed because the employers were stronger and willing to use the lock-out, and because public opinion has generally supported the proposition that the side paying the piper should call the tune. In the 1930s the demand side was given renewed stress, at least in principle, through judgements of the Labour Court.

Since the December Compromise the subsequent developments of the debate on job security illustrate four points. First, abuses occurred on both sides, through subtle pressures like blacklisting, blockades, and boycotts. Secondly, abuses varied with the level of economic activity. In boom conditions, when a shortage of labour existed, there were few complaints about employers exercising their prerogative harshly; when unemployment was high employers were frequently accused of abuses as they ran down their labour force. Thirdly, the discussion at LO congresses recognized that there was little point in trying to persuade SAF to modify its views on management prerogatives. More fundamentally, this was because some of the LO leaders accepted that, to quote Lindqvist, the right of the employer to lead and allocate the work 'must be admitted'.[1] Fourthly, LO's approach was therefore to try to have procedures introduced into contracts which would prevent abuses by employers, through providing recognized arrangements for handling lay-offs and dismissals and requiring employers to give reasons for dismissals. Successive LO congresses discussed various criteria that should be used in dismissing labour, the seniority rule, last in—first out, priority to local residents, and family responsibilities as a mitigating factor.

LO was successful in gradually bringing its point of view to the fore. The early discussions on industrial democracy, of which job

[1] See Casparsson, op. cit., I, 226. The 1961 LO congress discussion of this question marks a major shift in official LO policy, however. In addition to the modifications of the employers' prerogatives which it has succeeded in having introduced through the Basic Agreement, LO is now prepared to challenge the *principle* of the employer's prerogative. See *Fackföreningsrörelsen och företagsdemokratin*, especially pp. 62–74 (Stockholm, 1961).

security was an important aspect, recognized that a practical code was in fact growing up which involved a consideration of the reasons for dismissals. It envisaged that the proposed works councils would be suitable bodies for discussing dismissals.[1]

In the 1928 labour peace conference SAF's 'Article 23' was seen as a stumbling-block to co-operation, and the LO representatives hoped there could be consultation and discussions about management prerogatives. But von Sydow was not particularly conciliatory. The right to dismiss ought certainly to be exercised with caution and common sense, but it was out of the question for the workers to have any right of consultation in employment issues. This was quite irreconcilable with the economic laws of business activity. The Minister of Social Affairs (Lübeck) envisaged that Article 23 would eventually become a piece of paper and superfluous, because in practice each side had achieved its objectives.[2]

With the changes that took place in the 1930s, leading to the regulation of job security in Chapter 3 of the Basic Agreement, this is essentially what happened. LO's tactic of gradualism paid its way. But the path was not made easy by some of the doctrine on job security which the Labour Court espoused. In some of its early judgements[3] it set out 'the general legal principle' relating to the right to dismiss freely or to leave employment freely. The general principle it propounded was that the right of the employer to dismiss workers was unrestricted, unless contracts explicitly contained rules governing dismissals. Notice of termination could be given from either side, without stating reasons.

Four possibilities existed, according to Labour Court rulings:

(*a*) The collective contract contains no provisions about dismissals, in which case the general rule applies. Silence endorses.

(*b*) The parties to a contract can endorse the principle. SAF's 'Article 23' is then simply a precautionary measure, endorsing a general rule to which the workers as well as the employers are entitled.

(*c*) The parties can expressly agree to modify the principle, and had done so in contracts outside the SAF sector, e.g. by including seniority provisions, and organization clauses. Where the general principle was modified by such agreements the employer would be liable to state the real reasons for dismissal, in order to establish whether he had violated the terms of the contract.

[1] *S.O.U.*, 1923: 29, *Den Industriella Demokratiens Problem.*

[2] *Arbetsfredskonferensen i Stockholm*, November 30–December 1, 1928, p. 141 (Stockholm, 1929).

[3] E.g. Judgements 1932/100 : 1933/159 : 1936/121.

(*d*) The procedure of terminating employment without stating reasons, which also implied that the motives could not be probed, could not, however, be used indiscriminately by an employer, e.g. 'exclusively for an illegal or immoral purpose'.[1] This qualification to the general principle had to be judged in each case on its merits.

Undén, discussing Labour Court rulings at that time, suggested that the 'general principle' was a rule of interpretation, which could be modified by agreement, rather than a very valuable legal principle, the maintenance of which appeared to be of significant value to society.[2] It was permissive.

The meaning of the phrase 'of significant value to society' was indeed the heart of the controversy between employers and workers, both within and outside the Labour Court. The Court majority, excluding the workers' representatives, adhered to a legalistic freedom-of-contract approach, while the workers were much more concerned with what that freedom meant in practice. The whole LO approach was directed towards influencing the climate of opinion away from a contractual approach to labour services in the market. This indeed is the essence of LO's demands in 1961 for a new rule of interpretation on dismissals.

The Labour Court did not envisage that modification of Article 23 would be made other than by legislation, but such an approach was in keeping with LO's reluctance to have legal regulation of labour market matters. LO chose instead to seek to limit the absolute discretion of the employer in dismissals through discussion with SAF.[3] This approach accorded with the general 1936 congress theme of greater security in employment, and the SAF–LO labour market committee was a natural forum in which to pursue the tactic of persuasion LO had preached.

Chapter 3 of the Basic Agreement took up these problems associated with Article 23. Both the SAF and LO sides recognized that the methods and requirements for dismissing and laying off labour were the chief problems causing tension between management and

[1] Judgement 1936/121. Geijer, in Geijer and Schmidt, op. cit., pp. 132–5, concludes that the Labour Court has interpreted this 'law of morality' phrase so narrowly that it has not been very important in practice.

[2] Östen Undén, op. cit., p. 27 et seq.

[3] LO had consistently held to the view expounded at congress in 1909, that as the trade union movement became stronger it would be able not merely to rectify abuses but secure justice. True, it was committed by the 1912 congress, against the advice of the secretariat, to support unions which felt like making an issue of Article 23 with SAF. This formula was repeated in 1917, 1922, 1926, and 1931. But LO pointed out in 1936 (LO *kongress-protokoll*, 1936, pp. 282–94, and secretariat *utlåtande* no. 4) that no financial support had in fact been sought by member unions on this issue.

workers. Agreement was reached on some general principles and procedures, which try to take account both of the demand side, the employers' need for suitable labour, and the supply side, the workers' security of employment. Chapter 3 has been amended since the 1946 Agreement on Works Councils introduced provisions governing re-engaging, and the revised version is analysed here.

While SAF argued that the legal position governing the termination of collective agreements remained unchanged,[1] it recognized that the provisions of the chapter do involve a change in practice. They force the employer to be cautious and careful in making decisions affecting employment, and impose limitations on his freedom of action through the procedure agreed.

This covers dismissals, laying-off, and re-engaging of workers, but not a continuous reduction in working hours, such as short-time working. In principle, notice must be given for all types of reduction in the size of the labour force, both for objective reasons, such as a shortage of work, and for subjective reasons, e.g. if the employer considers a worker is unsuitable or lacking in skill. 'In principle the obligation to give warning and to consult exists irrespective of the reason for the measure.'[2] LO's new attitude to this whole question stems from its scepticism about whether this principle has been applied in practice.

Those covered by the provisions on dismissals and lay-offs are: (*a*) members of unions which have subscribed to the Basic Agreement; and (*b*) workers who have been employed for a minimum period of nine months. There are a number of specific exceptions: (*a*) workers engaged for a specified fixed period only or for the time required to complete a particular job; (*b*) a worker dismissed because of conduct which entitles the employer to revoke the contract of employment at once. The grounds are not specified, and there is a safeguard in the provision that such cases may be taken before the Labour Market Council by the union, if it considers appropriate; (*c*) lay-offs caused by fluctuations in the supply of work because it is seasonal or non-recurring in character; (*d*) when a lay-off is for a limited period not exceeding two weeks.

Three groups not covered by the agreement are: (*a*) unorganized workers; (*b*) salaried employees, who now have a separate agreement (discussed below); and (*c*) cases where action taken violates the 1936 Act guaranteeing the right of association or a collective contract, when the Labour Court, not the SAF–LO Council, is the final arbiter.

The rules provide a regular and minimum practice, but the parties to contracts are free to agree on more far-reaching limitations on the employer's prerogatives. In the co-operative movement, for instance,

[1] *Redogörelse för huvudavtalet*, SAF, p. 13. [2] Ibid., p. 14.

the details of the rules on job security are usually more favourable from the worker's point of view.

The notification procedure to be followed is that the employer gives two weeks' warning of his intention to dismiss or lay off workers to the local union representatives, *not* the individuals affected, though the names of those involved must be given. This period of warning is *in addition to* the period of notice of seven or fourteen days usually included in collective contracts. The intention is that this period should allow consultation to take place before the employer's intentions are made public.

This procedure channels communications through the unions, and makes it necessary to have a union representative in every workplace. The workers' side must inform the employer who their representative is in these matters. Under the Works Council Agreement this representative is to be a member of the Works Council, and either side can ask for the Works Council to discuss such questions without delay. If any emergency arises which the employer could not reasonably have foreseen (e.g. a cancellation of orders) and which necessitates lay-off within less than the two weeks' warning period, notice is to be given as soon as possible.

II. RE-EMPLOYMENT

In 1947 provisions on re-employment were included in this chapter of the Basic Agreement, to bring it into conformity with the 1946 Agreement on Works Councils, which extended the original Basic Agreement provisions to include re-employment of workers. If there have been dismissals or lay-offs to which the above provisions apply, the employer has to follow a specified procedure if the question of employing or re-employing labour of a corresponding kind should arise within four months. Before taking any action the employer must notify the local union representative of his intentions. He must also give the names of all the workers he considers should be employed or re-employed, whether they are organized and bound by contract or not. This is a safeguard against preferential hiring of non-union labour. If possible, notice is to be given at least one week in advance, and in any event before any labour is engaged or re-engaged. These arrangements mean that the employer cannot readily avoid revealing the reasons for any changes he is planning, and the successive stages for discussion ensure that he makes his reasons explicit. The stages in handling dismissals, lay-offs, and re-employment provide first for immediate local consultation between the employer and the local union representative. Negotiations can then follow at the national union level. The union thereafter has discretion to refer the matter to the Labour Market Council. A representative from each side at the national level sits with the Council on such cases.

The guidance given to the Council in assessing these cases is not a series of hard-and-fast rules, since opposing interests have in all probability to be weighed, but the consideration of what is *reasonable*. The Council is to endeavour to acquire a factually correct picture of all the circumstances in which the action cited was taken. The usual practice is for the SAF and LO secretaries of the Council to visit the workplace on a fact-finding mission. In appraising the position the Council is to take due account of: (*a*) the extent to which production is dependent on the skill and suitability of the labour employed—the employer's arguments; (*b*) the legitimate interests of the workers in having security of employment—the union side of the story. The most important point governing these provisions for security of employment is that productive efficiency is the primary objective, and has priority. But when an employer has to dismiss or lay-off workers because of a shortage of work he should, provided the choice is between workers who are equally suitable, take some account of length of service and any heavy family responsibilities. LO is now dissatisfied with this rule. It argues that priority should *not* be given to skill and suitability, since this is both wrong in principle and difficult to apply in practice, but that *all* aspects of the problem should be considered *equally* relevant.

In dealing with cases that come to it under this chapter the Council is intended to play a conciliatory role, through endeavouring to reach an agreed view which it then communicates to the two sides involved, but does not publish. The emphasis which the chapter places on balancing opposing interests through a conciliation process has meant that the Council has not devised any clear set of rules, e.g. for dealing with compensation in cases of unwarranted dismissals, or with reinstatement. The approach is pragmatic, and the emphasis on modification of the employer's prerogative rather than the development of new principles.[1]

Some gaps in the scope of these arrangements also lend point to the view that the employer's prerogative and the interests of production are still paramount. The chapter makes no provision for financial compensation during periods of lay-off from work. Nor does it

[1] Up to 1961, the Council had had about forty cases referred to it: of these the majority were settled by the parties or by the Council secretaries, before the Council had met to discuss them. Fourteen cases were examined by the Council. On one case no agreement was reached, and in thirteen the Council arrived at an agreed opinion. Seven of the cases dealt with dismissals of individual workmen for alleged negligence, and six cases concerned dismissals or lay-off because of a shortage of work. The cases are reviewed in Schmidt: *Tjänsteavtalet*, pp. 142–8, and in *Fackföreningsrörelsen och företagsdemokratin*, pp. 44–48 (Stockholm, 1961).

provide arrangements for compensation payment, severance pay, in the event of redundancy. These matters are still at the discretion of the employer. LO is now dissatisfied with this state of affairs. It argues that the modification of the employer's prerogative, and the balancing of interests through conciliation, does not go far enough. It wants to replace the existing arrangement with a new principle, which would require the employer to show *objectively acceptable grounds* for dismissals. How these would be defined in detail is in LO's view a matter for negotiation. Given a clearly defined set of objective criteria, LO would then change the function of the Labour Market Council from that of a conciliation body to an arbitration instance, with powers to issue legally binding decisions in disputes about lay-offs and dismissals. These criticisms mark a major shift away from the compromise thrashed out in 1938, which modified the sovereign position of the employer, but retained the emphasis on production as having priority over social and family considerations. LO is developing a full employment philosophy which advocates *both* a flexible economic structure, *including* a mobile labour force, and security of employment against *arbitrary* action by employers.

III. SALARIED EMPLOYEES

Salaried employees have had, and still have, much more job security than manual workers. Against the normal period of notice of seven or fourteen days for manual workers, the basic period of notice for salaried employees is one month from both sides, with longer periods of notice geared to length of service. It rises, for example, to a maximum of six months from the side of the employer and three months from the side of the employee. Individual arrangements for notice which depart from such collective norms must usually not be less favourable to the employee. It is possible for the employer to terminate the employment relationship at once where, to quote the metal trades agreement for salaried employees, an employee has 'been sentenced for a criminal offence, acted contrary to the law in the course of his duties, is guilty of gross negligence or lack of skill or if, despite reproofs, he has been guilty of repeated neglect or has otherwise materially neglected his obligations to the employer'.

This broad list of potential misdemeanours can clearly allow differences of interpretation, and the accusation of abuses has led in recent years to a clamour for safeguards against 'unjustified' dismissals of salaried employees.[1] In 1957 Riksdag motions asked for

[1] For a TCO study of the subject, see Lennart Geijer, *Rätten till arbetsplatsen*, TCO's skriftserie 6 (Stockholm, 1956). In December 1957, TCO produced a set of standard rules which it recommended its member unions to follow in obtaining

permissive legislation to protect salaried employees against unjustified dismissals, but they were rejected with the argument that this was a matter that ought preferably to be regulated by agreement. The Union of Clerical and Technical Employees in Industry and the Foremen's Union have subsequently succeeded in having some protection incorporated in their respective Basic Agreements. But it is a very limited protection.

The Union of Clerical and Technical Employees has recognized that cases of notices of termination of employment which it has felt compelled to bring to the attention of SAF employers have been few, and in its Basic Agreement and that for foremen the rules apply only to cases where there is *no* dispute about the legality of the notice of termination given by an employer. Cases of 'unjustifiable dismissal' are *not* covered. The agreed procedure is that each side has the right to take cases of notice of termination of employment of salaried employees with at least twelve months' service to their Labour Market Council for an expression of views, after local and central negotiations, *and* provided there is no dispute about the legality of the notice given. The rules suggested for the guidance of a Council are similar to those in the SAF–LO agreement, in that suitability of the employee is the primary criterion, and length of service and family responsibilities subsidiary considerations. One major difference from the SAF–LO procedure is that any pronouncement made by a salaried employees' Labour Market Council is made public.

One other significant difference in treatment, arising from the traditional distinction between salaried and manual employees, is that it is generally agreed that salaried employees cannot be laid off. There is no explicit mention of lay-offs in the rules devised for white-collar workers, and the implication of the provisions made in agreements for salaried employees in the event of disputes between manual workers and employers supports this point.[1]

In addition to these agreements for manual and salaried workers, protection against arbitrary dismissal is provided for certain categories of workers by legislation. The Seamen's Act provides safeguards, workers' safety representatives are protected, and arbitrary dismissal

security of employment for salaried employees through collective contracts. In principle, the rules were to apply to all salaried employees; at least fourteen days' notice of any dismissal was to be given to the local club or representative of salaried employees; dismissals that could not be justified on objective or subjective grounds were to be declared invalid; rules providing for damages should be incorporated. *None* of these provisions was incorporated in the agreement signed two days later by SAF and SIF which precipitated the breach within TCO.

[1] A typical formulation is: 'If a conflict has lasted for at least three months, and if it is not possible to provide full employment for salaried employees, salaries may be cut by 10% per month until they have fallen to 60% of their original level, with corresponding reduction in the number of working hours.'

is banned in circumstances connected with marriage, confinement, and military service.

VI. DEPLOYMENT OF THE LABOUR FORCE

In addition to the interests which the individual employer has in controlling and allocating his labour force, and the individual worker and union in obtaining job security, a wider perspective on the demand for and supply of labour immediately suggests that the rules discussed here are important for labour mobility as well. This has been increasingly recognized in the full employment society. Since 1944 there have been agreements between industry[1] and the National Labour Market Board, a government agency, setting out a procedure governing the closing-down and curtailment of productive operations. The essence of the agreement is that advance notice of such action is to be given to the authorities in good time, so that the labour exchanges can re-deploy labour in an orderly manner. Notice of anticipated dismissals or lay-offs takes place through management informing (in confidence, if it wishes) the county labour board or taking the matter up personally with the county labour director. Announcements of definite closure or a complete shut-down for more than fourteen days are to be given at least two months in advance, and similar notice, or as much notice as possible, is to be given where activity is to be curtailed, short-time working is planned, or there are to be abnormal reductions in a seasonal labour force. The country labour authorities inform the National Labour Market Board of reports received, so that a national picture of labour force changes is obtained. Within the firm, the Works Council will also take up the management's proposals.

The significance of the provisions in Chapter 3 of the Basic Agreement thus lies not only in the safeguards against arbitrary dismissals and the machinery devised for having warning and obtaining discussions on the dismissals. These are important in the light of the workers' traditional demands for security. Equally important, however, is the emphasis which the provisions lay on production, and flexibility in the use of labour. This, reinforced by the labour deployment provisions discussed above, has become increasingly recognized as essential, and as an important consequence of the shift to full employment. LO now argues that the hoarding of labour and the concealing of unemployment by short-time working are

[1] The signatories from the side of industry are SAF, The Federation of Swedish Industries, the Industrial Production Council, The Commerce Employers' Association, and the Co-operative Movement Bargaining Organization. The National Labour Market Board has urged groups not covered by the agreement to abide voluntarily by the procedures it sets out.

pernicious, and its policy is to encourage mobility through dismissals and transfers. The workers have the protection—though LO now wants more—against arbitrary action which the agreements discussed here give, and they can therefore afford to look at the problem of job security on the broader canvas of efficient deployment of labour. The Labour Court, too, has taken this point. As a rule, it argues, when a shortage of work can be expected to last for some time an employer should not lay-off workers. The correct thing is to dismiss them and thus inform them that they should seek work elsewhere.[1]

It can be said in conclusion that a comprehensive code has now been evolved in Sweden to protect workers against arbitrary action from the side of employers. Having provided the code, the labour market organizations can now afford to look at the deployment of labour in a more rational and economic manner, free from the preoccupations with the vexed questions of victimization and arbitrary dismissals.

[1] Judgement 1958/4.

CHAPTER XII

Works Councils

THE provisions of the Basic Agreement dealing with job security are confined to the specific issues of dismissals, lay-offs, and re-engaging of staff. But the scope of job security has now been widened, and given a more collective emphasis, through the movement towards industrial democracy. Worker influence in production and other problems of the firm, on which job security in the narrower sense ultimately depends, has become the focus of attention since SAF and LO concluded an agreement on Works Councils in 1946.

Industrial democracy is not a new issue in Sweden. It evolved naturally out of the new constructive era in industrial relations which began with the Basic Agreement, but this was in fact the third phase in debates about industrial democracy. In discussion of this theme in Sweden there has never been any great preoccupation with fundamental philosophical or moral concepts based on the Dignity of Man. The primary emphasis has been on practical matters, on increasing production, and on the contribution which the workers' influence on the running of a firm could make to increased efficiency. Swedish industrial democracy has a strong economic basis: soap-and-towel democracy is not dismissed out of hand, but is regarded as a means to increased production and thereby higher real incomes, rather than as an end in itself.

The first period when there was a lively interest in industrial democracy coincided with the post-war international boom in the subject after 1918. Various aspects of the problem were probed in Sweden, but one clear distinction was made which has persisted. When the minority social democratic government of 1920 appointed a committee of inquiry to study industrial democracy the emphasis was placed on stimulating production, and the committee was not empowered to discuss 'social ownership'. (This was taken up by a separate committee, and soon dropped.) There was little interest in the workers taking over production.

The committee produced a report[1] which led to abortive legislative proposals for advisory works councils. Some of its ideas, though tentative, developed an approach which finds echoes in the 1946 Works Council Agreement. It emphasized the twin requirements of

[1] *S.O.U.*, 1923 : 29 and 30.

the workers being given the opportunity to become acquainted with the economic position of the firm and with sales, technical, and financial administration, *and* on the workers equipping themselves to take advantage of the opportunity. The emphasis in the proposed works councils was on encouraging production, and the councils were to be internal to the firm, with no local, district, or national councils. The committee was critical of Whitleyism for not paying much attention to production problems, and for emphasizing the national councils rather than the works committees. It felt that in Sweden it was probably wiser to begin building from the bottom. At the works level, the councils were to be based firmly on the unions and have a worker majority, but no powers to make decisions. There were no provisions for co-determination on job security, the issue which the workers felt most keenly.

Interest in the unions was lukewarm. LO said it was prepared to accept legislation on the subject. But the unions were mainly preoccupied at the time with developing the system of collective contracts, which made considerable inroads into the employer's sovereignty. On the employers' side the fundamental objection made was that industrial democracy was not an appropriate subject for legislation, and the best path to follow was that of developing the collective agreements system. In fact, the time was not yet ripe for industrial democracy of the kind discussed in the commission report. With the benefit of hindsight, it can be seen that it was more appropriate for the Basic Agreement to come first.

The second phase began in 1928, when the new conservative government sponsored a conference to discuss the possibilities of voluntary co-operation to improve relations in the labour market and within enterprises. The background to this labour peace conference was the interest of Mr Lübeck, the Minister of Social Affairs, in promoting an understanding of economic and industrial subjects. The Mond conference also acted as a stimulus.

A report issued in 1929 by the delegation appointed after the conference emphasized the need for better information and better contact between management and men as two things which were essential for making labour relations more peaceful. Reports on accidents and industrial safety were subsequently produced by a smaller committee.

When the LO congress decided, against the advice of the secretariat, to withdraw from the committee after the Ådal incident, LO seemed interested in keeping the co-operation alive.

It is difficult to say what developments in this field might have taken place as a result of the labour peace conference if the Ådal incident had not occurred and the Great Depression had not arrived.

In addition, other problems soon became more pressing, e.g. the place of neutral third parties in industrial disputes.

The LO congress in 1936 marks the beginning of the third phase, and ideas of industrial democracy and collaboration were given a major stimulus by the form and content of the Basic Agreement. The whole atmosphere then became much more favourable for subsequent discussion of industrial democracy. LO and SAF reached agreement in 1942 on safety arrangements at the workplace, and in 1944 they signed an agreement on vocational training. Both required collaboration at the workshop level, as did the chapter of the Basic Agreement on lay-offs and dismissals. A more subtle pressure was the development by the social democratic party of an economic policy which aimed at ensuring that the workers obtained a fair share of any efforts they made to increase production and productivity.[1]

The general appraisal of the role of the trade union movement in society which the LO Committee of Fifteen undertook produced the dictum that the general process of democratization could not stop at the factory gates. Social and economic developments increasingly justified the demands of the unions that the workers should be guaranteed the right to participate actively in planning, and in solving the internal economic, technical, and administrative problems of the firm.

This impetus was lost in the war, however, although great interest was shown in the British joint production committees, until post-war development began to arouse new discussion. On what terms was the trade union movement prepared to help in achieving more efficient production? Should the workers have the right of co-determination in production problems? The Post-war Programme of Swedish Labour stressed economic democracy in the workplace both as an end in itself and as an aid to productive efficiency, and envisaged that the workers' demands for industrial democracy would be resolved by agreement, failing which by legislation.

Some thought was also being given to the matter on the management side, even before the war. The industrial democracy that mattered was that everyone in a firm should feel they belonged together. The impetus must come from management.[2] This was part of the new spirit of co-operation being fostered between the organizations. In 1945, too, employers examined the problem of improving

[1] Torvald Karlbom, in *Industriell demokrati*, p. 4 (Stockholm, 1946), suggests one of the reasons why LO and the unions had previously been content to approve industrial democracy in principle was that 'the strength of the parties in the labour market or on the political front has not until recent years been such that it "paid" to bring the question into the forefront of desirable reforms'.

[2] See Söderlund and Brunius, *Två anföranden i LO's skola*, July 19, 1937.

management-worker understanding through the provision of more information, and a report was produced.[1] A positive attitude was evolving in some employer circles to the problem of better contact, and 'an intelligent policy of adaptation'[2] was being pursued in response to worker claims for more influence. In 1945 also SAF agreed in principle to LO's request that the labour market committee should discuss industrial democracy. Nevertheless, many employers were very sceptical about such a departure.

Salaried employees also entered actively into the discussion of industrial democracy, and TCO appointed a committee to study the matter from the particular point of view of the white-collar worker. As a result, the Agreement on Works Councils which SAF concluded with LO in 1946 had a counterpart (but dependent at that time on the SAF–LO agreement) for salaried employees. Since 1958 the two agreements have been revised; the current version is analysed here.

I. OBJECTS OF WORKS COUNCILS

The Works Council Agreements set out limited and essentially practical aims for the Councils. They are meant to provide a framework within which constructive help can be given from all sides in improving the economic position of the firm, and in providing the employees with some insight into the working of the enterprise. The Council is not intended to be an instrument in bargaining about the distribution of the product. To put the point in another way, the unions are now so strong on the distributive side of the employment relationship that they can afford to adopt, and do adopt, a positive attitude to production problems.

Emphasis is placed on (*a*) the plant nature of the Council, the rule being that there should be one Council within each firm in any locality, and (*b*) the union basis, in that only organized employees are affected by the agreement and qualified to participate in the election of manual and salaried employees' representatives. The agreements apply only to firms in which at least half the employees belong to organizations that have accepted it (the 50% rule), but the high organization percentage and the industrial unionism principle make this rule unimportant in practice, at least for manual workers.

Councils are not compulsory, but are to be set up in enterprises employing at least fifty workers if the employer *or* the workers' local organization requests it. For firms with less than fifty workers the

[1] *Kontakt och samverkan inom industriföretagen. Riktlinjer för intern information.* SAF and The Federation of Swedish Industries (Stockholm, December 1945).

[2] The phrase occurs in *Metallarbetaren* (the journal of the Metal Workers' Union), 1946, no. 1, p. 3.

organized manual workers may select 'enterprise representatives' for consultative purposes if the branch of the union so desires.

The Works Council is an organ for *information and consultation*, and is thus purely advisory. The intention is that any important decision affecting the firm and its personnel should be preceded by consultation in the Council. It has the following tasks, which focus on the twin issues of production and workers' security:

(1) to maintain continuous co-operation between employer and employees in order to achieve the best possible production;
(2) to give employees an insight into the economic and technical conditions of operation and into the financial position of the enterprise;
(3) to promote security of employment for the workers, and safety and satisfaction in connexion with their work;
(4) to encourage vocational training within the enterprise;
(5) to work in other ways for good production and working conditions;
(6) to promote order and discipline in the workplace and work for good relations between management and employees;
(7) to promote economy in the use of personnel and material within the firm.

In order to fulfil its purpose of promoting production, the Council deals with questions of the technique, organization, planning, and development of production, with particular emphasis on utilizing the experience and insight of the employees. To provide it with an adequate diet, the employer is obliged to supply the Council with *continuous* production surveys, including reports of changes undertaken or planned, or other important alterations in operating or working conditions within the firm, and of new products, new methods of manufacture or operation, and other technical arrangements. Information is regarded as an essential prerequisite for insight and constructive help. However, the employer need not reveal information which could damage his business.

The employer also has obligations concerning the economic position of the firm. It is his duty to give the Council regular information about business trends and the state of the market in the industry, though with particular reference to the firm, and to supply information about the economic aspects of production and possible sales. LO has recently suggested that manpower surveys should also be included. The Council is entitled to obtain the balance sheet, profit and loss account, administration and auditors' reports, where the publication of these is required by law. Again, the employer need not reveal information which could damage the business.

The supplying of information by the employer has a counterpart in the work of the Council. On the basis of the information, the employees' representatives in the Council may make *suggestions* to the employer. Employees may also submit for the consideration of the Works Council suggestions for changes in methods of working or other arrangements or measures for the benefit of the enterprise. The Council has the right to assess the value of these suggestions and to consider whether the suggestions should be rewarded if the employer accepts them. An addition introduced in the revised 1958 agreement has endeavoured to strengthen the role of the Council in suggestions activity, by stating that the Council is enjoined to discuss the amount of a reward before the employer reaches a decision. The Council is also expected to discuss practical ways of running suggestions activity, e.g. through setting up a suggestions sub-committee. One limitation on suggestions by salaried employees is that suggestions arising out of the normal and special duties of the salaried employee cannot be taken up. Other suggestions by salaried employees may be examined by a suggestions committee or by the employer and salaried employee representatives, not by the whole Council.[1]

II. COMPOSITION

Membership of the Council is internal to the firm, and varies with the size of the labour force and the proportions of manual and white-collar workers. Where the manual workers form a majority they may elect a maximum of seven representatives and the salaried staff a maximum of five, depending on size. Where salaried employees form a majority of the staff the same maximum is set for both groups, three, five, or seven members, depending on labour force size. The employer can appoint a maximum of seven members, and has a *de facto* right to appoint the chairman from among his representatives.

[1] There is a narrow dividing line between suggestions and inventions in some cases. The Inventions Act of 1949 defines an invention as something that develops a new principle and can be patented. The main compulsory provision is that an inventor is entitled to a reasonable reward. Inventions are classified in four types, in three of which the employer has certain options on the use of the invention. The fourth category comprises inventions which have no connexion with the employer's activity and have not been developed in connexion with the employee's job. These clauses of the act are permissive and only apply where an agreement governing inventions is not in force. Since 1946 there have been successive agreements between SAF and the Union of Clerical and Technical Employees in Industry (and for supervisors) which regulate inventions made by salaried employees. An arbitration board with an impartial chairman is provided. In 1947 an advisory bureau for inventors, financed partly by the government and partly by the interest organizations, was set up which gives advice and information on patents and inventions, and assists in the development of inventions and the drawing up of applications for patents.

Neither the salaried employees nor employer side can form a majority group in the Council.

The employees' representatives are elected through their union branch for periods of two years, with only members belonging to a union which has signed the agreement having a vote. An indirect system of election may be used in larger firms. In the selection of members an effort is to be made to ensure representation of different kinds of worker and departments. LO recommends that at least one or two local union officials should take part, and this is in fact made necessary by the rules governing lay-offs and dismissals. Salaried employees' representation should always include a foreman.

The intention is that the Works Council should be called by the chairman to an ordinary meeting every three months, after due notice, with provision for fewer and more frequent meetings by mutual agreement. When special business comes before the Council it is possible for it to call on experts from within or outside the firm, and it is empowered to appoint sub-committees, e.g. to deal with suggestions. It can also set up sub-councils for departments within the firm.

As a contact organ the Council *as a whole* has the task of making the results of its work known in an appropriate manner to the employees, subject to the qualification that a Council member may not reveal or make use of any knowledge of a technical or economic nature which he has acquired by virtue of his office and which he knows to be a professional or business secret, or which the employer has particularly stipulated is not to be revealed. The revised agreement of 1958 suggests that at least once a year the whole staff of the firm should be given the opportunity to obtain some account of the Council's activities.

III. SPHERES OF INFLUENCE

The Works Council agreements have tried to clarify possible demarcation problems with other groups within the firm. The first and most important of these is that with the unions. The Council is not entitled to deal with disputes about collective contracts or the regulation of working conditions which are normally dealt with through unions. This intention, of preventing the Council from taking over recognized union functions, has proved workable in practice, because it has been brought into a discussion of potentially burning issues of union grievances. On security of employment, for example, the Council now forms an essential part of the machinery for handling both individual and collective job security for manual, but not salaried, employees. The person to whom the employer gives information about any planned changes in his labour force is one of the worker members of the Council, which may take up the matter on the request of either side. The Council discusses any proposed reductions or closures.

Another encroachment on trade union work could arise from the requirement that the Council is to promote good order and discipline as one means of encouraging production. The accepted view here is that it should confine itself to general questions of order and discipline, and avoid cases of individual breaches of discipline, which are taken up by the union and employer under the procedures of collective contracts.[1] Since it has no powers of decision, there is no question here of the Council becoming a court martial in front of which the foreman may be called to order, a fear expressed by the Supervisors' Union at the time the 1946 agreement was concluded.

The emphasis on production means that the Council is bound to have contact with, and it is intended to provide a focus for, committees in the firm set up under other central agreements, e.g. the 1942 safety agreement, the 1944 vocational training agreement, and the 1948 work study agreement. In matters of safety and health the Council co-operates with the safety committees and representatives. It is now urged to take an active interest not only in apprentice training but in all aspects of vocational training, and co-operate with the appropriate vocational training representative in the firm. He is called to attend Council meetings when it is discussing training questions. Under the work study agreement the Council can take up matters of *principle* concerning the arrangements for and practice of work study, but not questions which touch directly on wage-fixing. In all these contacts the Works Council is also a co-ordinating body. Disputes about spheres of influence have been avoided by making its central consultative position explicit in the agreements. In practice, however, the Council has not been given a very prominent role in co-ordination of this kind. It generally has little to do with work study problems.

IV. THE POSITION OF SALARIED EMPLOYEES

The original SAF–TCO agreement of 1946 on Works Councils was dependent on the SAF–LO agreement for its acceptance, validity, and content, and could only apply in firms where the SAF–LO agreement had been accepted. The salaried employees could not themselves ask for a Works Council to be set up. Since 1958 the revised SAF–TCO

[1] Alvar Odholm, *Kommentar till 1946 års avtal om företagsnämnder*, p. 31 (Stockholm, 1947), and Ernst Ahlberg, *Företagsdemokrati*, p. 87 (Stockholm, 1947).

agreement has existed in its own right, parallel to and not dependent on the LO agreement, and salaried employees organizable in TCO can take the initiative in forming a Council. The change illustrates the changing composition of the labour force in favour of salaried employees, and the growth in their numbers and strength of organization since the war.

Certain parts of the arrangements do not apply to salaried employees. The rules about security of employment apply to LO-affiliated union members only, and there are special provisions governing suggestions made by salaried staff. The 'in-between' position of salaried employees has led to some problems, arising out of the close historical relationship with employers, and also because of the channels of communication which the Works Council may both create and by-pass. Salaried employees were hesitant at first about participating in Works Councils, and their experience of and contribution to the working of the Councils have not been altogether satisfactory. It has not always led to greater interest and participation.

The foreman occupies the most delicate position of all the salaried employees, since by definition he is at one and the same time the firm's agent and the workers' link with higher management. Foremen were initially doubtful about the wisdom of the Works Council Agreement, though the Foremen's Union was in fact first in the field with an explanatory book about Works Councils,[1] and emphasized the positive contribution they could make. None the less, the foreman and the line system of communications can be by-passed by the Works Council, particularly in the conduct of suggestions activity.

V. CENTRAL ORGANS FOR WORKS COUNCILS

Under the Works Councils Agreement the central organizations assume the obligation of working for the acceptance of the agreement by their affiliates, and become bound by it as a collective agreement when their members ratify it. There has been some dissatisfaction in practice with the failure to place any explicit obligation on the national unions and associations to work actively in support of Works Councils, and the 1958 version of the agreements stresses the key position of LO national unions and SAF members in following and actively promoting local Works Council activity, and where possible appointing someone to be responsible for Works Council work in the union.

But no district, industrial, or national councils have been set up in the SAF–LO sphere.[2] The only central body with powers in this field

[1] Ernst Ahlberg, op. cit.

[2] The other SAF–LO agreements on particular problems have all established some sort of new central co-ordinating body.

is the Labour Market Council set up under the Basic Agreement. It acquired additional powers under the 1946 agreement:

(*a*) To act as a board of arbitration in disputes about the validity or correct interpretation of the provisions in the two agreements.
(*b*) To take up and settle disputes as to whether certain courses of action conflict with the agreement. Any disputes about the right of association remain the prerogative of the Labour Court.
(*c*) To act as a board of *reference* in disputes about dismissals, lay-offs, and re-engaging of workers.
(*d*) To promote and guide the activities of the Works Councils.

In fact, the Labour Market Council has not played the part of a continuing clearing-house for stimulating their activities, and SAF, LO, and TCO have each channelled their Works Council activity through special Works Council departments. The informal day-to-day contacts at this level make a formal central agency superfluous.

The absence of district or industrial councils from the SAF agreements has sometimes been deplored.[1] The big advantage claimed for co-ordinating boards at the industry level is that they would help to develop uniformity of procedure and stir up the laggards. This relates to the criticism that there is not enough exchange of good suggestions between firms in the private sector, because of business rivalries between privately owned firms, and this has sometimes been contrasted with the system-wide adoption of suggestions in the public sector, e.g. Swedish Railways.

On a larger canvas, councils have also been suggested as a means of exercising pressure for rationalization on less efficient and small-scale industries. Such uses of Works Councils in the SAF sector are not, however, in keeping with the letter or spirit of the agreement, which is essentially 'grass roots' consultation. The Works Council is not intended to exercise pressure. It is more appropriate, in the light of division of functions, for the trade unions to use their bargaining strength to promote rationalization of industry on the basis of the experience in productive efficiency which Works Councils give, rather than to use them explicitly as an instrument of controversial policy.

[1] In the co-operative movement and in State-owned companies central boards exist which have essentially the same function as the Labour Market Council under the Works Council agreement. Prior to 1958 there were agreements on Works Councils for most types of government activity, but in 1958 a new central agreement was concluded which provides more uniformity in arrangements than existed previously in government activity. The agreement sets out general provisions, which are supplemented at agency and departmental level by provisions to meet the special circumstances of each case. See *Svensk författningssamling*, 1958, no. 662.

It is not the intention that the sanctions of the Collective Contracts Act should be used for breaches of the Works Council agreements. SAF, LO, and TCO agree not to raise any such actions against one another, or at the national union level, since this would be contrary to the constructive spirit of the agreements. Failure to give notice of dismissals, laying-off or re-engaging of manual workers, and also (since 1958) failure to call the regular number of Council meetings, have, however, been specifically mentioned as examples of default which can lead to claims for damages at the local level. The idea here is to have in the background sanctions which will not be used, but which provide an incentive to make the agreement work.

VI. THE SUCCESS OF THE AGREEMENTS IN PRACTICE

The SAF–LO–TCO agreements were concluded at top level, and it has been necessary to conduct propaganda in favour of works democracy and provide instruction on the subject-matter of the agreement. This has not been wanting. In addition to the central organizations' special departments, some national unions and associations have full-time officials dealing with Works Council problems. Courses are held at all levels, an avalanche of printed material and films has been launched, a regular quarterly publication on Works Councils is produced by LO for general use, campaigns have been conducted, and national radio and television contests on suggestions activity have been sponsored by SAF, LO, TCO, and the Ministry of Civil Service Affairs. At the SAF college at Yxtaholm, where courses are provided for employer members of Works Councils, it is customary for trade unionists to lecture and take part in discussions.

The SAF agreements have been followed by similar arrangements in other sectors, central and local government, the co-operative movement, and in branches where non-manual work predominates, such as banking and insurance. But the SAF agreements set the pattern and are quantitatively the most significant.

Numerically, Works Councils developed very rapidly from mid-1948, and LO calculates that by 1959 there were about 3,700 Councils in sectors covered by its member unions, out of a possible estimated maximum of 4,000 Councils. By 1951 most industrial and government activity was well planted with Councils, and increases can only be expected in forestry, agriculture, building, commerce, and transport, all sectors where the units of production tend to be small and scattered. Progress with the establishment of 'works representatives' has been less satisfactory, in view of the large number of firms (nearly 8,000 in industry alone) in Sweden that employ fewer than ten workers.

Various surveys have been made in an attempt to discover how the work of the Councils is progressing and can be improved in the light of practical experience. The 1958 revision of the SAF agreements stemmed from such surveys. But it is extremely difficult to find precise measuring-rods for the success or failure of Works Councils. Most of the assessments use doubtful criteria. LO relies for its judgements on a standard report form which the branches send in to their national unions, but no standards are defined for assessing the activity and efficiency of Councils. The material is subjective and largely impressionistic, reflecting not so much how the activity of the Council is progressing, but rather how the workers' representatives in each Council think it should be conducted. Only the general tone of Works Council activity can be deduced from the intermittent reports, though this is of course useful in highlighting weaknesses in the formal arrangements of the agreements.

The difficulties become clear if some of the main points with which Councils are concerned are examined. There has been general disappointment on the LO side at the failure in many cases to meet at least four times a year, and thus provide for continuity in activity. But number of meetings is not a very reliable criterion. The agreement provides for fewer or more frequent meetings by arrangement, and the number of meetings does not of course give any test of quality and effectiveness. Clearly, however, regularity of meetings is important if the Council is to have any continuing perspective on the firm's activities. In general, large firms tend to have more frequent Council meetings than small firms, perhaps because the problems of communication are more satisfactorily solved in the latter. Failure to meet regularly is often the fault of an unenthusiastic chairman (employer).

It is also difficult to measure their success on the basis of specific tasks, like information and suggestions activity. Information has been one of the hoary chestnuts of the industrial democracy debate. Much of the demand for workers' participation has sprung from the feeling that the employer concealed essential information from his workers. Under the Works Council agreements information provides the staple diet of the Council, since it is on the basis of information that production and security of employment are to be discussed. LO reported in 1959 that about 80% of its Councils were satisfied with the quality of information. The workers' representatives in 50% of Councils reported that the timing of information was satisfactory, though this is a considerable improvement on earlier years, reflecting the efforts both LO and SAF have made to encourage information. LO has a research department which issues material, SAF publishes general accounts of the economic situation, and other organizations also participate in providing data about the economy. Legislation also encourages disclosure by employers of essential information. The Companies Act of 1948 applies to most of the economy, by employment and turnover, and it requires, within the framework of the balance sheet and profit and loss statement, that the administrative report should comment on and account for significant developments in the firm's activity during its financial year. Since 1950 disclosure of total income from sales, information on the rateable value and insurance value of property, machinery, and stocks has been required, in order to facilitate an analysis of asset structure. Even in firms which are not obliged by law to publish their accounts the Works Council is entitled to receive certain information.

Though the law has been developed in the direction of considerable social accountability for business firms the law and accounts can provide dull fare unless the employer fulfils the obligation, implicit in the Works Council agreement, of making information full yet simple. This can be costly, and involves great skill and a definite technique. More fundamentally, it must deal with the future as well as the past. But the obligation is not one-sided. The council members are expected to become aware of the law and accounting concepts involved, so that the information given may be understood and used to good purpose. Both SAF and LO make strenuous efforts to give guidance both in the giving and receiving of information. The seriousness of purpose here leads to the curious paradox of campaigning on the one hand for shorter hours and longer holidays, and on the other loading the spare time of the workers with exhortations to improve their grasp of business terms and operations.

At one point the information obligation places the workers' representatives in an ambivalent position, since the employer can divulge information to the Works Council with the proviso that it is confidential to it. The reconciliation in one person of the dual role of council representative and union official can be difficult. One early employer complaint, that the information given might be used in wage bargaining, is now less heard. The trends to national wage bargaining and the growth in professional expertise at the centre have made it clear that bargaining ammunition can be obtained from many other sources.

The counterpart of information is suggestions, on production and economic matters, social and safety questions. Production suggestions have predominated, while suggestions on economic matters have never been very great, and amenity suggestions, which began at a high level, tend to be non-recurring in character. Between 1954 and 1959 LO noted a tendency for the number of firms with suggestions activity, and for the number of suggestions, to fall, but in both

The 1961 LO report[1] on the subject clarifies the trade union movement's position. LO considers that there is a place for advisory, consultative Works Councils, whatever the type of business organization, and it recommends that the Councils should retain their existing status as advisory bodies. But it does not see the Councils simply as a meeting place for the polite exchange of views, but as an important forum and form for participating in the formulation of policy for the firm. LO envisages that consultation with the Council might be made obligatory, before management takes decisions, on a wide range of subjects which do not directly affect the management of production, sales, purchases, and accounting. Thus it clearly recognizes that the executive responsibility of management must reside in a single body.

On the wider, and wilder, claims to comprehensive co-determination LO makes three points which help to focus the debate. First, the trade unions already have co-determination on a range of issues, such as wages and hours, that are governed by collective bargaining, by law, and by social pressures on business firms. Moreover, progressive management has conceded that on such issues collective bargaining is constructive and helpful to management. Secondly, there are limits to co-determination on the part of the unions if they are to avoid the risk of a clash with fundamental trade union values. In matters of any economic significance, co-determination might place the unions in the incompatible positions of opposition and government at one and the same time. Nevertheless, LO considers, thirdly, that co-determination could conceivably be approached, *not* through the Works Councils, but through the development of some sort of corporate management, which would administer 'the common property of society', and be equally responsible to society, the employees, the consumer, and the owners of capital. But such a development would, in LO's view, necessitate a complete change in the existing organization of enterprises and in company law, which is based at present on the ownership of capital. It is in this direction, and not through Works Councils, that LO sees the long-term prospect of change to lie.

This approach is echoed in other quarters. The social democratic party is extremely empirical in its approach to co-determination, and envisages a type of economy with both a private and public sector, in many cases competing with one another. Recent writings from this quarter have stressed 'insight' and 'control', and pointed to a possible solution of workers' influence through private companies becoming foundations, without owners.[2]

[1] *Fackföreningsrörelsen och företagsdemokratin.*

[2] See, for example, Ernst Wigforss, *Socialism i vår tid* (Stockholm, 1952), and *Kan dödläget brytas?* (Stockholm, 1959): *Medbestämmanderätten i företagen* (a symposium) (Stockholm 1956): and *Inför 60-talet* (a symposium) (Stockholm, 1959), especially pp. 85–95.

VII. CONCLUSION

Despite the difficulties of finding reliable indicators of the success of the Works Council institution, it can be said that the 1946 Agreement has served a useful purpose in stimulating interest in the objectives it was designed to promote. It has helped to improve relations between business firms and their employees. There are several explanations for the overall vitality of the Councils. The Agreement is an astute one in the objectives it formulates, in the delimitation of spheres of influence, and in the organizational link with the unions on which it builds. The strength of the labour market organizations also explains its success. Historically, the development of joint consultation in Sweden has come about in the most practically acceptable fashion, *after* the employment relationship had come to be closely regulated by a strong system of organizations and collective contracts. Both sides know they have great bargaining strength and well-integrated organizations. They can now afford to allow Works Councils, and also the other special agencies for collaboration at works level, to develop as useful supplements and part of the superstructure. There is little likelihood of the Councils developing into local and independent cells.

The Swedes have not been slow to absorb ideas from abroad on industrial democracy, and British experiments with Whitleyism, Mondism, and Joint Production Committees have been influential. The German experience of co-determination has also been studied closely, if somewhat dispassionately. These foreign impulses have always been adapted, however, to the Swedish environment, and a strongly realistic strain has pervaded all the discussions of joint consultation. The idea of bargaining about distribution in one institution, the union, and promoting production through another institution, the Works Council, is proving fruitful.

PART V

Collective Bargaining in Action

CHAPTER XIII

Employment Agreements

IN this chapter we shall examine the main characteristics of the collective bargains through which the supply of and demand for labour services are regulated. Three main types of agreement are sufficiently distinctive to merit consideration: (*a*) collective contracts for manual workers; (*b*) collective contracts for salaried employees in the private sector, which tend to differ from (*a*) by *not* including salary tariffs; and (*c*) the salary plans which apply to many employees of central and local government. The differences within and between these groups in the degree of flexibility they permit, particularly on wage and salary rates, pose some of the most difficult problems for a comprehensive pricing or wages policy. Among such a mass of employment agreements we cannot hope to do more than discern and indicate broad classifications and contours.

We begin with the system of collective contracts for manual workers, which is the predominant system, both historically and quantitatively. The number of these collective agreements, and their coverage in terms of employers and workers, has increased steadily in the twentieth century, apart from a slight decline in the five-year period following the strike of 1909. It was the workers who took the initiative in demanding collective contracts, but the employers, after some early hesitation, quickly began to favour a wide coverage in contracts. The metal trades national agreement of 1905 was a landmark in setting out basic national wage provisions and bargaining procedures, and in 1907 SAF persuaded LO that sympathetic action was allowable for the purpose of extending the scope of contracts. In 1960 about 25,000 contracts were in force for LO unions alone. National agreements have come to dominate the bargaining scene. In 1907 there were only nine national agreements, but for LO unions alone 334 national agreements were in force in 1960, covering 64% (810,000) of LO members; 24% of LO members were covered by 18,000 local agreements (71% of the total), while local agreements explicitly depending on national agreements accounted for 27% of the agreements, but only 8% of the LO members.[1]

[1] The distinction between local agreements and local agreements *depending* on national agreements is more apparent than real. Many local agreements are to all intents and purposes dependent on national agreements, though the fact that they are concluded with unorganized employers, who may follow the big national agreements, makes them *formally* independent of national agreements.

District agreements have declined in importance, and are now insignificant.

The national agreement for the metal trades, which covers 160,000 union members directly, is the largest national contract. At the other extreme, the Building and Municipal Workers' Unions are by far the largest patrons of local agreements, accounting for 55% of the workers directly covered by local agreements. Again, however, in these two sectors the main terms of employment are settled nationally, and the agreements are only local in the formal sense, because of the nature of the employing authority or the structure of the industry.

There is great variety in the content of contracts, mainly because of the nature of the activity they cover but, by contrast to early agreements, the modern contract provides an extensive code of complex and detailed rules. A broad distinction can be drawn between general (non-wage) and wage provisions. Many of the general provisions reflect legislation on hours of work, holidays, accident and sickness insurance, and rulings of the Labour Court, while the rules of LO and SAF, and agreements between them, e.g. on the handling of dismissals and negotiating machinery, apprenticeships, safety rules for accident prevention, and work study, find expression in some form in agreements. The legislative provisions are often applied locally, by agreement between the parties about the allocation of hours of work, shift-working, and overtime, while national agreements usually deal specifically with clauses governing tools, dirty work, work carried on in another place, travelling time, and protective clothing. These general provisions are of course important for both the employer's costs and the worker's overall employment 'package'. But it is mainly with regard to the wage provisions that the collective contracts provide a wide range of different systems, varying in flexibility from agreement to agreement, and with differing degrees of centralized control over the wage systems used at local level.

I. METHODS OF WAGE PAYMENT

In systems of wage payment the main distinction is that between time wages and piecework, although the gulf between them is bridged to a very great extent by the fact that piecework rates are meant to preserve some relationship to time rates, while time rates are frequently supplemented by additional compensatory payment where the work cannot be measured by the piece and paid by the results achieved.

Pervading the whole wage system in Sweden is a positive attitude to and desire from all sides for piecework. Almost all collective contracts provide that piecework is to be used wherever possible.[1] In the 1880s and 1890s the trade unions were on the whole opposed to piecework, but they had to fight a campaign on two fronts, against employers who were interested in payments-by-results systems, and workers who opposed hourly wages because piecework gave greater individual freedom. When they had become strong enough to put forward and force through contractual proposals, the unions accepted piecework systems.[2]

The number of hours worked in industry by manual workers on payment-by-results systems, which are defined to include all wage systems where earnings are dependent on performance or product, is shown in the following table as a percentage of the total hours worked:

PERCENTAGE OF HOURS WORKED IN INDUSTRY ON INCENTIVE SYSTEMS

Year	*Male Workers*	*Female Workers*
1945	50	54
1950	59	59
1951	60	58
1952	59	57
1953	59	58
1954	60	59
1955	61	60
1956	63	60
1957	63	60
1958	62	61

Source: *Löner* Social Welfare Board.

By industry, piecework is most prevalent in dockyards, shipbuilding (88%), paper and pulp manufacturing, mining, iron, steel and copper works, and engineering, and is low in food processing, bakeries, and printing.

[1] The following eulogy, from the local authority sector, is typical: 'When work is paid by results on the basis of a well-constructed system of payment, an enhanced performance on the part of the worker can generally be expected, and the supervisor can devote himself more to the planning of the work and control of quality and less to supervising the workers. Even if the desire for higher wages is not regarded as the sole stimulus to enhanced performance—there are of course many reasons for a good performance apart from the desire to earn money—it must nevertheless be observed that performance wages play a large and important part in the Swedish labour market. It is now considered desirable wherever possible to endeavour to develop a greater interest in his work on the part of the employee by allowing enhanced performance to be reflected in higher earnings.' *Ackordshandledning*, p. 3 (Svenska stadsförbundet, 1959).

[2] Tage Lindbom, *Den svenska fackföreningsrörelsens uppkomst* (Stockholm, 1938), Chapter 7, Fackföreningsrörelsens avtalspolitik.

Despite the overall stability of the piecework percentage in the past decade there have been some significant increases in its use in bookbinding and in food and drink.

Wage payments in industry are usually based on the hour as the unit of time, though payment by the week occurs in some industries (e.g. printing), and in building the payment is eventually averaged out over the period of several months normally required to complete the job. The time wage takes two main forms. The *standard wage* states what the wage is per unit of time. Often the standard wage is no more than a high basic wage, which is supplemented by cash or percentage payments for skill. *Minimum rates* are common in a number of industries, e.g. the metal trades.

II. MINIMUM RATES

Minimum rates are the basic time rates, less than which no one must receive. They are collective in the sense that the labour force covered by a contract is divided into categories by skill, age, and sex, with lower rates for female than for unskilled and skilled male workers.[1] The division into categories is often quite crude, and may in machine-paced work simply be a broad division as between skilled workers (with age-experience classes) and unskilled workers. The newspaper industry agreement for compositors has seven categories, some of which contain various craft skill groups or semi-skilled groups. The metal trades agreement has two age-experience and four age categories for male workers, and four age categories for females, but makes no attempt to define a skilled worker beyond stating that he is someone who does work for which an apprenticeship or other training of three years is necessary.[2] The steel mills agreement gives detailed lists of occupations which are included in the two main skill groups covered by the contract. In nearly all contracts the minimum wage for any category is differentiated by cost-of-living zone.

The exact level of the minimum wage set as a floor for a category of workers or jobs tend to vary inversely with the prevalence of

[1] SAF and LO agreed in 1960 to remove sex categories from agreements over a five-year period. See below, p. 286.

[2] The historical explanation for the absence of craft designations in this agreement is that the Metal Trades Employers' Federation insisted, when the first national agreement was concluded in 1905, that payment was to be made by *skill* and *competence*, not by the material worked upon. A general definition of a skilled worker was also held to be impossible. See George Styrman, *Verkstadsföreningen*, pp. 130–1, 2nd edition (Stockholm, 1946). Since 1955 a more explicit job classification system has been permitted at the local plant level which takes account of some typical *job* evaluation factors, e.g. training and experience, judgement, initiative, responsibility required in doing certain *jobs*. Systematic job evaluation can also be used locally in accordance with the centrally agreed system.

piecework. In the food industry and brewing, where there is little piecework, a relatively high minimum weekly wage is set. Compositors have a very high minimum weekly wage. In engineering and the metal trades, where there is a lot of piecework, the basic minimum wage is set lower.

III. INDIVIDUAL SUPPLEMENTS

The minimum rates provided for categories are supplemented by provisions that allow for *individual* hourly wages, consisting of the minimum wage for the category plus an *unspecified* amount (a minimum sum or percentage) for each *individual* worker, based on his skill, experience, and competence. This gives the hourly rate *for each individual.* The national metal trades and steel mills agreements do not, for example, specify these rates, or define criteria for skill and competence in detail. They simply state that 'according to diligence and skill, the individual worker receives a higher wage, and competent workers who have worked several years in the industry enjoy a wage higher than the minimum'.

IV. PIECEWORK

Supplementary to the minimum wage provisions with additions for individual age and competence, and consistent with the desire for piecework, is the concept of *piecework compensation.* This is partly a technical payment made when the work does not lend itself to an incentive system, and partly a penalty payment which management makes because it has not introduced payment by results. Piecework compensation provides that workers who cannot be given piecework, temporarily or permanently, are to be paid an hourly compensation payment of an amount such that the total of the compensation plus the individual minimum hourly rate exceeds the latter by at least a certain sum or percentage. This compensatory payment is usually not so finely differentiated by groups and cost-of-living zones as the minimum wage categories, and thus it narrows differentials between workers who are not paid by results. The outcome is an effective guaranteed hourly rate.

Piecework Tariffs. Piecework tariffs are usually related to the individual hourly rate, which provides the basis for calculating piece rates. These are set so that they make it possible for the worker's earnings per hour to exceed the hourly rate by a certain percentage (varying with the level of the minimum), or make possible a certain level of earnings for a trained adult worker operating at normal speeds; or they may aim at giving a certain level of earnings per hour. These earnings are not guaranteed, but simply a guide to the earnings target, and again are usually less differentiated by groups than the minimum rates.

Systems for payment by results vary, but all are based wholly or in part on the quantity of work. Pure and direct piecework is used where there is a close and uniform relationship between input of effort and output of work. The building industry price lists provide a pure piecework system. But more common than pure piecework are *mixed* or *premium* piecework systems, which give scope for a variety of individual and group incentive methods, through a combination of a certain fixed sum of money per hour and a certain price per unit of quantity. The time taken to produce a unit then becomes fundamental, and gives rise to a great deal of time study. Systems with a low fixed part and a high variable piecework supplement are often intended to provide, and to show to the worker that they are providing, more scope for individual performance earnings than systems with a high fixed base and low piecework supplements according to the quantity produced.

From this array of clauses earnings per hour can under some agreements ultimately emerge, therefore, as individually determined wages that comprise (*a*) a minimum wage for the category; (*b*) an individual skill supplement; (*c*) piecework compensation when payment by results is not possible; and (*d*) piecework payment when the work can be measured or timed in a way that provides a reasonably uniform relationship between effort, time taken, and output of the individual, group, or factory. Overtime and shiftwork premiums vary a great deal between contracts. Overtime payment is usually stated to be a percentage addition, but there is tremendous variety in the detail which agreements give about the precise percentages, the number of hours for which particular percentages apply, and the hours of the day affected. Shiftwork premiums are such a vast bog that it is impossible to generalize. No particular system or payment is normal or typical.[1]

The significance of the various components of earnings in industry is shown in the table opposite.

Column *A* of the table also shows how important incentive systems are in enhancing earnings. In 1958 basic hourly earnings (concept *a*) for men were 17% higher for those paid by results than for those paid by time rates. There were important differences between industries, however. The paper and pulp industry had only a 3% differential of this kind, while in metals, mining, quarrying, wood manufacturing, and beverages and tobacco it was 20% or over.

[1] One of the conclusions of an inquiry conducted by LO in 1958 into shiftwork was that shiftwork premiums varied from 0 to 100%.
See *Fackföreningsrörelsen*, 1958, II, 196–205, especially p. 203.

COMPONENTS OF AVERAGE HOURLY EARNINGS IN INDUSTRY, 1958, FOR ADULT MALE WORKERS

	Percentages							Men	
	1	*2*	*3*	*4*	*5*	*6*	*7*	*A*	*B*
	Basic time and piecework rates	*Shift work*	*Overtime work*	*Public holidays*	*Vacations*	*Other benefits*	*Total*	*Basic piecework rates as percentage of time rates (a)*	*Percentage of total hours worked on incentive systems*
MEN									
1. Mining	90·4	0·8	1·5	0·0	5·6	1·5	100	122	66
2. Metal and Engineering Trades	89·4	0·7	0·8	2·9	5·9	0·3	100	120	68
3. Non-metallic Mining, Quarrying	90·7	1·3	1·1	0·4	6·1	0·4	100	126	64
4. Manufacture of Wood	89·5	0·4	1·6	2·6	5·7	0·2	100	120	58
5. Pulp, Paper, and Cardboard Mills	86·3	3·2	4·2	0·2	5·8	0·5	100	103	84
6. Manufacture of Paper Products, Printing and Allied Industries	85·8	4·8	3·4	0·0	5·5	0·3	100	116	10
7. Manufacture of Food	89·9	1·2	2·2	0·2	5·5	1·0	100	117	27
8. Beverages and Tobacco	89·9	0·8	1·6	0·2	5·5	1·8	100	122	24
9. Textiles and Clothing	87·6	1·9	0·8	2·3	6·0	1·7	100	107	58
10. Leather, Hair, and Rubber Goods	90·6	0·8	0·8	1·3	6·0	0·4	100	119	67
11. Chemicals and Chemical Products	88·4	2·7	1·4	0·5	5·8	1·4	100	108	54
12. All Industries	88·9	1·2	1·4	1·9	5·8	0·5	100	117	62

Source: *Löner*, 1958, Del II.

The Social Welfare Board classifies these components as follows:

wage concept *a*—column *1*.
wage concept *b*—*a*+columns *2, 3*.
wage concept *c*—*a*+*b*+columns *4, 5, 6*.

As column *B* shows, it is not always the case that piecework rates are high in relation to time rates in industries with a high proportion of piecework. While for industry as a whole 62% of hours worked by men were paid on incentive systems, some industries, such as beverages and tobacco, printing and food processing, had a very low percentage of piecework hours, but average or above average piecework rates in relation to time rates. At the other extreme, the paper and pulp industry had the highest proportion (84%) of hours worked on incentive systems, but piecework rates had the lowest premium (3%) over time rates. A great deal obviously depends on the extent to which the operative is able to affect the flow of output on incentive systems, and on the categories of workers in particular industries whose work can be brought into incentive systems of payment.

Size of firm has been shown to play an important part in the prevalence of piecework and overtime. Data of the type shown below are available only for the years 1950–3. The *pattern* suggested by these figures for 1953 also applies to the years 1950–2.

PIECEWORK AND OVERTIME BY SIZE OF FIRM, 1953

	No. of workers						
	1–10	*11–50*	*51–200*	*201–500*	*501–1000*	*over 1000*	*all*
PAYMENT-BY-RESULTS							
No. of firms (percentage of total) with incentive systems for men	35	60	84	92	94	100	59
No. of incentive hours (percentage of total hours worked) for men in these firms	50	53	63	68	75	77	68
OVERTIME							
No. of firms (percentage of total) with overtime working for men	38	75	93	96	95	90	68
No. of overtime hours (percentage of total hours worked) for men in these firms	2·6	2·6	3·1	3·9	3·8	3·3	3·4

Source: Social Welfare Board.

The emphasis on piecework clearly makes the arrangements for negotiating price lists and setting earnings targets fundamental. Three main approaches can be distinguished. First, national piecework price lists can be set, as in the building industry, a system which is discussed below. Secondly, piecework targets can be set in agreements, indicating the hourly earnings that locally negotiated piece rates should aim at. Thirdly, a formula may be used, as in the engineering and metal trades, which leaves the time for the job to be negotiated on the basis of work study at the plant level.

In the metal trades the following formula is given in the national agreement as a guide to the local piecework pricing taking place at the shop level through negotiations between the employer and the union branch or club:

$$X = t \times u \times \left(1 + \frac{s}{100}\right) \times \frac{p}{60}$$

where X is the piece rate in öre, t is the time taken for the operation in minutes, u is the equalization factor, s is the percentage addition for time lost, and p is the money factor in öre per hour. The time required for the operation is calculated by the mean value method. The equalization factor, u, is determined on the basis of the worker's performance during the observed study, and u is then $=1$ for the normal performance of an average experienced workman, >1 if the performance is better, and <1 if it is worse. The additional payment, s, for time lost is calculated in accordance with the necessary stoppages and wastage of time for the task being studied. The money factor, p, is arrived at nationally for different skills, age, and sex groups, and is usually less differentiated than the minimum wage categories. When a job is not studied by using the above formula, the money factor, p, is taken as the earnings target for the average worker with a normal performance.

Earnings can often differ from (exceed) those expected when money factors are set.[1] The time taken, t, may be reduced as the worker becomes more proficient at the task. The main criticism voiced against this type of formula in recent years, e.g. in connexion with the discussion of wage drift, has been that the time and other factors can in fact be faked (*fiffelfaktor*) in order to make X large enough to provide a level of earnings the worker will accept.

In the metal trades, departures from these formulae for calculating piecework rates can be allowed by the national organizations in exceptional circumstances, and other methods may be used locally by permission of the national organizations. Where group incentive schemes are in operation, the individual worker's share is determined in proportion to his hourly wage (which, as we have seen, is crudely weighted for skill and age) and the number of working hours he has participated in the job.

The building industry, like the metal trades, has a very differentiated range of products. Unlike the metal trades, however, where the main piecework price-fixing takes place on the individual shop floor, the building industry bases its wages system on *national* piecework price lists. In all, about 10,000 prices are listed in national piecework

[1] The 1948 agreement between LO and SAF on time and motion studies states quite explicitly that the use of such studies 'must not hinder the adaptation of piecework earnings to the zeal and skill of the individual worker'.

price schedules drawn up for the three main groups of jobs covered by the trades in the industry: masons and bricklayers, carpenters, and unskilled workers. Stockholm has separate price lists. All tasks covered by the price lists must be paid by results.

As tasks change and new methods are introduced, these price schedules are continually under surveillance by permanent price-list boards for each trade, and attempts have been made since 1956 to prune and simplify the lists, while retaining them as the basic feature of the wage system.

Because of the period of time required in building to complete most jobs before they can be measured for piecework payment on the basis of the price lists, the wages structure includes a basic straight hourly wage rate, which is dealt with very briefly in contracts. It varies for the skilled and unskilled groups, and is differentiated by cost-of-living area for each category.

Building work is carried out on the gang system. The worker is paid a *straight hourly wage* fortnightly in advance of the completion of the job. At the end of the job, or at three-monthly intervals, the work is measured and the price calculated by reference to the price schedules. Each worker then obtains a share of the proceeds (his *piecework earnings*) in accordance with (*a*) his trade, and (*b*) the number of hours he has participated in the task, less the amount he has already been paid fortnightly in advance.

The system has several interesting features:

(*a*) The total payment for the work is not directly related to the number of hours worked, but to the price set out in the price schedules. The workers thus have an incentive to complete the job quickly, since it is pure piecework.

(*b*) Jobs which are not carried out on the piecework scheme (covering on the average about 40% of the working time for the industry) are paid at an hourly rate, which is guaranteed if the job is *not* priced in the lists. In addition,

(*c*) When the number of hours worked by the gang and not paid by results exceeds one-third of the total during the job a piecework compensation rate is paid for those excess hours at the end of the job. This provides another time incentive, to try to have as many day-wage hours as possible recorded, while actually spending as much time as possible in doing piecework jobs. It is at this point that control of the wages system is weakest. So far, it has proved difficult to avoid this fall-back day wage, because of the difficulties of organizing a steady flow of materials and processes and therefore of piecework, and because the scarcity of labour encourages slackness in controlling hours.

(*d*) Workers who never have any piecework are automatically paid this piecework compensation rate in addition to their straight hourly rate.

(*e*) The division of the piecework surplus takes account of the skills as well as hours of the workers participating. The shortage of skilled workers has recently led (1) to the surplus shares being weighted more heavily in favour of skilled workers, and (2) to the division of the unskilled workers into three categories, in order to stimulate and reward specialization among them.

(*f*) The system can thus be made flexible to take account of demand and supply and of the prevalence of payment by results. Depending on the proportions of piecework to straight hourly rates in the three main craft groups, wage rounds allocate the total wage increases agreed in one or more of the following ways: (1) to straight hourly rates; (2) to the piecework price lists, either in the form of general percentage increases, varying for each trade, or in the form of revised rates for particular jobs in the lists.

(*g*) The main criticisms made of the building wage system are first, that earnings can vary considerably because of the organization of the work, which may facilitate or hamper rapid piecework. This is largely outside the control of the operative, as are other extraneous factors like the weather. Secondly, the incentive to work quickly on piecework to some extent simply shifts the point of supervision, from that of supervision of the execution of the work to close examination of it when it is completed. Thirdly, the price lists are criticized, not because they are national, but because they may not be adjusted quickly enough to changing techniques.

The interest being shown in other wage systems for the industry, and in work study, while retaining the essential piecework basis, suggests that employers and unions are now facing up to these problems, which have in the past caused a great deal of criticism of the building industry and its wage system.

In collective contracts in the public sector the attitude to piecework is just as positive as in the private sector. Local authorities have in recent years made big strides in introducing national job and/or price lists for piecework. In general, the percentage or cash supplements for piecework are more *specific* and closely regulated in the public sector, stating what the earnings level aimed at is, or the percentage supplements over time rates.

Piecework assessment is notoriously difficult, and the Swedish labour market has had its share of opposition to time and work study. The metal trades agreement provides rules to enable the workers to have some insight into the techniques used. They and their representatives are entitled to be given basic time-study data, and a bargaining procedure is provided for piecework disputes. Work study in general as an aid to wage determination has been made the subject of a special central Agreement of 1948 between SAF and LO. It provides for negotiating instances at different levels, and for a code of conduct for work study which was intended to overcome some of the distrust still prevailing at that time. It also places great emphasis on the psychological and physiological factors associated with work study, and stresses the importance of training for work-study personnel. There are similar work study agreements in public and co-operative employment, and in 1959 the building industry adopted the SAF–LO agreement as the pattern for its own work study agreement. One of the main difficulties has been the shortage of trained work-study personnel, a deficiency which has now been recognized and is being remedied through training courses. It is the system of payment by results itself, rather than work study as an aid to bargaining about rates, that has recently attracted most discussion.

V. WAGE DRIFT

The main advantages claimed for payment-by-results systems have been that they provide a productivity wage and a stimulus to production which straight time wages do not give, and that they eliminate the need for close supervision of the workers. There is now considerable criticism from both sides of the crudeness of the systems used, which has been shown up by 'wage drift'. The systems are flexible, by allowing increased effort and output and encouraging transfer to more productive jobs. But if the systems and rates are slack, and if the money factors are set at a low level, they can and do permit 'unjustifiable increases' as a result of '*fiffelfaktor*'.[1]

The phenomenon of 'wage drift' illustrates many of these problems. Wage drift can be defined as the difference between the actual earnings recorded in a sector during a period (e.g. a year) and the earnings which were expected to follow directly from the terms agreed under the contract for the period. It thus comprises the whole bundle of different kinds of wage changes (increases) which can arise in addition to these determined by, and following directly from, the agreement. Some of the components are:

(*a*) Increased effort on the part of the worker.

(*b*) Errors in estimating the outcome of an agreement. The complex agreements and wage structures often make it difficult to know what increase in earnings *does* follow directly from the agreement.

[1] For a criticism of these features of the metal trades wage system see the article by Åke Nilsson, chairman of the Metal Workers Union, in *Fackförenings-rörelsen*, 1960, I, 244–8.

(*c*) Small day-to-day improvements in production, e.g. organization, which improve earnings prospects for individual workers without piecework price lists being changed. Small technological changes taken individually may be small and insignificant, but taken together they may mean that rates are not changed when technological changes in fact warrant reductions in piecework prices. If there is a shortage of labour this may in addition be a direct inducement not to revise rates.

(*d*) Structural changes in production, by worker category, firm size and industry size. Workers move to tasks in the firm, in other firms, or other industries, that are already better paid.

(*e*) Deliberate upward revision of rates in setting new piecework prices, through slack rates or inefficient systems of piecework payment.

(*f*), related to (*e*): Black market extra payments, i.e. higher rates that are not the consequence of a change in work or in efficiency of work. This may be wage drift in a secondary or induced form, higher payment being made to hourly paid workers to restore differentials with piece-rate workers whose earnings may be creeping up under one or more of headings (*a*) to (*e*).

These induced wage changes may work their way through a firm's wages structure, through that of the industry and, in centralized bargaining at the SAF–LO level, may have an impact on the whole bargaining system.

In sum, certain of the forms of wage drift are earnings increases that result from better performance on the part of the workers, and these may be envisaged in the agreement or permitted by the structure of the agreement. The distinction between standard and minimum wage systems assumes that earnings will be above the minimum in the latter system. However, it is wage increases over and above 'legitimate' forms which are difficult to distinguish, and which attract the moral reproach of illegitimacy. Attempts are now being made to classify wage drift into *method* drift, which is technological and considered inevitable, and *market* wage drift, which indicates the equilibrium pricing of labour services taking place at the shop level. It has proved extremely difficult so far to separate and quantify the various wage drift components.[1] Wage drift is not confined to incentive payment systems, nor does it occur only among manual workers. Salaried employees in private industry may enjoy it, through their flexible salary system, through changing jobs, and obtaining higher

[1] *Löneglidning*, a report published by a joint SAF–LO expert committee in 1957, did not think it was possible accurately to distinguish the components.

starting salaries: while in the public sector it can occur in the form of upgrading.[1]

Some of the biggest stresses in the wages structure in post-war full employment have been caused through different systems of payment, and whether they allow earnings to drift upwards via the type of wage system used. Paradoxically, while there is much scepticism about the merits of payment-by-results systems, some of the strongest pressure to introduce such systems in recent years has come from groups which feel their earnings have lagged behind because they did not have flexible wage systems, e.g. the food industry,[2] and the compositors, who have argued in addition that the decline in their relative wage status has led to an exodus from the trade of the younger craftsmen.

While there has been no tendency for the overall percentage of payment-by-results to decline, greater emphasis is now being placed on a movement away from piecework systems to systems which give a more accurate assessment of performance. SAF stresses the need for flexibility and differentiation (though not necessarily wider absolute wage differentials), in the sense of rewarding skills. The existing piecework systems are not considered to be sufficiently precise and systematic in their present forms.

This point was recognized by the SAF–LO committee on female labour, which produced a report in 1951 arguing for the principle of wages in accordance with the value of the work performed.[3] Standardized wage rates make little allowance for regularity, steadiness in the job and trade, ability and willingness to undertake varying assignments, and all the other factors covered by the term 'interest in work'. Existing piece-rate systems did little justice to these factors. Logically, it argued, equal pay for work of equal value would mean differentiated piece rates. It went on to suggest—and recognized that this was a question that went far beyond its immediate interest in sex differentials—that wage differentials should be based on the nature of the job, *and* factors like regularity, adaptability, experience, length of service, training, and skill. The finer differentiation inherent in such a system was more suitable than the existing wage system for promoting production in a full employment society. This is essentially the crux of current discussion on revising wage systems, since it cries out for job evaluation and merit rating.

[1] For further data on wage drift in Sweden, see *Löneglidning*, SAF–LO, and Hansen and Rehn, 'On Wage-Drift', in *Twenty-five Economic Essays in Honour of Erik Lindahl* (Stockholm, 1956).

[2] There is a piquant contrast here with the inter-war years, when the food industry was one of the high wage groups in the unions' relative wages ladder. A branch of the Food Workers' Union argued that the reason for groups in export industries having relatively low wages was the use their wage systems made of payments-by-results! See LO *kongress-protokoll*, 1926, p. 175, motion no. 40.

[3] See *Arbetsmarknadskommitténs kvinnoutredning*, SAF–LO, 1951, p. 95 et seq.

There is accordingly a greater interest now in the use of work study, job evaluation, method-time-measurement, merit rating, and performance wage setting that is more 'scientific' in character. Since 1945 the metal trades agreement has sanctioned local systems of piecework pricing which allow a more differentiated wage setting where job evaluation can be used to take account of the nature of the job. The intention is to encourage skills. In building, too, there have been straws in the wind. Discussion of the building industry wage system has led to a number of experiments with new wage systems, e.g. 'the sliding premium piece rate', but all the experimental systems are still based on the national price lists. Work study is being used to rationalize the lists and to give added point to the intention that the system should reward performance.

VI. SYSTEMATIC JOB EVALUATION

The building industry is sceptical about introducing a systematic job evaluation scheme which might require as much constant reassessment as the present wage criteria, but it is at least interested in job evaluation as a possible approach. The same point can be made of industry as a whole. Ten years ago the attitude to systematic job evaluation was politely sceptical. LO endorsed a gradual approach.[1] Now there is greater interest at all levels in finding a more precise basis for wage differences than the rough-and-ready job classes explicit or implicit in most contracts. In 1957 LO estimated that job evaluation schemes existed in eleven unions covering 40,000 workers (3% of LO membership), and by 1959 covering 50,000 workers. Centrally agreed job evaluation schemes have been drawn up for the SAF General Group, for the metal trades, steel mills, and breweries, and a scheme developed by the employers' side is used in the paper industry. No system has yet been devised for use between groups and sectors. All the schemes have been applied locally, *and* jointly by management and workers.[2]

In the analysis of jobs, the requirements analysed are basic factors like training, experience, skill, responsibility, physical effort, mental strain, and working conditions. The Swedish systems developed so far mainly use a points system, and the qualities of particular jobs are weighted jointly in the attempt to find a measuring rod for judging the relative requirements of jobs when wages are being allocated. This assessment of jobs is quite separate from negotiations

[1] LO *verksamhetsberättelse*, 1951, p. 249, where it gave its views on a suggested job evaluation scheme for government employment.

[2] See LO aktuella frågor, no. 25, 1960—*Arbetsvärdering under debatt*, and Erland Lind, *Arbetsvärdering*, FKO meddelande, no. 32 (Stockholm, 1959), published by Ingenjörsvetenskapsakademien.

about the allocation of the wage bill and the rate at which payment for different jobs is graduated. It does not replace wage bargaining, but is intended to provide it with a more precise basis of knowledge about jobs and their characteristics than the crude classifications used in most contracts at present.

Complementary to job evaluation, which implies payment for the job according to the job requirements, is merit rating, payment for the job on the basis of individual performance. Assessment of the worker's performance can be based on a points system for evaluating factors like theoretical knowledge, practical experience, initiative, judgement, quantity and quality of work, economy in material, and utilization of machinery. Because many of these qualities of performance (e.g. quantity of output, efficiency) would be taken into account in a payment-by-results scheme, merit rating is likely to be used primarily for hourly paid workers with special skills. Systematic merit rating has only been tried experimentally so far, although the individual hourly supplements in collective contracts have long implied a rough-and-ready system of merit rating. The SAF General Group has worked out a scheme for manual workers, but not in collaboration with the unions, the Metal Trades Employers' Federation has constructed a scheme on a points basis, and in 1956 the Metal Workers' Union accepted merit rating in principle for hourly paid workers, but not for those paid by results. Merit rating is therefore not regarded as a substitute for payment by results, but as another aid to finding more precise measures on which to base differentiated payment by performance.

VII. COLLECTIVE AGREEMENTS IN THE PUBLIC SECTOR

There is much more uniformity about the general provisions of collective contracts in the public than in the private sector. In the main sectors of government activity like communications, covering railways, postal and telegraph services, power, roads, etc., and defence factories there are general rules for the whole sector, and these are supplemented by special contracts for each particular type of activity. The same is true of local government.

The general provisions cover negotiation procedures, dismissals, the right to organize, hours of work, shift work, overtime work, methods of calculating wage supplements, holidays, and a series of sections setting out the principles governing fringe benefits, which have traditionally been an important element in the employment package in public service. The social benefits cover accidents, sickness, confinement, military service, pensions and holidays, and the provisions usually run for a longer period than the wage terms of the contract. This helps to rationalize the bargaining process to some extent, for changes agreed in the general provisions can be easily incorporated in the special contracts.

Because of the general requirement of public accountability in government activity, the wage system is also tighter in public sector than in private collective contracts. The special contracts coming under the main agreements for public activity specify *in detail* the conditions and content for the particular types of activity they cover. For example, the contract for railway shopmen contains provisions arising out of the general agreement for government communications, and also provisions peculiar to that category. The workers are divided into skill groups, and *specific* percentage payments are set for shift work and overtime. Whereas the main agreement gives general provisions about wages, the particular contracts specify the rate for different groups. The central agreement for municipalities stipulates that the special provisions in the collective contracts for industrial, traffic, and other manual work coming under local authorities may not depart from the general provisions of the central agreement unless it expressly allows them to do so.

VIII. GEOGRAPHICAL DIFFERENTIALS

Geographical differentials designed to adjust wages for differences in the cost-of-living in different areas occur in most contracts and in salary plans.[1] Prior to 1914 geographical differentials occurred in some industries (e.g. metal trades and printing), but the first official classification of localities to serve as a guide to geographical real wages was produced in 1916, at a time of rising prices. This method of adjusting nominal wage rates in order to help to equalize real wages throughout the country among workers covered by the same contract has been used ever since, although the number of groups has been reduced, most recently in 1954 to four (three from 1962), in successive revisions of the official classification by the Social Board. The geographical differential (which is more accurately described as a statistical cost-of-living differential) was devised in the interests of equity, not to deal with local labour market recruitment problems, and can be (and has been) criticized from the point of view of subjective welfare. It is not easy to find an acceptable answer to the question which the inquiries pose: What does it cost in different areas to have the same standard of living?

Historically, there has been a tendency for the official geographical

[1] The cost-of-living zone problem applies not only to wage differentials. It arises in relation to taxation, pensions, government grants to local authorities, and thus has wide political implications. These are not discussed here.

differentials to narrow as regional differences in the cost of living declined, and the 1954 grouping provided for a span of 12%, by 4% intervals, between the cheapest and most expensive cost-of-living areas. This geographical differential is applied in its most rigid form in the public service, both on salary plan and collective contract employment. In the private sector almost every national agreement arranges its basic wage tariffs by reference to the Social Board inquiries, on the argument, which is supported by LO, that workers with similar jobs ought to be paid the same real wage in different parts of the country. However, there are considerable divergences from the 4% intervals and 12% range of the public sector, both in the differentials applied to the basic wage rates, and particularly in the differentials which emerge in earnings. In building, there is a 20% differential in the time wage plus piecework compensation between the highest group, Stockholm (which in this industry is placed in a separate class from the official grouping), and the lowest of the other four groups.

In principle, the geographical differential was not intended to be used as a market criterion, but it is so used in the private sector. Since 1957 the Civil Service salary plans have also been deliberately released from a strict adherence to the statistical index groupings for the explicit purpose of providing a market incentive to the lower salary groups. Civil Service unions argue, however, that this can only be one small factor in influencing the allocation of labour in local labour markets, and that other differentials are necessary if the public sector is to be able to compete with the much wider differentials which tend to prevail from group to group in sections of the private sector of the economy.[1]

IX. COLD REGION ALLOWANCES

Another form of geographical wage differentials is the cold region allowance, which occurs on salary plan and collective contract employment in the public sector. For the purpose of this payment the north of Sweden is divided into six cold regions, and within each region a *uniform* payment is made—presumably on the egalitarian assumption that in Kiruna cold feet are cold feet, no matter whose feet they are—to all who work in the type of employment covered, irrespective of their job, salary, or wage. Again, this particular payment is now being differentiated and graded by job and salary in

[1] An official committee which reported on the geographical differentials problem in 1957 favoured their abolition. See *S.O.U.*, 1957 : 42, *Löne-och skattegrupperingarna*. The problem is taken up in Chapter XVII for further comment.

order to provide an incentive for the recruitment and retention of labour in the far north.

Cost-of-living bonuses to allow for compensation for changes in the cost of living during emergencies have been used in some of the wage rounds since 1939, and are discussed in Chapter XV.

X. COLLECTIVE CONTRACTS FOR SALARIED EMPLOYEES IN THE PRIVATE SECTOR

These contracts have flourished remarkably since the legislation of 1936 encouraged bargaining by salaried employees. The main difference from manual workers' agreements is that they usually regulate general conditions of employment only, *not* salaries. General matters such as negotiation procedures, rights and duties in the event of a dispute between the employer and manual workers, procedures for dealing with inventions, are covered, as well as 'fringe benefit' provisions on holidays, sickness pay, and pensions. There can often be hard bargaining about these last provisions, since the law only provides a minimum, above which salaried employees wish to retain traditional fringe differentials. Formulae are given for percentage additions to salary for overtime working, but *not* the salary to be paid to categories of salaried employees or individuals. In principle, salaries in industry are negotiated locally and individually, in accordance with the policy that the great range in the position, duties, training, qualifications, age, and competence of salaried employees makes collectivized salary setting impossible and unacceptable.

Salary settlement is, however, far from completely atomistic. Uniformity is provided by organizations such as the Union of Clerical and Technical Employees collecting information from the individual members about the salaries carried by various posts in different firms, which it processes and makes available as a guide to them in negotiations.[1] SACO does the same.

Collectivism in a flexible form has been adopted in banking and insurance (here the employers are not members of SAF), where the type of activity makes possible a more uniform assessment of tasks and rewards than in industry. In banking, basic salary scales covering twenty-five years of service after a 2–3-year apprenticeship are provided for 'ordinary staff', with 4% geographical differentials. 'Promoted' employees are divided into five salary groups by function

[1] SAF also has extremely comprehensive salary statistics for its salaried employees, which can provide detailed statistical comparisons for the use of particular firms or categories of employees. A standard occupational classification system was agreed in 1955 by SAF and the Union, along with the Foremen's Union, and this provides additional standardization in making salary surveys.

and responsibility, and paid at least 10, 15, 20, 25, and 30% respectively above the tariff scales. Additional individual merit and responsibility payments are possible, at the discretion of the bank. In insurance, six salary classes with a length of service structure are established, with some overlapping between the classes, and employees are assigned to a class by job and qualifications. Salaried employees in the newspaper industry (which again is not in SAF) have salary tariffs for editorial staff.

Although the Union of Clerical and Technical Employees is opposed in principle to salary plans and tariffs, it has played a major part in the trend towards central salary recommendations since 1940. Central negotiations between SAF on the one hand and this union and the Foremen's Union on the other are now common. These negotiations lead to recommendations that general increases in salary of x% should be given throughout industry, and that individual age-experience and qualification increases should be adjusted by each firm. This means that the salary structure of each firm can vary from a statistical norm with the skill and age mix of its salaried staff. Normally, well-qualified salaried employees will receive the largest percentage increases within the firm, and the age-experience supplements will be greatest for the younger members of the staff. Thus considerable variety and differentiation of salary structure is possible for each firm, within the broad framework of general recommendations made at the SAF level, and salary drifting can readily occur.

SAF's policy is to favour individual differentiation of salary for all salaried employees, a policy accepted by the Union of Clerical and Technical Employees. The Foremen's Union has, however, tried to introduce a salary plan for foremen into the metal trades in recent years,[1] but the employers have resisted all attempts to develop a systematic grouping of foremen into salary groups. SAF has recently gone some way towards meeting the Foremen's Union's view that salaries should take more systematic account of job factors, through encouraging the use of aids like job evaluation and merit rating so that the system of setting foremen's salaries on an individual basis is an efficient one.[2]

Salary policy is a matter of urgency for the Foremen's Union, since almost the only remaining way in which the foreman can manifest his position, and secure a reward for his knowledge, experience, and judgement is through the salary he is paid. Most of his traditional differential benefits over the workers he supervises—pensions, sickness, and holiday pay—are being whittled away by social legislation. Meantime, most foremen have their salaries negotiated individually

[1] See Ernst Ahlberg, *Rätt Arbetsledarelön*, 2nd edition (Stockholm, 1954).
[2] *Arbetsledarlöner*, SAF (Stockholm, 1960).

or by the local club. Both the union and SAF collect and disseminate information about salaries as a guide to local bargaining.

XI. SALARY PLAN EMPLOYMENT IN THE PUBLIC SECTOR

The main feature of the bargaining pressures that can be used in concluding collective agreements is that economic sanctions are normally allowable, in both the private and public sectors. One of the traditional characteristics which is intended to distinguish employment on salary plan in the public sector is that such sanctions are very considerably restricted.

At the other extreme from the modified individual salary system in private industry, the terms of employees of the central and local government who are employed on 'salary plan' are just as much collectivized as those for manual workers through their collective contracts. Indeed, the salary plan system is much more tightly regulated than those manual workers' collective contracts, particularly those in the private sector, which allow scope for flexible wage supplements. The tightness of the salary plan system has made for considerable stresses within the national wage and salary structure.

Employment on salary plan in accordance with the terms of government regulations governing remuneration and conditions of employment is more common in the public sector than employment on collective contracts. Salary plan employment covers close on 300,000[1] and collective contracts 80,000 government employees. In local government the figures are approximately 90,000 and 110,000 respectively.

The broad distinction intended between employment on salary plan and on collective contract is that those employed under the terms of collective agreements can withdraw their labour. Most established civil servants are considered to be responsible officials and cannot use this sanction. However, this criterion of responsibility does not provide a clear demarcation line between the two forms of employment.[2] The general trend towards some form of collective contracts system for civil servants, which was discussed in Chapter V, will eventually simplify this issue.

The close regulation of both salaries and 'fringe benefits', duty allowances, and other remuneration, which the civil service salary regulations provide, can be illustrated by the main salary plan. Plan A, the structure of which was most recently revised in 1957,

[1] About 62,000 of these are employed in government-supported activity, e.g. primary school teachers and police.

[2] For the most recent report on this problem, see *S.O.U.*, 1952 : 3, *Löneplan eller kollektivavtal*.

covers over 90% of civil servants. It has twenty-six salary grades,[1] within each of which there are as a rule four salary classes. In all there are twenty-nine classes, since there is an overlap of classes between grades (e.g. grade 1 covers classes 1–4, grade 2 classes 2–5). The plan is systematized vertically so that each salary class has a salary differential 5·3% below the one above it. The top salary in any grade (covering four classes) is thus 16·7% above the lowest salary class in that grade.

Starting at the lowest class in a grade, there is promotion, usually at three-year intervals, from class to class, and advancement in some cases from grade to grade. In grades where advancement is infrequent personal up-grading by one grade can occur after fifteen years' service in the grade. Beginning at the foot of the grade into which he is recruited, the individual can move by the passage of time, through training, or promotion, at least some way up the salary plan. This provides a more refined grading system than a collective contract.

Each class within a grade receives a definite and fixed salary, which may not be varied up or down. Payment is by the grade of job, not by individual competence in the job, though merit can of course be reflected in the speed with which an individual progresses upwards through the grades. There is one horizontal differential, however, based primarily on the cost-of-living, but *not* (since 1957) solely on the criterion that the nominal salary is adjusted to give the same real wage, in the light of geographical fluctuations in the cost-of-living. Significantly, it has been adjusted in an effort to stimulate recruitment to the lower grades. The horizontal differential is now 16% in the lower grades, and is in part a town-country differential designed to stimulate recruitment in towns (generally the most expensive cost-of-living areas), and to compete with the private sector zone differentials, which are usually greater. In higher salary ranges, by contrast, where private differentials have been found to be less than those in the civil service, the zone differentials have now been reduced, and fall as low as 4%.

As was mentioned above, another market recruitment feature introduced in 1957 was that the traditional cold region allowance, paid on a flat *per capita* basis to all civil servants employed in one of the cold zones, has now been modified so that it is paid in proportion to salary.

Since 1957 the civil service salary plan has thus been made more flexible, and has features which appeal to all the civil service unions. SACO and SR are particularly pleased to have percentage

[1] The grades cover jobs ranging from a cleaner on a railway ferry to a bureau director. Job clusters make for a number of fairly self-contained groups of jobs and grades within the plan, with little vertical movement out of particular groups.

differentials between classes, while TCO and the LO cartel are more interested in the way in which the cost-of-living bonus provides a certain amount of compression of the salary structure in favour of the lower ranges.

XII. ALLOCATION OF JOBS TO GRADE

This now provides additional flexibility in the salary system. Grading of jobs used to take place at infrequent intervals through the appointment of a committee to make a thorough study of jobs and their grading, along the lines of a Royal Commission. A landmark in this procedure was that the committee appointed in 1949 for this purpose was empowered to negotiate with the unions about grading. Since 1957 a new approach to grading is being attempted. Periodic reviews did not take sufficient account of constant changes in the level and type of government activity. Grading questions are now divided into two main groups: A- and B-questions.[1] A-questions concern the placing in grades, on the basis of the existing grading norms, of jobs or groups of jobs as a result of changes in organization, or new activity. On these it is now recognized that the unions are entitled to be *consulted* before estimates are put before the Riksdag. B-questions involve new questions of principle about grading jobs—e.g. upgrading—and these are made the subject of *negotiation* during the year *before* which they are to be introduced. This too is an attempt to make the civil service salary and grading structure more responsive to changes in demand (government activity) and in the supply of the types of labour services wanted. B-list negotiations often cover large clusters of jobs in the plan. Employment on contract instead of salary plan has also been introduced in recent years, e.g. for civil engineers, to provide additional flexibility and competitiveness.

Broadly, local government employees whose conditions of employment are regulated by salary plan have followed the path marked out by the central government. A new salary plan similar to that in central government was, for example, introduced in 1957.

Two other aspects of employment agreements in Sweden are worthy of brief comment: profit-sharing and fringe benefits.

Profit-sharing does not strike a responsive chord in the hearts of unions and management. Apart from the usual arguments that profit-sharing identifies the worker too closely with the firm, and infringes solidarity, that profits fluctuate, that the share through profits is small, and that losses are not shared, the trade union movement takes the view that it is the function of the collective bargaining system to ensure a share in the profitability of economic activity.

[1] There are in addition C-questions, which refer to the general conditions of employment.

SAF considers that profit-sharing is a typical bargaining issue, and that profit-sharing schemes, of which few exist in Sweden, are contrary to the whole rationale of the collective bargaining system.[1]

There is a great range in different employment agreements both in the types of fringe benefit and their amount. Since about 1952 there has been a conscious effort on the part of the unions to obtain better social benefits, by legislation and through contracts, in the private sector. The public sector and the co-operative movement have traditionally been model employers in providing good social benefits, but various surveys made in recent years have suggested that there is a wider variety and greater prevalence of fringe benefits in the private sector than was generally supposed.

The most recent study made by SAF, for the year 1958, covered 93% of the staff employed by its member firms with more than 100 employees. Apart from confirming a tendency previously noted for higher fringe costs to occur in larger firms, this study found that, in addition to the cash wage paid for hours worked (which is the base used for the fringe cost calculations), fringe benefits averaged 19·9% of that base, and were 15·6% for manual workers and 29·2% for salaried staff. The big difference between the two groups arose mainly from the cost of pensions. Wages and salaries paid for the hours *not* worked (especially holidays, accounting for 6 to 7%) formed the largest fringe item for all employees, about 8 to 9% of the cash wage for hours worked.[2]

CONCLUSION

This discussion of the various forms of wage and other provisions which occur in the employment agreements of the Swedish labour market suggests that no characteristics can be singled out as having general validity. It is the differences rather than the similarities which are significant. There are, for example, considerable differences in the degree of control. The public sector provides the tightest system of agreements, with precise provisions on general clauses and detailed wage and salary scales. Salaried employees in industry have fairly standardized general and fringe benefit clauses, but individual salary provisions. Among manual workers in the private sector, there is great variety in both general and wage clauses, and the minimum wage system which occurs in many contracts gives the loosest arrangements both for rates paid and (in particular) the earnings obtained.

[1] For a study of profit-sharing in Sweden, see Torsten Skytt and Sven H. Åsbrink, *Vinstdelning och vinstandelssystem* (Stockholm, 1952).

[2] *Arbetsgivaren*, 1960, no. 11, p. 4.

It would be surprising if great uniformity could be discerned, since employment agreements have not developed in response to a deliberate and comprehensive national policy. What is surprising and suggestive in the private sector, *in the light of* SAF rules and the wages policy of solidarity espoused by LO, is the *laissez-faire* attitude to wages systems, whose merits and defects are only now being closely scrutinized. Even the LO unions and SAF Member associations have in many cases only the roughest of checks on the wages being paid at the plant level. The curious paradox of the wage contracts in the private sector is that the highly centralized organizations have allowed a very decentralized system of effective wage setting. This cannot be accidental. It suggests that these organizations cannot readily impose model wage structures and wage rates on the plant-level organizations. This is an important point, and one which will recur in Chapters XV to XVII, when we look at the problems which this wide variety in the methods of wage payments raises for any attempt to develop a systematic national wages structure and policy.

CHAPTER XIV

The Bargaining Process

PRIVATE and public arrangements for handling both justiciable and non-justiciable disputes have produced a very uniform and stable system of negotiation procedures.

Justiciable disputes arrangements can be dealt with quite briefly. The very nature of such disputes requires negotiation procedures which can deal with them promptly as they arise. Here the metal trades agreement of 1905 provided a framework which was to set a pattern for private arrangements. These have priority, for the legislation of 1928 specifically presupposes that private negotiation processes exist, and these procedures must first be exhausted at local and national levels before the Labour Court will take up a case.

Chapter 2 of the Basic Agreement builds on the private arrangements that had evolved, and tries mainly to ensure uniformity and codification of the provisions for handling disputes about working conditions. It provides first for local workshop negotiations, followed if necessary by negotiations at national union level. The emphasis throughout is placed on *urgency*, on having disputes made the subject of negotiation within two weeks at the local level and within three weeks of being requested at national level. Antiquated grievances cannot be taken up. If a dispute is not resolved by local and national negotiations, private arbitration or the Labour Court will provide a final settlement.

Private arbitration arrangements for justiciable disputes are quite common. We have already seen in Chapter X that the Basic Agreements developed for various groups of manual and white-collar workers provide detailed bargaining procedures, often for both justiciable and non-justiciable disputes. The building industry has a complicated system of private arbitration for handling piecework price disputes, made necessary by the prevalence of payment-by-results. Disputes about whether a price for a job has been fixed, or whether the job is to be carried out on time rates, are not taken before the Labour Court unless they cannot be divorced from other disputes before the Court. Instead, a permanent industrial arbitration board for price disputes, consisting of three representatives from the employers' side and three from the particular group of building workers (e.g. masons, carpenters) affected, plus an impartial chairman whom they choose, makes the final decision on disputes.

In local government it is not formally necessary for negotiations about justiciable disputes to be carried to the centre, e.g. to the Federation of Municipalities, though it usually happens that central negotiations take place at this level before a dispute between a local authority's wages and salaries board and a union or union branch is referred to the Labour Court. The Federation is anxious to introduce a formal requirement of negotiation at its level before cases can go to the Labour Court, in order to provide co-ordination of policy and interpretation. This is typical of the desire for order and uniformity in handling justiciable disputes.

In sum, the machinery for settling justiciable disputes is comprehensive, covering both private and public employment, it is swift, *and* it is peaceful.

I. NON-JUSTICIABLE DISPUTES

In these disputes, with which this chapter is primarily concerned, there are considerable checks and processes that must be exhausted before economic sanctions may be used. Negotiations must take place at local and central level, the parties may have to answer a call to mediation and to submit proposals for resolving a dispute, and they must give seven days' warning of direct action. In addition, the rules of organizations like LO and SAF provide powerful safeguards which govern the conditions on which their affiliates may commence the use of economic sanctions. But the important difference from justiciable disputes is that, unless by private arrangement, failure to agree on the solution of a non-justiciable dispute can lead to the use of economic sanctions. This is the fundamental collective bargaining rule of the labour market.

The main area of non-justiciable disputes is centred on the regularly recurring bargaining about new contracts of employment. We shall look mainly at collective bargaining for manual workers, and then very briefly at the procedures used for settling the terms of employment of salaried employees. The bargaining process is continuously evolving, and the main development in recent wage bargaining has been the central framework bargaining carried on at the SAF–LO level. However, it is not certain that this is a permanent innovation, and future bargaining may well alternate between centralized and union-level negotiations. Accordingly, it is worth saying something about bargaining at branch and union levels, though independent branch bargaining in particular is now rare and limited in scope.

II. BARGAINING AT BRANCH AND UNION LEVELS

The process is carefully controlled in union rules. Submissions to employers about drawing up or terminating contracts or for other changes in employment conditions can be made on the initiative of a national union or a branch, though it is much more likely in practice to be the former. Branches have a certain amount of initiative in negotiating and concluding contracts at the local level, but they are subordinate to the national union in that they can only propose changes after two-thirds of the members *affected* have decided in a *secret* ballot to do so, *and* the approval of the union executive has been obtained. When it asks for approval to begin negotiations the branch must submit a complete account of existing terms and the proposed demands. If an employer replies to a submission this must be passed to the union executive for its decision before the branch can take any further action.

When negotiations affect more than one branch the executive of the union is entitled to call (some rules say it must) a conference of delegates to discuss proposals. Usually these conferences are limited in size (e.g. to a maximum of 100), and only persons who are employed in the sphere to which the contract in question refers or is to refer, or who represent workers employed in that sphere, can take part in electing, and be elected, as delegates. The decisions of these conferences are only advisory: the union executive decides. A small bargaining delegation is elected at the conference to do the actual negotiating work with the employer. The Metal Workers' Union rules stipulate that working members and not officials are to form the majority of these bargaining delegations.

Formally, bargaining commences through the procedure of giving notice of termination of the contract, but in practice there is no difficulty about postponing the date for giving notice and prolonging the old contract until a new one is signed.[1] When bargaining has produced proposals for contracts, these are submitted to the members affected for examination, after which the union executive makes the final decisions about accepting them. All the forms used for consulting the union members are advisory. These forms vary, from a vote of the members affected to a delegate conference authorized to express views on behalf of the members. With the recent trend to

[1] Preliminary negotiations have sometimes been used in an attempt to reach agreement on a new contract without giving notice of termination of the existing contract. The object is to try to avoid the uncertainty associated with the termination procedure. Preliminary negotiations were first attempted in 1937. The rules of the Metal Workers' Union have since 1947 contained a provision that the results of preliminary negotiations do not go out to the members for a vote, but to the bargaining conference which drew up the proposals, after which the union executive has power to make the final decision. This rule is a reflection of SAF's insistence, when it agreed in 1937 to preliminary negotiations, that any results were not to be sent out for voting among the trade union members affected, since this introduced delay and uncertainty, which were inconsistent with the whole rationale of preliminary negotiations. See *SAF styrelse-och revisions berättelser*, 1937, p. 7.

centralized bargaining it is becoming more common for a conference to be called, in place of a voting procedure. The Typographers' Union has long followed the procedure of appointing a bargaining delegation for the period of years until congress next meets, and the Metal Workers' and Building Workers' Unions, for example, have recently introduced bargaining councils, appointed for a similar period, in place of *ad hoc* conferences.

If an employer has refused to negotiate, or negotiations do not lead to agreement, and if the workers wish to withdraw their labour, a secret ballot is taken. Even when the required two-thirds majority of those *affected* (not simply those voting) is obtained the union executive determines (through its power of veto, if necessary) whether and when a stoppage is to take place. The executive is entitled to decree a stoppage, and declare sympathetic action, whether or not it has been asked by the members, on the basis of the standard union rules governing strikes, lock-outs, blockades, or boycotts.

III. BARGAINING AT THE LO LEVEL

The full power of the LO rules revision of 1941 is brought to bear on wage bargaining procedures. In 1941 LO became entitled not simply to take part in the wage negotiations of affiliated unions, but also to present proposals for an agreement to the unions affected. Support can be withdrawn if the union(s) concerned object(s) to LO's proposals, but only if the conflict gives rise to, or can be feared to lead to, considerable inconvenience for other affiliated organizations, for the trade union movement as a whole, or for vital social interests. In developing a practical programme for bargaining, the 1951 LO congress agreed to set up a Wage Policy Council, now composed of seven members (a majority) of the secretariat. After a slow start it has gradually acquired increasing significance in co-ordinating the bargaining proposals which filter up through the unions. The bargaining conferences of individual unions are still important, however, particularly when LO agrees that a case has been made for trying to deal with particular groups' problems outside any general bargaining recommendations it may make.

On the employers' side bargaining preliminaries are usually much less publicized, but just as intensive and thorough. Since the 1914–18 war SAF has had annual discussions on bargaining policy for the ensuing year with its Member associations. It has not always practised a central co-ordinated approach, but it has (since 1905) been able to exercise strong powers over the contracts concluded by its Members and Partners. Employer bargaining delegations are usually compact, and often empowered to conclude agreements without reference to bargaining conferences, and in almost every case without reference back to the Partners of an association.

Given this framework of rules and institutions, and remembering that the government provides a mediation service, what is the procedure followed in arriving at contracts in the private sector of the labour market?

Almost all contracts now run for one or two years. This is mainly a reflection of the trend towards centralization that developed immediately before the Second World War, of the annual war-time index wage negotiations between LO and SAF, and, in recent years, of the period SAF and LO consider appropriate for the contracts they recommend.

The formal period of notice of termination of contracts is usually three months. In 1959 55% of LO contracts, covering 76% (972,000) of the members, had a period of notice of three months, and 29% of contracts, covering 14·3% of members, a period of notice of two months. The number of contracts with a period of notice of one, four, or more months' notice is thus small. Some contracts provide that notice of termination must not only be in writing but must, in order to be valid, be accompanied by proposals for a new contract. When negotiations have been conducted at the union level contracts have tended to expire at the end of the calendar year, except for 'seasonal' industries like forestry and building, but the experience of SAF–LO level bargaining suggests that the long-drawn-out negotiations are shifting the time-table forward to February.

A fairly definite annual or biennial fixture list can be traced for the timing of negotiations. That described here is typical for a wage round conducted at the LO–SAF level.

(1) During the early summer members of the government, employers, and union leaders begin to reflect in public speeches on the major aspects of wage bargaining for the coming calendar year, and to discuss the order of priorities among wage increases, pensions, shorter hours, and other demands that may be expected to arise. There may be a preliminary and informal exchange of views between SAF, LO, and (on occasion) TCO leaders.

(2) The representative assembly of LO meets. This is a practice which LO began in 1937 as part of the change-over to the wages policy of solidarity. General information about the economic situation is given, nowadays usually in the name of the LO Wage Policy Council, and the policy that seems advisable for the coming wage round is thrashed out on the basis of the economic situation and of the demands the unions have in mind. Any statements which the assembly formulates—these have been made public since 1947—are expressed as *recommendations* to the unions when the bargaining is

expected to take place at union level. If the outlook is uncertain the assembly may postpone making a definite policy statement until November. Since 1948 the council of TCO has normally met in the autumn as well for bargaining discussions.

(3) Informal discussions involving Ministers, LO, SAF, TCO, and the Federation of Industries may be held to discuss trends in the economy.

(4) In October or November the National Institute of Economic Research publishes a report,[1] which contains an *ex-post* analysis of economic trends and an assessment of likely developments in the coming year. This forms the basis for the autumn debate on the economic situation in the Riksdag. The Institute's views have varied in the direct references made to wage determination. In 1955, for example, the Institute pointed out that 'there is no objectively given scope for wage increases independent of the economic policies pursued',[2] while in 1959 it called down the wrath of LO upon its head by putting forward strong arguments for the view that it might be necessary to prolong the 1959 wage contracts in order to avoid cost inflation in 1960.[3]

(5) For agreements expiring at end-December the usual time for giving notice is September 30th, though the date can be postponed by mutual agreement, and the unions begin to draw up the line of advance which, in consultation with the branches, they have in mind for the coming year.[4]

[1] Since 1960 the Institute has begun the practice of making more frequent, quarterly, reviews.

[2] See *Meddelanden från konjunkturinstitutet*, *Serie* A : 28, 1955, p. 71. A similar point was made in 1956, *Serie* A : 29, 1956, p. 85.

[3] See *Meddelanden från konjunkturinstitutet*, *Serie* A : 32, 1959, pp. 127–30.

[4] The 1961 LO congress agreed to write into the LO rules the following procedures for conducting bargaining. The secretariat discusses the bargaining outlook well in advance of the date for giving notice of termination of the majority of the collective contracts of the affiliated organizations, and then recommends to the representative assembly that negotiations on new contracts should either be conducted centrally or for each contract area independently. Before the assembly meets for this purpose advisory conferences of union chairmen are held. If the assembly decides to accept a recommendation from the secretariat that negotiations should be conducted centrally the organizations affected are asked whether they approve the recommendation. If the secretariat thereafter considers that central negotiations are possible it is responsible for appointing a bargaining delegation and executing the negotiations.

When central negotiations are to take place the secretariat can ask the organizations affected for power to reach agreement with the employers' associations involved about postponing the dates for giving notice of termination and of expiry of all the contracts covered by the negotiations. If at central negotiations, agreement is reached between the delegations on each side the agreement is to be submitted to the representative assembly, which has to decide whether it approves or rejects it. Its decision is communicated to the organizations affected, and they have to decide, in accordance with their rules, whether or not they approve the agreement for their part. The secretariat is informed immediately of their decision.

(6) Advisory conferences of union chairmen and the secretariat are held, and the assembly of LO then meets again. It may recommend 'restraint', 'moderation', make policy declarations about prices, cost-of-living, women's wages, and other major facets of the bargaining pattern as it interprets them. It will also decide whether it wants to bargain centrally with SAF, or at union level.

(7) In December the unions submit demands, and bargaining begins. When bargaining is being conducted centrally at LO and SAF level each side will nominate a delegation consisting of about twenty-five persons, e.g. on the LO side the secretariat and some union chairmen plus the LO bargaining experts.

(8) In January the national budget division of the Ministry of Finance presents a report on economic trends (an Economic Survey) which may or may not give estimates of the likely scope for increases in incomes.[1]

The finance minister presents his fiscal budget to the Riksdag, and discusses the requirements for economic equilibrium in the light of the budget report. He may suggest what level of nominal wage increases is reconcilable with stability. On occasion, as in 1955, he has issued a severe warning about the limited scope for wage increases.[2]

(9) When bargaining is centralized, LO and SAF will eventually produce a framework agreement in which they recommend the level of earnings increases to be aimed at by the unions in their various agreements. (The details of these agreements are discussed below, in

[1] The following sample of its techniques is typical. In 1952 (see Översikt över det ekonomiska läget, *Meddelanden från konjunkturinstitutet*, *Serie* B : 14, 1952, it was pointed out (p. 64) that no estimate of private consumption had been made because wage changes were unknown. It added: 'Preliminary assumptions or arithmetical examples have proved of more harm than use, since they are readily considered as an authoritative pronouncement of an economically correct development of wages.'

Nationalbudget för år 1957 (*Serie* B : 21), p. 84, discussed three alternatives for income developments during 1957, because the outcome of wage negotiations was still unknown. No estimate of trends in private consumption was therefore made.

The preliminary national budget for 1959 (*S.O.U.*, 1959 : 31, p. 94) gave two alternatives for wage magnitudes in 1959, but stressed they were hypothetical. The preliminary budget for 1960 (*S.O.U.*, 1960 : 8, p. 52) used as a hypothesis for its calculations of wage movements the assumption that wage costs would rise in step with the increase in productivity. The preliminary national budgets presented in January have always suffered from the disadvantage of being drawn up (except when two-year wage contracts were in force) *before* the wage round had really begun in earnest.

[2] The 1955 pronouncement produced an equally sharp retort by the chairman of LO, Mr Strand, who was also a member of the Riksdag. In his view, there was no point in asking the unions to exercise 'restraint' for the purpose of maintaining equilibrium when booming economic activity and high profits had *created* disequilibrium, e.g. in the wages structure. See *Första kammarens protokoll*, January 19, 1955, pp. 17–22.

Chapter XV.) Alternatively, if bargaining has been decentralized throughout the round, the first of the important contracts, usually in the metal trades, will be concluded by about the end of January, and other agreements then follow in quick succession, frequently after use has been made of the mediation facilities provided by the government. Delay in concluding new agreements is usually not inconvenient, since it is the normal practice to postpone the date of expiry of the old contract until a new one has been concluded, and to back-date wage increases.

(10) Salaried employees in central, municipal, and private employment negotiate their increases. Since 1947 a general principle accepted for civil servants has been that their salaries should be kept in line with general wage movements.

(11) Agricultural price-fixing *used* to be a major sector for *bargaining* on income levels. The objectives for agricultural policy agreed in 1947 were largely social in character, and aimed at providing the agricultural population with a reasonable standard of living in relation to other sectors. In terms of detailed costing, both farmers and workers had a common interest in raising wages, since wage costs were automatically offset in farmers' cost calculations. A less rigid system was introduced in 1956, and since 1959 a further change has introduced a six-year agreement for agriculture which uses the incomes of industrial wage-earners as a direct guide for farming incomes. Thus, the consequences for farm incomes of changes in earnings in industry are now known in advance, and the emphasis for agricultural incomes is on fact-finding rather than bargaining.

This time-table has not hitherto been systematically drawn up, e.g. as part of a national wages policy, but has developed in a purely pragmatic way in response to institutional and market pressures. There has been a tendency for the institutional pressure groups to seek an advantageous place in the income queue, which has in turn led to the idea of equity in income distribution becoming very marked. Such equity is explicit policy only in the case of farmers, but it has gained wide acceptance in an informal way.[1] It is of course not simply institutional forces that explain the time-table. In the case of

[1] See, e.g. *Mål och medel i stabiliseringspolitiken, S.O.U.*, 1961 : 42, p. 85. 'In round numbers we can reckon that over 2·5 m. workers and salaried employees (about 2 m. of them organized) and about 350,000 farmers with family helpers have their incomes linked or related in various ways to the trend of incomes of industrial workers in the more profitable sectors. This amounts to 2·9 m., i.e. the largest part, of the working population. In addition there are over 900,000 old age pensioners. The only large group not included are professional people and *entrepreneurs* outside agriculture.' The issue was put somewhat more strongly by Erik Lundberg in *The Business Cycle in the Post-war World*, p. 72 (London, 1955): 'the strong inflationary bias of the Swedish economy, which is so well organized that only a small proportion of the population is left out and can be cheated.'

civil servants there is a market basis for their attempts to find a place in the time-table which does not lead to too much lagging in income developments.

IV. STAGES IN THE BARGAINING PROCESS

The actual process of bargaining between the parties may take various forms and pass through successive stages, somewhat along the following lines.

I. In December the first general meeting is held of the bargaining delegations from each side. In key industry negotiations LO and SAF would probably be represented, and would in any event be closely in touch with the bargainers on their respective sides. The leading employer delegate is usually appointed chairman, and a general discussion takes place in which each side puts its arguments about the economic situation in the light of wage and other statistics and the proposals and counter-proposals, which have usually *not* been made public in advance. This stage is essentially exploratory, each side trying to assess the strength and weaknesses of the other. Concessions are never made at this stage. Once this stage is well begun a general rule followed is that no publicity is given to the talks, and certainly not to any offers that may be made. The Press endures this embargo, but on the whole dislikes it.

This first phase may be the only one at which the large bargaining delegations actually meet and participate in the general discussions. Subsequently, and particularly in the LO–SAF central bargaining rounds, they may be employed in small groups in resolving special problems affecting particular contracts or clauses in contracts.

After the general discussion, the parties adjourn to separate rooms, and the chairman, who is at the same time an employer representative, communicates with each side separately, and through smaller groups of two or three members of the large delegations on each side. In SAF–LO bargaining, the 'small delegations' comprise the chairman, managing director, and deputy-managing director of SAF, and the chairman, vice-chairman, and secretary of LO. It is unusual for the parties to find a solution at once, and after a day or two the discussions will be adjourned.

II. At the second stage the isolation in separate rooms is resumed. Direct agreement between the parties may well be reached at this stage, and the vast majority of bargaining encounters end without additional stages being necessary. But if no agreement can be reached, several procedures are possible:

(*a*) Notice of direct action can be given. This is unlikely at such an early stage.

(*b*) The chairman can declare that the negotiations have broken down.

(*c*) The parties can agree to ask an impartial chairman to lead the negotiations. This is a highly flexible arrangement devised by the labour market organizations themselves, and not part of the 'official' mediation machinery. But it is much used. An impartial chairman may have been called in from the beginning of bargaining, and the parties may choose as an impartial chairman one of the official mediators, who will subsequently adopt the rule of a mediator if he cannot produce agreement as an impartial chairman. The impartial chairman may in this respect simply be a safeguard introduced by the parties to ensure that they obtain the special mediator they want, although they themselves cannot formally appoint a mediator.

III. If the impartial chairman has not succeeded in bringing about agreement, the bargaining moves to the mediatory stage. It is also possible for stage II to be by-passed, and for a special mediator to be brought in fairly early in the negotiations. Mediators may be introduced in various ways. A district mediator may be called in; in law he may step in on his own initiative if the dispute seems likely to be serious, but this is extremely unlikely in practice. When a special mediator is asked for, he may be drawn from the ranks of the district mediators and is then appointed by the Social Board (quite informally, particularly if he has already been acting as impartial chairman). But a special mediator can also be drawn from outside the ranks of the district mediators, in which case he will be appointed by the government on the recommendation of the Social Board.

In cases where a major dispute threatens the government may appoint a mediation commission. Special mediators and mediation commissions are intended to be *alternative*, not successive instances, in order not to undermine the position of the special mediator, but in practice they are sometimes used as successive stages. If they are, then the special mediator continues to participate, usually as chairman of the commission and always as a member.

IV. When the mediators have taken up and worked on the outstanding problems certain alternatives become possible. The mediator(s) may adjourn negotiations and send the parties a proposal for settlement. This is very rare. Alternatively, the mediator may, after putting out feelers, present a written proposal for settlement. This is (in theory) the critical point in mediation, for there is no mediatory function beyond this stage. However, recent experience belies this argument, for in the 1956 central negotiations LO did not accept the first proposal put forward by the mediation commission, while in 1959 both LO and SAF rejected the first proposal. The mediators tried again. The other alternatives, if no agreement is reached, are either a strike or lock-out (or both) after seven days' warning, or (and, as has been argued, this is *extremely* unlikely) emergency legislation or reference to the Labour Market Council under Chapter 5 of the Basic Agreement. In most cases the mediators will be successful in bringing about agreement.

If a proposed solution has been accepted by the parties at the bargaining table, they are then given time to consult their members. In central bargaining between LO and SAF the parties may reach preliminary agreement, though the agreements are technically only recommendations, and report back within a few days after consulting their members, e.g. the LO representative assembly.[1] When bargaining is conducted at the level of national unions and SAF Members, there has until recent years been a broad contrast between the two sides, in that the employers' representatives had a mandate to arrive at agreement at the bargaining tables (since SAF was usually represented at the table), while the LO union had to consult its members in one way or another. The trend in recent years towards the use of bargaining delegations and conferences on the union side is gradually removing the discrepancy, and reducing the delay which this caused in the past. Apart from the dilemma of union democracy,[2] the really serious bargaining disadvantage of delay from the workers' side was that the employer had not necessarily made his last offer when there was danger that the union bargainers might have to come back and, like Oliver Twist, ask for more. The workers' bargaining delegation has on occasion been placed in an ambivalent position, and the mediation system can also be thrown into disrepute. The building industry dispute of 1933 vividly illustrated this dilemma for the unions.

How good a bargaining system is this? The negotiation system in the private sector can best be evaluated from the vantage-point of the central bargaining system SAF and LO have devised since 1956, since it was intended to eliminate some of the disadvantages of high-pressure bargaining at the union level in the post-war years.

(1) The system was, and still is, undoubtedly time-consuming. If bargaining occurs each year—there have been two-year central agreements for 1957–8 and 1960–1, and a wage freeze in 1949–50—the bargaining process may take the greater part of the year, and leave little time for other problems of labour relations. This has been one of the points argued in support of longer-period agreements.

(2) When bargaining is conducted at union level, the timing of

[1] One feature of central SAF–LO bargaining is that union-level bargaining may have been going on simultaneously to iron out particular problems.

[2] The power of veto of union executives, the needs of representative democracy on the one hand versus demands for member influence on the other, have been discussed in Chapter I, on LO and union rules.

bargaining often counsels delay, until changes in the internal economy and international situation have become clear. There is a natural tendency to wait and see, and in particular to use the metal trades industry as a wage leader. In 1950–1, when prices were rising very rapidly, the outcome of union-level bargaining was partly dependent on the time at which agreements were concluded. It has on occasion paid to malinger.[1]

(3) The negotiations were and are frequently physically exhausting. One of the techniques practised by mediators has been to have all-night sessions at critical stages of the negotiations, not only because this makes the parties more amenable to (or, perhaps more accurately, less able to resist) conciliation, but because an agreement may be in sight, or the mediators and parties may have other negotiations to attend the next day. Complaints made against the system because of the strain it puts on officials of both sides, and the related point (under (1) above) that negotiations are time-consuming, are understandable, but the negotiation system is not intended for their ease and comfort, but for settling terms of employment for their members.

(4) A related point is that the bargaining process is frequently described as a tribal ritual. It is argued that the parties could often arrive at agreement sooner were it not that the members of each side have become so accustomed to witnessing the hard grind of prolonged negotiations and all-night sittings that they would feel their negotiators were giving in too easily if agreement were speedily reached. This is a half-truth at best, because there may be genuinely complex matters to resolve. The attempts now being made to bargain for the whole of the SAF–LO sphere through one central agreement usually involve immense technical problems for wage-setting in the whole of the private sector, and indeed the whole economy, which cannot be resolved without careful exploration. In the early post-war years the problems of central and long-term agreements were considered technically insuperable. Here at least there has been progress in the sense of endeavour.

(5) One aspect of rationalization in recent years has been the increased use of joint statistical data, particularly on wages. Many unions now collaborate in producing joint statistics, and the SAF statistics on wages are now generally accepted for official and for bargaining purposes. Bargaining has become more and more factual, where *ex-post* items are concerned.

(6) Bargaining is becoming increasingly a matter for the small

[1] The strike-lock-out in the foodstuffs industry in 1953 was an example of the problems that may arise in an unco-ordinated, drawn-out wage round. SAF dug in its heels about wage increases for food workers which would have led to higher food prices, since earlier contracts had been concluded on the assumption that food prices would not rise.

band of leaders on each side. SAF and LO bargaining delegates are usually on very friendly personal terms, inspired by mutual respect and by the common desire to conclude a peace treaty. This spotlighting of the *élite* on both sides brings into sharp relief the necessity for the good internal communications and orderly discipline which were highlighted in Part I as features of the labour market organizations. (In addition, of course, the employer and union at the local level can, as wage drift suggests, often pursue a fairly independent line in giving effect to a central agreement.)

(7) The mediation system occupies an important position in the bargaining process. The system is flexible, as was noted in Chapter VI, and dependent for its success on mediators who can find acceptable solutions to awkward bargaining problems which the parties are not able to resolve without outside assistance. The mediator's job calls for considerable skill and the feel for a situation, since his success depends very much on timing, experience, and understanding of the individuals on each side of the bargaining table. There have, however, been some significant shifts in the uses made of the mediation system in the post-war period.[1]

The use of district mediators has declined in the past decade, with the growth in national agreements and the increasing degree of organization on both sides. The following figures, which are not always complete, must be interpreted with caution, since they indicate the number of cases where negotiations took place before district mediators, but do not tell us anything about the way in which the district mediator may use his influence and give advice, apart from leading formal bargaining sessions.

NEGOTIATIONS BEFORE DISTRICT MEDIATORS 1945–59[2]

Number of cases reported			
1945	344	1952	230*
1946	359	1953	150*
1947	397	1954	187*
1948	347	1955	182*
1949	149	1956	160
1950	127	1957	98
1951	238*	1958	101
		1959	94

Source: Mediation Office. * Known to be incomplete.

[1] The figures given here have been made available by courtesy of Mr Carl Chr. Schmidt, head of the official Mediation Office.

[2] By way of comparison, the mediation service handled an average of 208 disputes annually in the period 1915–37. See Robbins, op. cit., p. 175.

USE OF SPECIAL MEDIATORS 1945–60

	Appointed by government (*a*)	*Appointed by Social Board* (*b*)	*Total*
1945	17	30	47
1946	26	33	59
1947	28	31	59
1948	25	49	74
1949	3	7	10
1950	13	11	24
1951	16	39	55
1952	12	43	55
1953	28	45	73
1954	22	29	51
1955	19	39	58
1956	4	9	13
1957	1	10	11
1958	2	3	5
1959	0	15	15
1960	3	23	26

(*a*) Persons other than district mediators appointed by government on recommendation of Social Welfare Board.
(*b*) District mediators, whom the Social Welfare Board can appoint directly as special mediators.

The main features of this table are that, as was to be expected, special mediators were little used during the wage freeze years (1949–50), and they have been less frequently used since 1956, when the new pattern of central LO–SAF negotiations began to take shape. The last two central agreements, for 1959, and for 1960–1, have, however, allowed express exceptions to the central framework agreement, and this gives scope for the renewed use of special mediators. Disputes concerning salaried employees account for a considerable share of mediation activity in recent years.

The number of mediation commissions,[1] which are always appointed by the government, nearly always on the recommendation of the Social Welfare Board, tells the same story:

1945	12	1953	19
1946	24	1954	18
1947	33	1955	27
1948	38	1956	5
1949	2	1957	9
1950	4	1958	1
1951	23	1959	9
1952	10	1960	15

[1] It should be noted that mediation commissions are not necessarily *alternatives* to special mediators, but sometimes a subsequent instance.

The increased use of statistics and of economy-wide bargaining have in some respects tended to make the mediator's role less obvious. Will he then become superfluous? The answer on the evidence so far is—no. The parties to central agreements have on occasion, e.g. SAF and LO in 1959, needed the good offices of a third party to bring about agreement, despite the fact that they take a professional pride in exhausting all other possibilities, except direct action, in their bargaining interchanges. The essential point about mediation, however, is that a skilful mediator will be able to convince the parties that all the possibilities for reaching agreement have *not* been exhausted.

The mediation system is unlikely to become superfluous if centralized bargaining becomes customary. There are three main reasons. Firstly, the system has tremendous resilience and flexibility. The use of the government commission in 1955 provided evidence of flexibility, even though in principle the establishment of such an additional mediatory instance is inadvisable. The system can be adjusted to the needs of the parties *and* in consultation with them. Secondly, the central agreements are themselves often flexible, leaving scope for union-level bargaining; nor are they comprehensive enough to debar salaried employees in the private and public sectors from seeking to push claims which necessitate ultimate use of the mediation facilities. Thirdly, it is likely that the mediation system will be given an additional load if responsible civil servants are given the right to bargain collectively, and to use the mediation facilities.

One post-war criticism, particularly when wage bargaining was unco-ordinated, was that there were too few mediators (the number of district mediators was increased from seven to eight in 1950). Paradoxically, however, the high-pressure negotiation system would lose much of its effectiveness if there were too many mediators, precisely because they have a scarcity value over the period when the bargaining season is at its peak. The parties could afford to abandon some of their sense of urgency if mediators were freely available.

A good deal of the negotiation procedure is sanctified by habit, practice, and tradition. It can be exhausting, but the main merit is that the parties have become accustomed to it psychologically, and this is a good climate in which to bargain. The justification for the system is that it now produces results with comparatively little direct action, though the sanction of economic coercion has not been abandoned, and is always present as an ultimate threat. The negotiations in 1955 and 1959 illustrate this point.

It should also be remembered that, prior to the centralized bargaining, only the awkward cases came to the notice of the public, and to mediation or direct action, while hundreds of local and some national agreements were regularly concluded without fuss. One of the aspects of the new centralized negotiations is that the public is aware of the bargaining process to a greater extent than ever before. This, too, is a pressure on the parties to agree.

Bargaining for salaried employees in both the private and public sectors has become more centralized since 1945, and the process has usually been timed to follow after bargaining in the SAF–LO sector. But whereas prior to 1939 only LO and SAF had developed a powerful bargaining system, the rise of salaried employees' organizations has produced additional strong bargaining institutions. In both central and local government employers' organizations have deliberately co-ordinated bargaining. On the side of the unions, the main salaried employees' union in the private sector, the Union of Clerical and Technical Employees, has tried to follow a mixed policy of centralized bargaining on general provisions and mainly a flexible decentralized bargaining policy for salaries. In the civil service, there has been a very conscious trend since 1957 to increase the bargaining strength of the TCO civil service section by building up fighting funds, and establishing a bargaining council drawn from the unions in the civil service. Throughout the economy the bargaining system is thus becoming highly integrated and collectivized. The chronicle of the wage rounds since 1939 which follows in the next chapter shows the bargaining process at work in the context of a full employment economy.

CHAPTER XV

Wage Rounds 1939–60

SINCE 1939 the goals of wage bargaining have been fashioned primarily with reference to LO's avowed wages policy of solidarity. One of the main reasons for the reform of LO rules in 1941 was the adoption of a deliberate wages policy of solidarity, which at that time was conceived as 'helping the worst-paid groups of workers', mainly those employed in agriculture and forestry. The theme can be traced back to the LO congress of 1922, long before wages policy became so inexorably associated with full employment.

At that time the trade union movement made the first of a series of pronouncements on the subject of rationalization of production through improvements in production techniques and work simplification. The attitude which LO adopted then and has maintained ever since was overwhelmingly positive, in recognizing that this was inevitable and also necessary for improving the living conditions of the workers. At the same time, LO stressed the need to provide safeguards for the workers, which has since been reflected in the central agreements on job security, workshop safety, vocational training, works councils and work study.

Having declared its positive attitude to productive efficiency in 1922, the trade union movement faced up to the question of what its policy on wages should be when productivity varied greatly between sectors, when some types of production could be rationalized, while others were unsuited to intensive methods of production. Early discussion of solidarity recognized the problem, but did not produce a satisfactory policy for dealing with differing capacities to pay in different industries. This is hardly surprising. What the policy of equity in wages policy involved was nothing more or less than a complete reform of the bargaining behaviour of trade unions, supplemented by social policy measures when the market pricing process could not be conditioned by union behaviour alone to setting equitable wages. This was a vast undertaking, for solidarity in wage bargaining coheres more naturally at a craft or industry than a class level. Some solidarity was indeed practised at those levels in the 1930s.

Three main strands can be distinguished in the early discussion of solidarity and the policy necessary to achieve it. They are still apposite.

(*a*) If capacity to pay differed between industries, then the group which could enjoy higher wages by exploiting the economic strength of employers in their industry ought deliberately to refrain from doing so, in order to help 'badly paid' groups. It was recognized that this might not happen at all, but simply mean that profits would rise in the prosperous industries where bargaining pressure was not being fully applied. It was hoped that purchasing power might in some vague sense nevertheless be transferred, at least to closely related groups.[1]

(*b*) In pursuit of solidarity, it had been agreed since the 1922 LO congress that priority in strike support should be given to badly paid groups.

(*c*) In addition to the reform in 1941 of the organization and constitutional powers of LO in support of the wages policy of equity, the point was made that the unions might not be able to reform the wages structure without some help from social policy measures.[2]

[1] This is argued in vague terms in one of the early tracts on equity in wages policy. See Albin Lind, op. cit., pp. 22–24. His conclusion was that only unified leadership could achieve the tightly geared planning and division of labour that must form the basis for an equalizing policy such as this. Previous LO discussions had always recognized the practical difficulties in the way of such a policy. In 1931 the LO secretariat doubted whether in fact, if the possibilities existed (i.e. capacity to pay) for better-paid groups of workers to improve their position further, it would be possible to prevent this by conference decisions and constitutional provisions, or by drawing attention to their relatively favourable position. It might well lead to a split in the movement and to its disintegration. 'To persuade the workers or others to refrain, through affiliation to an organization, from having their wages raised when the possibilities for this exist, and at the same time to pay dues in this organization, is quite simply unthinkable.' LO *kongress-protokoll*, 1931, p. 51 et seq.

In 1926, likewise, the LO secretariat had argued that it was impossible to work out common wage provisions for all workers in Sweden, since capacity to pay differed from industry to industry in accordance with economic conditions. Who was badly paid in fact depended (and still depends) on the state of the economy. In 1922, when wage solidarity first became a topic for debate and discussion, export industries were less well-placed for paying higher wages than certain domestic industries. See LO *kongress-protokoll*, 1922, motion 144, and secretariat *utlåtande* no. 23, p. 284. SAF argued at that time that wages policy should be based on the ability to pay of the export industries, which were then less profitable than, for example, foodstuffs, a predominantly sheltered industry.

One of the most interesting points about the 1931 declaration in particular is that it is the exact opposite of a view sometimes expressed at the present time by trade unionists, who claim that the trade union movement would disintegrate if LO were to abandon its wages policy of solidarity. The 1931 argument is that the movement would disintegrate if solidarity were pushed too far! It explicitly provided some scope for egoism in wage bargaining by the unions.

[2] This was very clearly recognized by motion no. 224 at the 1936 LO congress, which stressed that social policy would be necessary to supplement the internal adjustments the trade union movement could make by its own efforts. This difficulty, and the need for social policy to overcome it, is stressed by the committee whose report was the basis of the 1941 reform. See *Fackföreningsrörelsen och näringslivet*, pp. 186–7. 'Equalization of wages within a particular industry can probably be achieved by exclusive use of trade union action, but the resources of the trade union movement are inadequate for the purpose of eliminating wage

Subsidies to agriculture, housing, and fiscal policy appear in the discussion as necessary aids to help the badly paid groups. Wages policy and social policy were to be complementary, a combination which appeared a natural alliance at a time when big social reforms were being planned by the social democratic party.

By 1939, therefore, the trade union movement was developing an equitable approach to wage determination, on the premiss that relative wages were not to be based on capacity to pay. At first the alternative criteria given for guiding wage claims were imprecise and did not go beyond exalting those of low degree in the relative wages scale. Later analysis has tried to expand the meaning of solidarity to include reference to the nature of the job, its requirements, and to manpower criteria, with overriding consideration being paid to the low relative position of female workers.[1] The forms in which the policy has been applied and the machinery used have varied during and since the war.

The wage goals of salaried employees' organizations have been much less complex than those of LO during the period. Their primary aim has been to retain or restore traditional differentials over manual workers. Nevertheless, different salaried employee groups have pursued significantly different objectives. SR is concerned to restore the pre-war position of senior civil servants, SACO emphasizes the importance of reimbursement to university-educated persons for the cost of the training they undergo, while TCO, as the largest and as a vertical organization, has been much more concerned than the others with the broad mass of salaried employees.

Both the problems of wages structure and the general level of wages are vividly illustrated by the wage bargaining that has occurred since 1939. An analysis of these rounds sheds light not only on the way in which LO has tried to pursue its wages policy of solidarity, but on the wider issues of wage determination for the whole labour market.

differentials between different industries and sectors of the economy. In the last resort it is the profitability of the sectors which sets the limit to what the trade union movement can achieve. An industry with a stable market and a large demand can naturally pay better wages than a branch which is enduring a hard and often precarious existence. In the latter industry the workers do not, however, obtain better wages simply because their comrades in a more favourable branch refrain from exploiting their opportunities to improve their position further. An equalizing wages policy can only be achieved here by means of social policy measures.' Union and political action must therefore be complementary. At the same time it was argued that it was in the interests of the trade union movement not to let wage differentials widen but, on the contrary, to make them as uniform as possible. No criteria were given at that time for assessing the precise meaning of 'uniformity'.

[1] See in particular LO *Fackföreningsrörelsen och den fulla sysselsättningen* (Stockholm, 1951), especially pp. 149–55.

I. WAGE ROUNDS SINCE 1939

At this stage the material discussed will be primarily institutional and descriptive of bargaining events. In the two chapters which follow the significance of these wage rounds for the wages structure and for the whole system of collective bargaining will be analysed.

From the outbreak of the Second World War until 1944 wage bargaining centred on index agreements between LO and SAF to compensate for changes in the cost-of-living, and to avoid the necessity for direct government control of wages. The index agreements for 1940–4 took the form that wages were adjusted to changes in the cost-of-living, but (*a*) retrospectively, and usually at six-monthly intervals (for 1940 every quarter), and (*b*) without giving full compensation for rising living costs. The first index agreement, for 1940, was the most favourable one for the workers, for in addition to quarterly index adjustments it provided for about 75% compensation for rising living costs. Civil servants agreed in 1940 to accept only 50% compensation, and this helped to bring agreement on similar less favourable partial compensation in the private sector. Technically, the index agreements were constructed in such a way that they allowed wages to fall retrospectively if the cost-of-living fell, but in fact this clause was never used. The cost-of-living was stabilized for the period 1943–5 by a rigid price and income stabilization policy.

While there was some union-level bargaining throughout the war this was moderate in amount, and in 1942–4 SAF and LO tried to control it by taking up outstanding issues in conjunction with the central index negotiations. During the wage-price freeze agreed from late 1942 there was explicit exemption for badly paid groups, in accordance with LO's wages policy of solidarity.

In the wage negotiation rounds since 1945 a variety of approaches has been tried, in the light both of the state of the economy and the outcome and experience of preceding rounds. Four main groups can be identified:

(*a*) Bargaining by individual unions, on the basis of general LO recommendations, for the years 1945 to 1948, for 1951, and for 1953, 1954, and 1955.

(*b*) A period of wage freeze for 1949–50.

(*c*) Centrally negotiated agreements between LO and SAF in 1952 and 1956,[1] regarded as exceptional arrangements.

[1] It is arguable that the 1956 round should be included under group (*d*). The reasons for regarding it here as exceptional are the luke-warm pronouncements on centralization by the then LO chairman (Mr Strand) and the hope expressed by the managing director of SAF (Mr Kugelberg), after the 1956 round was over, that the exceptional, co-ordinated agreement of 1956 would not need to be repeated. See *Arbetsgivaren*, 1956, no. 3, p. 2.

(*d*) Centrally negotiated SAF–LO agreements, for 1957–8, 1959, and 1960–1, which are no longer regarded as exceptional.

What are the highlights of these variations on the collective bargaining theme?

When bargaining has been carried on by the individual LO unions they have enjoyed considerable variety in the recommendations LO made to them. For 1945 LO anticipated that real wages would rise through stable money incomes and falling prices.[1] For 1947 a general wage offensive was signalled, but stress was laid on the need to avoid endangering price stability.[2] 'Great restraint' was recommended for 1948, but big claims were made and conceded,[3] although SAF made a public declaration in favour of stabilization and tried to co-ordinate its bargaining front. LO has consistently and constantly tried, during and since the war, to give prior consideration to lower-paid groups of workers—though it has not always defined who they were—and to women workers. For 1947, for instance, a successive closing of differentials between the sexes in accordance with the principle of 'equal pay for equal performance' was recommended.

The wage restraint period, 1949–50, had some significant features. It was on the initiative of TCO, which took the lead in 1948 by accepting an unchanged bonus for civil servants, that a stabilization policy was agreed among all the interest groups, including farmers, for those years. No contractual increases were permitted, though wage drifting allowed some rises in the private sector; the government used subsidies to hold down the cost-of-living after the

[1] See LO *verksamhetsberättelse*, 1944, pp. 18–19. As well as having an honoured place in Swedish economic theory, this was a policy recommendation of the Post-war Programme of Swedish Labour. The stability of the cost-of-living index in the period 1943–5, and the existence of strict price controls, made it seem a reasonable policy at the time. In later years LO has again campaigned for lower prices. In 1954 it made no recommendations to the unions for wage increases, but issued a strong statement condemning price inflexibilities downwards. Effective control of monopolies was also stressed in the LO wages declaration for 1955.

[2] 'One of the fundamental elements in trade union tactics is that good economic conditions with high and stable employment ought to, and will, be used to raise wages.' Stability in the price level must not, however, be endangered. It 'seemed' that in most branches of the economy adjustments in the wage-level would be possible without this justifying demands for higher prices. At the same time LO sought an extension and increase of the wartime cost-of-living bonus, which became consolidated from May 1947. See LO *verksamhetsberättelse*, 1946, p. 35.

[3] Part of the explanation for this was the profit time-lag from 1946. The National Institute of Economic Research pointed out, *Meddelanden från konjunkturinstitutet*, *Serie* A : 15, p. 23, that the good profit statements published for 1946 did not signify that there was scope for increases in wages in 1948. Salary increases in 1947 for civil servants also provided a stimulus.

1949 devaluation and on the outbreak of the Korean war in order to prevent price rises. SAF and LO agreed a cost-of-living reopening clause for the second year of stabilization, 1950, but this was not needed. The wage freeze began to thaw out early in 1950.

At the end of the wage freeze, the individual union-level bargaining for 1951 produced chaotic wage movements, depending on how far groups had lagged during the freeze (closely dependent on the structure of the wage provisions in their contracts), the timing of their new agreements, and the rapidity of price rises, which were accentuated by the removal of subsidies. The government deliberately chose a once-for-all upward adjustment of the cost and price level.

The experience of 1951 led, at the request of SAF, to the first centrally negotiated peace-time agreement between LO and SAF, for 1952. It tried to steer wage movements by dealing with four main aspects: (*a*) protection against price changes during 1952 by a consumer price index clause, though this did not cover the consequential increase in prices (estimated at 3%) arising out of the agreement itself; (*b*) scope for unions to negotiate compensation for any lag behind the cost-of-living in 1951 and earlier years; (*c*) a share in the increase in production during 1951 and anticipated for 1952 through general wage increases; and (*d*) adherence to the wages policy of solidarity, by raising women's wages more than those of men and providing a minimum cash increase in contractual wages of 25 öre an hour.

This was the first centrally negotiated agreement for wage increases in peace-time, and it differed from war-time index agreements by aiming not simply to compensate for rises in living costs, but to pursue an active policy of drawing up targets for wage increases all along the SAF–LO line. Significantly, it did not deprive the unions of some scope for bargaining about the division of increases in their particular contracts.

Neither side considered that the procedure used for 1952 set a precedent. SAF had not originally envisaged a co-ordinated bargaining round for 1952, because the wage structure had in 1951 become so distorted that in its view central bargaining would put enormous stresses on the employers' organizations. But it decided to insist on co-ordinating wage bargaining in one general agreement as a condition of meeting LO's request for a cost-of-living clause to protect real wages against price rises. Each had difficulties in getting groups to toe the line, SAF with depressed textiles, and LO with the unions in the booming paper and pulp industry. LO argued that it did not have the constitutional powers to arrive at an agreement on behalf of the unions which deprived them of their right to seek compensation for lagging.[1]

The next centrally negotiated agreement was for 1956, after a lull of three years in which new experience was gained of the difficulties of relying on general recommendations to the unions, when the profitability of sectors and the structure of agreements made it possible to obtain both official and unofficial increases in wages. For 1953 and 1954 there were moderate wage demands—the pressure on resources was much less than in 1950–1. For 1953 LO recommended the unions not to put forward demands for general wage increases, although, as in 1948, when it had urged restraint, it allowed some departure by suggesting negotiations on general provisions of contracts. In 1953 SAF refused to have any truck with an index clause, and tried to force wage cuts in certain industries. The metal trades set the pattern for most agreements through prolongation for the year, but negotiations proved difficult in some sectors, and there was a mixed strike-lock-out in the foodstuffs industry for five weeks before agreement was reached. LO made no specific recommendations for 1954, but hoped for higher real wages via price falls. For 1955 wage demands by both LO and TCO groups were badly out of alignment with the restrained policy and 'limited scope' recommendations of LO, and the somewhat more aggressive recommendations of TCO,[2] and there was an imminent threat of a lock-out on a wide

[1] After the 1952 agreement Axel Strand, the LO chairman, stated that 'LO did not aim at such a high degree of centralization in wage-fixing for the future. The 1952 negotiations did not lend support to the idea of continuing along the same lines, not simply because of the experience gained from negotiating with the employers, but because the negotiations *within* the union delegations should have made it clear that the movement was not constructed and was not ripe for negotiations of this kind.' The structure of agreements, and the variation in conditions between sectors, also argued against such an approach. He also doubted whether a free and more differentiated wage round would have been more costly. See *Aftontidningen*, February 22, 1952.

[2] See LO *verksamhetsberättelse*, 1954, p. 4, for the statement by the representative assembly on 22/9/54. 'The representative assembly considers that economic developments will permit a limited improvement in the standard of wage-earners for 1955 as well, and that this improvement should be possible without a general rise in prices, because of the current improvement in efficiency in the economy. It is important that particular attention should be paid to women's wages in the coming wage round.' TCO pronounced that 'an improvement in the salaries of white-collar workers is called for, and that economic conditions for this exist. The salaried employee group demands its share of the improved production results through its wages being brought into line with the general trend of the economy. This has not been the case in recent years, but a palpable lagging—due primarily to the more rigid pay system—has emerged for the salaried groups, some of whom have not even been compensated for the slight increase in the cost of living. A greater advance is desirable in sectors where salaried employees' wages are unsatisfactory in relation to other sectors, or where lagging has been particularly large. This applies also to women's wages, to which special attention must be paid.' TCO *styrelsens och revisorernas berättelser*, 1954, p. 34.

front by SAF. Total increases of 8–10% were obtained throughout the year, 5–6% by agreement. Salaried employees obtained somewhat more.

The 1955 experience produced a reaction for 1956, when once more overall recommendations to the individual unions were abandoned, and a central agreement was arrived at by SAF, LO, and TCO after prolonged negotiations and resort to a mediation commission. SAF initiated this approach by inviting LO and TCO for discussions in June 1955, and later LO and TCO had discussions with the government on economic policy, e.g. with regard to the bad harvest. The main factors behind the approach for 1956 were (*a*) the failure of the unions to heed restraint for 1955, and (*b*) the development of relative wages in 1955, which had in fact eliminated some of the most keenly felt inequities in relative wages and improved the prospects for a uniform settlement for 1956.

The centrally negotiated agreement recommended that average hourly and piecework earnings should be raised by 3·7% or by 16 öre per hour, whichever was the greater. This 'broken line' approach catered for LO's principle of wages solidarity, the flat rate of 16 öre applying in fact to all groups of female workers. For TCO groups salaries were increased by 4%. The LO unions were left some initiative in being allowed to discuss exactly how the increases should be allocated in their particular agreements. There was thus no guarantee that every individual would in fact obtain the increases stipulated. The main features of this agreement were that TCO participated directly in the bargaining for the first (and so far the only) time, and that the central agreement set the target indirectly for all other groups of employers and employees, whether in private or public services, through the three top organizations agreeing to work for the adoption of these principles elsewhere.

Both the 1952 and 1956 co-ordinated wage rounds were felt at the time to be exceptional and unlikely to be repeated. SAF 'in principle' disliked a comprehensive bargain, since it did not take account of differing profitability in different sectors. TCO opposed any rigid approach, and objects still to the feature that wage drift, which is less prevalent among salaried employees than manual workers, closes salary-wage differentials during the course of agreements to the disadvantage of salaried staff. It also prefers straight percentage increases, which avoid awkward problems of internal relativities. Civil service salary differentials are now based on percentages. The LO congress of 1956 was generally more sympathetic towards co-ordination, as a result of the 1952 and 1956 experience, but LO argued that in future co-ordination more flexibility should be sought which would give greater freedom of manœuvre to the individual unions.[1] It was agreed that wages policy would have to be practised in more standardized forms.[2]

II. THE NEW TREND TO REGULAR CENTRAL BARGAINING

It is too early to judge how permanent a change has taken place in bargaining techniques since 1956, but it does seem that, with the centrally co-ordinated two-year agreement for 1957–8 between LO and SAF, central bargaining is now looked upon as a desirable and promising, not an emergency approach. Central agreements have also been reached for 1959, and for the two-year period 1960–1. It is also wise to remember that in these years there have been a number of particularly ticklish bargaining problems, connected with issues like the reduction in the working week from 48 to 45 hours, the national superannuation scheme, and a turnover tax. These have favoured a central and comprehensive solution.

The bargaining for 1957 did not begin as central negotiations, though SAF was keener than LO to have them, but after three unsuccessful attempts to bargain at union level the negotiations were shifted to the SAF–LO level. In the two subsequent rounds both sides have been in favour of central negotiations from the start.

The three agreements have taken the form of central *recommendations* to the SAF and LO member groups to increase *average* hourly *earnings* by specific percentages or cash sums in each year, e.g.:

	1957	*1958*	*1959*	*1960*	*1961*
For hourly paid workers	2% or 10 öre	3·5%	2%	18 öre	19 öre
For workers paid by results	2% or 10 öre	2%	1·5%	3%, min. 16 öre	3%, min. 16 öre

These are agreed *average* changes, expressed in relation to current earnings, and they do *not* guarantee that everyone obtains these

[1] See LO *kongress-protokoll*, 1956, secretariat *utlåtande* no. 2, p. 141.

[2] It is difficult to say how much significance ought to be attached to the change in the chairmanship of LO at the 1956 congress, when Axel Strand retired and Arne Geijer succeeded him. Geijer argued (op. cit., p. 163) that there was now greater acceptance of co-ordination among the unions, and that wages policy would now have to be pursued along more uniform lines. In a policy speech after his election, Geijer said (ibid., p. 502 et seq.) that co-ordination could not be precisely defined, but must take the form which circumstances at any one time required. It was important to retain the freedom of the labour market. But this in turn involved sharing responsibility for the trend of the economy. This pronouncement is much more favourable to co-ordination than the doubtful views expressed by Strand on various occasions. The 1961 LO congress accepted the *principle* of co-ordinated bargaining without a murmur, and devoted its wage bargaining debate almost entirely to the problem of finding the best form for conducting centralized negotiations.

increases. In other words, they provide the *cost framework* for union-level bargaining, but the precise division of the centrally agreed general increases is left to the parties to particular contracts. This provides the flexibility which is generally regarded as essential for obtaining the consent of the unions to co-ordinated bargaining at all. Thus there is scope for union-level bargaining about the allocation of increases, e.g. between systems of payment, between male and female workers, etc.[1]

There are two forms of control on this union-level bargaining. First, a clause has been included in each central agreement which provides that the small LO–SAF delegations will settle (i.e. in practice arbitrate) any outstanding disputes if agreement has not been reached at union level within a period of (usually) three to four weeks. This is in effect a guarantee of peace. So far few disputes, mainly on small issues, have been outstanding for settlement in this way. This is hardly surprising, since the whole system of framework bargaining would be undermined if the careful aggregative costing on which it is based were to be upset by major deviations at union level. The second check is provided by the procedure of dealing with specific and difficult problems that arise in the bargaining build-up at union level *before* the central bargain is struck. The treatment of particular issues, which are handled by the small delegations or at union level, can be very time-consuming. In 1959 about fifteen special cases were reviewed before the central agreement was concluded, while in 1960 about fifty cases calling for special treatment were submitted by the unions. This second check therefore endeavours to iron out the difficult problems in advance, so that when the central agreement is signed it is reasonably certain that there are no outstanding major issues.

Much of the criticism directed against the central agreement of 1956 related to its rigidity, and the subsequent central agreements have tried to introduce greater flexibility by allowing exceptions to the general recommendations. For 1957–8 larger increases were permitted for 'low-wage groups', which were not specified. In the two later agreements a more systematic treatment has been attempted by specifying the groups which are not included in the master recommendations. Such groups are of course *not* bound by the peace obligation affecting those *within* the direct coverage of the agreement.

LO and SAF undertake to work for their general framework agreement being applied elsewhere in the labour market.

No special treatment for female workers was specified in the 1957–8 agreement, apart from any preference that might be shown

[1] The text of the 1960–61 central agreement given in Appendix 4 illustrates the structure of these agreements.

them when the overall increases were allocated at the union-level bargaining, and LO was unsuccessful in having any specific provisions relating to women's wages written into the agreement for 1959. But the poor achievements of LO's policy of closing sex differentials (discussed in Chapter XVI) led to a new approach in 1960. For the 1960–1 agreement a most significant clause was included which has enormous implications for the future structure of collective contracts. The SAF–LO committee of 1951 on female labour had suggested the abolition of the categories 'male' and 'female' in collective agreements, and argued for a wage system based on the value of work performed by the individual worker. Following this principle, the 1960–1 agreement provided that over a transitional period of five years the structure of agreements is to be changed, by discussion at union level, in such a way as to dispense with the designations 'male' and 'female' in the categories used in contracts. They are to be replaced by job classes.

The central agreements have not always used the mediation facilities. Since 1956 a mediation commission has been used only in the 1959 round. The nature of the opening gambit in the wage round has also varied. For 1957–8, when LO initially envisaged union-level bargaining, a specific 5% or 25 öre bargaining ceiling was eventually recommended for the unions. No specific demands were made for 1959, because LO, like everyone else, wanted to wait for a clearer picture of economic trends to emerge before putting forward any precise proposals. In complete contrast, LO made very detailed bargaining and procedural proposals from the start of the 1960 round, and SAF also produced specific counter-proposals. Other points worth noting are that TCO has not participated in central bargaining since 1956, and, of the last four agreements, only the 1957–8 agreement has contained a cost-of-living reopening clause (which was not needed). It is also noteworthy that the 1959 agreement showed it is possible to bargain centrally even when there is a slackening in economic activity.

For salaried employees in private industry wage rounds have tended to follow the pattern set by the negotiations between LO and its unions on the one hand and SAF on the other. In war-time, SAF adopted the policy for salaried employees of sending out circulars to its Partners recommending cost-of-living bonuses similar to those for manual workers and individually determined merit and seniority increases. A ceiling salary set for compensation for the cost-of-living was raised in 1946, and the bonus was gradually absorbed into basic salaries by 1951. In the post-war years of centralized SAF–LO bargaining, SAF has issued circulars to its Partners recommending specified general percentage increases for salaried employees, supplemented by individually determined seniority and merit increases. In years when the manual workers' bargaining has been carried on at union level, salaries for staff in industry have been determined by local bargaining.

Some important landmarks are noticeable in the bargaining rounds since 1955, when the Union of Clerical and Technical Employees in Industry began a more independent and aggressive policy, instead of being content to follow. SAF resisted a central recommendation for general salary increases for 1955, but the union was successful in its tactics of obtaining increases through attacking some of the largest individual firms (e.g. ASEA, the large electrical concern). In subsequent years general recommendations, with scope for individual supplements, have been produced, but in a variety of bargaining circumstances.

In 1956 salaried employees were included in the overall bargain struck by SAF, LO, and TCO for that year, but in the later centralized rounds TCO and its unions have stayed outside. For 1957–8 the Union of Clerical and Technical Employees bargained on its own with SAF; in the 1959 round and for 1960–1 it was joined in bargaining by the Foremen's Union. In the three agreements since 1957 the union has obtained general plus individual increases. These individual seniority and merit supplements allow considerable flexibility, and scope for demand and supply to operate in the salary structure, as the following figures show:

	1958	*1959*	*1960*
		Percentages	
Centrally negotiated general increases	3·5	1·9	3·5
Total increases obtained	6·4	4·7	7·4

In addition to the flexibility suggested by these figures, the union has on each of these three occasions succeeded in winning agreement that badly paid firms and groups should obtain more than the recommended general increase in salaries. In 1960 the problem of lagging salaries for male salaried employees over fifty years of age and females over forty-five was tackled by allowing a general increase of 1·5% to be allocated among these two groups by local bargaining. Thus central bargaining has not eliminated the salary differentiation sought by the union.

The extension of social benefits among manual workers to include many of the salaried employees' traditional fringe benefits has also produced important and separate bargaining rounds in recent years. In 1955, after the national health scheme was introduced, the union was able to ensure that salaried employees retained the same standard of sickness benefits as before. In 1959 it forced a break-through against the narrowing holidays-with-pay gap by obtaining an improvement in holiday provisions for white-collar workers in industry. In 1960, following the start of the national superannuation scheme, the union brought off a remarkable coup. It succeeded in negotiating a new general pensions scheme for salaried employees in industry, and also obtained total increases of about 15%: 8% being previous superannuation contributions, and 7% to maintain the total of their employment package relative to manual workers.

Thus the union has not by any means played follow-my-leader with LO. Nor has SAF been able to divide and rule. The Union of Clerical and Technical Employees has not allowed itself to be dismissed as a poor relation at the bargaining table.

When we look at bargaining rounds for public employees, it is also true that civil servants, for example, have not always been content to follow the pattern set by SAF and LO for the private sector. The public sector has not simply been a wage follower, in crisis and in peace: it has sometimes acted as a stabilizer, and on occasion as a wage-leader.

In 1940 the civil service gave a lead in damping down automatic demands for wage increases to compensate for rises in the cost-of-living, by accepting partial compensation on the basis of the revised 1939 salary scales. In 1944, on the other hand, it was salary increases for lower-grade civil servants employed on salary plan which helped to set a precedent, and (along with local authorities and agriculture) generated a more active wage round for 1945 than SAF relished.[1]

New salary scales agreed for civil servants from 1947 provided a flexible system which was designed to keep civil servants in line with general developments in the economy, and not simply the cost-of-living. (The interpretation of 'general developments' has subsequently provided a bone of contention between the government, arguing that this means that civil servants follow the trend of wages in industry, and civil service unions, arguing in terms of gross national product. Economic self-interest is evident in the respective arguments. GNP at market prices rose by 400%, hourly earnings for adult male workers in industry by 340%, between 1939 and 1959.)

The system helped in turn both to stabilize and provoke wage rounds. In 1948 TCO took the initiative in developing the economic stabilization programme for 1949 and 1950, by agreeing that its civil

[1] See SAF, *styrelse-och revisions berättelser*, 1944, p. 14. 'Even if there was justification for raising the salaries of some groups of government employees this could surely have waited until the ordinary session of the Riksdag in 1945.'

service members would accept a lower cost-of-living bonus for the second half of 1948 than that to which they were entitled, provided other groups agreed to stabilization. Civil servants were quickly off the mark when the end of stabilization was envisaged in 1950, with demands that they should be compensated for the lag in their incomes because of their altruism in 1948 and the absence of wage drift.

From 1951 civil servants succeeded in obtaining agreement that their salaries should be the subject of periodic revision, which in fact has meant annual review, and their bargaining rounds have followed the pattern set each year by the negotiations in the private sector. In two respects civil service bargaining has raised awkward questions. The amount of the bonus during the 1951–2 inflation was of the order of 15–20%, which had a bad psychological effect on other parties, and raised the question of automatic machinery for adjusting civil service salaries. Secondly, and related to this, the annual adjustment of job grades through B-list negotiations machinery has not succeeded in giving civil servants regular compensation for the absence of wage drift in their employment. The Ministry of Civil Service Affairs has tried always to limit the annual increases given to civil servants to the amount set out in the SAF–LO central agreements, but this makes no allowance for the earnings drift which in fact ensues in the private sector. On one occasion, December 1956, the civil service unions were able to insist on obtaining compensation (*nollställning*-parity) of 7% rises for the earnings drift in the private sector since November 1954, *before* SAF and LO began their bargaining which led to the 1957–8 agreement. At the time this was considered a sensible way of differentiating the wage round to take account of the wage drift problem. But an attempt by the civil service unions to do the same again before the 1959 SAF–LO negotiations failed, because the bargaining climate was unfavourable, LO in any event obtained a meagre agreement, and the government could therefore resist the claims of civil servants for 'restoration of parity'.

One of the major issues in the wage rounds which build up the wages and salary structure is therefore the inflexibility of civil servants' scales of pay compared with those in the private sector. Until some more regular and automatic adjustment machinery is devised—and the frequent re-grading of jobs does not in itself provide this—period explosions and attempts to restore parity must accordingly be expected in good bargaining years. Paradoxically, however, it is in good bargaining years that wage drift is likely to be greatest, opening out the differentials against the civil servants on fixed salaries. To close these, as in 1956, requires a major upward adjustment of civil service salary scales.

The experience of the wage rounds since 1939 suggests a number of significant points.

(1) It now seems clear that SAF and LO are setting the bargaining pattern for the whole economy, although their common coverage is no more than one-third of the labour force. But it is by no means the case that salaried employees in the private and public sector are always content to follow in the wake of the SAF–LO agreement.

(2) It is proving difficult for TCO to participate formally in this centralized bargaining, because of the heterogeneous coverage of TCO groups. Salaried employees in industry want flexibility through decentralization and are unwilling to collaborate with LO. The public employees in TCO are reasonably sympathetic to co-ordination with the SAF–LO bargaining, provided that some means can be found of overcoming the disadvantages they suffer through their rigid salary systems. At present they are reluctant to take part in negotiations for agreements lasting for more than a year, since they wish to have frequent opportunities of obtaining the parity with the private sector which wage drift tends to destroy during the course of agreements. Until these issues are resolved for TCO groups, it is difficult for it to participate in central negotiations. At the moment it cannot speak with a voice representative of all its major groups. From the side of SAF, moreover, it is doubtful whether it sees any advantage in bargaining with TCO rather than with the Union of Clerical and Technical Employees and the Foremen's Union.

(3) The centralized SAF–LO wage rounds put the parties under tremendous pressure to agree, with or without the use of mediation. SAF could not readily contemplate a lock-out of all its Partners' employees. This does not mean that no conflicts are possible, because both sides sometimes wish to exempt groups from the uniformity of the central recommendations. This could lead to small-scale conflicts, while the general agreements serve to limit the area of potential conflict. The power of the small delegations on both sides then becomes very great,[1] both as a result of the bargaining techniques that have evolved and through their being used when necessary as an arbitration instance, something which, as we saw in Part II, has been foreign to the thinking of SAF and LO in the past. Needs drive when full employment is a must.

(4) This increasingly professionalized bargaining nevertheless does provide some scope for differentiation, for union-level decisions about the allocation of the common pot, and for exceptions to the general agreement's rules. 'Centralized differentiation' is flexible

[1] The small delegations are known colloquially and collectively as *domkapitlet* (lit., the cathedral chapter), which suggests that its powers are not altogether of this world.

enough to leave responsibility for the precise treatment of wage and other issues to union-level bargaining. In this way, too, LO can put some of the responsibility for the pursuit of solidarity on the unions.

(5) LO is now tending to abandon its 'compensation complex' of insisting on cost-of-living clauses in the central agreements. The 1960–1 agreement had no reopening clause, and one of the main benefits which the employers' side sees in contracts running for more than one year can now be reaped, namely, that wage costs are known for a period ahead and pricing and output policy can be planned accordingly.

(6) Wage drift remains the fly in the ointment. Since 1958, however, there has been explicit recognition of its inevitability by providing *ex ante* that workers paid by time are given higher contractual increases than those paid by results, on the assumption that the latter will be able to push up rates outside the contract. In previous years LO had sometimes simply suggested that contractual rates should be adjusted towards 'the rates being paid in practice'.

An evaluation of these wage rounds since 1939 poses two main groups of questions. First, how successful has wages policy been in providing a wages structure which accords with the demands of the various organized groups? Secondly, what conclusions can be drawn from this experience about trends in collective bargaining? We shall look in the next chapter at the statistical evidence which is available for assessing the first question, and in the last chapter the implications of these wage rounds and wage statistics for collective bargaining will be examined.

CHAPTER XVI

Wage Changes and Wages Structure, 1939–60

IN this chapter we look at the evidence that is available for illuminating the previous discussion of wages in quantitative terms. Much of this statistical data is imperfect and crude, but we can at least hope to see some of the orders of magnitude which have been significant in the labour market since 1939.

The framework for this analysis is provided by figures for the size and composition of the national product. Table 1 shows the balance of resources since 1939 at current prices. The first point is that inflation has clearly been at work in an economy where GNP increased more than fivefold between 1939 and 1960 in money terms. Another significant feature is the shift in resource use to the public sector. Both public investment (line 6) and public consumption (line 9) have been very expansive. Public investment increased from 6·8% of GNP at market prices in 1939 to 13·1% in 1960. Private investment, on the other hand, has been very stable throughout, at about 17–18%, except for the years 1946 and 1947 (20·3%). Together, private and public investment, including inventory charges, have increased their share of GNP from 26·3% in 1939 to 33·7% in 1960.

Private consumption has suffered the main impact of this shift to higher investment ratios and increased public activity. In 1939 private consumption accounted for 66·2% of GNP, but by 1960 its share had dropped to 54%. The importance of imports and exports for the Swedish economy is brought out by lines 2 and 7 of Table 1. The export-import boom in 1951 at the time of the Korean crisis, the imports boom in 1947, and the severe controls on imports in 1949 are significant highlights in the changes in these items. Discussions of resource use in Sweden can never ignore her dependence on developments in the international economy.

Table 2 shows post-war changes in some of the main economic indicators. The largest changes in GNP at current prices, in the cost-of-living, and wages, and the lowest level of unemployment, were recorded in 1951. But the effect in volume terms of these once-for-all upward movements in money indicators was negligible. The explosion

TABLE 1

BALANCE OF RESOURCES, 1938/39 AND 1946–60

	Current Prices Millions of Crowns		*Index, 1939=100, based on current prices*															
	1938/39	*1960*	*1938/39*	*1946*	*1947*	*1948*	*1949*	*1950*	*1951*	*1952*	*1953*	*1954*	*1955*	*1956*	*1957*	*1958*	*1959*	*1960*
SUPPLY																		
1. GNP at Market Prices	12713	68500	100	182	195	219	230	245	300	328	338	356	386	418	450	468	499	539
2. Import of Goods c.i.f.	2256	14890	100	151	232	220	192	271	408	397	362	407	458	507	557	543	552	662
3. Decrease in Stocks	—	—																
4. Total Supply	14969	83390	100	177	201	219	224	250	316	339	345	364	397	432	466	480	508	556
USE																		
5. Private Domestic Gross Investment	2227	12760	100	193	226	217	216	251	298	310	334	359	380	419	438	478	511	552
6. Public Domestic Gross Investment	863	8990	100	209	242	296	323	356	443	581	657	684	714	780	866	904	1003	1045
7. Export of Goods, f.o.b., and Net Services	2213	14440	100	149	171	205	218	284	458	413	384	408	448	511	564	541	565	656
8. Private Consumption	8418	36960	100	176	193	210	213	230	259	285	296	312	333	359	377	402	419	440
9. Public Consumption	998	8860	100	223	245	284	302	318	393	470	511	531	578	632	706	766	835	886
10. Increase in Stocks	250?	1380																
11. Total Use	14969	83390	100	177	201	219	224	250	316	339	345	364	397	432	466	480	508	556

Source: Based on *Nationalbokföring för Sverige 1938/39, 1946–1959*, Table 1A: *Meddelanden från konjunkturinstitutet* (Mfk), *Serie* B: 30, 1960, and *The Swedish Economy*, *August 1961* (Mfk).

TABLE 2

POST-WAR ECONOMIC INDICATORS

Percentage increase on previous year (except line 5, current year)

	1947	*1948*	*1949*	*1950*	*1951*	*1952*	*1953*	*1954*	*1955*	*1956*	*1957*	*1958*	*1959*	*1960*
1. GNP at current market prices	7	12	5	6·5	22	9	3	5	8	8	8	4	7	8
2. Volume GNP	—	6	7	4·5	0	3	3	7	3	3·6	3·5	0·9	5	4
3. Hourly earnings in industry, men	14·1	8·3	3·0	3·9	20·6	18·2	3·6	4·4	8·5	8·1	5·7	5·4	4·5	7·1
4. Cost-of-living	5·0	2·7	2·0	1·3	15·5	7·8	1·0	1·0	2·5	5·4	4	4	1·0	4·0
5. Unemployment	2·8	2·9	2·9	2·3	1·9	2·6	2·8	2·6	2·5	1·7[1]	1·9	2·5	2·0	1·4

Notes. Line 1 based on Table 1.
Line 2 based on OEEC *General Statistics Bulletin.*
Line 3 taken from Table 5.
Line 4 based on Table 6, column 1.
Line 5 *Unemployment in Trade Unions to 1955.*

[1] From 1956 unemployment among members of Unemployment Insurance Funds.

of 1951 was the main reason for the co-ordination of 1952; but in that year the rises in money wages and cost-of-living were quite out of line with the other indicators. Co-ordination of wage bargaining in 1952 was largely intended to cater for the compensation complex by providing increases for the 1951 laggards. Judged by the performance of the indicators in 1953, the 1952 round did provide a steadying influence; 1953 was a year of rising unemployment, little bargaining, the lowest post-war increases in earnings, and of a favourable development of the volume of output, which was continued into 1954. The recovery of 1954 and rising volume of GNP produced another free wage round in 1955, which gave considerable money increases to catch up with the volume increase; 1956 again gave large increases, as did 1960.

1958 was the second year of a two-year contract, with the money earnings increases outpacing the performance of volume and unemployment indicators, and the cost-of-living having to carry the pressure of higher wages costs when output was stagnating.

By contrast to these free and co-ordinated wage rounds of various years, the restraint period of 1949–50, and the years 1953–4, when bargaining was either very limited or non-existent, gave a combination of the smallest post-war money wage increases and big upward changes in volume. But the restraint of 1949–50 led to the deluge of 1951 (though the Korea effect complicates the picture), while the 1954 revival led to a bargaining race in 1955.

There is no clear pattern from these indicators of a systematic pursuit of co-ordinated bargaining. Each year has had its own problems, *and* has had to reconcile the events of previous years with bargaining pressures that seek to exploit or obtain compensation for them.

What has happened to the wage share during this period? Table 3 attempts an answer.

There has been a marked upward shift in the wage share. The years 1947, 1950, 1952, and 1953 show the most significant shifts on preceding years. In terms of bargaining arrangements, it is not possible to see in these figures any correlation between free bargaining and upward movements, or co-ordinated bargaining and upward shifts; 1947 was a 'free year', when the wage share rose 4 points from 63 to 67: in the wage freeze years 1949–50 the wage share fell 3 points. The free wage round of 1951 did not restore the 1947 position, however. It was the centralized wage round of 1952 which provided the next upward shift. Since that round was flexible in the manœuvrability it allowed to individual unions, it cannot be regarded as providing proof that co-ordination *per se* improves the wage share. This conclusion is supported by the figures for the years since 1955

TABLE 3

WAGES AND SALARIES AS PERCENTAGE OF GROSS AND NET NATIONAL PRODUCT

	1938/39	*1946*	*1947*	*1948*	*1949*	*1950*	*1951*	*1952*	*1953*	*1954*	*1955*	*1956*	*1957*	*1958*	*1959*	*1960*
1. Of GNP at factor cost, *net* of depreciation, repairs and maintenance	58	63	67	67	66	64	64	69	71	72	73	73	73	73	73	—
2. Of GNP at factor cost, *before* providing for depreciation, repairs and maintenance	49	53	56	56	55	53	53	57	58	58	59	59	59	59	59	60

Source: (1) *Nationalbokföring för Sverige*, *1938/39*, *1946–1958* (Mfk), *Serie* B: 28, p. 6°, Table 2, line 6, and (for depreciation) Table 14, Account VI, line 8.

(2) Ibid., p. 6°, Table 2, line 4, and (for 1959) (Mfk), *Serie* B: 30, p. 10°, Table 2, line 4. For wages and salaries, ibid. (1958), p. 42°, Table 14, Account IV (households), item 4, and (1959) p. 48°, Table 15, Account IV, item 4.

TABLE 4

TRENDS IN FACTOR INCOMES

	Current Prices Millions of Crowns		*Index, 1939=100, based on current prices*														
	1938/1939	*1959*	*1939*	*1946*	*1947*	*1948*	*1949*	*1950*	*1951*	*1952*	*1953*	*1954*	*1955*	*1956*	*1957*	*1958*	*1959*
Wages and Salaries	5761	33,975	100	196	224	250	258	271	328	387	401	426	467	502	540	565	590
Income of Private Entrepreneurs[1]	1510	5,414	100	193	208	227	242	265	305	334	332	344	345	351	359	352	359
Net Interest and Dividends[2]	211	458	100	67	70	69	72	81	118	142	179	166	227	212	213	225	217
Direct Corporate Taxes	224	1,670	100	234	251	268	377	371	472	762	581	645	692	835	847	857	746

Source: op. cit. (Mfk), *Serie* B: 30, 1960, Table 15.

[1] Including net farming and forestry incomes. This item is considered highly unreliable by the Swedish national income Sources and Methods study. See *Nationalbokföring* 1946–1950 (Mfk), *Serie* B: 13, 1951, p. 25.

[2] Residual, after taking account of interest and dividend payments and receipts by households, central, and local government. There is in addition a 'regular residual' item in the private enterprises account, on which (Mfk), *Serie* B: 13, p. 26, comments that 'as long as this residual item cannot be allocated any discussion about income distribution which is based on the national accounts is beset by great difficulties, and must be qualified by reservations because of wide margins of error'.

(which was a 'free' year), for the co-ordinated bargaining since 1956 has been associated with great stability in the wage share.

The wage share cannot be looked at in isolation, however. Unfortunately, statistical data on other factor shares are too imperfect to provide a reliable explanation of the shifts in the share of wages in the national income, but from Table 4 we can see some significant pointers to the changes in income distribution implied by Table 3. Net interests and dividends of the private sector have shown the greatest propensity to lag behind other factor incomes. But it is the shareholders who have suffered, rather than the firms themselves. Business investment has maintained a high private investment ratio (Table 1, line 5), despite—or perhaps because of—the pressure from wage costs and from direct corporate taxes. Since 1938 private business firms have enjoyed favourable depreciation treatment for new investment, though the arrangements are now not quite so lenient and the investment reserve system has also been changed. But the broad policy throughout has been to discourage consumption through dividend distributions, and to maintain a high level of investment.

The failure of the incomes of private entrepreneurs to keep pace with wages and salaries is ascribable to the reduction in the number of farmers and to full employment of the labour force.

In sum, there is a complicated pattern of economic forces and policy measures at work affecting income distribution and factor shares, and the data are too unreliable to enable us to do more than indicate these broad trends.

WAGE CHANGES SINCE 1939

The main questions arising out of the earlier discussion of wage rounds and wage agreements are first, the impact of centralized bargaining on wage changes and wage structure, and second, the relative importance of solidarity and the market as determinants of wages structure. These two main aspects can be traced in the subsequent discussion of wage data.[1]

[1] Note on wage statistics. Prior to 1954 the Social Welfare Board statistics for wages in mining and manufacturing were based on data covering about 85% of the total number of workers included in the Board of Trade's (Kommerskollegium) industrial statistics. Larger establishments were better represented than smaller, because of the poorer response (on a voluntary basis) from smaller firms. The surveys asked for information about number of workers, number of hours worked during the year, total wages paid—with a breakdown for time and piecework basic rates, overtime, shift pay, holiday and sickness pay, and payments in kind. Separate data were collected for adult men, women, and for juveniles.

In 1954 an agreement was reached between the Social Welfare Board and

The standards by which solidarity is adjudged successful or otherwise are not always clear, and open to controversy. It is arguable, for example, that it is naive to identify solidarity solely with the closing of all wage differentials. Much of the LO analysis of solidarity is now concerned with making the wage structure more equitable in the sense that it is more *rational*, the criteria for this being derived from job requirements. This approach is a job evaluation rather than a statistical exercise, and it can lead logically to the conclusion that a group of wage earners that is statistically below the average level of earnings in industry is not necessarily badly paid, if the job requirements are not exacting.

Despite this, there is a broad acceptance that wide statistical wage differentials *are* inequitable, and, in addition, LO itself, in the reviews of wage developments which it presents to its congresses, has hitherto always judged the success of solidarity by reference to *wage statistics* and the various types of statistical differential discussed here.

Table 5 shows the year-to-year movements since the war in average hourly earnings for male and female workers in manufacturing industry, the sector in which particular wage rounds take shape. As the table shows, there is no strong evidence to suggest that the level at which bargaining takes place has a significant effect on the amount of wage increases obtained. The two years in which total increases and wage drift were largest, 1951 and 1952, were respectively free and co-ordinated bargaining years; 1947, the year of the next largest increases, was a free round. Nor has co-ordinated bargaining been associated with *small* increases. Increases since 1956 have not been notably smaller than in other years, with the exception of 1947, 1951, and 1952. Co-ordinated bargaining has not, on the evidence so far, been more successful in obtaining or preventing wage increases. This is hardly surprising, for three main reasons. First, each year is a unique complex of economic, bargaining, and other circumstances. Secondly, as Chapter XV showed, co-ordination of bargaining has been attempted only in a pragmatic fashion and on a hand-to-mouth

SAF whereby SAF collects the reports on wage data from Partners in mining and manufacturing, building and construction, inland transport, petroleum distribution and stevedoring. The Social Board collects data from non-SAF firms. The total number of man hours reported in 1958 was 84·5% of the man hours, according to the Board of Trade's survey of industrial production and employment in 1958.

SAF in fact makes two wage surveys for manual workers each year. In addition to the annual survey outlined above, it collects wage data for the second quarter of the year in order to have up-to-date information for wage bargaining. This material is processed to give hourly earnings statistics by Member association, contract, worker category, and wage items.

These second quarter statistics are normally used by mutual agreement in the centralized wage rounds. In addition, about two-thirds of the workers covered by SAF now have their wage statistics compiled *jointly* by the unions and the employers' associations.

TABLE 5

ANNUAL INCREASES IN HOURLY EARNINGS[1] IN MANUFACTURING INDUSTRY, 1945–60

	Percentage increase on previous year's average earnings														
	1946	*1947*	*1948*	*1949*	*1950*	*1951*	*1952*	*1953*	*1954*	*1955*	*1956*	*1957*	*1958*	*1959*	*1960*
ADULT MALE WORKERS															
Total	8·0	14·1	8·3	3·0	3·9	20·6	18·2	3·6	4·4	8·5	8·1	5·7	5·4	4·5	7·1
Of which by agreement	3·2	9·7	4·5	0·2	—	14·3	11·6	1·1	1·5	4·3	4·1	2·1	2·4	1·6	3·6
Wage drift	4·8	4·4	3·8	2·8	3·9	6·3	6·6	2·5	2·9	4·2	4·0	3·6	3·0	2·9	3·5
ADULT FEMALE WORKERS															
Total	9·5	18·1	10·5	3·8	3·4	20·6	17·1	2·7	4·1	9·1	8·4	5·6	4·7	3·9	7·9
Of which by agreement	5·4	14·0	6·0	—	—	16·3	13·8	0·8	2·5	6·6	5·5	3·1	2·5	1·8	4·6
Wage drift	4·1	4·1	4·5	3·8	3·4	4·3	3·3	1·9	1·6	2·5	2·9	2·5	2·2	2·1	3·3

Source: Swedish Employers' Confederation.

[1] Time and piece rate and shift pay.

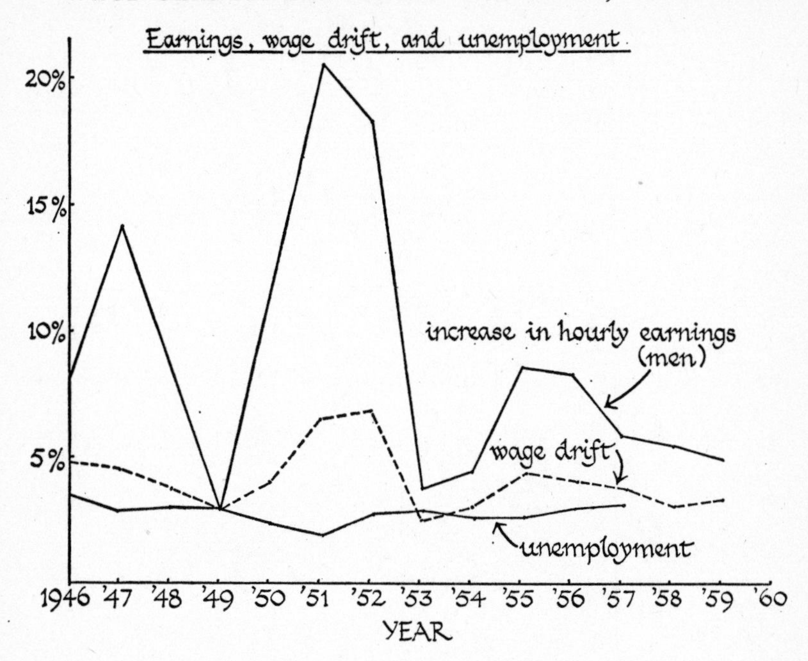

Notes: earnings and wage drift statistics taken from Table 5.
Unemployment statistics from Table 2, line 5.

ad hoc basis. No long-term *systematic* attempt has been made to use centralization as the mechanism for steering wages. Thirdly, even if it had, wage drift emerges clearly as a force which can considerably amend the contractual bargains struck. This is particularly significant in the case of sex differentials, for attempts to close the gap by awarding larger contractual increases to women than to men (in all years except 1953) have, in seven years out of fifteen since 1946, failed to give larger *total* earnings increases for women than for men.

How significant is the state of the labour market in determining the rate at which wages have changed? The answer is by no means clear cut, as the above chart indicates. Indicators of the demand for labour are very imperfect. That used here, unemployment in trade unions, is not comprehensive, but is the only available unemployment series for years before 1955. Vacancy statistics are not used because it is not known what proportion of all vacancies is reported to the Labour Exchanges or filled with their help. Nevertheless, unfilled vacancies do of course tend to correlate with unemployment among trade union members; unfilled vacancies rise as unemployment among trade union members falls.

TABLE 6

WAGE AND SALARY CHANGES, 1939–60 FOR SELECTED GROUPS

(Index, 1939=100)

I

1	2	3	4	5	6	7	8	9	10	11
Year	*Cost-of-Living (a)*	*Hourly Earnings in Mining and Manufacturing (b)*		*Hourly Earnings in Agricul-ture (c)*	*Daily Earnings in Forestry (d)*	*Hourly Earnings in Building (b)*	*Hourly Earnings in Public Works (State)*	*Hourly Earnings for Manual Workers in Local Government Service (f)*	*Salaried Employees in Industry Clerical Staff(e)*	
		Men	*Women*	*Men*	*Men*	*Men*	*Men*	*Men*	*Male*	*Female*
1939	100	100 (1·34)	100 (0·84)	100 (0·67)	100	100 (1·89)	100 (1·48)	100 (1·78)	100	100
1940	113	109	110	108	116	98	—	105	106	107
1941	128	117	119	122	137	103	121	112	114	115
1942	138	128	130	136	162	112	131	120	124	125
1943	140	133	135	151	163	122	134	125	132	132
1944	139	137	140	158	162	126	137	127	134	138
1945	139	142	150	181	178	130	141	133	140	144
1946	139	153	163	202	206	147	157	146	151	153
1947	146	175	193	219	225	157	172	167	164	173
1948	150	190	213	264	242	172	186	186	175	186
1949	153	196	221	275	230	176	192	193	182	194
1950	155	204	229	285	290	182	197	193	189	203
1951	179	246	275	325	409	223	230	231	218	235
1952	193	293	325	408	390	269	273	262	257	282
1953	195	307	338	413	414	289	294	271	265	291

1954	197	320	352	424	443	303	309	280	279	301
1955	202	346	382	466	462	316	330	296	309	333
1956	213	376	415	496	488	340	349	312	330	352
1957	222	399	440	528	503	365	372	—	350	374
1958	231	423	465	558	518	386	393	—	369	390
1959	234	443	486	584	557	407	411	—	385	403
1960	243	472 (6·32)	518 (4·35)	646 (4·33)	614	440 (8·32)	442 (6·54)	—	409	426

II

Percentage Changes

1939–45	41	42	50	81	78	30	41	33	40	44
1946–50	12	44	53	57	63	40	40	45	35	41
1951–55	28	70	67	64	59	74	62	53	64	64
1956–60	20	36	36	39	33	39	34	—	32	28

Source: Social Welfare Board Statistics.

Notes on series: (*a*) excluding taxes and social benefits.
(*b*) average hourly earnings including all supplements (concept *c* of official hourly wage statistics).
(*c*) including value of benefits in kind. Break in series in 1954, when methods of collecting data changed.
(*d*) estimates by regional forestry inspectors of normal daily earnings of fellers, weighted average.
(*e*) annual earnings, 1939–47, monthly earnings, 1947–59, for office staff. Basis of collection changed in 1947 and 1955.
(*f*) change in series in 1951. Series under revision since 1956.

General Note: Average hourly earnings in crowns are given in brackets for years 1939 and 1960 in columns 3, 4, 5, 7, 8.

The chart shows earnings changes are much more volatile than the moderate changes from year to year in unemployment. A slight fall in the level of unemployment is associated with big changes in earnings, e.g. in 1947 and 1951–2 (the latter a quite exceptional period); and the rising unemployment of 1952–3 is associated with small wage increases in 1953. By contrast, in 1956 unemployment rose slightly above the 1953 level, but wage increases were much greater than in 1953.

Wage drift might appear to throw light on the sensitivity of wage changes to scarcity of labour. The market hypothesis would suggest that wage drift falls as unemployment rises, and vice versa. This is true of 1953, when wage drift was small and unemployment rising. It is true also of 1951–2, but in the opposite direction, when wage drift was high and unemployment low. In 1946–7, however, both unemployment and wage drift fell. A significant point that emerges from 1951–2 and 1955–6 is the *lag* in wage drift, which remained high after unemployment had begun to rise. Wage drift is only in part a market phenomenon. Together with the large fluctuations that take place in money earnings, this point suggests that the market sets the general direction of change, but the build-up of bargaining rounds and the compensation complex can frequently give rise to earnings increases and wage drift which are much more violent than the actual marginal changes in employment.

One of the strongest policy pressures on the wages structure since 1939 has been LO's wages policy of solidarity, and in Table 6 wage and salary movements since 1939 for selected groups are presented. The material permits only broad conclusions, since changes in earnings are affected by shifts in the size, age, skill and qualification mix, hourly and piecework payments, and also by changes in the basis of compilation of some of the series since 1939. Since 1945 all the groups have improved their real position compared with cost-of-living movements, and the years 1947, 1951, and 1952 again stand out as years of large money changes in pay. By sector, the general point to be noted is that the low-wage groups of 1939 have improved their position relative to others.

There has been a general compression of the earnings structure, favouring agriculture, forestry, and both manual and clerical female workers. Public sector employees, whose hourly rates were well above the average for industrial male workers in 1939, have fared worse than workers in industry. Salaried employees in general have lost ground. The unfavourable relative movement of *hourly* earnings in building should be treated with caution; it was only in the period 1939–45 that a relative decline occurred, because of building controls, and in addition one of the most important changes in that industry has been the increase in the average number of hours worked per annum, which sheds quite another light on the building worker's relative position. Even so, his hourly earnings still put him at the top of the wage scale.

The breakdown of increases by percentages over several years which is given in Part II of Table 6 provides a more instructive view of the relative wage and salary movements. It can be seen at once from these figures that the improvement in the status of agricultural and forestry workers took place during the war, when production in these sectors was buoyant. Since the war there has been little further improvement in their relative status, and since 1950, indeed, they have fared no better than industrial workers. The same point is true of the sex differential for manual and clerical workers. In war-time, and up to the year 1950, women obtained larger increases than men, but in the period 1951–60 women have obtained smaller total percentage increases than men. This break around 1950 in the closing of differentials accounts for much of the gloom which LO felt in 1956 about the success of its wages policy of solidarity.[1]

When wage movements since 1939 for male manual workers in industry are studied by sector, in Table 7, the same general tendency towards compression in the wages structure is evident. The largest increases in hourly earnings (column 4) have been obtained by the three worst-paid groups in 1939—non-metallic mining and quarrying, manufacture of wood, and textiles. The high wage industries of 1939, paper and printing in particular, and mining, have lost ground. An explanation is to be sought not simply in terms of solidarity. The market has some suggestive indicators as well.

The outstanding example of market forces is non-metallic mining, where a very big drop in manpower since 1945 has been accompanied by high productivity per man-hour and large wage increases. Capital investment was heavy in this industry soon after the war.[2] Manufacture of wood shows a big drop in manpower, a poor performance by volume and productivity, but large wage increases. In beverages and tobacco, there has been a small decline in manpower, a high productivity increase, but low wage increases. Leather, etc., shows a similar drop in manpower, the largest productivity increase, a large increase in volume, but poor wage increases. The pulp and paper industry shows a rise in manpower, 'average' productivity and volume increases, and considerable improvement of its relative wage position. The chemical industry has expanded most rapidly in volume terms, but with only a small increase in labour force, and the relative

[1] See LO *kongress-protokoll*, 1956, p. 127 et seq. The gloom was still as widespread at the 1961 congress. *Kongress-protokoll*, 1961, p. 146 et seq.

[2] See *S.O.U.*, 1957 : 10, *Balanserad Expansion*, bilaga 7, especially Table 1, p. 113, for statistics to support this point.

TABLE 7

EARNINGS, PRODUCTION AND PRODUCTIVITY IN MANUFACTURING

1	2	3	4	5		6	7		8	
	Hourly Earnings Men		*Percentage Increase by 1959 over*	*Rank*		*Manual Labour Force in 1945 as percentage*	*Productivity per man hour in 1958 (1939=100)*		*Volume of Production in 1958 (1939=100)*	
Industry	*1939*	*1959*	*1939*	*1939*	*1959*	*of 1958*	*Index*	*Rank*	*Index*	*Rank*
1. Mining	1·72	7·48	335	2	6	80	139	9	139	9
2. Metal and Engineering Trades	1·39	6·21	347	4=	5	80	155	8	210	2
3. Non-metallic Mining, Quarrying	1·12	5·51	392	9	1	160	223	2=	177	6
4. Manufacture of Wood	1·10	5·32	384	11	2	120	138	10	128	11
5. Pulp, Paper, and Cardboard Mills	1·28	5·79	352	7=	3=	80	176	5	180	5
6. Manufacture of Paper Products, Printing and Allied Industries	1·79	6·46	261	1	11	85	114	11	181	4
7. Manufacture of Food	1·39	5·32	283	4=	9	105	156	7	153	8
8. Beverages and Tobacco	1·45	5·36	270	3	10	108	223	2=	169	7
9. Textiles and Clothing	1·11	5·02	352	10	3=	111	165	6	132	10
10. Leather, Hair, and Rubber Goods	1·28	5·56	334	7=	7	107	235	1	204	3
11. Chemicals and Chemical Products	1·37	5·74	320	6	8	92	220	4	284	1

Source: Social Welfare Board Statistics, and *Statistisk årsbok*, 1959, 1960.

TABLE 8

RELATIVE WAGE POSITIONS IN INDUSTRY. ADULT MALE WORKERS

(Average Hourly Wage in Industry in each year=100)

	1939	*1941*	*1942*	*1943*	*1944*	*1945*	*1946*	*1947*	*1948*	*1949*	*1950*	*1951*	*1952*	*1953*	*1954*	*1955*	*1956*	*1957*	*1958*	*1959*	*1960*
1. Mining	129	122	123	122	121	120	118	121	125	126	129	125	126	127	127	126	125	126	126	126	126
2. Metal and Engineering Trades	105	106	106	106	106	105	104	103	103	105	105	104	106	106	105	105	105	105	105	105	104
3. Non-metallic Mining, Quarrying	84	83	86	88	90	91	92	94	93	93	92	92	92	92	93	94	93	93	93	93	95
4. Manufacture of Wood	83	81	82	83	83	86	89	89	89	89	88	89	87	87	90	90	89	89	89	90	90
5. Pulp, Paper, and Cardboard Mills	96	92	92	89	89	89	93	94	93	92	92	98	97	96	98	100	100	99	98	98	99
6. Manufacture of Paper Products, Printing and Allied Industries	129	128	128	126	128	126	124	123	121	118	120	115	113	111	111	110	110	109	109	109	109
7. Manufacture of Food	105	101	100	100	99	98	98	96	96	96	95	94	91	91	89	91	89	89	89	90	90
8. Beverages and Tobacco	109	110	105	103	101	102	98	98	98	95	93	93	93	91	92	93	92	90	89	90	93
9. Textiles and Clothing	84	83	85	85	87	89	91	92	93	93	92	91	87	86	86	86	86	85	85	85	84
10. Leather, Hair, and Rubber Goods	96	98	98	98	100	100	99	100	101	102	101	97	94	95	95	94	94	94	94	94	95
11. Chemicals and Chemical Products	103	104	102	100	101	102	102	102	102	101	101	99	99	100	100	99	100	99	98	97	97
12. Average Hourly Earnings (*c*) in Industry	1·33	1·56	1·70	1·78	1·82	1·90	2·04	2·33	2·53	2·61	2·72	3·30	3·92	4·11	4·29	4·64	5·04	5·34	5·67	5·93	6·32

Source: *Löner*, Del. 11, 1958, Table 17, and *Löner*, 1952, Table 19. Stencilled data for 1959 and 1960.

wage position of the workers has deteriorated since 1939. This is perhaps the best example of a heavily capitalized industry.

From Table 7, therefore, we cannot, on the one hand, draw broad conclusions which point generally to a market explanation of wage increases. On the other hand, the 'solidarity' approach which appears at first sight to explain the closing of the wages structure must be considerably qualified in the light of this evidence. A fuller explanation of the wage changes would require a more detailed study industry by industry than the statistics permit. A capital/output approach would be helpful, but cannot be attempted because of the conceptual and statistical difficulties.

Relative wage positions play an important role in the tightly organized Swedish labour market, with its emphasis on solidarity. Table 8 (for men) shows that the very slight general tendency to compress the wages concertina in industry (from 129–83 in 1939 to 126–84 in 1960) has been accompanied by some major shifts in relative wage positions. While bargaining units do not coincide precisely with the industrial classification the prevalence of industrial unionism makes this a minor qualification.[1]

Mining has maintained its position throughout as the wage *élite* of industry. The metal and engineering trades have shown a stability which is to be expected in view of the heavy 'weight' carried by this sector in industrial activity. The stability suggests also that the 'black market' wage drift '*fiffelfaktor*' so frequently associated with this particular industry's wage agreements are not an outrageously destabilizing influence. Non-metallic mining and quarrying verifies the analysis of Table 7 by showing considerable improvement in relative wage terms. The improvement in the wood manufacturing industry occurred between 1944 and 1946. The pulp industry lost ground in war-time, when it was cut off from foreign markets, but the most significant feature here is that the relative improvement effected in 1951, during the Korean boom, has been maintained. Such once-for-all major shifts in the wages structure can help some groups, just as, in the case of printing, the upheaval in the wages structure in 1951 hastened an already deteriorating position. The drastic drop from its 1939 position of eminence alongside mining has led to considerable agitation in the printing trades for a reform of the wages system which allows payment by results to enhance earnings. The foodstuffs industry has drawn similar conclusions about its payments system from its fall since 1939. Here the strike-lock-out of 1953 did nothing at all to slow down the process of decline down the relative wages

[1] The earnings statistics on which Tables 8 and 9 are based have not been revised by the Social Welfare Board to take account of small changes (e.g. between 1951 and 1952) in industrial classifications.

ladder. Beverages have lost ground steadily. In textiles, the relative position steadily improved until the crisis in the industry in 1952–3. Leather began to lose ground at the time of the 'Korea effect' on the wages structure. Chemicals has shown the greatest stability in its relative position.

Some other features are worth noting. Not only did the Korean upheaval provide a major upward shift for the pulp industry, and accentuate the downward drift in printing, food manufacturing, and the leather, hair, and rubber goods industry. This 1951 displacement of the wages structure was not eliminated by the co-ordinated round of 1952. It is too early to judge the effect on relative wage positions of the centralized bargaining practised since 1956, but there has been a suggestive stability in relative wage positions since that year. Finally, it again appears that solidarity has had limited success in compressing wage differentials, and has not offset market forces operating in different sectors; or, if the solidarity issue is put in another way, solidarity is not inconsistent with sharp movements in the wages structure.

The relative wages structure for female workers in industry has been compressed more than that of men since 1939, with a range in 1939 of 123–82, against 108–88 in 1960. Table 9 shows the developments. The decline in the relative position of beverages accounts for the narrowing of the range at the upper end, and this is in fact the only sector where there has been a large change in relative position (apart from mining, which is not a significant employer of female labour). The metal and engineering trades show less stability for female than male workers, and a slight downward tendency. Non-metallic mining and wood manufacturing show the same upward trend as men's position, leather and chemicals great stability, while pulp fluctuates more than men. By contrast to their male counterparts, women in printing and food manufacturing have not experienced a sharp fall in relative positions. Table 10 shows that in both industries the female labour force is above average, and it is in these two industries that the woman worker's wage as a percentage of the male worker's has shown the greatest increase since 1939. Textiles, which is predominantly a women's industry, does not show the same post-1952 downward trend for women as for men, and Table 10 shows increased female participation in hours worked and a significant closing of the sex differential since 1939. Apart from the pulp industry, the Korea displacement effect noticeable in the men's relative wage structure left hardly any impact on women's relative positions.

Table 10 throws more light on women's wages with regard both to sex differentials and the relative weights of female and male participation in the various sectors of industry.

TABLE 9

RELATIVE WAGE POSITIONS IN INDUSTRY. ADULT FEMALE WORKERS

(*Average Hourly Wage in Industry in each year=100*)

	1939	*1941*	*1942*	*1943*	*1944*	*1945*	*1946*	*1947*	*1948*	*1949*	*1950*	*1951*	*1952*	*1953*	*1954*	*1955*	*1956*	*1957*	*1958*	*1959*	*1960*
1. Mining	99	97	95·4	97	96	83	82	86	84	83	89	89	92	91	90	—	89	87	85	83	88
2. Metal and Engineering Trades	114	113	111	111	109	108	104	104	102	103	105	105	108	110	108	107	108	108	109	109	108
3. Non-metallic Mining, Quarrying	82	80	82	85	86	86	88	91	90	89	89	90	91	91	91	92	92	92	91	90	91
4. Manufacture of Wood	89	90	91	89	90	89	95	95	95	94	95	96	94	96	96	99	99	100	99	101	101
5. Pulp, Paper, and Cardboard Mills	102	93	94	94	92	91	94	100	101	101	98	104	106	105	103	104	104	103	102	101	101
6. Manufacture of Paper Products, Printing and Allied Industries	114	107	108	108	108	108	109	110	108	105	106	108	110	109	109	109	109	109	110	109	107
7. Manufacture of Food	104	101	101	102	100	98	101	100	98	99	97	99	98	100	99	100	99	99	99	100	100
8. Beverages and Tobacco	123	132	127	122	118	114	110	107	106	103	101	103	106	104	105	105	104	103	103	103	110
9. Textiles and Clothing	94	95	95	96	98	98	99	99	99	100	100	99	97	97	98	97	97	97	97	96	96
10. Leather, Hair, and Rubber Goods	100	102	100	101	99	98	98	100	100	102	102	99	98	99	98	99	99	99	99	99	99
11. Chemicals and Chemical Products	99	100	99	97	98	99	96	96	95	96	97	97	100	101	101	101	102	102	101	101	101
12. Average Hourly Earnings (*c*) in Industry	0·84	1·00	1·09	1·13	1·18	1·26	1·37	1·61	1·79	1·86	1·92	2·31	2·73	2·84	2·96	3·21	3·49	3·70	3·91	4·08	4·35

Source: *Löner*, Del. 11, 1958, Table 18, and *Löner*, 1952, Table 20. Stencilled data for 1959 and 1960.

TABLE 10

SEX DIFFERENTIALS IN INDUSTRY

	Women's Hourly Wages (c)[1] *as percentage of Men's*							*Hours worked by Women as percentage of Total Hours worked*	
	1939	*1947*	*1950*	*1952*	*1954*	*1956*	*1958*	*1952*	*1958*
1. Mining	48	49	48	51	49	50	46	1·0	1·1
2. Metal and Engineering Trades	69	69	71	72	71	71	72	6·4	6·1
3. Non-metallic Mining, Quarrying	62	67	68	69	68	69	68	7·2	8·0
4. Manufacture of Wood	68	74	75	75	74	77	76	2·5	2·9
5. Pulp, Paper, and Cardboard Mills	67	73	76	76	72	72	72	7·4	8·0
6. Manufacture of Paper Products, Printing and Allied Industries	54	60	62	68	68	69	70	18·5	16·6
7. Manufacture of Food	63	72	72	75	76	77	77	26·0	28·3
8. Beverages and Tobacco	71	76	77	79	79	79	80	32·0	28·8
9. Textiles and Clothing	71	75	76	78	78	78	79	58·0	61·1
10. Leather, Hair, and Rubber Goods	66	69	71	72	71	73	72	32·0	32·0
11. Chemicals and Chemical Products	61	65	68	70	70	71	72	19·0	17·7
12. All Manufacturing	63	69	71	70	69	69	69	16·8	16·4

Source: *Löner* and *Lönestatistisk årsbok*, various years.

[1] *Note*. This comparison, based on hourly earnings concept (*c*) is *less* favourable to women workers than a comparison based on concept (*a*) (basic hourly and piecework rates), since proportionately more men than women are shift workers and/or work overtime, e.g. in 1952 women's wages, concept (*a*), were 70·8% of men's wages, and 69·6% of concept (*c*). In 1958 the percentages were 70·2 (*a*) and 69 (*c*). The discrepancy is to some extent offset by the fact that women's holiday and sickness pay (which enter into concept (*c*)) are a slightly more significant part of concept (*c*) than in the case of men.

As Table 6 suggested, the closing of the sex differential occurred between 1939 and 1950, and since 1950 there has been great stability in this particular differential for industry as a whole. Again, however, an aggregative observation of this kind is misleading. In the industries where the hours worked by women form a significant proportion of the input of labour services, differentials have continued to narrow since 1950 (e.g. in printing, food manufacturing, beverages, textiles—the largest group, and chemicals). Leather, etc., is the exception.

Three significant points emerge from this data on women's wages in industry. First, the LO wage policy pronouncements on 'badly paid female groups' are relevant to fairly clearly definable groups in particular industries. Yet LO has often been vagueness itself about this policy, by making women's wages a *general* issue instead of specifying the concentrations of female workers in particular industries. To the unions the issue is not of course solely an economic one. A hard core of justice underlies the propaganda for reducing sex pay differentials; and women can in addition make a significant contribution to trade union numbers and finances. Secondly, the downward trend in labour force participation among female manual workers makes it difficult to conclude that this limited success in narrowing sex differentials is to be ascribed to the policy of solidarity, rather than to the impact of market forces. The significance of the market is indicated by a third point, that (as Table 5 showed) attempts to weight contractually agreed increases in favour of women workers have been made nugatory by wage drift. Justice (and a desire to increase trade union membership among women workers) may point in one direction, but the market has not always concurred.

GEOGRAPHICAL DIFFERENTIALS

The use of cost-of-living zones arrived at by official inquiry was originally intended to provide an element of justice in civil service salaries against the harsh dictates of geography and of forces outside the control of the worker. Private industry took up the zones, and has adapted them to suit particular needs. The geographical differentials which emerge in industry are only partly explicable by actual differences in the cost-of-living, since the zones are not always followed precisely in industrial agreements, and, more important, the differentials set for different zones frequently differ from the rigid standard (at present a 12% range) used in the public service.

Geographical differentials are in fact a mixture of equity and plant location factors. Differences in wage settings between firms and industries, in the wage and skill mix, and in methods of wage payment,[1] also operate to blur the pristine concept of justice dispensed by cost-of-living bonuses determined according to the expenses of living in particular localities, and zone differentials must be treated with caution when solidarity and the market are discussed in this context.

TABLE 11

GEOGRAPHICAL DIFFERENTIALS IN INDUSTRY

Hourly earnings (c) of adult male workers in industry in lowest cost-of-living zone as percentage of those in highest

	1939 %	1946 %	1952 %	1958 %
1. Mining	40	65	63	70
2. Metal and Engineering Trades	57	70	75	77
3. Non-Metallic Mining, Quarrying	53	74	68	70
4. Manufacture of Wood	58	85	84	86
5. Pulp Factories	80	82	86	92
6. Printing	51	65	79[2]	74
7. Manufacture of Food	66	70	81	82
8. Beverages and Tobacco	64	67	79	80
9. Textiles and Clothing	62	75	79	80
10. Leather, Hair, and Rubber Goods	70	80	83	88
11. Chemicals and Chemical Products	59	79	83	84
12. All Manufacturing	52	67	72	74
WOMEN (all industries)	71	76	77	82

Source: *Löner* and *Lönestatistisk årsbok*, various years.

The statistics of Table 11 show a very considerable closing of this differential since 1939, particularly during the war. Since 1946 (line 12) the rate of closing differentials has proceeded much more slowly. During the period there has been a significant reduction in the actual inter-zone differences in living costs, and for this reason alone the zone differentials must be expected to narrow. But differentials are still in general much larger than the 'just wage' basis intends. The rigid civil service differential range of 12% is met in industry only by pulp factories and leather. Why have geographical differentials closed as *little* as they have done since 1939?

The answer is to be sought in the market, in plant size and location, type of wage system, structure of labour force, and local labour market conditions. It is true that the market has helped to narrow geographical differentials by the pressure which the drift from the land and agricultural policy have put on the wages structure of rural

[1] The significance of size of firm for the amount of piecework and overtime can be shown in official data for the years 1950–3, the only years for which such material was analysed. The 1953 statistics are given in the table on p. 242.

[2] Includes paper-manufacturing.

labour markets.[1] But there is no reason in principle to expect demand and supply to operate in the same direction as the cost-of-living concept, which is meant to provide the hard core of zone differentials. The point is well put by the experience of the civil service—the rigid zone differentials are considered by TCO to hamper recruitment to the government service in localities where the zone differential cannot readily be adjusted to the market in the way it can in private industry.

Data on plant-level differentials are much too scanty to permit any systematic analysis. Average hourly earnings for adult workers in industry have only been analysed in official wage statistics for the years 1947–50. Some trend in the period 1939–46 for the gap between small and large firms to narrow has been noted.[2]

SALARIED EMPLOYEES IN INDUSTRY

The upswing in the numbers and proportions of salaried employees in the whole labour market has been noted at various stages of this study. In industry, the number of manual workers increased by 24,000 (4%) to 676,500 between 1948 and 1958, while the number of salaried employees rose by 54,000 (40%) to 187,400 in the same period, and their proportion of the employed labour force in industry increased from 17% to 22%. The metal and engineering trades account for 51% of salaried employees in industry, and printing and chemicals also have high white-collar manual worker ratios.

It is important to ask how this shift has affected the wage and salary structure, although the *discontinuities* in the statistical data for the period 1939–59 make the answers even more tentative than usual.[3]

[1] The actual shift from country to town has, however, been much less in the post-war period than this argument often allows. E.g. the division of manual workers in industry proper between rural areas and towns changed in the following way between 1946 and 1958:

	1946		1958	
Rural districts	263,500	40·4%	254,500	37·6%
Towns	389,000	59·6%	422,000	62·4%

[2] See LO *Fackföreningsrörelsen och den fulla sysselsättningen*, 1951, pp. 117–19: and Gösta Rehn, Unionism and the Wage Structure in Sweden, in *The Theory of Wage Determination*, edited Dunlop (London, 1957), for a discussion of this point. The data are also reproduced in Reynolds and Taft, *The Evolution of Wage Structure*, p. 246 (New Haven, 1956).

[3] Beginning in 1913, the Social Welfare Board made annual surveys of salaries in mining and manufacturing industry, covering annual salaries paid to a few categories of employees and figures for the average number of employees. For the years 1947–54 summary data were collected referring to the month of September, and including basic salaries, extra shift pay, overtime, holiday and sickness pay, and the value of benefits in kind. In 1955 a new procedure was introduced by agreement between the Social Welfare Board and SAF, along the same lines as the 1954 agreement for manual workers' wage statistics. SAF collects statistics for salaried employees of its Partner firms on an individual basis—in fact SAF's statistics for salaried employees are now more detailed and

TABLE 12
MAJOR GROUPS OF SALARIED EMPLOYEES IN INDUSTRY, 1958

	Men		*Women*		*Total*	
	Total '000s	*Percentage*	*Total '000s*	*Percentage*	*'000s*	*Percentage*
Technical	37·5	29·7	2·3	5·8	39·8	23·9
Foremen	34·9	27·7	1·0	2·5	35·9	21·5
Office	41·1	32·6	35·7	88·1	76·8	46·1
Sales	8·1	6·4	0·9	2·2	9·0	5·4
Other	4·5	3·6	0·6	1·6	5·1	3·1
Total	126·1	100	40·5	100	166·6	100

Source: *Löner*, 1958, Del. 1, p. 6.

With that clear warning, we can obtain a broad picture of trends. Table 12 classifies those salaried employees in industry in 1958 covered by the salary statistics by major occupational groups and by sex. Clerical staff account for 46% of the total, and form the largest group for both sexes. But the overwhelming majority (88%) of female staff are clerical workers, while the male staff is fairly evenly divided among technical, foremen, and clerical staff. Technical staff have shown easily the most rapid rate of growth in numbers since 1939 (probably about 300%), though the lack of a figure for industry proper in 1939 makes it difficult to say precisely what the increase has been. Clerical staff in industry has grown by about 130%, with roughly the same change for women and men.

In Table 13 series are given for salary changes since 1939. A comparison with Table 6 shows that not even those salaried groups that have improved their relative position among white-collar workers —female technical staff, and to a lesser extent (at least till 1955) women clerical workers—have approached the increases obtained by manual workers. The position of salaried employees *vis-à-vis* wage-earners has deteriorated. The percentage breakdown of increases given by groups of years in Table 6, Part II, does not suggest that salaried employees have been able in the past decade to halt the trend, despite their organization efforts. In the past ten years female white-collar workers have indeed lost ground relative to female manual workers in industry. This can be explained at least in part by

differentiated by individual than those for manual workers—and the Social Welfare Board collects similar data for non-SAF firms outside SAF, but excluding public corporations. The two sets of statistics are then combined. The data now refer to employees in August of each year, and overtime is excluded. For 1958 the statistics covered 167,000 salaried employees. These statistics are not comparable with those collected by the Union of Clerical and Technical Employees in Industry, which has about 100,000 members.

TABLE 13

SALARIES IN INDUSTRY, 1939–60

(*Index, 1939=100*)

	Male			*Female*		
	Technical	*Foremen*	*Clerical*	*Technical*	*Foremen*	*Clerical*
1939	100 (546)	100 (412)	100 (381)	100 (200)	100 (257)	100 (197)
1940	106	106	106	107	106	107
1941	113	113	114	121	112	115
1942	123	122	124	131	120	125
1943	129	126	132	135	127	132
1944	130	130	134	146	135	138
1945	133	134	140	152	139	144
1946	139	144	151	160	149	153
1947	148	155	164	186	170	173
1948	159	164	175	195	184	186
1949	161	168	182	210	190	194
1950	171	174	189	215	197	203
1951	194	204	218	259	230	235
1952	225	244	257	305	267	282
1953	229	244	265	321	268	291
1954	238	254	279	328	276	301
1955	258	272	309	360	301	333
1956	272	295	330	378	318	352
1957	290	315	350	402	337	374
1958	307	330	369	415	351	390
1959	320	341	385	428	362	403
1960	340 (1856)	362 (1491)	409 (1560)	452 (904)	382 (983)	426 (839)

II

Percentage changes

1939–45	33	34	40	52	39	44
1946–50	29	30	35	41	42	41
1951–5	51	56	64	67	53	64
1956–60	32	33	32	26	27	28

Source: *Löner* and *Lönestatistisk årsbok*, various years.

Note. These series must all be used with caution. The basis of collecting salary statistics was revised in 1947 and 1955. Moreover, only the series for clerical workers is based on data for industry proper throughout the period: the statistics for technical staff and foremen for the period 1939–46 cover other parts of the private sector besides industry proper.

Monthly salaries in crowns are given in brackets for the years 1939 and 1960.

the conditions of supply, for the number of female manual workers has tended to move downwards, while the supply of female office staff has increased (partly for social reasons). Female technical staff, on the other hand, who are predominantly technical assistants, have been more successful in improving their position.

They have had particular success in closing the sex differential, for between 1939 and 1960 the salaries of female technical staff increased from 37% to 49% of the salary of their male counterparts. For clerical staff the sex differential closed only slightly, from 52% to 54%.

The penalty of the rapid increase in male technical staff seems to have been a sharp loss of their 1939 position as the cream of the salaried grades in industry, their salaries dropping from 133% to 119% of clerical workers'. The number of male foremen has increased at a somewhat faster rate than clerical staff, but their poor performance compared with clerical staff in obtaining increases provides some explanation for the foremen's disquiet about the existing (individual) system for determining their salaries. In sum, the clerical worker, who had the lowest salary in 1939, has gained most ground compared with male technical staff and foremen.

These are of course extremely broad general conclusions, and it should be remembered that each individual group of employees discussed here (e.g. technical staff) contains within it an extremely wide range of skills.

Solidarity has not been a conscious policy on the part of salaried employees in pay determination, but the general closing of differentials which pervades the wages structure seems also to have influenced salary differentials. If we abstract from the moment for the undoubted influence of demand and supply, quality and skill, this suggests that it may not be solidarity *as such* that is the really significant factor in closing differentials in both the wage and salary structures. The tremendous upward movement in money GNP since 1939 may *in itself* have an equalizing tendency. It is the lowest-paid groups, e.g. clerical workers among salaried employees, who appear to be worst hit by inflation, and it appears equitable to award them higher increases, irrespective of whether these are already being pursued as part of a deliberate policy of solidarity (as with LO), or are primarily incidental to the rapid changes taking place in money terms. Against that, it can be argued that high income groups paying high marginal rates of tax under a progressive tax system are equally entitled to ask for 'equalizing' wage increases. SACO, for example, has long endeavoured to compile salary statistics that indicate incomes *net* of direct taxation.

Statistics for civil servants' salaries over a long period are not considered reliable, because of quality changes in the nature of jobs and job gradings, and in various forms of pay allowance which do not enter into the statistics for basic salaries. If, with these qualifications in mind, certain groups of government employees are followed through the period, we find a considerable closing of vertical differentials, and also a definite tendency to lag behind income trends in industry.

	1939	*1959*
Civil servants, grades 4–12	100	373 (1958)
Railway porter	100	319
Senior schoolmaster	100	294
Under secretary	100	278

The relative absence of wage drift in public employment is a big obstacle to government employees maintaining their relative income positions.

SUMMARY

The first main question posed with reference to wage experience since 1939 was the significance of the various forms that wage rounds took. There is no strong evidence that free or centralized bargaining is 'superior'. Centralized bargaining has not followed any theoretical postulate or objective, but rather a rule-of-thumb treatment of the wage problems of a particular year as they presented themselves to the bargaining parties. Co-ordination has not been used systematically, and there is no strong evidence in terms of the wages share, closing of differentials, or the 'tranquillity' of wage increases to point conclusively towards a preference for co-ordinated bargaining. Even if centralization had been planned systematically to steer the course of wages, wage drift proves an Achilles heel, so that the outcome is frequently different from the policy.

The second main issue, that of the relative importance of solidarity and demand and supply, is even more complex. Again, wage drift blurs the picture, and *appears* to swing the scales conclusively in favour of a market explanation. But not *all* wage drift is caused by the market. Induced or secondary wage drift can occur because solidarity requires a particular framework of wage differentials. Yet solidarity itself appears to have only limited, and perhaps negative, powers, in the sense that it acts as a restraining influence against wider differentials. The market and the changes in demand and supply offer at least as good arguments and explanations. Sex differentials have shown some response to solidarity, but also considerable sensitivity to market impulses, while the limited closing of inter-industry and geographical differentials reflects a complicated range of forces, mainly economic, at work.

CHAPTER XVII

Wages Policy

THE material of the four preceding chapters amply testifies to the seriousness with which the familiar dilemmas of full employment wages policy have been tackled in Sweden. The outstanding issues of practice and policy are analysed in this chapter.

I. THE WAGES POLICY OF SOLIDARITY

Chapter XVI suggested that some progress was made during the war and in the immediate post-war years in narrowing inter-industry differentials, sex differentials, geographical differentials, and the industry-agriculture differential, and in compressing the salary structure; but the evidence adduced is not entirely helpful to LO's original wages policy of solidarity. LO has in recent years been somewhat gloomy on the subject, and the reasons it puts forwards for the disappointing success of solidarity are worth examining. It ascribes the earliest post-war success in narrowing differentials to the general boom and excess demand conditions that prevailed in the economy, but argues that solidarity has subsequently had to contend with wide differences in the profitability of sectors.[1] Export and heavy goods industries have been more profitable than domestic and consumer goods industries. This is in fact an 'auld sang', for the whole pre-war debate on solidarity focused on the intricate problems of conducting wages policy on lines other than capacity to pay.

LO argues that solidarity is only possible if there is a stable economy.[2] This argument requires examination. It is true that the

[1] See R. Meidner, Löneutveckling och lönepolitik, in *Fackföreningsrörelsen*, 1955, I, 516. 'It is no exaggeration to state that the task of establishing just and reasonable relative wages between different groups is still in the main unresolved.' This was not regarded as a reason for abandoning this policy, since (*a*) at best, solidarity has prevented even larger differentials than existed at the beginning of the war; (*b*) there has often been a lack of balance in the economy as a whole (an argument less relevant since 1956 than at the time Meidner was writing), and (*c*) a lack of balance in the *structure* of the economy. Structural problems were given great emphasis at the 1961 congress, primarily through the report on *Samordnad näringspolitik*.

[2] 'Economic stability is a prerequisite of a rational trade union wage policy, and LO has appealed to the government on various occasions for firm measures to achieve this stability. If society does not succeed in its task of ensuring a tranquil rate of economic development, with moderate profits and equilibrium

past two decades have brought changes in money GNP which can fairly be characterized as incompatible with the stability LO desires. Since the fall in the value of money has not occurred discreetly behind the veil of a Keynesian money illusion, the period has undoubtedly been turbulent and abnormal in the pressures generated from the side of income distribution. But, in addition to the argument of experience, there seem to be strong grounds on which LO's policy of solidarity is open to objection.

First, is this declared prerequisite of stability possible as a long-term objective in a country so dependent on the course of the international economy, unless controls (which LO opposes in principle) are used to insulate the domestic economy? And, if they are, are they not likely to have a harmful effect on economic growth? On the basis of twentieth-century experience, there is no general presupposition that Sweden can insulate herself successfully from the international economy, or that it would be in the long-term interests of wage-earners for her to do so.

Secondly, would the stability *per se* for which LO yearns be conducive to rapid growth? Is it disequilibrium and instability that promote growth; are 'growth points' indicative of disequilibrium; or does growth flower best in equilibrium and stable economic conditions? The literature of economics is full of the clamour of discordant voices on this question, but the possibility—to put it no more strongly—that stability may mean a slower rate of expansion must be recognized. LO economists are of course not so naïve as to have overlooked this difficulty, and claim to have met it in two ways, which are essentially *complementary*. The first, which gets round the stagnation difficulty by developing a policy designed to promote the mobility of labour, is, however, important enough to deserve separate and wider treatment, and is discussed below, p. 329.

The other approach sees not only equity advantages in the wages policy of solidarity, but *economic* advantages. Solidarity helps to provide a flexible industrial structure by exercising steady pressure on low-wage, high-cost firms to rationalize or be exorcized from the market. This promotes a more efficient use of scarce resources. Analytically, the sequence of the argument is that growing industries with high profits raise wages (demand pull). But the acceptance of solidarity leads to *consequential* (cost push) wage increases in other sectors. LO accepts price increases as one likely outcome of this squeeze, but places greater emphasis on the way in which wage

in the labour market, the trade unions face formidable difficulties in carrying on their wages policy of solidarity successfully.' LO *kongress-protokoll*, 1956, p. 140. A similar attitude is adopted in *Fackföreningsrörelsen och den fulla sysselsättningen*, 1951, p. 147, and in the English version, *Trade Unions and Full Employment*, 1953, pp. 90–91.

solidarity helps to promote an efficient structure of the economy. Inefficient firms are forced to become more productive, or go to the wall (the 'expulsion effect'), thereby releasing resources for other, expanding sectors. This process is reinforced by a vigorous policy aimed at promoting a mobile and adaptable labour force.

LO argues that, when there is high employment, it is not possible to use adjustments in relative wages, the market mechanism, to allocate the labour force. Pressure through solidarity, backed by labour market policy, is considered a more effective way of encouraging growth.

In practice, this policy means accepting the structure of the economy which is dictated by expanding sectors such as the ore-based and timber-based industries, helping low wage groups in service and other industries by accepting that wage increases will mean price rises, and encouraging the shift of resources out of industries in which the pressure of wage costs makes Sweden less competitive internationally into the growing sectors.

This analysis may well underestimate the pressure on the price level from domestic service industries indulging their compensation complex under the banner of solidarity. It is important, for example, to ask how these consequential wage increases are financed. If they are conceded, they may be financed through running down liquid balances, borrowing, and, in the public sector, by government borrowing. In either event a rise in the money price level is likely. Alternatively, if they are not conceded, but thwarted by a restrictive economic policy, solidarity is hampered (at least in money terms). It is difficult to resist the view that the former alternative has generally been chosen, for the labour market now has such built-in compensating policies and mechanisms through its wage-determining institutions that any widening of differentials in response to growth points immediately leads to a consequential increase of wages in other sectors. This *may* promote solidarity, but at the expense of the price level and of the stability LO desires. For this reason LO is confronted with a formidable campaign of educating its members to understand what appropriate and equitable differentials are, in order to avoid these consequential inflationary cost and price rises. This is perhaps the greatest incentive behind, and the most challenging task for, the new move to co-ordination through the LO Wage Policy Council.

A third difficulty about solidarity as a policy is that it throws a great burden on wages as the determinant of the structure of the economy and of the distribution of income. Whether this is appropriate involves value judgements. More fundamentally, it does not follow that the structure of the economy which solidarity would promote provides for a more efficient use and combination of resources than the admittedly sluggish pricing process of the market, or that a wages policy of solidarity is a sufficient instrument of income distribution policy.

Other aspects of solidarity deserve comment. The policy has suffered from a lack of facts and data about the job requirements and labour supply to particular occupations which determine wage differentials, and has worked with extremely undifferentiated statistics about these wage differentials. Wage statistics for assessing relativities have been crude, and have been used for rough-and-ready comparisons, with considerable weight being given to traditional differentials. The central wage policy recommendations of LO have often been vague. The precise meaning of 'equity', 'lagging', 'groups with unfortunate experience in recent years', 'restraint', and 'priority' is liable to lead to wide misinterpretation. LO has been slow to develop any precise criteria. Job classification and evaluation of the Dutch type have been dismissed as too grandiose and inflexible, yet the criteria which have emerged—nature of the job and its requirements—cry out for the use of more 'scientific' standards. The work of the LO Wage Policy Council and the tighter co-ordination of claims since 1956 suggest that these deficiencies are now being tackled.

This leads to another aspect of solidarity. Despite the great formal powers vested in SAF and LO, complete and rigid control over wage-fixing is neither attempted nor possible. For its part, LO argued in both 1951 and 1956 that its formal powers were adequate. Wages policy should be based on voluntary co-operation of unions, and on their understanding of the common interests of the trade union movement. The dilemma is again plain. Too much formal central control is distasteful to 'democratic' trade unionism, though this issue was formally resolved in favour of 'representative democracy' by the 1941 LO constitutional debate. Too much rigidity is also bad for the reputation of LO and the unions, since the actual bargaining is then shifted to the local level, and LO and the unions—not to mention SAF—appear as obstacles to wage increases which employers are willing to concede, rather than as agents bargaining on behalf of the workers and the individual Partners of SAF. The attempt to provide both a lead and a leeway for local deviations in the early post-war wage rounds by making only vague pronouncements was not successful. Even the central agreements so far have also had to allow a suspiciously large and increasing number of exceptions to the general SAF–LO framework agreements.

A feature of solidarity which has been neglected is its *social policy* manifestations.[1] Originally, social policy was looked on as an indispensable supplement to solidarity, but hitherto all the emphasis has in fact been placed on the wage negotiation aspects. If a social minimum wage is held to be necessary then the possibility of a national minimum wage, which LO supported for a time in the 1930s for agricultural workers, could be re-examined, and social and fiscal policy measures could be employed to exalt those of low degree in the income distribution hierarchy. To put the point in another way, it is asking a lot of wages policy to make it do a job which already poses formidable problems for fiscal policy.

It is curious and paradoxical that the homogeneous trade union movement in Sweden should seriously fear that the only alternative to solidarity and co-ordination must be a split in the movement if wage differentials become too wide. There is little risk of the Swedish trade union movement disintegrating because of lack of solidarity, and indeed the emphasis placed on the concept probably does more to encourage an awareness and envy of relative wages than existed before the wages policy of solidarity was mooted.

That is by no means the end of the story. The most fundamental feature of solidarity is that it has changed its spots. While LO continues to assess the success of solidarity in the light of the size of wage differentials, it has since the war added a new interpretation of the term. There has been a growing recognition on the part of LO that solidarity does not simply mean the whittling away of *all* wage differentials, but the development of a rational wages structure, in the sense of moving towards wage differentials that are considered to be just and acceptable, in the light of varying job requirements. The meaning of solidarity has gradually evolved from the crude pre-war income redistribution idea of equity to a rough-and-ready job evaluation basis.[2] Solidarity now means a general ideological position of *narrow* wage differentials, unless a case can be made out for wider

[1] Some recognition of its importance is once more apparent, however, in speeches by Arne Geijer (p. 164) and Torvald Karlbom (p. 167) at the 1956 LO Congress. Karlbom argued that 'we must take account of common interests and try to co-ordinate our wages policy, and then, in conjunction with the political wing of the labour movement, endeavour to achieve what we cannot obtain solely by means of wages policy'. The use of fiscal policy as an alternative and more appropriate route to equity is also suggested by Bent Hansen in *Recept mot inflation*. 'Sex professorer har ordet', p. 51 (Stockholm, 1957).

[2] See *Fackföreningsrörelsen och den fulla sysselsättningen* (1951); and R. Meidner, in *Fackföreningsrörelsen*, 1957, I, 128. 'The goal of the wages policy of solidarity is a rational wages structure where the reward for labour is reasonable in relation to the nature of the work, the necessary qualifications, the conditions of work, and other circumstances. 'Rigid öre and percentage increments' are in the long run an obstacle to the attainment of this goal. . . . This differentiation is not the same as that which would be justified by differing capacities to pay.' Clearly, solidarity in terms of nature of work, qualifications, etc., may differ vastly from solidarity as originally conceived in terms of a just wage.

differentials, and the use of job evaluation to provide rational support for a range of differentials which is *accepted* as equitable. This more subtle concept of equity is essentially grounded in the ideas about 'equal pay for work of equal value' which LO and SAF agreed for women workers in 1951.

Paradoxically, this shift in the interpretation of solidarity has made it much more acceptable to SAF as a criterion.[1] Like LO, SAF is not now interested in founding its wages policy exclusively on capacity to pay, for under full employment conditions this would mean a much wider range of wage differentials, which would infringe the solidarity of employers' organizations no less than the class solidarity of trade unions.

SAF and LO could therefore agree broadly on their economic interpretation of solidarity, and the development of centralized bargaining since 1956 is intended to provide a central forum in which a workable arrangement can be found for wage determination to be based on this new concept.

Even given this measure of agreement between LO and SAF about equal pay for work of equal value, however, it does not follow that their respective members unions and Partners find this acceptable. SAF and LO may unite about one view, whilst their members seek to employ, and by wage drift succeed in doing so, a wages creed which uses demand and supply as the basic criteria. The difficulties can be illustrated by reference to two of the applications of 'equal pay for work of equal value', first the sex differential, and then the reform of the wages structure.

II. EQUAL PAY FOR WOMEN

Sweden has never ratified the I.L.O. convention (no. 100) on equal pay,[2] and the labour market organizations have argued that this is a collective bargaining issue, to be resolved at the bargaining table and not by law. The essence of LO's equity policy with regard to women's wages is the cry for justice. LO has consistently tried in the post-war years to give priority to women in the formulation of wage demands, and this has often been reflected in higher contractual

[1] See the address by Mr Kugelberg, the managing director of SAF, entitled 'Lönepolitik i ett progressivt samhälle—Wages Policy in a Progressive Society'—in *Nationalekonomiska föreningens förhandlingar*, 1955, Femte Häftet, for a statement of this broad agreement.

[2] That does not mean that Sweden has not been sympathetic to, and moved some way towards, greater opportunities for women in the labour market. Moreover, Sweden stands high in the international league table for sex differentials. The fundamental reason for not ratifying is the point repeatedly stressed in this study—that, in the eyes of the labour market organizations, the terms of employment are a collective bargaining, not a legislative issue.

increases for women than for men. But the market has not followed the contractual rates.

The 1951 report of the committee on questions of female labour probed more deeply than the shallow slogan of 'equal pay for equal work', and formulated the criterion which has since become explicit, that there should be equal pay for performances of equal value. From the point of view of the employer, this means that his labour costs should be the same, irrespective of who does the job, a man or a woman. It also means that the wage system must take account of a number of factors which the employer has insisted are relevant to costs and to the wage differential issue in any form, but particularly in the sex differential form, e.g. regularity, and period of gainful employment, which influence the value of the employee to the firm. These are important for the employer's costs, and he is therefore interested in adjusting the wage in accordance with this very comprehensive concept of cost per unit of output.

The 1960 agreement between LO and SAF to remove the sex categories in collective contracts over a five-year period is a major step away from the value-judgement type of sex differential. In fact this is now regarded as one particular aspect of the move towards more individualized and differentiated wages in the light of job evaluation and merit rating criteria. But it does not follow that a wage system using such criteria will inevitably narrow the sex differential. Many of the job evaluation and merit factors, e.g. criteria which take account of service, regularity, independence, may simply serve to justify the sex differentials more 'scientifically' than has been the case so far. Differentials can still exist, but in fact be more rationally justified, e.g. because women have simpler jobs. All that may happen is that the employer re-classifies the jobs and the labour force. Demand and supply will still be critical. The outlook for the fair sex does not therefore automatically become set fair. As was suggested in Chapter XVI, the shift of women to clerical employment and the decline in the participation of women in manual work may well be the important, and the economic, factor in future trends in the wage and salary differentials between the sexes.

III. SYSTEMATIZING THE WAGES STRUCTURE

The technical construction of wage and salary contracts encourages many stresses in the wages structure, either through the direct scope for wage drift which the drafting of some agreements allows, or through the indirect inducement to seek compensation which the rigidity of other agreements demands. The importance of basing contract clauses on minimum or standard rates, the use of incentive schemes and the significance of employment on salary plan or on collective contract, have only recently begun to attract serious constructive comment as important aspects of the wages policy programme. As a first approach to a solution, there is now greater acceptance of work study, job evaluation, and merit rating for providing more precise criteria for wage differentials than the prevailing loose incentive systems of payment. This point has already been discussed in Chapter XIII. Both sides stress that the suggested reform in the direction of more individualized wage settings means a system of wage differentials based on the nature of jobs and their requirements, and on the job performance. This need not conflict with solidarity, for it does not necessarily mean *wider* wage differentials, but simply more acceptable differentials, in the sense that they conform with some sort of concept of equity endorsed by both sides. This is clearly a very long-term reform, which in essentials resembles the Dutch system of job evaluation.[1]

Reform of the wages structure does not of course stop at manual workers. Some of the greatest problems arise from the systems of payment used for the growing numbers of salaried employees. For white-collar workers employed in either the private or public sector one general feature which provides an impetus to salary claims is the spread of social benefits to manual workers. The salary differential has increasingly to carry the main weight of the distinctiveness of salaried as against manual employment. The differences between the private and public sector in the rigidity of the terms of employment of salaried employees also pose problems. In industry, the salary structure is at present flexible, and it can adjust fairly quickly to any changes in differentials which LO bargaining or wage drift bring about. In future, however, the shift in the labour force towards salaried employment may mean a tighter control over salaries and more collectivism in this salary system. It is not too fanciful to envisage a future where wage determination for manual workers is becoming more individualized, while for salaried employees in industry it becomes more collectivized.

For public employees the main difficulty is that of obtaining parity to compensate for the rigidity in their system of payment. Flexibility could be introduced in two ways. The phenomenon of retrospective parity could become acceptable as a general and frequently recurring device. This would have weaknesses if the arrangement were purely automatic, and it would be misunderstood by other groups if it were construed as a regular invitation to bargain. Alternatively, local salary supplements or a larger number of salary plans could be

[1] The job evaluation gospel has also been preached in the recent stabilization policy report. See *S.O.U.*, 1961 : 42, pp. 283–5.

introduced to meet the needs of public employees in particular local labour markets. Some combination of the two seems likely: (*a*) occasional general revision of civil service salaries to restore parity, and (*b*) greater flexibility than at present in allowing local pay supplements.[1] The current system of cost-of-living bonuses does not do this adequately.

IV. ZONE DIFFERENTIALS

The civil service rigid zone differential is an equity concept, providing compensation for the cost-of-living, and working in particular local labour markets in a very crude and imperfect way. It loses much of its effectiveness by the fact that if government varies it to stimulate recruitment the private sector is likely to respond by doing the same to its already less rigid system of zone differentials.

The zone differential introduces yet another social justice criterion into the wages and salary structure and, on ideological grounds, is considered to have one great advantage. It gives the worker a choice of locality for his occupation, secure in the knowledge that rough justice will be done by the zone differential, which ensures that he obtains much the same real standard in one part of the country as another. Whether this also ensures the efficient distribution of the labour force is, however, another question. Little is known about the part played by this differential in influencing mobility of labour and location of industry.

V. THE WAGE DRIFT

The figures given in Table 5 of Chapter XVI show that the amount of wage drift has varied in the post-war years, averaging about 3–4% per annum (a residual figure). It has been large even when large contractual increases were obtained, e.g. in 1947, 1951, 1952, and has been least, not when wages stabilization or co-ordination was being attempted, but in periods of difficult economic conditions, such as 1953 and 1954. Wage drift to a large extent represents the triumph of sectional, plant-level and individual bargaining, and capacity to pay over co-ordinated solidarity and an equity approach to wage determination. In some measure it is the factor which brings demand and supply of labour into equilibrium in sectors where the structure of agreements makes this possible. We might be tempted to conclude, therefore, that wage drift provides flexibility, and prevents the unions from dictating too rigid and equitable a structure of wage rates. But

[1] Some possibilities are examined in a recent report, *S.O.U.*, 1957 : 42, *Löne- och skattegrupperingarna*.

there is a very strong built-in propensity to restore the position at the next wage round, because groups which cannot obtain wage drift during the period of an agreement try to have compensation included in the terms which are agreed for their sectors in the following wages season. The spread which wage drift introduces into wage differentials may be only temporary.

LO economists argue that in any case wage differentials are a poor incentive for encouraging the most efficient use of scarce labour services—an argument discussed below in connexion with labour mobility. This in principle provides another reason for trying to eliminate wage drift. But the damping down of wage drift faces formidable economic and institutional difficulties. Institutionally, bargaining at the level of the union or the industry cannot readily adjust the wages structure at the bargaining table to the precise circumstances of each plant, and the problem is immensely more complicated in the centralized, albeit differentiated, SAF–LO bargains. Economically, wage drift can arise because even at the plant level there is imperfect knowledge about the markets for labour services. In theoretical terms, the marginal productivity wage for the period of a contract is not known *ex ante* when the contract is concluded. Both the institutional forces and the imperfect knowledge of the market lead to a formalized set of prices for labour services, and these are then corrected in local markets in the light of marginal productivity. Productivity components of wage drift are then quite legitimate. This is unexceptionable in terms of the economist's particular equilibrium analysis, even if there were 'black market' prices —since these may also be manifestations of demand and supply—but it is the consequential and secondary wage increases inspired by wage drift which cause the trouble for stability. The long tail ends up wagging the dog.

It is arguable that under full employment wage drift would in fact be very much greater if the institutions did not set a pricing framework, and if bargaining were decentralized and based on capacity to pay. Indeed, this argument provides the whole rationale of the gradual evolution towards the current series of centralized bargains struck between LO and SAF. Both sides have good grounds for pursuing solidarity in this matter. SAF's appeal to employers has always been based on the stability of wages and the uniformity which unity could give, while LO's appeal to the common rule has long been evident.

The new trend of co-ordination holds out some hope of striking a balance, on the one hand between excessive rigidity and centralism which invite deviation through wage drift and on the other decentralization which produces violent swings in relative wages that neither employers' organizations nor unions can accept as consistent with their rationale. SAF and LO hope to damp down wage drift in this way, to crib, cabin, and confine it within fairly predictable limits. But the approach presupposes no violent fluctuations in the demand for labour, and therefore an economic policy that eliminates excess demand, and it also leans heavily on the projected reforms of the wages structure which are now common currency.

VI. ADAPTABILITY AND MOBILITY OF LABOUR

Both LO and SAF accept the argument that in principle the main burden for full employment stability must rest with an economic policy which controls the aggregate level of demand. But an 'active labour market policy' is now considered an important part of policy, and the trade union economists have long recognized that measures to promote labour mobility are essential when the market, via wage differentials, is not allowed to serve as the incentive to mobility.

The wages policy of solidarity involves two important points which focus on the mobility of labour. In the first place, and on ideological grounds, large wage differentials are not acceptable as a stimulus to labour mobility. Secondly, wage differentials are not *in fact* considered to serve the function allotted in the pricing system to relative price and wage differences as a means of promoting mobility. The empirical evidence for this second argument is not, however, well founded in *Swedish* studies.[1]

An active labour market policy designed to stimulate *both* occupational and geographical mobility is therefore canvassed in the trade union movement as a complement to solidarity. Such a policy serves two objects: (*a*) it allows the unions to continue to argue in favour of solidarity by putting the onus on mobility, not wage differentials, and (*b*) it satisfies what is also considered to be an ideological objective, that of allowing and encouraging workers to choose jobs freely.

The forms for labour market policy have now begun to adjust to the full employment society. The trade union economists were preaching mobility as a necessary complement to solidarity in 1950 and earlier, but it is only since the recession of 1957 that labour market policy has abandoned the narrow and traditional view that it was primarily anti-cyclical, designed to relieve distress in time of

[1] There have been few studies of labour mobility in Sweden. See Rudolf Meidner, *Svensk arbetsmarknad vid full sysselsättning* (Stockholm, 1954) for a study of the labour market (particularly mobility and turnover) during the period 1945–50, and the study by The Industrial Research Institute of mobility in a local labour market (Norrköping) made by interview in 1958. See Bengt G. Rundblad, Arbetskraftens rörlighet, in *Industriproblem*, pp. 117–31 (Industriens utredningsinstitut, Stockholm, 1960). Meidner found (op. cit., p. 198) that the limited data available justified the view that 'the wage is an important, but by no means the dominating factor' in determining labour mobility.

unemployment through public works, relief works, and cash supplements. In the early post-war years the whole emphasis was on the phenomenon of over-mobility as one of the accompaniments (usually regarded as an unfortunate by-product) of full employment, rather than on an active policy to encourage adaptability as one means to a flexible industrial structure.

Emphasis is now being placed on the development of an official long-term selective labour market policy, which is considered to have an important place in a full employment economy. The anti-cyclical emphasis has been replaced by a more comprehensive view of adaptability and structural change. Labour market policy is not considered an effective weapon against *over*-full employment. But, provided monetary and fiscal policy create the overall climate of high employment, labour market policy can be a useful aid in taking care of pockets of unemployment by helping people away from sectors and areas with poor employment prospects to those with a high demand for labour. It is considered as a correction factor, operating at the margin in a flexible and selective way.[1]

Three main classes of measures are distinguished in the adaptability policy: (*a*) those that promote mobility, (*b*) those which create employment, and (*c*) measures which provide financial help to the unemployed. Training and re-training schemes, measures to encourage mobility through travel and removal allowances, family allowances, temporary housing, housing subsidies, in some cases financed out of funds that would otherwise have been paid out in unemployment benefit, are now being increasingly regarded and used as the primary weapons of this more active labour market policy. In addition, there is a growing awareness of the need for regular and rapid manpower appraisals, through an improvement of the six-monthly qualitative studies of the employment situation made by the National Labour Market Board, through the Business Tendency Surveys begun by the Institute of Economic Research in 1954, and through American-type labour force investigations.

The need often expressed for a long-term labour force plan harmonizing with the structure of industry is only part of a large range of economic policy questions. It has been generally recognized that the need for an active labour market policy arises from an economic policy that provides full employment in both factor and product markets, and that it has to be dovetailed with monetary and fiscal policy in the wide sense, and in particular with complementary parts of policy such as the location of industry and housing policy.

The unions see labour market policy as part of their overall

[1] For an exposition of what is now a widely accepted policy weapon, see *S.O.U.*, 1961 : 42, Chapter X.

strategy of a flexible economy and a wages policy of solidarity; movement of labour through this policy, rather than via wage differentials, promotes solidarity and reduces wage drift. It is arguable, however, that the unions' ideology of equity in wages policy throws too great a burden on an active labour market policy. A number of points can be made about this theme.

(*a*) The paucity of empirical material about mobility, and in particular about wage differentials as an inducement to mobility, suggests that LO's policy views on mobility derive primarily from an ideology of solidarity rather than adequate factual data.

(*b*) The existence of wage drift suggests that the wage may be an important factor in *retaining* labour. There is not enough reliable evidence available to know whether it *attracts* labour.

(*c*) Local measures to stimulate employment must be selective and detailed. LO is on record as preferring generally operating rather than specific measures.

(*d*) No adequate analytical framework, e.g. a regional input-output table, is as yet available in Sweden for pursuing a labour market policy as ambitious as that advocated by LO.

In sum, not enough is known about the effects of LO's wages policy of solidarity, however limited its success in practice, in discouraging mobility, about the role of wage drift, and not enough is known about the general determinants of mobility for the wage rate to be cast aside as an insignificant price indicator. At the same time, the labour adaptability policy cannot be dismissed as a mere trade union device. *All* the interest groups agree it has an important function as a correction factor in the economy. Disagreement lies in the explanations given for the lack of mobility which the policy is designed to remove, and in the range of objectives which it is intended to attain.

VII. ALTERNATIVE POLICIES FOR WAGES

The *experience* of wages policy under full employment has been based on the premise that the free system of collective bargaining was worth preserving for its own sake. Both sides have, however, accepted the point that wages bargaining may have to be conducted in such a way as to restrain the exuberance of their member groups. LO has been slow to match its general recognition and sophisticated analysis of this problem with actual bargaining reforms, and a good deal of tentative and unsuccessful post-war experience has preceded the current method of bargaining at the LO–SAF level. Many, but not all, of LO's difficulties here are ascribable to its strongly held view that government economy policy must accept the primary responsibility for determining the overall climate of economic activity. LO has, for example, canvassed a particular type of economic policy, which uses fiscal measures to provide the level of profits in the economy that LO regards as a necessary prerequisite for the trade unions being able to co-ordinate their wages bargaining successfully.[1] But in addition the co-ordination practised by LO and the criteria it has used have often been very half-hearted and half-baked, and much of the criticism of the free collective bargaining system has had legitimate grievances about the manner in which the unions, e.g. in 1952 and 1955, flouted the government's pronouncements about the appropriate level for wage changes. On the other side, LO complained in 1953 that its restraint recommendations for that year were undermined by an insufficiently restrictive economic policy.

Discussion of wages policy outside the immediate labour market interest groups has not felt bound to respect the autonomy of the free collective bargaining system. Two proposals, by Professors Hansen and Östlind, propound approaches which mean that voluntary bargaining is allowed to continue, but its results are corrected by an outside agency—the government. LO sets out in its analysis from the given institutional conditions and then asks how economic policy is to be framed in order to make it possible for the trade union movement, in its existing form, to pursue a long-term wages policy which will assist monetary stability. Hansen asks how the government can persuade a centralized trade union movement to choose the wages policy that the government finds advisable in a particular situation.[2] His central assumption is that the government always has at its disposal sufficient means to neutralize the effects on the value of money and on employment of any changes in money wages. The government takes charge of the task of income distribution through the use of monetary and fiscal policy.

In practice the government would issue a declaration at the beginning of wage negotiations, stating clearly what economic policy

[1] This is the essence of the policy recommendations of *Fackföreningsrörelsen och den fulla sysselsättningen*. Excess demand is to be eliminated by indirect taxes which mop up excessive profits, and the government uses the increased tax revenue to finance local investment where unemployment tends to emerge. Having had profits deflated in this way to make it possible to co-ordinate wages policy so that inflationary wages increases are neither conceded nor demanded, LO can then, it is argued, face up to the task of co-ordinating relative wages.

For discussion of LO's proposals, see op. cit., and the English edition, *Trade Unions and Full Employment*, LO, 1953 : *Wages Policy under Full Employment*, edited Turvey (London, 1952): Bent Hansen, *The Economic Theory of Fiscal Policy* (London, 1958), Chapter XVII: and *International Labour Review*, 1959, LXXX, nos. 4 and 5, Wages Negotiations and Wage Policies in Sweden.

[2] Hansen, loc. cit.

would be put into force on various alternative changes in wages, while maintaining full employment and monetary stability. If the government felt that the *status quo* in money wages was best for its economic policy objectives it would point out EXPRESSLY IN ADVANCE that fiscal policy would be conducted in such a way as to give wage-earners the greatest disposable income if the *status quo* were preserved. For example, if the unions did not change money rates the government would ensure that real incomes rose by (say) $x\%$. If money wages changed, either up or down, they would rise by less. If the workers demanded increased money wages, increased taxation would be threatened. By this policy, the course of money and real wages would be divorced.

Hansen solves the dilemma of responsibility for stable money policy by placing the onus fairly and squarely on the government, while the labour market parties are not required to be socially responsible, or show restraint, but to devote themselves exclusively to obtaining the highest possible living standard. His policy is not necessarily hostile to profits, since the government enforces the level of profits it sees fit.

Östlind puts forward[1] for discussion (he is by no means certain that it is practicable) an alternative to the *laissez-faire* attitude to the labour market institutions. Wages negotiations should continue to be carried on at union and local levels by the parties concerned. If bargaining produced larger income increases than the government policy of preserving monetary stability (which is the criterion Östlind has in mind) could accept, the government would decree that all wages (including wage drift) should be reduced by a certain percentage. If, for example, the average wage level rose 3% above the level consistent with monetary stability, the 'reduction coefficient' by which wages would be multiplied would be 0·97. The government would thus fix the absolute wage level, while each union could still try to advance its relative position by group bargaining in the light of bargaining power, capacity to pay, and employer resistance. To encourage the parties to negotiate as though their negotiations were final, rather than preliminary to government action, the government could introduce uncertainty about its corrective action by sometimes permitting flexibility in the coefficient. In Östlind's view, this prescription retains the advantages of decentralized bargaining and a free labour market. This is a doubtful claim. Both the Hansen and Östlind proposals make the government clearly responsible for the overall money and real wage levels, and bargaining becomes a preliminary to government policy decisions.

[1] See *Recept mot inflation. Sex professorer har ordet*, p. 114 et seq. (Stockholm, 1957)—Kan arbetsmarknaden göras mindre inflationistisk?

The value judgements of the advocates of 'free collective bargaining' do not accept encroachment in this direct way, though they can not of course deny the relevance of economic policy. The really significant issue highlighted by all these proposals is the role of general economic policy versus the role of wages policy. Hansen and Östlind use economic policy in a retrospective manner to correct the wages set through bargaining. LO, on the other hand, takes the view that it should be the *continuing* function of economic policy to set the framework for income determination, which is still carried on by free bargaining agents. The advantage of the LO scheme is that it provides explicitly for the continued existence of free labour market groups.

The debate on the allocation of responsibility for the various parts of income determination policy has now been clarified, and positions have crystallized, through the publication of the official Stabilization Report. It states explicitly that it sees no reason to interfere with the freedom of contract of labour market organizations.

'If this freedom is exercised by organizations with authority and a sense of social responsibility it means that there is a collective acceptance of responsiblity for an important sector of the economy, and this has been, and will remain, an important asset in the development of Swedish society, both through the division of power and responsibility which it involves and through its being a voluntary undertaking.'[1]

A consequence of this is that both the government and central organizations like LO and SAF will have to strive to ensure that their policy is generally acceptable to their members, and not imposed upon them. It is considered to be of fundamental democratic value that the member groups should have to be consulted on policy. In addition, the risk of clashes within the organizations is lessened when consultation and not coercion is the guiding rule.

The report recommends, therefore, that the government should continue to avoid direct intervention in collective bargaining through either permanent or temporary compulsory arbitration.[2] It ought to endeavour to influence wages by the same methods as have hitherto been employed, i.e. by using economic policy to exercise an indirect influence over wage determining forces, by making available information as a guide to wage deliberations, and, when appropriate, promoting agreement about voluntary co-ordination of the policies of organizations on the labour market and elsewhere, both with one another and with government policy.

In a word, it is proposed to continue the system of collective

[1] *Mål och medel i stabiliseringspolitiken, S.O.U.*, 1961 : 42, p. 35 (para. 18).
[2] Op. cit., p. 270.

bargaining institutions whose development and policies we have traced throughout this book. Pragmatism and gradualism still reign supreme. Nobody denies from the side of the labour market organizations that there are still potential explosive forces in the wage and salary structure. Nobody can deny that progress to their solution has been extremely slow. But the intention is to explore the co-ordinated bargaining now practised by LO and SAF as the most promising avenue for reconciling the sides of the Uneasy Triangle of full employment, price stability, *and* free collective bargaining. This does *not* mean that collective bargaining in its existing forms is Untouchable and sanctified, but that the parties will be left to develop and adapt collective bargaining practices and content in order to meet their share of responsibility.

VIII. THE MACHINERY OF WAGES POLICY

The organization of wages policy in Sweden rests on the foundation of a private system of government for the labour market. In principle, SAF and LO operate wages policy in the light of the government's overall economic policy, though it is not always evident where each side thinks the division of function between government policy and the labour market begins and ends. Given agreement in principle about this division of function, informal exchanges of views are the best safeguard against such misunderstandings.

The authority of the private organizations is not all-powerful. Despite the steady historical build-up towards the power centres of LO and SAF, there is considerable flexibility and decentralization of activity. Moral suasion is the main disciplinary pressure rather than directives. The current method of bargaining shows this compromise at work. SAF dare not allow capacity to pay to have its head; and the widening of wage differentials which resulted would be unacceptable to LO's solidarity outlook. The mixture therefore provides solidarity at the central level negotiations, wage drift at the level of the firm, and an active labour market policy to overcome any rigidities in the structure of the economy. 'Economy wide' bargaining keeps the main pressures between manual, white-collar, and public employees in check, but is sufficiently flexible to allow some deviations without there being too much risk of conflict. The inter-dependence of the bargaining system provides checks and balances.

The economic time-table (discussed in Chapter XIV) on which wage rounds are based does not provide for close synchronization of budgetary and wages policy. This is only in part accidental; there are deliberate reasons as well. Some attempt has been made to iron out some of the awkward policy clashes, particularly in the case of agricultural price-fixing. Until recently this was not well co-ordinated but the six-year agreement for farm incomes now permits an accurate appraisal of the consequences for farm incomes of any wage changes in industry. Very deliberately, however, there has been no great support for a policy which suggests 'the scope for wage increases' in explicit percentages. There are two reasons. The economic reason is that economic forecasting is not generally regarded as sufficiently sophisticated for the wage rounds to be geared tightly to the budget or to the economic surveys of the Institute of Economic Research. The presentation of alternative surveys by different bodies enables the various interpretations to be examined critically for strengths and weaknesses. Such a debate is valuable, not only because it clarifies assumptions, but because it brings out the different policies that are being suggested for the use of resources. In 1959, for example, the LO economists' view of the economy's prospects was more optimistic than those of the national budget and the Institute—and in retrospect LO's assessment proved to have been more realistic. This then is a *flexible* approach to the economic aspects.

But there is another reason. The debate is considered to be valuable as an integral part of *democratic government*. This is the whole rationale of the bargaining time-table, and to seek to systematize it too far would mean that the organized system of pressure groups would be deprived of a fundamental liberty—even if this liberty is destined to manifest itself in the sordid business of income maximization.

CONCLUSION

This analysis of collective bargaining in action cannot conclude with the peroration that Swedish bargaining arrangements provide a cure-all, or a grandiose blueprint for a national wages policy. The current practices have been moulded by the particular combination of institutional arrangements in Sweden—the power of SAF, industrial unionism, solidarity, mediation, and the resistance to arbitration that stems from a clear distinction between justiciable and non-justiciable disputes. The system has weaknesses, and defects, e.g. in the woolliness about solidarity, in the reluctance to question seriously the usefulness of incentive systems, in the curious gaps in wage statistics, and in the very imperfect knowledge about local labour markets on which much policy is based.

It may appear therefore that the primary lesson of Swedish collective bargaining is a negative one. It illustrates the complexity of the problems and the pitfalls of national wage policy panaceas. But some positive lessons can also be learned. It is useful to have a flexible framework of institutional bargaining arrangements, rather than a master plan operated through a Grand Palaver, since the power of labour market organizations is not static but, as in the case of salaried employees, is continually evolving. There is wisdom in keeping the government outside the formal bargaining machinery, rather than having it as the presiding genius, for it has not shown that it is in a better position than any other body to determine a 'correct' level of wages, even for its own employees. There is sense too in not gearing collective bargaining too closely to imperfect forecasts of future economic trends.

The past few years have seen considerable clarification of the place that monetary and fiscal policy occupy as the basic weapons of economic policy, with price, wages, and labour market policy as important sub-areas of policy within the general framework of economic activity. To mould collective bargaining practices and wages policy into their allotted place in the organized Swedish full employment society is the challenge facing the labour market organizations.

EX POST

A RETROSPECT on collective bargaining in Sweden at once poses the need for criteria to be used in assessing it. It is easy, if one takes a Swedish outlook, to fall into the habit of criticizing some parts of the system because they are not so fully developed as others. There is a distinct danger of judging the government of TCO, for example, from a lordly LO and SAF eminence, just because they appear to have more powerfully integrated constitutions. If, on the other hand, one takes an international standpoint, there is the dilemma of choice, between a general eulogy—such as the I.L.O. provided for the Swedish system at its 1961 conference—and a diffuse barrage of praise and condemnation, all selected according to one's particular national or academic perspective. There are no absolute standards in assessing the competence or maturity of a collective bargaining system. An eclectic approach will be taken in this retrospect.

Clearly, the Swedish system has developed a nexus of extremely powerful organizations, with clearly formulated rules. It is true, as we have seen, that rules *per se* are not enough, and that they cannot stem the tide of economic forces, or harness them to private ends. The lines of communications within the organizations are clearly marked, and the different levels of organization and government have a well-defined place. This has meant that clear centres of bargaining power can be readily developed, in both the private and public sector, to meet the needs of a central or of a decentralized system of bargaining. The structure of unionism has been adapted to meet the needs of productive activity, and internal demarcation problems have now become secondary to the prime objective of promoting productive efficiency. Here perhaps we can discern a maturity which is the culmination of efficient and effective policy on the part of employers and unions.

Grievance handling is well regulated in the system, both by private arrangements and through the machinery of the Labour Court. The law, as we saw, has aimed at developing the collective contracts system as a private system of government in the labour market, even for groups of employees, such as the civil servants, who have traditionally been agents of, rather than bargainers with, the government. The absence of legislation, judged at least by international standards, makes it crystal clear what the alternatives to agreement are in the event of non-justiciable disputes. This has led the parties, under the threat of law, to work out for themselves a code for industrial peace through the Basic Agreements which control sanctions, protect neutrals, and society, and endeavour to resolve the vexed questions of job security.

The habit of positive discussion which these Basic Agreements have fostered can again be awarded a high rating on an international perspective. It is broadly accepted that one of the main problems of industrial relations is that of effective communications. To have achieved the kind of rapport which now exists at all levels of Swedish labour relations as a result of the Saltsjöbaden discussions of the 1930s is clearly an efficient outcome, even if it cannot be quantified. The same is true of the Works Council and other collaboration agreements, which make for a positive outlook; it may not be easy to measure their impact, but they surely have some positive usefulness which works its way through to productivity.

Productivity is indeed the basis of many of the institutional arrangements. The wage system is intended to be adaptable so that it can reflect enhanced performance, and, while in full employment it may do this too readily through wage drift, this is undoubtedly the correct emphasis in the wage aspects of a labour relations system.

On the test of industrial stoppages, days lost through disputes, Sweden stands high. But this is both a narrow and doubtful measuring rod. It is narrow because it takes no account of the output lost through unrest prior to and subsequent to an actual stoppage, and it is doubtful whether in fact the alternative of the strike-lock-out is always more costly than (say) a cost-push wage increase. No great importance is attached here, therefore, to statistics of stoppages *as such*. But, as has been stated, the Swedish system performs well in the arrangements it makes for channelling grievances and alerting the organizational links about impending disputes, and this is an important point at which to dispel embryonic unrest. Other statistical assessments would be desirable, but are just as limited. It is not possible to relate the system of collective bargaining directly to changes in national product, and establish a causal connexion. As we saw, changes in the wage share may be a function of the level of employment and of government policy on income determination and resource use, rather than of trade unionism working through pressure on wage costs.

It would be a grave disservice to the Swedish system to label it as 'mature'. Does not maturity precede ripeness and 'the season of mists and mellow fruitfulness'? A retrospect is not the same as a post-mortem. Indeed the retrospect leads naturally into a prospect, and a number of fascinating questions immediately spring to mind about the Swedish system.

The first is that of the changing composition of the labour force, with all its implications for LO, and its relations with TCO in particular. Undoubtedly, the white-collar worker trade union movement will go on expanding, not least among university-trained employees, and there will be changes in the present arrangements whereby TCO, SACO, and SR are rivals for the favours of salaried employees. Trade unionism among salaried employees will present a greater challenge to LO's leadership in the future than it does at present. How is LO placed? In certain respects it is responding already, by simplifying the structure of unionism, and merging into larger and more effective groupings of industrial unions. It has flown kites in support of more collaboration with TCO, but has not, to judge from its scant discussion of these problems at its 1961 congress, formulated a policy to meet any challenge that may come.

A major obstacle to LO–TCO collaboration is the avowed political allegiance of LO, and the explicit political neutrality of TCO and all the other salaried groups. How likely is LO to give up its historical alliance with the social democratic party? Not at all, on the evidence so far. An LO congress does not permit itself the luxury of ardent political demonstration. It allows the social democratic Prime Minister to address it and refresh its ideological zeal with reminders of the spiritual bond between the industrial and political wings of the working class movement, is aware of the distinction between industrial and political action, but has no cause to change the present political system when its alliance allows it to use both the political avenue and the industrial route to better conditions of employment. LO's political unionism is good business!

The development of a middle-class party appealing to salaried employees might force LO to change, but the outlook for this is distinctly dim. In the foreseeable future LO will continue as a trade union grouping with a clear social democratic anchorage, and for that reason collaboration along practical lines—such as consultation on wage policy—is the most that can be expected of LO–TCO interchanges.

On the employers' side some change can be looked for in the private sector through the absorption into SAF of those groups presently co-operating with SAF on a consultative basis—commerce, shipping, and agriculture—but no formal merger can be expected between private and public sector employers. Increased pressure from salaried employees is likely to bring about more explicit collaboration, however, between SAF and the employers' organizations in central and local government.

Throughout the history of Swedish collective bargaining the broad contrast between employers and unions has been that the employers defended the *status quo*, while the unions attacked. It is true that SAF was instrumental in the early days in forcing through its policy on the management's prerogatives, and in using lock-outs to hold and repel pressure from the side of wages. But increasingly the full employment society has put the initiative in the hands of the unions in the sellers' market. (This makes it much easier to criticize LO than SAF!) How has LO responded? Is there indifference, even stagnation, in LO's outlook? The answer here is emphatically in the negative.

Since it published its report in 1941 analysing the role of trade unions in society and the economy, LO has produced two reports dealing with the major issues of economic and social policy. Its 1951 congress debated the report on Trade Unions and Full Employment that subsequently won international acclaim for its perception and breadth of view. It bids fair to continue this stimulating tradition, for the highlight of the 1961 congress was the report on Economic Expansion and Structural Change produced by the LO economists. LO emphasizes the need for flexibility in the Swedish economy, and has accepted, indeed preached, the necessity for adaptability, not least on the part of the worker. A typical outlook is that of the Textile Workers' Union, which suffered greatly in the 1950s from structural changes in the economy. Here the decline of the industry has not produced a stubborn opposition to change, but an acceptance of the challenge to adapt.

This outlook can of course be assessed from another standpoint, if the report on structural change is considered simply an eleventh-hour attempt to save the skin of solidarity in wages policy. Then LO could legitimately be accused of conservatism. But the charge can be repulsed on three good grounds. First, the whole tone of the report is liberal in its economics. Secondly, it has forced employers to clarify their policy, and, thirdly, it issues a challenge to salaried employees' organizations to become as sophisticated and stimulating in their policies. LO remains an impulse-giver. Here there is no sign of stagnation. LO itself would not consider these pronouncements as signs of 'maturity', for its outlook has never been static, but always dynamic and forward-looking.

The future of wages policy points to more and more co-ordination, and some approximation to a national labour market-wide bargaining system, even if LO and SAF still set the basic pattern through agreements for industry. But the existence of wage drift at the local level at least poses the question of the role to be assigned to decentralization. It is clearly not an *alternative* form for wages policy, but a supplement to the type of economy-wide bargaining now being evolved. LO and SAF have explicitly taken account of the need for local differentiation in all the recent central bargains about average movements in earnings. The fact that there has been excessive drift at plant level is not a reason for giving up the practice of central bargaining, but for making the central agreements more differentiated, and for tackling wage drift through economic policy. In addition to the overwhelming historical and institutional pressure that has shifted the main weight of wage determination to a national plane, the 'common rule' has now become nation-wide for many groups. Income solidarity, not only wage solidarity, is a fact. To turn the tide of group pressures back towards the plant would be impossible. Instead, the Swedes have chosen, with their usual empiricism, to endeavour to find arrangements that satisfy national claims for solidarity and at the same time allow some individual expression in a decentralized supplementary policy of wage-setting at the local level.

A great deal of the undoubted Swedish success in seeking to progress through discussion must be ascribed to a healthy respect for education. If the education manifested itself only at the level of the LO and SAF leaders and their research staffs there would be an obvious danger that an *élite* of technocrats would come to dominate collective bargaining. The emphasis on skilled manpower at the LO, SAF, and union levels of activity is of course remarkable in itself, and undoubtedly an eye-opener in an international context.

But in fact the emphasis on education is broadly based. The articulateness of trade unionists, for example, is impressive, but no accident. The informed discussion and evolution of policy stem from a large investment in education on both sides at all levels of labour market activity. This is perhaps the fundamental key to Swedish success in moulding a collective bargaining system that is heavily collectivized, yet flexible and responsive to new ideas from all levels and sources. Here, surely, lies the value of Swedish experience.

> On a huge hill
> Cragged, and steep, Truth stands, and he that will
> Reach her, about must, and about must go.
>
> (Donne, *Satyre* iii)

APPENDIX 1

LO Unions, 1960	*Membership ('000s)*
Garment Workers' Union	36·1
Sheetmetal Workers' Union	4·2
Bookbinders' Union	12·3
Brewery Workers' Union	7·9
Building Workers' Union	143·8
Civil Servants' Union	8·2
Amalgamated Unions	15·1
Electricians' Union	22·0
General Factory Workers' Union	67·5
Building Maintenance Workers' Union	27·3
Hairdressers' Union	5·0
Prison Warders' Union	2·5
Civilian Personnel in Defence Establishments	18·0
Insurance Employees' Union	10·0
Foundry Workers' Union	11·6
Miners' Union	14·3
Commercial Employees' Union	98·8
Hotel and Restaurant Workers' Union	26·0
Railwaymen's Union	58·0
Municipal Workers' Union	119·1
Agricultural Workers' Union	28·1
Lithographers' Union	5·8
Food Workers' Union	38·9
Metal Workers' Union	286·0
Bricklayers' Union	15·3
Musicians' Union	17·2
Painters' Union	22·0
Pulp and Paper Workers' Union	51·0
Postmen's Union	22·1
Upholsterers' Union	5·0
Seamen's Union	15·8
Shoe and Leather Workers' Union	10·1
Forest Workers and Raftsmen's Union	39·7
Chimneysweeps' Union	1·1
State Hospital Staff Union	9·9
Stoneworkers' Union	4·7

Telecommunication Workers' Union	19·5
Textile Workers' Union	36·7
Tobacco Workers' Union	1·6
Transport Workers' Union	47·2
Wood Industry Workers' Union	64·3
Typographers' Union	17·1
Waterpower Personnel Union	1·8
Road Construction Workers' Union	17·3
	1485·9

APPENDIX 2

Swedish Employers' Confederation—SAF Member Associations, 1961	*Total Employees ('000s)*
General Group	87·6
Bakery and Confectionery	14·8
Road Transport	22·4
Master Tinners and Platers	3·6
Breweries	7·0
Glass Bottle Manufacturers	0·9
Building	72·6
Building Materials	20·8
Chocolate Industry	4·8
Clothing Retailers' Workshops	0·4
Electrical	17·1
Tanners	2·4
Glass	4·4
Glaziers	1·2
Bookbinders	6·4
Lithographic Printers	3·5
Paper Package	5·7
Typographic Printers	8·9
Grängesberg Mining Group	1·9
Hotel and Restaurant	19·5
Iron and Steel Works	62·5
Ready-made Clothing	29·1
Flour Millers	1·2
Food Producers	30·2
Mineowners, Central Sweden	5·4
Automobile Servicing and Retailing	30·0
Stevedores, North Sweden	1·7
Paper Mills	28·1
Pulp	25·2
Petroleum	7·3
Plumbing	13·6
Saddlery and Upholstery	2·1
Leather Goods	4·3
Shoe Manufacturers	6·5
Master Blacksmiths	3·4

Stone Industry	3·0
Sawmills	17·8
Stevedores, South Sweden	4·2
Textiles	36·8
Peat Industry	0·1
Market Gardeners	1·8
Wood Products	26·4
Metal Trades	257·4
Civil Engineering	18·8
	922·8[1]

[1] Of whom 216,000 are salaried employees.

APPENDIX 3

TCO Unions, 1960	*Membership ('000s)*
Union of Clerical and Technical Employees in Industry	107·0
Foremen's and Supervisors' Union	42·9
Union of Municipal Employees	32·5
Union of Commercial Employees	24·7
Federation of Civil Servants	22·3
Union of Nurses	19·0
Union of Infant School Mistresses	12·8
Union of Elementary School Masters	12·5
Union of Civilian Employees in Defence Forces	12·0
Union of Bank Employees	11·0
Union of Insurance Employees	10·2
Union of Elementary School Mistresses	9·7
Union of Handicrafts' and Skilled Trades' Teachers	9·5
Union of Non-Commissioned Officers (lower ranks)	9·2
Union of Policemen	8·3
Union of Non-Commissioned Officers (higher ranks)	6·1
Union of Chemists' Assistants	4·6
Union of Telephone Employees (women)	4·6
Union of Customs Officers	3·5
Union of Journalists	3·3
Union of State Waterpower Department Employees	3·3
Union of Navigation Officers	3·2
Union of Post Office Employees (women)	3·0
Union of Railway Clerks and Supervisors	2·6
Marine Engineer Officers' Union	2·5
Union of Hotel and Restaurant Employees	2·3
Union of Telegraph Office Employees (women)	2·0
Union of Organists and Choirmasters	1·8
Union of Foremen Printers	1·6
Union of Elementary School Superintendents	1·2
Union of Agricultural Supervisors	1·2
Union of Theatrical Employees	1·1

Union of Ship Stewards	0·7
Union of People's High School Teachers	0·6
Union of Milk Controllers' Assistants	0·6
Union of Teachers of the Deaf and Dumb	0·1
	393·5

APPENDIX 4

Text of Central Wage Agreement between SAF and LO for 1960–61

SAF and LO arrived at the following agreement on March 18, 1960.

The parties bind themselves to work for the prolongation of those agreements which have been terminated, or which, if terminated, would expire before September 30, 1960, for a period of two years from the normal date of expiry of the agreements. The following provisions are to apply:

A. *Wages*

For the first year of the agreement:

A sum is placed at the disposal of the parties to particular contracts such that the average level of earnings per hour worked by adult workers at the date of expiry is raised by 3 %, minimum 16 öre, for workers paid by results, and by 18 öre an hour for workers paid by time wages.

The calculation of this sum is to include the amount necessary to increase the average earnings of juvenile workers by the same percentage figure as that for adult workers covered by a contract.

The parties to each particular contract can agree as to the precise allocation of wage increases within this cost framework.

Changes in wage tariffs which exceed the adjustments of earnings and in the general provisions of contracts which have financial implications are to be accommodated within the cost framework indicated. However, this does not apply to changes in subsistence, travel and tools allowances, or to compensation for other direct outlays which arise from higher costs that have occurred since these were last adjusted.

For the second year of the agreement:

A sum is placed at the disposal of the parties to particular contracts such that the average level of earnings per hour worked by adult workers at the date of expiry is raised by 3 %, minimum 16 öre, for workers paid by results, and by 19 öre per hour for workers paid by time wages.

The calculation of this sum is to include the amount necessary to increase the average earnings of juvenile workers by the same percentage figure as that for adult workers covered by a contract.

The parties to each particular contract can agree as to the precise allocation of wage increases within this cost framework.

Notes:

In applying this agreement the following points are to be observed:

(*a*) Where information about earnings and the total number of hours worked on time wages and by payment by results is necessary for the purpose of applying this agreement, the parties to contracts are entitled to agree about the statistics to be used. If they fail to reach agreement the SAF statistics for the second quarter of 1959 and 1960 are to be used.

(*b*) By earnings on time and piecework is meant, unless the parties agree otherwise, earnings according to columns 4 and 5 respectively of Table 5 of the statistics for the second quarter of 1959 and 1960, augmented in each case by the wage paid for public holidays given in column 8.

(*c*) Increases in pay for public holidays are to be deducted from the cost framework even where the increases are automatic.

(*d*) The bonuses paid for overtime work, shift work and for work done at inconvenient hours and on Sundays, which are not shown in column 4 or 5, are to be raised by the same percentage as average earnings, even where this does not occur automatically, and without deduction from the permissible amount, unless these supplements exceed it.

In the case of tugs and lighters covered by the SAF General Group the provisions to be applied, from July 1, are those stated in the agreement reached by the parties on March 4.

(*e*) In the case of mixed incentive payment systems the cost is to be determined by treating the fixed part as time wage and the flexible part as payment by results. Where this gives rise to difficulties the fixed part is to be increased by the same percentage as the time wage and the flexible part by the same percentage as the increase in payment by results.

(*f*) Previous practice will be followed in any recalculation of weekly and monthly wages which the application of this agreement necessitates.

B. *Women's wages*

SAF and LO are agreed on the principle of equal pay for equal performance suggested by the 1950 committee on female labour. The parties recommend their affiliated organizations to change the structure of their agreements in accordance with this principle over a five year period, so that they dispense with the designations 'men' and 'women' and replace these with job classes. In this revision particular regard should be paid to the need for differentiating wages. During the coming contract period discussions should take place at branch level about the new provisions in contracts, and this reform is to be regarded as a technical problem. Should the reform entail higher costs, it is to be made the subject of the ordinary negotiations on new contracts. All provisions in collective contracts which prevent equality of treatment of men and women in doing the same kind of work should be eliminated.

C. *Working hours*

The parties are agreed that reductions in the hours of work and in the disposition of working hours should be made in such a way as to avoid interruptions in production. Variations in hours of work at different periods and at different periods of the year are permissible, and in addition firms covered by the same contract can arrange the hours of work to suit their own circumstances.

Note: The parties have agreed to ask the Labour Protection Board to discuss with them the provisions of the Workmen's Protection Act dealing with night work and the employment of women.

D. *Particular common contracts*

This agreement also applies, unless specific provision to the contrary has been made in contracts, to contracts which have already been arrived at, and to questions already regulated in them. The negotiations on contracts for market gardens covered by SAF will be concluded after the agricultural price agreement has been settled. Any disputes that arise between the parties to these contracts which they cannot themselves resolve will be settled jointly by SAF and LO.

E. *Negotiations at union level*

SAF and LO bind themselves to work for the bargaining at union level concerning the application of this agreement being concluded as soon as possible, and by April 9, 1960, and one month before the provisions covering the second year come into force, at the latest.

Any disputes outstanding between these organizations which they have not settled by the dates given above will be resolved jointly by SAF and LO.

F. *Contracts outside the common coverage of SAF and LO*

SAF and LO undertake to work for the principles governing this agreement to be applied for other groups besides those directly affected by the agreement, with the exception of those contracts specifically named in the minutes of the negotiations.

G. *Acceptance of the agreement*

Each party undertakes to inform the other by March 21, 1960 at the latest whether this agreement has been accepted.

INDEX

Agreements
See Collective contracts; Individual Employment contract
Agriculture, 267, 336
Ahlberg, E., 223n, 224n, 254n
Amalgamated Unions, 65
Arbitration, Act on Central Arbitration Board, 145, 155, 162; Act on Special Arbitrators, 145; under early agreements, 144; under Basic Agreements, *see* Basic Agreements
Article 23 (now 32), 48, 78, 205; and Basic Agreement, 208. *See also* Job security
Association, right of, before 1936, 124; contractual basis, 125; legal basis and scope, 127; Act of 1936, content, 128–9; penalties, 129; Labour Court and, 128–9, 132; public servants, 132. *See also* December Compromise
Associations, economic and idealistic, defined, 118; legal status, 119

Bank Employees, Union of, 96, 101n
Bargain, right to, customary right, 124–7; legal right, 129–30; public servants, 132–6; *see also* Registration Procedures
Bargaining, procedures and process, 268; at SAF-LO level, 263; union rules on, 261; place of mediation in, 269; salaried employees, 275, 286–8; civil servants, 288–9; system evaluated, 270. *See also* Centralized Bargaining, and Negotiations
Basic Agreement, SAF-LO, background 169; content, 174; coverage, 191; direct action controlled by, 176–81; essential services, 183; dismissals, lay-offs, etc., 208; negotiation procedures, 260; neutrals, 177; success of, 191, 201; Labour Market Council and, *see* Labour Market Council
Basic Agreements, for Co-operative Union, 194–5; newspaper industry, 196–8; salaried employees, 198–200; state-owned companies, 193
Bergendal, Prof., 170, 176n, 178n, 179n
Blockades and Boycotts, under Basic Agreement, 177, 179; Collective Contracts Act, 150; LO rules on, 43
Branch Union, *see* National union
Branting, H., 26
Bricklayers' Union, 34, 65
Budget, fiscal, and national, 266
Building Employers' Federation, 81
Building industry, adjustment of piecework disputes, 260; dispute in 1933–4, 34–5; piecework system, 243–5
Building Workers' Union, 44–5, 65, 236, 263

Cartels, 59–60
Casparsson, R., 26n, 34n, 206n
Central agreements, LO-SAF, (1952) 281, (1956) 283, 284–5, text (1960–1), app. 4; salaried employees, 286–7
Central Employers' Federation (CAF), 63n, 78n, 84
Centralized bargaining, 281–6, 290, 334; TCO and, 283, 290. *See also* Bargaining, and Negotiations
Chimney Sweeps' Union, 46
Civil servants, 86–7, 267; bargaining rights, 86–7, 132–6
Civil Service Affairs, Ministry of, 87, 134–5, 289
Clerical and Technical Employees in Industry, Union of (SIF), 93, 98; assets, 101; as focus for private sector, 111; Basic Agreement, 198–200; job security, 213; relations with TCO, *see* TCO; salary policy, 254; salary rounds, 286–8
Closures, 214
Closed shop, 54; *see also* Open shop, Union shop
Co-determination, *see* Works Councils
Cold region allowances, 252, 256, 327
Collective affiliation, 27–8
Collective Bargaining Board, Government, 87–8
Collective Contracts, duration 264; notice of termination, 264–5; numbers, 235; in public sector, 87–8, 250; salaried employees, 253; Supreme Court Ruling, 120; types, 235
Collective Contracts Act, direct action prohibited by, 150; LO protests, 146; obligations on parties, 54, 153; parties bound, 149; provisions, 147; SAF views, 146; sanctions, 152–4; superiority of collective norms, 148; sympathetic action allowed, 151–2; unorganized workers, 149; union section's status, 57n

Commercial Employees, Union of, 44, 56, 57, 59
Commission (Nothin), *see* Nothin committee
Committee of Fifteen (LO), 18, 35; flexible union rules, 51; industrial democracy, 218; non-justiciable disputes, 143; open shop, 48; wages policy, 277
Communism, and trade union movement, 27, 29, 53n
Companies Act, 11, 228, 231
Conflicts, *see* Stoppages
Constitution, Swedish, 124
Co-operative Union, Bargaining Organization, 90; Basic Agreement, 194–5; Union shop, 48; works councils, 230
Cost of living, clauses, 279, 281, 291; post-war changes, 294, 302
County Councils, Federation of, 88
Craft Unionism, 61, 97, 107
Croner, F., 92, 93, 94, 95n

DACO, 96
Dahlström, E., 93n
Damages, 129, 153, 154, 226
December Compromise, 79, 125, 206
Dehlgren, S., 196
Demarcation disputes, *see* LO, TCO
Dental Federation, 107
Deployment of labour force, 214
Direct action, under Collective Contracts Act, 150–3; under Basic Agreement, 176–81
Dismissals, *see* Job security
Domkapitlet, 290n
Durham, H. E., 140n, 142n

Earnings, *see* Wage earnings
Economic Freedom Ordinance, 11, 124
Edström, J. S., 69n, 72n, 172, 193
Ekblom, O., 134, 135, 136, 140n, 160
Emigration, 11
Employers' Confederation, *see* SAF
Employment in Industry, 15
Equal Pay, *see* Women's wages
Essential public services, attempts to define, 182–4, 187–8; electricity power supply, 185; food processing industry, 187; protection under Basic Agreement, 184; in public sector, 187–9
Establishment, size of, in industry, 15
Eviction Act, 163

Factory Workers' Union, 57, 61, 65
Female labour, SAF-LO committee on, 192, 248, 286, 325
Food processing industry, 187, 271n, 277n, 282
Food workers' union, 59, 65, 248n
Foreman, defined, 129; works councils, 223
Foremen's and Supervisors' Union, 98; assets, 101; Basic Agreement, 200; salary policy, 254, 287
Forslund, A., 172, 173
Foundry Workers' Union, 48n, 59, 62, 65, 69
Franchise, political, 17, 69
Fridell, F., 230n
Fringe benefits, 258

Galenson, W., 172n
Garment Workers' Union, 45
Geijer, Arne, 189n, 284n, 323n
Geijer, L., 212n; and Schmidt, F., 132n, 148n, 151n, 158n, 161n, 208n
Geographical differentials, 251, 312–14; in civil service, 252, 256
Gilds, 11, 23
Graduate Engineers, Association of, 107
Great Strike (1909), 17, 32, 33; and organization of LO, 62; SAF and, 77; legal case arising out of, 120
Gulbrandsen, O., 12n

Hallendorff, C., 32n, 70n, 124
Hansen, B., 248n, 323n, 332–4
Hansson, Per Albin, 170
Hansson, S., 44n, 124n, 126n
Heineman, H., 120n
Holidays Act, 160n
Hotel and Restaurant Workers' Union, 45, 59
Hourly wage rates, *see* Wage payments
Hours, 236, 284
Höök, E., 14n, 93n

I.L.O., 324, 338
Impartial chairman, 269
Individual employment contract, 147–8
Industrial democracy, *see* Works Councils
Industrial unionism, 61–6, 97
Interest (*intresse*) disputes, *see* Non-justiciable disputes
Inventions, 221n
Iron and Steel Works Association, 81

Job evaluation, 238n, 249, 326
Job security, 205; Basic Agreement provisions, 209; closure and deployment, 214; criteria for, 211; dismissals and lay-offs, 208; re-engaging, 210; protected by law, 213; salaried employees, 105n, 212–13

Jonasson, S., 94n
Journalists' Union, 96
Justiciable (*rätts*, rights) disputes, 115; characteristics, 138–9; settlement by private arrangement, 260; before 1928, 144–5; under Collective Contracts Act, 146–63

Karlbom, T., 31n, 218n, 323n
Kugelberg, B., 72n, 279n, 324n
Kärrfeldt, E. D., 162

Labour Court; provisions of Act, 156; composition, 155; additional functions, 160; number of cases, 158–9; LO views on 146, 162; proceedings, 156–7; principles developed, 157–8; precedents, 161; reservations, 158n
Labour Court Judgements; employees' work obligations, 66n; Holidays Act, 160; right of association, 128–9, 132; shortage of work, 215; status of union section, 57n; termination of employment, 207; unorganized workers, 149; unresolved disputes, 151; 200 crowns rule, 154
Labour force, by sector, 13; by industry, 15
Labour Market Board, *National*, 214, 330
Labour Market Committee (LO-SAF), 35, 173, 192: (SAF-SIF), 198: (SAF-Foremen's Union), 200
Labour Market Council (LO-SAF), composition and functions, 174–5; activities under Ch. 4, 181; essential public services, 184–7; job security, 211; works councils, 225: (SAF-SIF), 198–200: (SAF-Foremen's Union), 200
Labour peace conference (1928), 169–70, 207, 217
Lawyers' Association, 107
Lay-offs, *see* Job security
Libel, 163
Lind, A., 35n, 277n
Lind, E., 249n
Lindbom, T., 237n
Lindhagen, A., 159, 161
Lindqvist, H., 27, 33, 58, 62n, 142, 146, 206
Lithographers' Union, 46
LO: founded, 25; objects, 36–7; relations with party, 25–9; membership, 29; growth, 30; member unions, 44–5; executive machinery, 37–9; congress, 37–8; representative assembly, membership, 38, and negotiations, 264; list of chairmen, 38n; powers of chairman, 38; secretariat, composition and powers, 38–44; centralization, 32–3, 39; internal disputes, 39; wages policy and negotiations, 40–1, 263, 265, 266; demarcation disputes, 64; expulsion of unions, 51; procedures in disputes, and conflict support, 41–4; conflict support, 41–4; strike permission, 41–2; lockouts, 43; blockades and boycotts, 43; organization plan and industrial unionism, 40, 61–6; finances and dues, 31; investment of funds, 46–7; Press Fund, 28: cartels, 59–60; local central organizations, 58–9; relations with TCO, 95, 104, 340; National unions, *see* National Unions
Local government; employees' bargaining rights, 133, 136; employers' organizations, 88–90; justiciable disputes, 261; piecework, 237
Lock-outs; number, *see* Stoppages; LO and, 43; SAF and, *see* SAF; sympathetic lock-outs permitted by law, 151–2; under Basic Agreement, 177
Lübeck, S., 207, 217
Lundberg, E., 267n

Mackmyra, 124
Marine Engineers, Union of, 96, 101n
Mediation Act, provisions 139–43; obligations to bargain, 130, 141; sanctions, 141
Mediators, functions 141–2; role in bargaining, 269; district mediators, 139, 272; special mediators and mediation commissions, 140, 269, 273; government commission, 140n; mediation service in post-war bargaining, 272–4, 290
Medical Association, Swedish, 107
Medical Board, 184
Meidner, R., 319n, 323n, 329n
Member (SAF), *see* SAF
Merit Rating, 250
Metal trades, 236, 238, 243
Metal Trades Employers' Federation, 61, 68, 81, 238, 250
Metal Workers' Union, 34, 44, 46, 48n, 54n, 56, 59, 62, 65, 250, 262, 263
Minimum Wages, *see* Wage payments
Mobility of labour, 320, 329
Mondism, 169, 217
Municipalities' Federation, 88–90, 261, 237
Municipal Workers' Union, 44, 236
Möller, G., 130, 131, 146, 170, 178n
Möller, Y., 189n

National agreements, 235–6
National income, 292–5; wage and salary share, 295–8
National Institute of Economic Research, 265, 266, 280n, 336
National Unions (LO), 44; size, 44; dues, 45; assets, 46; objects, 52; compulsory rules, 47–52; open shop, 47–9; right and obligation to transfer, 49; right of veto, 50–2; rules on wage bargaining, 261, 270; Members, rights, 52–5; obligations, 55; organization, 52; congress, 52; chairman, 52; branches, 44, 55–6; clubs, 56–7; sections, 57; district organization, 57; inter-union cartels, 59–60
Navigation Officers, Union of, 101n
Nazis, 53n
Negotiations: preliminary, 262n; stages, 268; timetable, 264; *see also* Bargaining, and Centralized bargaining
Negotiation procedures: SAF-LO agreement of 1908, 145; under Basic Agreement, 260
Neutrals in labour disputes, *see* Third parties
Newspaper industry, Basic Agreement, 196–8
Nilsson, Å., 246n
Non-justiciable (*intresse*) disputes, 115; characteristics, 138–9; LO statement on, 143; Nothin committee discussion, 144; settlement, 261
Nothin committee, 34–5, 41n; impetus to Basic Agreement, 172; idealistic associations, 121; non-justiciable disputes, 144; essential public services, 182–3, 187–8; voting procedures, 50
Notice, *see* Closures, Stoppages, and Warning Act
Nurses pay dispute, 189

Odholm, A., 223n
Ombudsman, 158, 161
Open shop, LO and, 47–9; SAF and, 48n, 49; *see also* Closed shop, and Union shop
Organization clauses, 48, 128
Organization Plan, *see* LO, and TCO
Overtime, *see* Wage payments

Partners (SAF), *see* SAF
Penal code, 163
Pensions, 29, 288
Picketing, 180
Piecework, *see* Wage payments
Police pay dispute, 188
Population, 12
Post-war Programme of Swedish Labour, 218, 280n
Productivity, 306
Profit-sharing, 257
Protection at workplace, 192, 223
Protective work, 180–1
Public sector, *see* Civil servants, Local government
Public servants, special bargaining position, 86–90, 132–6

Railways, Swedish, 184–5, 225, 230
Re-engaging, *see* Job security
Registration prodecures for bargaining, 131–2
Rehn, G., 248n, 314n
Retaliation, regulated by Basic Agreement, 177
Reynolds and Taft, 314n
Rights (*rätts*), *see* Justiciable disputes
Road Transport Association, 81
Robbins, J. J., 120n, 125n, 135n, 272n
Rundblad, B. G., 329n
Rural Councils, Federation of, 88

SACO, 106–8, 110, 111, 278
SAF, constituted, 70; objects, 70; organization, General Meeting, 71; Council, 71–2; Board, 72, powers, 73; list of managing directors, 72; powers of managing director, 73; Members, 71, 73; size of, 81–2; Partners, 71, 72, 73, 75; size of, 82–3; disciplinary control over, 76; finances, annual dues, 74; insurance, 74; Guaranty Fund, 74; insurance Fund, 74: mutual insurance scheme, 70; rules on lock-outs, 70, 75–6; lock-outs as a tactic 77; lock-outs of salaried employees, 80; rules on collective contracts, 78; Departments, 83; General Group, 71, 81, 250, app. 4; Trade Groups, 80; Council for Personnel Administration, 83; salaried employees, 79; industrial unionism, 61, 67; industrial disputes, 75; consultative council, 85, 155; relations with other employers, 84–6, 91; *see also* Article 23
Salaried employees: definition of, 94; numbers, 14, 92, 314; in industry, 93; collaboration among, 109–12; collective contracts, 253, in banking and insurance, 253; industrial democracy, 219; job security, 212–13; right of association, 125; reorganization, 110–12; *see also* SACO, SAF,

Salaried employees—*contd.*
SR, Clerical and Technical Employees, Foremen's and Supervisors' Union
Salaries, in industry, 314; for civil servants, 317
Salary plan, 255–7
Salary policy, 254, 278
Sawmill Worker's Union, 59, 65
Schmidt, Carl Chr., 132n, 272n
Schmidt, F., 54n, 120, 128, 149n, 181n, 211n: *see also* Geijer and Schmidt
Seamen's Act, 213
Secondary School Teachers' Association, 107
Seniority, *see* Job security
Sex differentials, *see* Women's wages
Shop stewards, 57
SIF, *see* Clerical and Technical Employees in Industry, Union of
Sjöberg, S., 104n
Skytt, T. and Åsbrink, 258n
Social democratic party, and early trade unions, 24; ties with trade unions, 26–7; collective affiliation, 27–8; philosophy, 170, 231
Solidarity, wages policy of, 33, 276–8, 318, 319–24
SR, 108–9, 110
Statistics, wage and salary, 253n, 271, 298n, 314n
Stensland, P. G., 95n
Stoppages of work, statistics, 17; under Basic Agreement, 177; sympathetic, 151–2; notice of, 131, 140; in LO and SAF rules, *see* LO, SAF
Strand, A., 266n, 279n, 282n, 284n
Strike breakers, legal protection, 163; under Basic Agreement, 179
Stripa conflict, 169
Styrman, G., 238n
Supreme Court, *see* Collective Contracts
Sydow, H. von, 70, 72n, 74, 172, 207
Sympathetic stoppages, *see* Stoppages
Syndicalism, 29, 33
Söderlund, G., 79n, 127n, 130n, 172, 173, 218
Sölvén, A., 36n, 40n, 183, 184, 186n

TCO, founded, 96; membership, 97; member unions, 102–3; objectives, 98; political neutrality, 98; solidarity, 106; organization, 98; finances, 101; Guaranty Fund, 101n; bargaining rules, 99; demarcation disputes, 104; organization plan, 103; local committees, 103; civil service section, 100, 105, 111; relations with LO, *see* LO; with Union of Clerical and Technical Employees in Industry, 98n, 99, 105, 212–13
Telegraph Board, 185
Third parties in labour disputes, neutrals protected, 178; non-neutrals defined, 179
Tingsten, H., 69n
Transport Workers' Union, 61, 153, 162, 196
Turvey, R., 332n
Typographers' Union, 46, 57, 263

Undén, Ö., 153n, 208
Unemployment, 294, 301, 304
Unemployment Insurance Funds, 46n
Union shop, 48; *see also* Closed shop, and Open shop

Veto, right of, 50–2
Vocational training, 192, 223

Wage earnings, 299; by sex, 300; components, 240
Wage drift, defined, 246; components, 246; compensation for, 289; figures, 300; significance, 248, 291, 304, 327
Wage payments: methods, 236; prevalence of piecework, 237; piecework compensation, 239; tariffs, 239: piecework formulae in metal trades, 243; in building, 243; minimum, standard rates, 238; individual supplements, 239; overtime, 240; piecework and overtime by size of firm, 242; shiftwork, 240; fiffelfaktor, 243, 246, 308; *see also* Cold region allowances, Geographical differentials, Wage drift
Wages policy: LO powers, 40–1; Cooperative Union, 195; salaried employees', 254, 278; machinery for future, 335–41; alternative, 331; *see also* Solidarity
Wage Policy Council, 263, 264
Wages, relative, men, 307–9, women, 309–12
Wage rounds, 279; and restraint, 280; centralized, *see* Central agreements, and Centralized bargaining
Wage share, 295–8
Wages structure, 325
Wage systems, 236; in metal trades, 238–43; in building, 243; for salaried employees, 253, 255
Warning Act, 140–1
Westerståhl, J., 116n, 146n, 170n
Wigforss, E., 231n

Women's wages, 300, 309–11, 324
Works Councils, 192, 217: Agreement (SAF-LO), 219–20; composition, 219, 221; numbers, 226; information, 227; Labour Market Council and, *see* Labour Market Council; suggestions activity, 221, 228; foremen, 223; salaried employees, 223; co-determination, 230
Work study, 192, 223, 245

Ådal, 18, 170, 217
Åkarp act, 163
Åman, V., 29n, 189n, 205n
Åsbrink, *see* Skytt

Örne, A., 230n
Östlind, A., 332–4